AGAINST THE GRAIN
SELECTED ESSAYS

AGAINST THE GRAIN

SELECTED ESSAYS

Iain Provan

Edited by Stacey L. Van Dyk

Regent College Publishing
www.regentpublishing.com

By Iain Provan

Against the Grain: Selected Essays
Copyright © 2015 Iain Provan

All rights reserved. No part of this publication may be reproduced, stored in a retrieval system, or transmitted, in any form or by any means, electronic, mechanical, photocopying, recording or otherwise, without the prior written permission of the author, except in the case of brief quotations embodied in critical articles and reviews.

Published 2014 by Regent College Publishing

Regent College Publishing
5800 University Boulevard, Vancouver, BC V6T 2E4 Canada
Web: www.regentpublishing.com
E-mail: info@regentpublishing.com

Regent College Publishing is an imprint of the Regent Bookstore <www.regentbookstore.com>. Views expressed in works published by Regent College Publishing are those of the author and do not necessarily represent the official position of Regent College <www.regent-college.edu>.

ISBN 978-1-57383-520-6

Cataloguing in Publication information is on file at Library and Archives Canada.

This book is dedicated to:

Robert Gibson
Richard Sturch
Donald Guthrie

Teaching is not a lost art, but the regard for it is a lost tradition.
Jacques Barzun (1907–2012)

CONTENTS

Preface   xi

Permissions and Acknowledgements   xvii

Essays

1. Reading Texts Against a Historical Background:
   The Case of Lamentations 1 (1990)   1

2. Past, Present, and Future in Lamentations 3:52–66:
   The Case for a "Precative Perfect" Re-examined (1991)   16

3. The Messiah in the Book of Kings (1995)   29

4. Why Barzillai of Gilead (1 Kings 2:7)?
   Narrative Art and the Hermeneutics of Suspicion in
   1 Kings 1–2 (1995)   51

5. Ideologies, Literary and Critical: Reflections on
   Recent Writing on the History of Israel (1995)   63

6. Foul Spirits, Fornication, and Finance: Revelation 18
   from an Old Testament Perspective (1996)   90

7. Canons to the Left of Him:
   Brevard Childs, His Critics, and the
   Future of Old Testament Theology (1997)   108

8. The End of (Israel's) History?
   A Review Article on K. W. Whitelam's
   The Invention of Ancient Israel (1997)   144

9. The Historical Books of the Old Testament (1998)   163

10.	In the Stable with the Dwarves: Testimony, Interpretation, Faith, and the History of Israel (2000)	180
11.	To Highlight All our Idols: Worshipping God in Nietzsche's World (2000)	212
12.	On "Seeing" the Trees While Missing the Forest: The Wisdom of Characters and Readers in 2 Samuel and 1 Kings (2000)	247
13.	The Terrors of the Night: Love, Sex, and Power in Song of Songs 3 (2000)	272
14.	"All These I Have Kept Since I Was A Boy" (Luke 18:21): Creation, Covenant, and the Commandments of God (2002)	293
15.	The Land is Mine and You are Only Tenants (Leviticus 25:23): Earth-Keeping and People-Keeping in the Old Testament (2006)	317
16.	"'How Can I Understand, Unless Someone Explains It to Me?' (Acts 8:30–31): Evangelicals and Biblical Hermeneutics" (2007)	346
17.	"Unscripted, Anxious Stutterers": Why We Need Old Testament (Hi)story (2008)	393

Endnotes 417

Index of Authors 541

Select List of Iain Provan's Publications, 1988–2014 561

Preface

It was in the summer of 2012 that I first formed the idea of a collection of my essays—not a comprehensive collection, but a broad sampling from all but the most recent (which may be found simply listed at the back of this volume). Having formed the idea, I began to think about a possible title. At the time, I was hiking the northern half of the West Highland Way in Scotland, between Tyndrum and Fort William, a distance of about forty-four miles. Since I was hiking from north to south, whereas most people follow the guidebooks and hike from south to north, I only ever encountered other travellers in the middle part of the day as we met head-on in pursuit of our quite different goals. If the trail was narrow at these points, this created some temporary difficulty as we edged past each other, bumping each other with our often bulky backpacks. And it struck me, as I walked, that my decision to hike in the opposite direction to everyone else was fairly typical of my approach to life in general, and my approach to academic life in particular. It has all been pretty much "against the grain." I am told by my parents that this could have been predicted. Perhaps all children exasperate their parents with the endlessly repeated question, "but why?" Apparently I was particularly exasperating, however, and I have persisted on this pathway through life for a longer time than many. Show me a settled opinion, particularly one that is dogmatically or even arrogantly held—a truth regarded as self-evident, that all right-thinking people should believe—and I will probably respond, "but why?" I do not think that I was fully conscious of the extent to which this has been true of my academic life until I reviewed the essays in this volume. I encounter here essays that on the whole are marked by an evident desire to question received truths within the Academy—truths about how best to read poetic or apocalyptic texts, not least in relation to historical backgrounds; about how to do history itself; about how best to read various narrative sections of the Old Testament, and about how far historical-critical theorizing helps us in this task; about how to do biblical theology; and so on. I also encounter here essays marked by an evident desire to question received truths within the (especially evangelical) Church—that other "tribe" to which I have belonged, as an often dissenting voice, these past several decades. Clearly, I am just a very difficult person. I do not follow the guidebooks, and I bump others on the way with my backpack.

There are many people who share some of the blame for this unfortunate state of affairs, and this book is dedicated to three of them, each of whom I first met a long time ago. I think of all of them often, and with a thankful heart, although I am quite sure that the survivors in the group have no idea of the impact they have had on me. The first I have not seen for forty years. He is Mr. Robert Gibson, my high school history teacher at Paisley Grammar School in Scotland, who first taught me how to think critically, and thereby changed my life. The second I have not seen for thirty-five years. He is the Reverend Dr. Richard Sturch, former rector of the parish of Islip in England and the 1996 UK *Mastermind* champion. He greatly sharpened my critical thinking skills by way of his undergraduate philosophy classes at the London School of Theology (as it is now). His penetrating lectures on logical fallacies have lived long in the memory, and his "A" for an essay of mine on the ontological argument (which I felt I understood while writing the essay, but which became a fog again once I had submitted it) remains one of my most treasured undergraduate "possessions," not least because it greatly increased my academic self-confidence. The "third man" I last saw in 1981, and he is now deceased. He is Dr. Donald Guthrie, a New Testament scholar who also taught at the London School of Theology, and who at a crucial point in my post-college life instructed me, as an undergraduate major in New Testament and Systematic Theology, to proceed to a doctorate and to make Old Testament Studies my focus. I did as I was told, because of my enormous respect for the man. If he had not instructed me to do this, I would never have thought of the possibility. Even if I had thought of it, I would have lacked the confidence to proceed. Because of Dr. Guthrie, I applied to the University of Cambridge, was accepted, and the rest is history. It is the combination of critical thinking and Old Testament studies, made possible by these three men among others, that has so often got me into trouble since.

Finally, I want to extend a big thank you to my wonderful research assistant Stacey L. Van Dyk. Stacey has functioned as the editor of this volume, and it has not been exciting work. The essays themselves have been reproduced here in all substantial respects just as they appeared in their original published forms, so there was nothing that needed to be done with the content. What she *did* need to do, however, was to convert all sorts of files (some quite ancient) into Word, fix all the mistakes that occurred in the process, and then begin to make smaller changes in pursuit of a general consistency of style throughout the volume (e.g. rendering Hebrew words into transliterated form; imposing a consistent *SBL* style on journal abbreviations). Anyone who has ever attempted such a task will know all too well just how truly tedious it is. I am most grateful to Stacey that she took it on, and completed it with such attention to detail. I myself added a small number of further edits in pursuit of an even style across the breadth of the volume, while also taking the opportunity to correct a few instances of extreme lack of clarity and ridiculous punctuation, as well as random infelicities of other kinds. I am glad to discover that my writing style has improved somewhat over time. Such interventions were modest, with the intention of making the volume more readable, without disturbing the originals more than was absolutely necessary.

Iain Provan
Vancouver, April 2014

Permissions & Acknowledgments

"Reading Texts Against an Historical Background: The Case of Lamentations 1" was originally published in the *Scandinavian Journal of the Old Testament* 4 (1990): 130–143.

"Past, Present, and Future in Lamentations 3:52–66: The Case for a 'Precative Perfect' Re-examined" was originally published in *Vetus Testamentum* 41 (1991): 164–175, and is republished in this volume with the permission of Brill Publishing.

"The Messiah in the Book of Kings" was originally published in *The Lord's Anointed: Interpretation of Old Testament Messianic Texts*, edited by P. E. Satterthwaite, R. S. Hess, and G. J. Wenham (Carlisle: Paternoster/Baker Academic, 1995), 67–85, and is republished in this volume with the permission of Paternoster Press and the Baker Publishing Group. Copyright © 1995 Paternoster/Baker.

"Why Barzillai of Gilead (1 Kings 2:7)? Narrative Art and the Hermeneutics of Suspicion in 1 Kings 1–2" was originally published in the *Tyndale Bulletin* 46 (1995): 103–116, and is republished in this volume with the permission of the Tyndale Bulletin administrators.

"Ideologies, Literary and Critical: Reflections on Recent Writing on the History of Israel" was originally published in the *Journal of Biblical Literature* 114 (1995): 585–606.

"Foul Spirits, Fornication, and Finance: Revelation 18 from an Old Testament Perspective" was originally published in the *Journal for the Study of the New Testament* 64 (1996): 81–100.

"Canons to the Left of Him: Brevard Childs, his Critics, and the Future of Old Testament Theology" was originally published in the *Scottish Journal of Theology* 50 (1997): 1–38, and is republished in this volume with the permission of the editors. Copyright © 1997 *Scottish Journal of Theology*.

"The End of (Israel's) History? A Review Article on K. W. Whitelam's *The Invention of Ancient Israel*" was originally published in the *Journal of Semitic Studies* 42 (1997): 283–300, and is republished in this volume with the permission of the editors.

"The Historical Books of the Old Testament" was originally published in *The Cambridge Companion to Biblical Interpretation*, edited by J. Barton (Cambridge: Cambridge University Press, 1998), 198–211, and is republished in this volume with the permission of Cambridge University Press.

"In the Stable with the Dwarves: Testimony, Interpretation, Faith, and the History of Israel" was originally published in *Congress Volume: Oslo 1998*, Papers of the 16th Congress of the International Organisation of the Societies for Old Testament Study, edited by A. Lemaire and M. Sæbø (Leiden: Brill, 2000), 281–319, and is republished in this volume with the permission of Brill Publishers.

"To Highlight All our Idols: Worshipping God in Nietzsche's World" was originally published in *Ex Auditu* 15 (2000): 19–38, and is republished in this volume with the permission of Wipf and Stock Publishers (www.wipfandstock.com).

"On 'Seeing' the Trees While Missing the Forest: The Wisdom of Characters and Readers in 2 Samuel and 1 Kings" was originally published in *In Search of True Wisdom: Essays in Old Testament Interpretation in Honour of Ronald E. Clements*, edited by E. Ball (JSOTSup 300; Sheffield: Sheffield Academic Press, 2000), 153–173, and is republished in this volume with the permission of Bloomsbury Publishing (of which Sheffield Academic Press is an imprint).

"The Terrors of the Night: Love, Sex, and Power in Song of Songs 3" was originally published in *The Way of Wisdom: Essays in Honor of Bruce K. Waltke*, edited by J. I. Packer and S. K. Soderlund (Grand Rapids: Zondervan, 2000), 150–167. Copyright © 2000 by J. I. Packer and S. K. Soderlund. Used by permission of Zondervan (www.zondervan.com).

"'All These I Have Kept Since I Was A Boy' (Luke 18:21): Creation, Covenant, and the Commandments of God" was originally published in *Ex Auditu* 17 (2002): 31–59, and is republished in this volume with the permission of Wipf and Stock Publishers (www.wipfandstock.com).

"The Land is Mine and You are Only Tenants (Leviticus 25:23): Earth-Keeping and People-Keeping in the Old Testament" was originally published in *Crux* 42:3 (2006): 3–16.

"'How Can I Understand, Unless Someone Explains It to Me?' (Acts 8:30–31): Evangelicals and Biblical Hermeneutics" was originally published in the *Bulletin for Biblical Research* 17 (2007): 1–36, and is republished in this volume with the permission of the editor.

"'Unscripted, Anxious Stutterers': Why We Need Old Testament (Hi)story" was originally published in *Sapientia Logos* 1 (2008): 12–36, and is republished in this volume with the permission of Hokma House, an educational and research organization (Jos, Nigeria).

1

READING TEXTS AGAINST A HISTORICAL
BACKGROUND: THE CASE OF
LAMENTATIONS 1

This essay is the published form of only the second conference paper of my academic career.¹ I came to write it as a result of a fortuitous series of events in terms of timing and placement. In 1986–1988 I was teaching at King's College, London, as a temporary replacement for Dr. Michael Knibb, who was on research leave. One of my colleagues was Professor Ron Clements, who at that time was the Old Testament editor for the New Century Bible Commentary Series. The author whom Ron had originally assigned the volume on Lamentations had not been able to produce a manuscript, and Ron offered the project to me. As a very new Ph.D. in my first academic appointment I jumped at the chance. I wrote much of the commentary during 1988–1989, while benefiting from a postdoctoral fellowship in the University of Wales and living in Bangor. The volume eventually appeared in 1991, by which time I had taken up a permanent appointment at the University of Edinburgh (1989–1997). Along this winding way I was able to publish several essays relating to puzzles I encountered in reading either Lamentations itself, or the scholarship concerning Lamentations, or both. This essay concerns the question: how easy or difficult is it to read history out of poetry? It is the first essay I ever published in a peer-reviewed journal, appearing originally in 1990 in the recently-founded Scandinavian Journal of the Old Testament, *and that is why it appears first in this volume.*

It has been the universal assertion of critical scholarship for most of the modern era that if we are properly to understand biblical texts we must discover and understand the historical context in which they were originally written. Only when we have established what they meant in their original setting may we then go on to ask about their possible contemporary value. One consequence of this emphasis has been that an enormous, some would say disproportionate, amount of effort has been put into the dating of texts; and principal among the factors which have been understood as helping us to determine date has been the historical allusions believed to be made by the texts themselves. These allusions may not of themselves settle the question of the precise date and context of a text, but they are fundamental to the whole quest, since they give us a *terminus a quo*, a secure point from which to begin our discussion. Only when this has been established may we then move on to enquire precisely how long after the events alluded to the particular text might have been written; and only then, and in conjunction with other discoveries such as the genre of the text, shall we know how to use the text correctly for such purposes as historical reconstruction or theology.

Now this way of approaching biblical texts has, of course, been much criticized in recent years, to the extent that one feels somewhat old-fashioned even beginning a paper descriptively in such a way. It is, nevertheless, an approach still much in evidence in scholarly work worldwide, and especially in Europe; and it is not my intention to argue here that it is entirely or even generally without validity. This paper is not an attack on the historical-critical method *per se*.[2] It is, rather, written, for better or for worse, from within the historical-critical camp; and it has an "even if" flavor. The conviction which lies behind it is this: that when one is even a little aware of some of the issues that have been raised by the newer *literary* critics, certain important questions arise in relation to the nature of biblical texts as literature which need to be addressed by historical critics *even if* they do not wish to take on board the whole philosophical and methodological package. It is to two of these questions that I should like to devote my attention here. The first is this: are some texts, particularly poetic texts, quite so susceptible of dating, even quite general dating, as is often assumed by practitioners of the historical-critical method? It is my belief that scholars, in their eagerness to find a context in which to place texts, have frequently overreached themselves, making assumptions that do not stand up to critical examination and ignoring the limitations that the literary qualities of some texts impose upon us. My second question follows on from this: does it matter, and if so, in what sense does it matter, if we cannot date such texts precisely? Is it really always necessary to have a particular historical background in mind in order properly to understand a text? The way in which these questions are phrased should make clear that I am primarily addressing fellow historical critics. I hope, however, that the paper will nevertheless be of some interest to those who are, so to speak, sailing on a different ship, for it represents a sincere, if modest, attempt to build something of a bridge between two sets of scholars who often do not seem to have much to say to each other. The text I should like to take as a "case-study" for the examination of the issues mentioned is Lamentations chapter 1.

On the Dating of Biblical Poetry

Most scholars agree that Lamentations 1 looks back to the events surrounding the fall of the Judean state in the early decades of the 6th century BC. Dissenting voices include Morgenstern,[3] and Treves,[4] who think that events in the early 5th century and the mid-2nd century BC, respectively, are in view. Neither position has attracted support. Most have read the poem specifically against the background of the events of 587/586 BC.[5] Jerusalem suffered a siege at this time, a possible background for the references to famine (1:11, 19–20; cf. 2 Kgs 25:1–3); she was defeated by an enemy and many of her people exiled (1:1, 3, 5 etc.; 2 Kgs 25:4–12), including leaders (1:6; 2 Kgs 25:18–21); erstwhile friends seem to have abandoned and betrayed her (1:2, 7–9, 17 etc.; cf. particularly the Edomites, Jer 27, Obad 7–14; Ps 137:7); the temple precincts were entered by foreigners and its treasures plundered (1:10; cf. 2 Kgs 25: 9, 13–17); and we may well imagine that all this caused disruption of cultic life (1:4). Some have followed Rudolph,[6] on the other hand, in reading the poem against the background of the events only of 598/597 BC. His main argument is that, though it describes the *capture* of the city, as well as entry into and plunder of the temple, it mentions the *destruction* of neither (cf. 2 Kgs 24:10 ff.). Rudolph further maintains, firstly, that the emphasis upon captivity that is to be found in the first poem, in contrast to the second and fourth poems, makes better sense against the background of these events, since the captivity of 597 was worse than that of 587 (2 Kgs 24:10–17); and, secondly, that the various references to the "friends" and "neighbors" are also more easily understood thus. There is evidence that Judah's neighbors were Babylon's allies in 597 (cf. 2 Kgs 24:2; Jer 35:11; Ezek 19:8), but no such evidence exists for 587. Brunet[7] occupies a mediating position here, arguing that the poem looks back on some of the events of 587 (e.g. the fall of the city) but not on others (e.g. the destruction of city and temple).

The precise *terminus a quo* of the poem is thus a matter of dispute among those who regard it as having an early 6th century background, though this is not so disputed as the date of the poem's *composition*. This has been variously given as shortly after 597 (Rudolph, Weiser, Haller); in the same month as the fall of Jerusalem in 587 (Brunet); shortly afterwards (i.e. during the exile: Kraus, Gottwald, Hillers, Brandscheidt, Renkema); and in the early postexilic period (Kaiser). The dates after 587 BC are, of course, arrived at on the whole by arguments unconnected with the question of historical allusions in the text. Those who wish to argue for a date close to 587 stress such things as the style of the poem (the description of events is said to be "fresh" or "vivid"[8]) or its general tone (there is no trace of the kind of hope that appeared in later exilic times, that things would soon change for the better). Those who wish to argue for a *later* date stress such things as the supposed literary links with other later books, positing dependence upon these.[9]

Let us briefly examine these latter arguments first of all. They are all, it seems to me, entirely inconclusive. There is on the one hand little evidence that the links with other Old Testament material that exist are literary rather than simply traditional, and certainly no indication, if literary influence were to be granted, of the direction of that influence. It is clear on the other hand, first, that the "freshness" and "vividness" of the poem may have more to tell us about the creativity and imagination of the author than about when he lived; and secondly, that the lack of any explicit hope in the poem may be explicable in terms of the particular perspective of the author, or the specific use to which it was intended to be put, rather than in terms of the general context in which it was written. To assume that all the individuals or groups of any given period shared the same outlook is an obvious error; and we know that the poem was in later times used liturgically on days of mourning, by people who could not generally be described as lacking a future hope. One thinks here, for example, of the use made of the poems in the

Book of Lamentations by Jews in their services on the 9th of Ab, and by Christians in the *Tenebrae*, the Matins-Lauds services for the last three days of Holy Week. Mournful and hopeless songs have their place even in a generally optimistic, eschatologically-oriented community. Even if it were to be granted that the *terminus a quo* of the poem is 597 or 587 BC, then, the evidence does not seem sufficient for any conclusion to be drawn as to its date of composition. But how strong is the evidence that one or other of these dates should indeed be taken as the *terminus a quo*?

The question here is a fundamental one: is Lamentations 1 really literature of a kind that allows the reconstruction of the specific historical circumstances that might lie behind? There are, it seems to me, two different types of problems with the material from the point of view of a historical reading, both to do with the nature of the language in the poem, and both all but universally overlooked by scholars when they have read it in the past. The first is this: how can we be sure that a concrete reality of the type sought by those who are looking for history in the text in fact lies behind the text at all? Poems are, after all, works of literary art; and many literary critics would, of course, say that it is a mistake to read them as if they had any reference outside themselves. As E. M. Forster puts it: "We have entered a universe that only answers to its own laws, supports itself, internally coheres, and has a new standard of truth. Information is true if it is accurate. A poem is true if it hangs together. Information points to something else. A poem points to nothing but itself."[10] If it is difficult to accept such absolute distinctions, it is at least clear that there is a real difficulty, because of the nature of poetry, in distinguishing which parts of Lamentations 1 may be taken as having a referential function in a historical sense and which may not. Modern translation and comment often seems to overlook this difficulty. It resists, on the whole, the temptation to historicize in such an extreme way as Morgenstern did,[11] when he insisted that there was "a very reasonable probability" that the *mnḥm* in the phrase *'yn-mnḥm* ("no comfort") that recurs throughout the poem was actually the proper name of a king, Menachem, who ruled over the Jewish community in Palestine in 486–485 BC. One suspects, however, that such resistance to historicizing has more to do with the fact that there is no historical evidence that such a king existed than it has to do with qualms about whether the language can be treated in this way. When the poem *can* be read against the background of known events, resistance to historicizing crumbles.

For example, the third line of verse 1 has often been translated as referring to Jerusalem's vassalage (cf. for example RSV's "She that was a princess among the cities has become a vassal"); and commentaries then relate this in a concrete way to the events of 597 or 587 BC.[12] Is it not questionable, however, whether the latter half of the verse is *meant* concretely, particularly when it is realized that the Hebrew word *ms* usually indicates a relationship between master and servant in which forced labor is imposed on the latter (e.g. 1 Kgs 5:27), and thus that the NEB's "She that was a princess among the cities has been put to forced labor" is a much better translation of the line? The theme of the stanza is reversal. Zion is pictured as one who was "full of people" or perhaps "mistress of people,"[13] but is now "lonely," because she has been bereaved of these, and has become as vulnerable as "a widow" was in the ancient Near East. She is further pictured as one who was "great/mistress among the nations" and "princess among the provinces,"[14] but has now become a slave.[15] Are we really justified in interpreting this allusion to slavery in a concrete historical way if we are not also prepared to enquire into the identity of the dead husband who has left a widow? This question gains even more force when it is realized that the contrasting of former glories with present desolation and humiliation is a common element in Old Testament laments and funeral songs. And indeed, more generally, it is clear that *much* of the material of Lamentations 1 is paralleled both in such Old Testament texts and in laments from other parts of the ANE.[16] Accounts of suffering were clearly, to some extent at least, written up in a stereotypical manner, without thought of the immediate "facts." This being the case, how are we to know when concrete reality lies behind the text and when it does not? To take another example: are the "friends" of Zion who are mentioned in the poem historical friends who might in principle be identified, as most commentators have assumed; or are they present simply because abandonment by friends is a traditional theme in laments (e.g. Ps 38:12), and its presence is expected here also as a way of stressing a feeling of isolation? The answer is not obvious; and arguments about whether the friends are Edomites, Syrians or Judeans[17] therefore seem premature.

To what extent we should look for concrete historical reality behind texts of this type at all is thus a difficult question to answer. A second problem is this: even if we were reasonably sure that concrete historical reality lay behind at least some details of the text, how confident could we be about reconstructing that reality? On the one hand, the language of the poem is clearly largely metaphorical; and it is not always as clear as is often assumed exactly for what the metaphors might stand. It is not by any means clear, for example, that 1:6 actually refers, as has often been suggested, to the exile of all the community's leaders. If it does, then the "all" of the first line is plainly an example of hyperbole, of which more in a moment. But I would suggest that the Masoretic Text's depiction of these leaders as stags[18] fleeing before the hunter, finding no pasture and consequently being weak, fleeing without strength before the pursuer, could just as well be taken as metaphorical of their experience of the aftermath of defeat in battle as of their experience of exile. The "departure of majesty" might not refer to their departure from the city, but to the humiliation of the city in the light of these events. Similarly, the "precious things" mentioned in verse 10 might refer to temple treasure, but it need not. The meaning of the first line may be "the enemy has stretched out his hands over everything that she holds dear (in general)," one such thing being the sanctuary. Alternatively, the reference may be more specifically to people: the enemy has not only entered the city to seize "her precious ones" (*mḥmdyh*, cf. Lam 2:4, where *mḥmdy 'yn* certainly refers to people rather than to things), he has also violated her sanctuary. On the one hand, then, the language of the poem is clearly metaphorical; and metaphorical language has a capacity for ambiguity.

On the other hand, the language is clearly often hyperbolic. For example, verse 3 tells us that Judah has gone into exile, a statement that stands in some tension with others in verses 4, 11, 19–20 (which suggest that some, if not many, people remained in Jerusalem). It is, further, a statement that, to our knowledge, exactly corresponds to reality at no point in Judah's history: that is, it was never true, not even in 587 BC,[19] that Judah as an entity went into exile. Verse 4, with its reference, at least in the Masoretic Text,[20] to the priests and maidens who remain in the city being in mourning, is itself in tension with verses 18–19, where the maidens have gone into captivity and the priests and elders have died. Verse 19 is further in tension with regard to this last claim, that the priests and elders have died, with verse 6, if that verse is taken as saying that *all* the leaders of the community have gone into exile ("From the daughter of Zion has departed all her majesty"). Verse 15, similarly, has the young men killed in battle, verse 18 has them carried off into exile. Now, of course, I am being pedantic: the reader knows that such exactitude is not required of this kind of writing, that it is perfectly acceptable for the author to engage in hyperbole. Exaggeration is a natural tendency of the distressed and of authors trying to communicate distress. But such a lack of exactitude is a serious problem for the person who wishes to reconstruct the historical reality that might have generated the poem. If it is the case that the language of the poem is frequently and demonstrably hyperbolic, how could we ever know *how much* inexactitude is actually present at any given point? How could we know which details could be used for historical reconstruction and which not? And how could we then be sure which particular historical background is in view? For it is the detail of texts, not their generalities, that enables us to form an opinion about this.

The nature of the language in Lamentations 1, then—its stereotypical nature, the use of metaphor and hyperbole—limits us in what we can safely say about its historical background. It certainly seems impossible in the light of this to make any decision between 597 and 587 BC. Indeed, it does not seem to me that we can even be sure that it must be one of *these* sets of events that lies behind the poem. After all, the generalities of Lamentations 1—defeat, captivity, hunger[21] and so on—if these are all intended here as historical happenings rather than literary fictions, are things that were part and parcel of life in the ANE, and they would have been experienced by Judeans both before and after these dates. There is at least one passage in the books of Kings that refers specifically to enemies entering Jerusalem and the temple precincts in the period prior to 597 BC (2 Kgs 14:8–14), and a second passage that implies that this happened (1 Kgs 14:25–28).[22] The first records the taking of booty and the capture of an unspecified number of people, the second only the taking of booty; and it might well be that if we had fuller accounts of these events, we would find yet further parallels with our poem.[23] At the other end of the time scale, the events in 167 BC, when Jerusalem was attacked by Apollonius on the orders of Antiochus IV Epiphanes, come even more forcibly to mind. From the point of view of historical allusion, there would appear to be nothing in Lamentations 1, given its literary character, that would forbid us connecting the poem with any of these occasions; for we cannot get beyond the generalities of the poem with any confidence. Even verse 3, with its "Judah has gone into exile," is of no help here. I have already noted that "Judah" must be regarded as hyperbolic whichever historical background we read the poem against; and I should add here that several commentators on this verse have argued that "exile" refers to voluntary migration rather than to forcible removal.[24] The phrase might imply no more, then, than that a number of Judeans fled in the face of the advancing enemy, or in the aftermath of the city's defeat. If skepticism still remains that exaggerated language of this type could have been used of much less significant events than those of the early 6th century, consider 1 Maccabees 1:38–40, a passage that refers to the aftermath of the attack on Jerusalem by Apollonius in 167 BC, and that reads in JB's translation as follows:

> The citizens of Jerusalem fled because of them, she became a dwelling place of strangers; estranged from her own offspring, her children forsook her. Her sanctuary became as deserted as a wilderness, her feasts were turned into mourning, her sabbaths into a mockery, her honor into reproach. Her dishonor now fully matched her former glory, her greatness was turned into grief.

Verse 53 adds that in the circumstances, Israel was forced "into hiding in all their places of refuge." There was, of course, no depopulation of

Jerusalem of the proportions of 597 or 587 BC in 167 BC. The reader of these verses in 1 Maccabees 1 would, however, be forgiven for thinking that there must have been; and the warning is apparent for all readers of Lamentations 1. The text will simply not bear the weight of the fine distinctions that have to be drawn if one position with regard to historical background is to be maintained over against another. I would submit, then, that if the author of Lamentations 1 had specific historical events in mind when he wrote this poem, then they are now forever veiled by the language of the poem itself. And I would further suggest that when scholars have believed themselves capable of identifying the historical background of the poem, they have only really been reading it against one possible background that they happen already to favor for other reasons of which they may or may not be consciously aware.

On the Necessity of Dating Biblical Poetry

Of course, the process of bringing together historical event and text in order to make sense of both is a very natural one, and has gone on throughout the ages. Other backgrounds for the text are found, for example, by the Targum, which sometimes understands it (cf. the Targum to vv. 18–19) against the background of the events of 609 BC (Josiah's death at Megiddo, cf. 2 Kgs 23:29–30) or 70 BC (the destruction of Jerusalem by the Romans). Important events, like important people, tend to attract texts to themselves that may originally have had nothing to do with them. If the historical critic decides that the recovery of the *original* background of such a text is impossible, what are the consequences of this? Does it matter?

It clearly matters from the point of view of someone who wishes to use the text for the purposes of historical reconstruction of one kind or another, whether a history of Israel or of Israelite thought or religion.

And here lies a warning for all who wish to use the biblical texts for this purpose: we need to be more sure than we have sometimes been that they may indeed be safely so used. But does it matter, even granted the historical critic's own emphasis upon the importance of the historical context of a text, from the point of view of *meaning*? The answer seems to be no. An appreciation of what might have been *meant* by a text like Lamentations 1 is by no means dependent upon knowledge of exactly which *particular* events prompted the author to write and when he did his writing. The text is clear enough whether it was written in 850 BC or 450 BC, to take two dates at random; and it might well be argued, indeed, that the lack of any evidence that the author felt it important to give us specific information about date and background is an indication that he himself was not so much interested in the significance of particular historical events as he was concerned to portray an aspect of general human experience. As Cohen[25] puts it, he "may have been attempting to confront catastrophe as an absolute." The author laments not only the fall of this city, "but also all falls from divine grace, all disasters inflicted upon a sinful humanity."[26]

Failure to find a specific historical context for texts like Lamentations 1, then, does not threaten the historical-critical endeavor. For what is essential to this endeavor is that a text is first of all read as a document from the past, before being read as a document for the present, and with a due appreciation of the distance between these two poles. A very general view of the original context as "ancient Israel" will suffice in this case. Indeed, and here the newer literary critics have something very important to say, an obsession with searching for more *specific* historical details in the text may actually lead us to miss the point. If I cannot agree with Forster's absolute distinction between information and poetry that I cited earlier, it is at least clear that poems do not exist *primarily* to impart information; they are not in the end reducible merely to statements. To steal an example from John Barton,[27] we could not without great loss replace Tennyson's poem *In Memoriam* by a sentence such as "I am extremely sorry that my friend has died." And so it is with Lamentations 1. As blindness to the qualities of language may lead us to make questionable assertions about the historical reference of the text, so over-interest in the possible historical reference of the text may lead us to fail to reflect upon the qualities of its language.

Lamentations 1 is more than simply a mine out of which information may be quarried: and to lose sight of this, to read the text simply for information, is to lose sight of its power and pathos, its ability to draw us into the experience that it describes and transform our own experience by so doing. It is these features, indeed, that can help us as modern readers, if we are at all interested in the *theological* enterprise, to overcome a dilemma with which the poem confronts us. For the perspective on human experience and particularly on suffering that is evident here is one that most modern readers, of religious faith or not, would find it difficult to accept: that is, that suffering comes about as the result of sin. This is not an explanation of suffering with which a modern reader would always (if at all) be content: the problem of suffering cannot be reduced to simple equations. There is already a hint in the text itself, of course, that the speakers, the narrator and Zion, do not quite see eye to eye on this matter. As with Job, the perspective of the sufferer and that of the observer on the suffering are different. The last verse of the poem (v. 22) hints that the sufferer herself, as opposed to the more detached narrator, has begun to realize that traditional explanations of suffering do not quite meet her own particular situation. She feels that she is no worse than her enemies, and therefore that the current situation, in which she suffers while they do not, should not be allowed to continue. The key to a modern handling of the text lies in the recognition that we are being drawn by it into a debate. We are being invited, I would suggest, along with the other onlookers described in the text, to empathize with the suffering individual of the poem, to feel the sense of isolation and abandonment that suffering often brings. We are further being invited to learn from her experience, to participate in her attempt (and that of those who observe her plight, represented by the narrator) to relate her experience to the reality of God. The poem reminds us in a forceful way of the challenge of suffering to faith, and invites us to feel and to ponder its significance. The history of Lamentations 1 thus turns out not to be as important for its interpretation as its poetry. Its theological utility is not just a matter of its content, but also of its style.

In the case of Lamentations 1, then, the specific historical background of the text is unclear. This is a disadvantage if we wish to reconstruct history from it. It does not seem to matter in other respects, however, and indeed, if we are overly concerned to use the poem simply to gain information about its background, we may actually miss the real point. Even if we are convinced, then, of the general value of the historical-critical method, it is not always desirable, even if it is possible, to read texts against a historical background.

2

PAST, PRESENT, AND FUTURE IN LAMENTATIONS 3:52–66: THE CASE FOR A 'PRECATIVE PERFECT' RE-EXAMINED

Although this essay comes second in this volume, the paper upon which it is based was actually the first that I ever read at an academic conference; it was delivered a few weeks before its successor (now reproduced in chapter one above).[1] Like the first essay, this one arose out of my work on Lamentations for the New Century Bible Commentary Series, and specifically out of my curiosity concerning a number of Qal verbal forms in Lamentations chapter three that are difficult to understand in a "normal" manner. This observation set me off on a quest to discover whether belief in a "precative perfect" in biblical Hebrew could be justified, which among other things led to substantial amounts of detective work in the British Library in London, reading through Hebrew grammar after Hebrew grammar from the nineteenth century to the present day to find out when the idea first appeared and what scholars over the years have had to say about it. The prevailing view at the conference, as I remember it, was that it was "impossible" that a "precative perfect" should exist. My own continuing view is that sometimes impossible things are nevertheless true, that one needs to look and see whether this is so, and that when one does so in this particular case, one comes to a surprising (and positive) conclusion. The editors of Vetus Testamentum *must have thought there was something to my argument, because they published the essay in 1991.*

The possibility of the existence of a "precative" perfect in Biblical Hebrew—a verb in the perfect used as an optative to express a wish or a hope—was, so far as I have been able to discover, first seriously discussed in the middle of the 19th century by the grammarians Gesenius, Ewald and Böttcher,[2] though the idea had already appeared in the work of earlier scholars such as W. M. L. de Wette, in his commentary of 1811 on the Psalms.[3] In the 5th edition of Ewald's Hebrew grammar, the first in which the author seems clearly to envisage such a use of the perfect, we find the following:

> Das *Perf.* kann, kräftiger als sonst und wie im Ausrufe gesprochen, auch ohne weitere Umbildung zum Ausdrucke des Willens des Redenden dienen, indem nichts als die lebhaftere Farbe der Rede den besondern Nachdruck anziegt ... diese Farbe der Rede im Arabischen recht eigentlich zum Ausdrucke frommer (religiöser) Wünsche dient ... Daß auch im Hebr. das Perf. so gebraucht werden konnte, folgte sicher aus einzelnen Ausdrücken die sonst unverständlich bleiben.

The essentials of the case for the existence of a precative perfect in Hebrew as it has been argued ever since by scholars are clearly presented in Ewald's words: first, that in a number of Old Testament passages, satisfactory sense may not be made of the Hebrew unless the perfect verbs are precative; and secondly, that there exists support from the cognate languages for such a use of the perfect. Arguments along these lines have met with a mixed reception among Old Testament scholars. Among the older students of Hebrew grammar and syntax not already mentioned, König, Davidson and G. R. Driver[4] all refer to the idea of a precative perfect favorably, though differing in the passages in which they believe the form actually occurs. All three are marked out by their conviction that the evidence from the cognate languages can be even more strongly stated than it was by Ewald, Davidson going so far as to say that the precative perfect "is common to all the Shem. languages in some shape" and that "it would be strange if Heb. altogether wanted this usage." A significant minority of more recent scholars, particularly those working in the Psalms, have also responded positively to the idea, notably M. J. Dahood,[5] who claimed that Ugaritic, too, has a precative perfect, and that in the Old Testament psalter alone there are 89 examples of the form to be found. Dahood has been followed to a degree by such scholars as A. A. Anderson and P. C. Craigie in their own commentaries on the Psalms.[6] The precative perfect has not been without its supporters, then. The reaction of the majority of scholars, however, has from the very beginning been one of skepticism. S. R. Driver is one of the earliest of the skeptics,[7] and the influence of his arguments against acceptance of a precative perfect in Hebrew has been immense, to the extent that even in quite recent work, and in spite of all interim developments, it is often considered sufficient in refutation of the concept simply to cite his *Hebrew Tenses*, along with perhaps one of the older grammars that depend upon it.[8] Driver argued, on the one hand, that the parallels from the cognate languages were weak,[9] and, on the other hand, that the perfect verbs of the Old Testament taken as precative by Ewald and others readily admitted of explanation by other means. He himself preferred to explain them in terms of other uses of the perfect that he did accept. Other scholars have explained at least some of the examples in terms of textual corruption. We may note, for example, the treatment of Psalm

4:2 and 7:7 in *BHS*. The possibility that the precative perfect existed in Biblical Hebrew, Driver maintained, could therefore all but be excluded. This is a conviction that is still widely shared today.

Now it is no part of my intention in this article to join the argument over the appearance or nonappearance of the precative perfect in languages cognate with Biblical Hebrew. Whatever the truth with regard to this—and there is no lack of modern support among those best qualified to judge for the contention that it does so appear, particularly in Ugaritic[10]—it is clear that internal evidence must in any case be of primary importance in determining whether the precative perfect is to be found in the Old Testament. One could well believe that precative perfects appear in the cognate languages and argue still, as W. H. Bellinger has recently done,[11] that the precative perfect is "an imposition on Hebrew from other Semitic languages which has not been substantiated from the Old Testament." The cognate languages give us a plausible context in which to argue the case; but internal evidence must be of primary importance. It is the question of whether such evidence exists that will once again be addressed in this article. Because of the way in which the debate has developed, however, it is necessary, before turning to specifics, briefly to consider what kind of evidence one might expect to find. Our starting point here is, it seems to me, crucially important. Scholars who have followed S. R. Driver have argued that because possible examples of the precative perfect in Hebrew can be explained by other means, we need not admit that this form exists at all. This does not seem to me the correct way in which to frame the argument. It is, after all, self-evident that the perfect verbs under consideration can be explained in other ways. If alternative explanations of these verbs were inherently and obviously implausible, they would not have been widely accepted. The fact that such alternatives exist is not, however, sufficient reason for rejecting the possibility that any given perfect verb is nevertheless precative. There seems little good reason for placing the burden of proof in such cases upon the new proposal rather than upon traditional views. Our system of Hebrew grammar was not, after all, handed down from above on tablets of stone like the commandments. It is, on the contrary, an artificial construct, a way of looking at things which can and does change. This itself may seem self-evident; yet it is a fact of which scholars often seem to have lost sight in the debate under discussion here. The question in the case of any individual passage is not, "should we accept a new proposal where alternative proposals already exist?" but rather, "which of the several proposals that have been made, including the new one, makes best sense of the passage overall?"

A Key Passage: Lamentations 3:52–66

The present article will ask this question anew of one passage, Lamentations 3:52–66, which appeared on Ewald's original list of passages which were *unverständlich* without resource to the concept of a precative perfect. This was, in fact, one of the key passages in the early discussion about the form, Böttcher and Davidson also citing it as one of their proof texts, and S. R. Driver feeling compelled to address himself to it specifically in refutation. One might have expected, then, that more recent scholars working on Lamentations 3:52–66 would have felt constrained at least to mention the theory, if only to dismiss it. This has not, however, generally been the case. Of the major post-war commentaries on Lamentations, only those of Wiesmann, Rudolph, Lamparter, Gordis and Hillers do so, only the last two of these positively; and of the monographs, only that of Gottlieb (also positively).[12] For the most part the earlier debate has simply been ignored. I shall argue, however, that, if it is the case that Ewald has fallen prey to the scholarly affliction of over-certainty which manifests itself in the too frequent use of words like "unintelligible" and "impossible," then at least it would be true to say that all the alternative possible understandings of the perfect verbs in Lamentations 3:56–61 involve us in exegetical implausibilities.[13] The acceptance of these verbs as precative perfects, on the other hand, results in an entirely coherent reading of Lamentations 3:52–66 and of the chapter as a whole. The balance of the internal evidence, in other words, favors our acceptance of the existence of this form in Biblical Hebrew.

The crucial question of interpretation in Lamentations 3:52–66 is this: are two situations of distress described in this passage, or only one? The vast majority of commentators have thought two, differentiating between past distress from which deliverance has already taken place, and present distress in the midst of which God's help is now sought. Among those who hold this view we may note, for example, Kraus, Weiser and Kaiser.[14] This is also the understanding of the passage implicit in the translations offered by the major modern English versions (RSV, JB, NEB, NIV). On this view, there is an element of thanksgiving in the passage, the memory of past deliverance functioning as an encouragement in the midst of present troubles. These present troubles are, it is argued, certainly in view by verse 63, though there is disagreement among commentators as to the precise point of transition between past and present. Indeed, it is the difficulty of finding any plausible point of transition that constitutes the main objection to such an interpretation of the passage.[15]

One older suggestion is that the transition in thought occurs between verses 58 and 59: this is the view of Zenner and Wiesmann.[16] The perfects of Lamentations 3:52–8 describe past distress and deliverance from distress, those of verses 59–61 God's seeing and hearing present distress without yet having acted to relieve it. The author pleads that he would now act (*špṭh mšpṭy*): "judge my cause," verse 59 (if we accept the Masoretic Text's imperative here as original).[17] It has to be said, however, that it is not a natural reading of the text to break it at this point, differentiating between "You have taken up my cause" in verse 58 and "You have seen the wrong done to me" in verse 59. Nor is the distinction particularly between God's seeing and his acting convincing. The fact that God is asked again to "behold" (*hbyṭh*) the author's suffering in verse 63 renders such exegesis strained—it implies that the author does not, in fact, believe that God has yet seen his plight. Moreover, analysis of *r'h* elsewhere in Lamentations 3 and, indeed, in the remainder of the book, does not suggest that such a distinction is otherwise in view when the verb is used. The closely preceding verse 50, in fact, clearly implies that the author of our poem believed that "seeing" and deliverance go hand in hand. The point at which God takes notice is the point at which lament may cease. Gottlieb makes this point generally with regard to the use of both *r'h* and *šm'* in Old Testament laments. More recent exegetes (for example, Kraus, Weiser, Kaiser, Brandscheidt) have, accordingly, preferred to see the transition as lying somewhere in verses 60–3.[18] It may immediately be granted that the correction of the imperative in verse 59 to a perfect that is necessary to make this view at all plausible has textual support. The LXX and Peshitta both read the verb here as a perfect. It is stretching credibility, however, to suppose that the oppression of verse 63 is different from that of some or all of the remainder of verses 60–2. There is no hint in verses 60–3 that all the third person masculine plural suffixes (*nqmtm* and *mḥšbtm* in v. 60; *ḥrptm* and *mḥšbtm* again in v. 61; *whgywnm* in v. 62; and *šbtm*, *wqymtm* and *mngyntm* in v. 63) do not refer to the same people and the same situation.

The artificiality of differentiating between two situations of distress in the passage is, then, all too apparent; and it seems better to attempt an interpretation of it that does not have recourse to such a strategy. Rudolph ([n. 12] 233, 236–237) is one among several commentators who have, more plausibly, argued that only one period of oppression is in view. His position is distinctive, however, in that he argues that the whole passage, and not just part of it, is a *Danklied* referring to past suffering and deliverance. The *Bittgebet* identified in the closing verses of the chapter by most other scholars does not exist. The imperfect forms *tšyb*, *ttn* and *trdp* in verses 64–6 he explains as forced upon the author by the acrostic structure of the poem. As in Lamentations 2:22a (*tqr'*), the verbs must begin with the *taw* of the imperfect, even though they refer to the past. The imperatives of Lamentations 3:59 and 63 (*hbyṭh*) he emends to perfects. This is certainly one way of resolving the problem. It is not convincing, however. The emendation of the imperative in verse 63 to the perfect has no textual support, as Rudolph himself recognizes, and this alone makes his understanding of the following imperfects improbable. It is more likely that these refer to the future, like *tb'* in Lamentations 1:22, and that the chapter ends, like chapter 1 and other Old Testament laments (e.g. Pss 25, 44, 79), with a plea for future action. If Lamentations 3:52–66 does refer to only one situation of distress, then, it must be distress currently being endured, rather than distress already past. The solution must be sought in a recasting of the first part of the passage rather than the second.

Careful analysis of Lamentations 3:56–7 provides additional evidence which points in this direction. In most treatments that regard at least verses 55–8 as referring to the past, verse 56b (*'l-t'lm 'znk lrwḥty lšw'ty*) is regarded as containing the content of a past plea to God: thus the RSV's "thou didst hear my plea, 'Do not close thine ear to my cry for help!'" This is obviously not impossible. There is, however, no parallel to such a construction elsewhere. We do occasionally get a reference back to what the petitioner said or thought before prayer began, analogous to what we find in verse 54 (cf. Ps 31:23). In no other address to God in the Old Testament of which I am aware, however, is a statement that he has heard (*šm'*) a petition followed by a citation of that petition. If such a reading were accepted, then, we would be dealing with a unique form. There are, on the other hand, many parallels to pleas to God in the present in which verbal or nominal forms from *'zn* are used;[19] and the other imperatives in the section (v. 59, if original, and v. 63) both express pleas in the present of this kind. Verse 59 provides a direct parallel (perfect followed by imperative). Similarly, the phrase *bywm'qr'* addressed to God (v. 57) nowhere else refers to the past, but always to the present (Pss 56:10, 102:3; cf. also Ps 136:7). A present casting of the whole passage allows renderings of both this phrase and verse 56b which are more consonant with other Old Testament evidence than those which are usually suggested.

If the general case for a present casting of Lamentations 3:52–66 is sound, the question then arises as to how, exactly, the perfect verbs are to be explained. One possibility is that the perfects not only of verses 59 ff. (with Zenner and Wiesmann), but also of verses 52–8, are true perfects rather than simple pasts: "you have heard my plea," "you have come near," "you have redeemed my life," etc. The passage then tells us that though the poet has asked for God's help, and God has initiated such help (vv. 52–62), deliverance has not yet occurred (vv. 63–6). It is immediately clear, however, that one of the weaknesses of the Wiesmann/Zenner theory reappears here in aggravated form. We now have a passage in which God is said not only to have heard and spoken, but also to have acted already, and yet in which deliverance is still in the future.

Such an interpretation would also require us to take verse 56 (assuming that the arguments above with regard to its present casting are accepted) as first stating that God has heard the poet's plea and then asking him to hear it. On both counts, this alternative must be rejected, and so, for the same reasons, must the suggestion of B. Albrektson,[20] who thinks that a present tense is appropriate throughout these verses.

It seems clear, then, that only a future reference for the perfect verbs of verses 56–61 really does them justice. The distress, though caused by past actions (vv. 52–4), is indeed being endured in the present, and the call from the poet (v. 55) that God should respond to this situation is no doubt being uttered in the present. As D. Michel[21] has shown, the perfect of Heb. *qr'* in appeals to God in the Psalms must often be translated as a present tense, as in Pss 17:6, 88:10, 119:145–6, 130:1, 141:1. The poet's plea is uttered in the present; God's hearing, seeing and acting, however, must be understood as future events. We are thus able to accept verse 56b as a present cry for relief, while at the same time accepting that there is only one situation of distress and one enemy in verses 52–66, and that verses 64–6 look to the future. The text so understood fits in well with the flow of thought in the poem as a whole, with several links back to earlier sections connecting the speaker's experience here with his and the people's experience as described earlier.[22] The speaker is still trapped like an animal (vv. 52–3; cf. v. 47); God has not yet responded to prayer (v. 56; vv. 8, 44); he needs someone to achieve justice for him (vv. 58–60, esp. *rbt 'dny ryby npšy* in v. 58; cf. vv. 34–6, esp. *ryb* in v. 36); God has not yet "seen" the situation (vv. 59–60; cf. vv. 49–50); the taunts of verse 30 continue (v. 61), he is still the "burden of their songs" (*mngyntm* in v. 63; cf. *ngyntm* in v. 14); God must now "pursue" the enemy as he had "pursued" his own people (*rdp*, vv. 66 and 43).

The idea that perfect verbs standing alone can have a future reference is, of course, not alien to traditional Hebrew grammar. The existence of a "perfect of confidence" or "prophetic perfect" is generally accepted by scholars, Gesenius-Kautzsch (§ 106 *n*, note 2) stating that the perfect is used in such circumstances "To express facts which are undoubtedly imminent, and, therefore, in the imagination of the speaker, already accomplished." Gottlieb (60), indeed, mentions this form as a candidate for verses 56 ff., apparently seeing little difference between this form and the "precative perfect." The interchange between perfect, imperfect and imperative he explains in terms of vacillation in the man praying between trust and hope. It must be questioned, however, whether such a reading of the passage is any less artificial than the others already examined above. Verse 56 again provides us with the litmus test, for the two parts of this line are best understood, if both refer to the future, as strictly parallel ("hear my plea; do not close your ear to my cry for help"). Such a combination of a request that God should hear (*šmʿ*) a prayer with a request that he should use his ears (nominal or verbal forms of the root *ʾzn*) is common elsewhere in the Old Testament (e.g. Pss 17:6, 39:13, 54:4, 89:9, 130:2, 143:1), and Psalm 130:1–2 is particularly close to the sense which we are suggesting for Lamentations 3:55–6 taken together:

šyr hmʿlwt mmʿmqym qrʾtyk yhwh ʾdny šmʿh bqwly thyynh ʾznyk qšbwt lqwl tḥnwny

A Song of Ascents. Out of the depths I cry to you, O Lord! Lord, hear my voice! Let your ears be attentive to the voice of my supplications!

qrʾty šmk yhwh mbwr tḥtywt qwly šmʿt ʾl-tʿlm ʾznk lrwḥty lšwʿty

I call on your name, O Lord, from the depths of the pit! Hear my voice! Do not close your ear to my gasping, my cry for help!

There is of course a difficulty with the rare *rwḥh* in Lamentations 3:56, a word otherwise appearing only in Exodus 8:11, where it seems to have the meaning "relief, respite." My translation here takes its cue from the Vulgate's *a singultu meo*, assuming the root to be *rwḥ*, "to breathe."[23] Whether this is correct or not, the common elements in the two passages are clear enough: the allusion to the depths, the plea in the present to God using the perfect of *qr'*, the request that God should hear the poet's voice (*šm'*), and the parallel request that he should use his ears. Psalm 102:2–3, in addition, is similar in sense to our suggested reading of verses 56–7 taken together:

yhwh šm'h tplty wšw'ty 'lyk tbw' 'l-tstr pnyk mmny bywm ṣr ly hṭh- 'ly 'znk bywm 'qr' mhr 'nny
   Hear my prayer, O LORD; let my cry for help come to you! Do not hide your face from me in the day of my distress! Incline your ear to me; answer me speedily in the day when I call!

qwly šm't 'l-t'lm 'znk lrwḥty lšw'ty qrbt bywm 'qr'k 'mrt 'l-tyr'
   Hear my voice! Do not close your ear to my gasping, my cry for help! Come near in the day when I call! Tell me not to be afraid!

The common elements here are the request that God would hear (*šm'*) his cry for help (*šw'h*), the accompanying reference again to the ear (*'zn*), and the request that God would act on the day when the poet calls (*bywm 'qr*). Lamentations 3:56 taken in this way makes much better sense than it does as a statement of assurance immediately followed by a plea. We should, then, resist this final attempt to allow an explanation of the perfect verbs in Lamentations 3:56–61 within the framework of traditional Hebrew grammar. The prophetic and precative perfects should be clearly distinguished; and it is the latter whose presence should be accepted in this passage.

Conclusion

All the traditional renderings of the perfects in Lamentations 3:56–61, then, involve implausibility. They require that we accept unique forms of expression and strained or tortuous exegesis, sometimes involving unsupported emendations. If we interpret these verbs as precative perfects, on the other hand, then without going beyond the available textual and formal evidence, we obtain a coherent and straightforward reading of Lamentations 3:52–66, and indeed of chapter 3 as a whole. The balance of the internal evidence, in other words, favors our acceptance of the existence of the precative perfect in Biblical Hebrew.

3

THE MESSIAH IN THE BOOK OF KINGS

Around 1992, I received an invitation from Professor Bob Hubbard, Old Testament editor of the New International Biblical Commentary Series, to write the commentary on 1–2 Kings. This was a great opportunity to bring the expertise I had gained in these books from a technical point of view, in completing my Ph.D. dissertation, into conjunction both with my developing narrative-critical interests and my theological commitments, and to "see what happened." The commentary was published in 1995, and it was followed in short order by a guide to 1–2 Kings in the Sheffield Old Testament Guides series, published in 1997. One of the interpretive issues that faces every reader of 1–2 Kings concerns the authors' perspective on the future: are they fundamentally pessimistic about it, or is there a future hope embedded in the books? If there is, does it involve a royal figure, and can it rightly be called a "messianic" hope? This essay arose out of my reflections on these questions, and like the commentary, it was originally published in 1995, in a volume entitled The Lord's Anointed: Interpretation of Old Testament Messianic Texts. *The attentive reader will notice in the essay a pronounced development in my thinking, relative to the two preceding essays, in the direction not only of narrative-critical but also of canonical reading.*

The book of Kings may not immediately strike the reader of this essay-collection as very promising territory in which to hunt for messianic secrets. The *a priori* implausibility of the venture (as it might seem to many) has as much to do with the general trend of scholarly thinking about messianism in the Old Testament in the last three hundred years as it has, more particularly, with the recent history of interpretation of the book of Kings itself.

On the one hand, there has been something of a general reaction in Europe (and later elsewhere) since the beginning of the eighteenth century against those reading practices of the early and medieval church which found references to a Messiah widely scattered throughout the Old Testament, even in places where the "plain sense" of the Hebrew text could not obviously support the interpretation offered. As early as 1724 the Deist Anthony Collins, in his *Discourse of the Grounds and Reasons of the Christian Religion*, argued that the New Testament interpretation of even fairly important "messianic" passages (e.g., Isa 7:14) could not be sustained in terms of the literal, historical sense of those passages. The force of this kind of criticism was keenly felt by all those for whom the "plain meaning" of the Old Testament was important, whether they were Protestant Christians intent on reading it as Scripture or other interested parties intent on reading it simply as historical artifact. In fact, Collins' view of the proper method of approach to the Old Testament—that it must be studied historically in the first instance without reference to the New Testament—in due course became the dominant view not only in the universities but also in the Protestant Christian Church, right across the theological spectrum. The corollary was the birth of a discipline of Old Testament Studies that saw as its first task the explication of the Old Testament texts in their own terms rather than in relation to either New Testament or Christian theology;

and one of the consequences of this was a significant reduction in the number of Old Testament passages that could "safely" be claimed as messianic. The burden of proof now fell firmly on those who wished to claim that passages had this character, particularly when it was realized the extent to which the language and imagery that they contained could be explained in terms of high concepts of kingship that Israel shared with her neighbors. How far were "messianic" passages truly messianic, then, and how far did they concern kings of actual historical experience described in idealized (but fairly stereotypical) language? Increasingly the tendency was to assume the latter unless the former could be proved "beyond reasonable doubt." A broad scholarly orthodoxy on the question emerged, in which it was claimed that the majority of the passages that popular theology had interpreted as messianic were in fact concerned with the kings of historical experience, the ideal of kingship becoming the expectation of a future Messiah only in the postexilic period.[1] It is no surprise that in this general context the book of Kings, which is itself in large measure a *description* of the kings of historical experience, should not immediately be thought of as a book where messianism might be found.

Nor has the recent history of interpretation of the book of Kings itself encouraged readers to think of it as a messianic book to any great degree. The extent to which the book looks to the future at all has in fact been questioned, most famously by Martin Noth,[2] who argued that Kings was a fundamentally pessimistic work designed simply to tell the story of Israel's downfall and of the end of her monarchy. Even those who have disagreed with Noth, however, in arguing for a future hope in Kings, have not generally highlighted messianism as an important strand of that hope.[3] The notable exception has been von Rad,[4] who finds an unresolved tension in the book between judgment and hope, the latter being a messianic hope based on the promise to the house of David of an everlasting dynasty. The closing verses of 2 Kings (25:27–30) represent a hint that the Davidic line will one day be restored through a descendant of Jehoiachin, who remains alive in Babylon. Many commentators, however, find the hope allegedly present here so muted as to be virtually unexpressed; and many, therefore, have found it difficult to follow von Rad on this point.[5] If hope exists at all in Kings, it has been "democratized." Kingly figures belong to the unsatisfactory past from which Israel must now break free in corporate dependence upon the God who restores from exile.

It might seem, then, that the climate is not favorable to the project in view here. Yet the climate is itself changing once again with regard to the way in which Old Testament narrative texts are being read. If it is true that post-Enlightenment Old Testament scholarship has, on the whole, read these texts piecemeal, believing them to be composite and largely incoherent entities and focusing upon the parts rather than the whole; then it is equally true that in the past two decades narrative criticism has subjected the assumption of incoherence and its allied exegetical practices to searching critique.[6] There has been a recovery of a sense of the whole, where books like Kings are concerned; and with that, a recovery of the sense of the literary artistry which binds the whole together.[7] Again, if it is true that the past three hundred years has seen the gradual breakdown of the Bible story as the defining story of Western culture— the unified narrative whole that set the context for individual human narratives coming generally to be understood, rather, as a collection of unrelated fragments requiring recontextualization by the individual reader in order to be properly understood—then it is equally true that in the past two decades this fragmentation of the Bible (book separated from book, author set against author) has come under intense scrutiny.

Is it really the case that individual Old Testament books are read with greater integrity if they are read in isolation from their neighbors in the first instance? Is it really the case that we gain a more "objective" grasp of what an Old Testament book has to say if we try to bracket out wider contexts of interpretation while we are reading it? Skepticism is, in fact, increasingly voiced in respect of the historical-critical method in areas quite other than the traditional conservative heartlands.[8] Why should we believe that the most appropriate way to read a book like Kings is in isolation from the remainder of the Old Testament, when the high level of intertextuality that exists between Kings and other Old Testament books itself invites us to do otherwise?[9] Why should we believe at all that books like Kings are read more "objectively" if read in conscious disregard of the New Testament and of Christian theology, when all readings are so obviously affected by the contexts in which they are carried out and when noncontextual reading is impossible? These are good questions; and in the absence of satisfactory answers, many have begun to wonder whether "historical" reading of the Old Testament as it has been widely practiced in the modern period is a good thing.

The climate is changing; the burden of proof has been more fairly distributed; and it is as the chilly winds of change are blowing and the baggage is being shared around that we come to reexamine this question of messianism and the book of Kings. Is messianism after all to be found in this book? My brief answer is in the affirmative; my lengthier and more detailed answer will occupy the remainder of this essay.

2 Kings 25:27–30

I begin where von Rad placed so much of his emphasis—at the end. How is 2 Kings 25:27–30 to be read? It might be taken simply as the final nail in the coffin that the authors have so skillfully been preparing for Israel throughout the preceding chapters of the book. Solomon's glory has in the end departed to Babylon. The empire has dissolved. The Babylonian king has destroyed Solomon's city, his palace and his temple; he controls his empire, and he possesses all his wealth. Now Solomon's last-surviving successor (so far as we know) sits, amply provided for, at the Babylonian king's table—the great symbol of imperial power (cf. the reference to Solomon's table in 1 Kgs 4:27). He sits; he eats; and then (it is implied) he dies. The exiles (it is also implied) ought to behave in the same way, accepting the advice of Gedaliah to the people in Judah: "Settle down … serve the king … and it will go well with you" (2 Kgs 25:24).

Yet in the context of the book of Kings taken as a whole, it is difficult to believe that this is all there is to it; and that is the immediate context, of course, in which 2 Kings 25:27–30 must be read. We cannot read the final words of the story without due attention to all the words that have preceded them and prepared us for them. The first thing to notice here is the simple fact that the authors of Kings have chosen to tell us that Jehoiachin lived on at all (in contrast to Jehoahaz, 2 Kgs 23:34), when they could have allowed him to dwell in obscurity (with Zedekiah, 2 Kgs 24:18–25:7). They did not need to recount this part of Jehoiachin's tale. They have also chosen to contrast the fate of Jehoiachin's family (exile, 24:15) very clearly with that of Zedekiah's (death, 25:7). It is Zedekiah, and not Jehoiachin, who ends up effectively as the "eunuch in Babylon" that Isaiah had foreseen (20:18), a mutilated man deprived of heirs who might later claim the throne. Jehoiachin, by contrast, has living descendants. The significance of this mere fact is more clearly seen when we consider, first of all, the general theme of promise as it appears in Kings; and secondly, the whole movement of the narrative in 2 Kings up to this point.

Promise is a much more prominent theme in Kings than has sometimes been supposed. The two most important divine promises referred to are those given to David, on the one hand, and to the patriarchs, on the other. The promise to David, that he should have an eternal dynasty, appears in Kings in a curiously paradoxical form. For much of the narrative it provides us with an explanation as to why the Davidic dynasty survives, when other dynasties do not, *in spite of* the disobedience of David's successors (e.g., 1 Kgs 11:36; 15:4). It is viewed, in other words, as unconditional. Judah's fate is not to be the same as Israel's, Jerusalem's fate is to be different from Samaria's, because God has promised David a "lamp," a descendant who will always sit on his throne. Thus when Solomon sins the Davidic line does not lose the throne entirely, but retains "one tribe" (1 Kgs 11:36) in the meantime, with the prospect of restoring its dominion at some time in the future (1 Kgs 11:39). When Abijam sins, likewise, his son still retains the Judean throne (1 Kgs 15:4). The background here is evidently the promise to David as it is recorded in 2 Samuel 7, where the sins of David's descendants are to be punished by the "rod of men" rather than by the kind of divine rejection experienced by Saul (2 Sam 7:14–16). It is this promise that makes the ultimate difference between Davidic kings and those of other royal houses throughout much of the book of Kings; that makes the Judean dynasty unshakeable even while the dynasties of the northern kingdom are like "reeds swaying in the water" (1 Kgs 14:15). The dynasty survives *in spite of* the disobedience of David's successors. At other times in Kings, however, the continuance of the dynasty is seemingly made *dependent* upon the obedience of David's successors (1 Kgs 2:4; 8:25; 9:4–5). The promise is treated as conditional, rather than unconditional. There is thus a tension between law and grace where David's dynasty is concerned, a tension that is never fully resolved. A similar tension is apparent when we turn to the other great promise referred to in the book, the promise to Abraham, Isaac, and Jacob of descendants and everlasting possession of the land of Canaan. This is a promise, too, that influences God's treatment of his people in the story (2 Kgs 13:23, and implicitly in 1 Kgs 4:20–21, 24; 18:36); and it is a promise that lies in the background of Solomon's prayer in 1 Kings 8:22–53, as he looks forward to the possibility of forgiveness after judgment. Yet it is a promise that seemingly finds itself in conflict with the facts as the book of Kings closes, when disobedience has led to expulsion from the land and exile in a foreign empire.

Keeping these tensions in mind, let us now turn to the movement of the narrative in 2 Kings. Throughout the initial stages of this second section of the book, the reader still awaits the judgment that Elijah has prophesied will fall upon Ahab's house (1 Kgs 21:17–29)—judgment unexpectedly delayed, in the first instance, by Ahab's own repentance when confronted by its announcement. The delay is sufficiently long to allow the kingdom of Judah to be drawn into Israel's sins. After two relatively righteous kings (Asa, Jehoshaphat), we discover in 2 Kings 8:16–29 that Judah has found herself with two kings who share with Ahab's children both their names (Jehoram, Ahaziah) and their penchant for idolatry. The disease in Ahab's household has proved infectious, carried south by his daughter (2 Kgs 8:18). Intermarriage has again wreaked its havoc (cf. 1 Kgs 11:1 ff.; 16:31–33). Yet God has promised David a "lamp" (2 Kgs 8:19). Here we find the reappearance of the motif mentioned above which has already been seen twice in 1 Kings (11:36; 15:4), the reappearance of the promise that makes the ultimate difference between Davidic kings and others.

It is certainly this promise that makes the difference in 2 Kings 9–11. When we are told about the Judean Ahaziah in 2 Kings 8:25–29, it seems at first that the promise is under threat. Although we anticipate that it will hold good for Jehoram's son as well as for his father, we note that it is not explicitly repeated in 8:25–29; and it is somewhat disconcerting to read in verse 26 that Ahaziah added only one year of life to the twenty two that had passed by the time he succeeded to the throne. Did he die without an heir, we ask? What of the Davidic line after him? It is particularly disconcerting when we read alongside this information, in verse 25, that he came to the throne in Jehoram of Israel's twelfth year; for we know from 2 Kings 3:1 that Jehoram only ruled for twelve years. We are in the last moments of the house of Ahab, and it seems that the house of David, mixed up through marriage with this other, most wicked of royal houses, is to be caught up in the judgment. When we then read in 2 Kings 11:1 that after Ahaziah's death Athaliah the queen-mother "proceeded to destroy the whole royal house," it seems that the end has indeed come. Yet this is not quite so. One royal prince remains to carry on the line (11:2); and against all the odds, he survives six years of his grandmother's "foreign" rule to emerge once again as king in a land purified of the worship of foreign gods (11:3–20).

The significance of this for our reading of the end of the book of Kings becomes apparent once we have grasped how it is that Hebrew narrative in general works and how it is that the Ahab story in particular provides the framework within which 2 Kings 21–23 must be read. At the level of generality, one of the striking things about biblical storytelling is its use of narrative patterning. The biblical story is quite self-consciously told in such a way that events and characters in the later chapters recall events and characters in the earlier chapters, by way of comparison or contrast. We are thus invited to read the various chapters of the story together in order to gain a fuller understanding of what is being said overall. Within the book of Kings itself, for example, the kings of Judah are everywhere compared and contrasted with David (e.g., 1 Kgs 15:3, 11), while Jeroboam is painted in the colors, first of Moses, and then of Aaron (1 Kgs 12).[10] What is interesting in regard to 2 Kings 21–23 in particular is that the characters of both Manasseh and Josiah are drawn there so as to remind us, each in its own way, of Ahab. Manasseh imitates Ahab by building altars to Baal (2 Kgs 21:3; cf. also the Asherah pole in 1 Kgs 16:33) and by worshipping idols (2 Kgs 21:11; cf. 1 Kgs 21:26). The judgment that will fall on Jerusalem because of Manasseh's sins is to be analogous to what happened to the house of Ahab (2 Kgs 21:13). That was judgment, of course, that completely destroyed the royal house (1 Kgs 21:21–22; 2 Kgs 9–10; cf. 1 Kgs 14:10 and 21:21 for the only occurrences prior to 2 Kgs 21:12 of "I am going to bring ... disaster"). It seems from this that the Davidic line is to end after all, divine promises notwithstanding. It seems that there will be no escape, on this occasion, like the narrow escape of 2 Kings 11:1 ff.—that this time, identification with Ahab will lead the house of David to Ahab's fate. What is said about the righteous Josiah does nothing to dispel this impression. Huldah's words to him in 2 Kings 22:15–20 simply confirm what we already know from the unnamed prophets of 2 Kings 21. It is true that because Josiah has humbled himself before the LORD (v. 19), he will not personally see all the disaster that is to fall on Jerusalem. There is to be a delay of the kind that we saw with Ahab, whose house was also spared for a while because he tore his clothes and "humbled himself" (1 Kgs 21:27–28). Manasseh's grandson, in other words, is now being treated, as his grandfather was, like Ahab. Josiah's reaction makes a difference—but only to him. The judgment that has been announced will still surely fall, as it fell on the house of the apostate predecessor.

These parallels drawn between the house of David and the house of Ahab in 2 Kings 21–23 clearly imply that the destruction of David's house will be total. There will be no escape of the kind that occurred in Athaliah's day. The full significance of the mere mention of Jehoiachin and his family in the closing chapters of Kings now becomes apparent. He reappears in the narrative, in fact, in a manner strikingly reminiscent of the appearance of Joash after that earlier destruction of the "whole royal family." He survives like Joash, unexpectedly, in the midst of carnage; and he represents, like Joash during Athaliah's reign, the potential for the continuation of the Davidic line at a later time, when foreign rule has been removed. All is not yet necessarily lost, after all; the destruction of the family of the "last king of Judah" (Zedekiah) does not mean that there is no Davidide left. As the prayer of Solomon in 1 Kings 8:22–53 looks beyond the disaster of exile, grounding its hope for the restoration of Israel to her land in God's gracious and unconditional election of Abraham, Isaac and Jacob (cf. also 1 Kgs 17:36–37; 2 Kgs 13:23; 14:27); as it refuses to accept that God's words about the rejection of people, city and temple (e.g., 2 Kgs 21:14; 23:27) are his final words; so too 2 Kings 25:27–30 in its narrative context hints that the unconditional aspects of the Davidic promise may even still, after awful judgment has fallen, remain in force. They express the hope that grace may, in the end, triumph over law; the hope that, God's wrath having been poured out upon good Josiah's sons, his (admittedly wicked) grandson might still produce a further "lamp for Jerusalem," as his (equally wicked) forefathers did (1 Kgs 11:36; 15:4; 2 Kgs 8:19). These closing verses of the book thus hang on tenaciously, in difficult circumstances, to the words of 2 Samuel 7:15–16: "my love will never be taken away from him ... your throne shall be established forever."

Can such a hope reasonably be described as "messianic"? It is certainly a hope focused on the unforeseen future, a time which is not this time. There is no sense in the book of Kings that the king of the future is anything other than a distant prospect. It is equally clear that the king who is sought is an ideal king. The book of Kings always measures its monarchs in terms of the ideal, finding almost all of them wanting in serious respects. The two least criticized, Hezekiah and Josiah, together with the early Solomon (criticized, but nevertheless blessed by God to an unparalleled extent) are themselves interesting, to the extent that they may be taken as indicating the shape of the ideal towards which the authors of Kings were looking. A full answer to our question requires a closer look in the first instance at the way in which the reigns of these kings are described.

Solomon, Hezekiah, and Josiah in Kings

The early Solomon, we are told, inspired by the wisdom which comes from above (1 Kgs 3), rules over a well-ordered, happy and prosperous kingdom (1 Kgs 4:1–20). Even though the people are as numerous as the sand on the seashore (a fulfillment of the Abrahamic promise in Gen 22:17), his wisdom is of equal measure (1 Kgs 4:29). He is fitted for the task. Here is government by the righteous person whose prospering is allied to the people's rejoicing (Prov 29:2), rather than government by the wicked person who makes the people groan (Prov 29:2; cf. 1 Sam 8:10–18). Solomon's reign extends, indeed, over all the kingdoms from the Euphrates to the land of the Philistines, as far as the border of Egypt (4:21, 24)—a large area, corresponding to the ideal extent of Israel's dominion as promised to Abraham in Genesis 15:18, and apparently corresponding also to a very great extent to the area of David's dominion as we may deduce it from texts such as 2 Samuel 8:1–14 and 2 Samuel 10. The countries in this region, we are told, brought tribute and were Solomon's subjects all his life; and so it is that an enormous quantity of food flows into the kingdom from outside, with the result that all Israel, from Dan to Beersheba, lived each man under his own vine and fig tree. That is to say, they lived under God's blessing (Joel 2:22; Mic 4:4; contrast Ps 105:33, Jer 5:17), having a degree of economic independence (cf. 2 Kgs 18:31 for an explicit threat to such independence). This fits in very much with the thrust of 1 Kings 4:7–20 (that Solomon's economic arrangements were not oppressive, and that his subjects were happy and prosperous under his rule); and, indeed, it gives us the broader context in which to comprehend these verses. It is at least partly because of the flow of goods into Israel from outside that the system of districts described in 1 Kings 4:7–19 does not create economic difficulties for the people (v. 20). If this is indeed the line of argument here, then it is no surprise that, having described the broader economic picture, the authors should then return in verses 27–28 to the local position. It is because of Solomon's international position that the district officers are able to do their job in the way they do. The picture painted here is, then, a glorious one. It is very much the picture that the book of Micah paints of the kingdom of the "last days," in which swords are beaten into ploughshares; in which every man will sit under his own vine and fig tree, with no one to make them afraid; in which the nations come in pilgrimage to Zion (Mic 4:1–5). The gathering around Solomon's table that is described in 1 Kings 4 in essence represents a kind of proto-messianic banquet, with Solomon presiding as the ideal king.

Hezekiah appears in the narrative of Kings in a context where the long-term absence of a king who is truly "like David" has raised questions about Judah's future. Judah has most recently known a thoroughly bad king, unlike David in every respect (Ahaz, 2 Kgs 16:2); and the account of that king's reign, together with the account of Israel's exile in 2 Kings 17, implies that Judah may also be heading for exile—unless she heeds the prophetic warnings she has received and turns away from her sins. It is at this point that we are presented with a king who resembles David more closely than any Davidic king so far—the second David, who does what is right "in accordance with everything David did" (2 Kgs 18:3). His religious faithfulness is impressive. Coming at the end of the long line of kings during whose reigns the high places "were not removed" (1 Kgs 15:14; 22:43; 2 Kgs 12:3; 14:4; 15:4, 35), Hezekiah at last addresses this issue (2 Kgs 18:4), reforming Judean worship and making it what it should be. There was no one like him among all the kings of Judah, we are told, in the way that he trusted in the LORD (v. 5). This is evidenced in the way that he held fast (*dbq*) to God throughout his life, keeping the law of Moses, in contrast to Solomon, who in his old age "held fast" to foreign wives (*dbq*, 1 Kgs 11:2; cf. also Jehoram in 2 Kgs 3:3) and broke this law. The consequence of Hezekiah's religious faithfulness was that his military exploits paralleled David's in a way that was not true of any of the rest of his descendants, including Solomon. Only of David and Hezekiah among the Davidic kings is it said that "the LORD was with him" (v. 7; cf. 1 Sam 16:18; 18:12, 14; 2 Sam 5:10) and that the king was successful in war (*śkl*, v. 7; cf. 1 Sam 18:5, 14, 15). Only David and Hezekiah, furthermore, are said to have defeated the Philistines (*nkh*, v. 8; cf. 1 Sam 18:27; 19:8; etc.). As similar to David as he was, he was by the same token utterly dissimilar to Ahaz; for he would not continue to serve the king of Assyria (*'bd*; contrast Ahaz's description of himself as "servant" of the king of Assyria in 2 Kgs 16:7), but rebelled against him. Foreign influence or domination, of whatever kind, was rejected.

This in turn leads on to the Assyrian invasion of Judah (2 Kgs 18:13–19:37), where the matter of Hezekiah's "trust" is the central issue (cf. the use of *bṭḥ* in 18:5 and in 18:19, 20, 21, 22, 24, 30). Are the Judeans wise to trust in the unseen LORD, when the all-too-visible

Assyrian army stands at Jerusalem's gates with overwhelmingly superior numbers in its favor? The Assyrian commander suggests not, holding out the prospect that surrender will lead the people only into Solomonic bliss (v. 31) and later into a new "promised land" like their own (v. 32; cf. Deut 8:7–9). He presents the God of Israel as simply one of many powerless gods (the argument of vv. 33–35), and offers the king of Assyria in his place as the true provider of material blessings and of life itself. This blasphemy is compounded in 19:10–13, where the argument is subtly different. In 2 Kings 18:28 ff. it is Hezekiah who is deceiving the people about what will happen if they trust the LORD. In 19:10 ff. it is Hezekiah who is himself deceived by the God in whom he trusts. This is a god, avers Sennacherib, who is not only weak, but duplicitous; and like the deities of all the other conquered lands, he is a god who will be destroyed. The word of the "great king" (18:19, 28) thus uttered is met in turn by the word of the LORD through the prophet Isaiah in response, first, to Hezekiah's messengers (19:2–4), and then to his memorable prayer (19:14–19), which affirms his belief that the LORD is God alone, creator of heaven and earth and God over all the kingdoms of the earth. Sennacherib's blasphemy and pride will lead to his downfall (19:5–7, 20–34). Although he imagines that what he has accomplished in his military campaigns has been achieved in his own strength,[11] in reality the LORD ordained and planned it all. Assyria was merely the rod of his anger. Now the judgment of the all-knowing God will come upon Assyria instead; and Sennacherib will be forced to abandon his campaign before an arrow is fired, a shield raised, a siege ramp built against Jerusalem's walls. The LORD will protect Jerusalem completely, saving the city for the sake of his own reputation and for the sake of David his servant. The "great army" outside Jerusalem's gates is duly decimated by the angel of the LORD; and Sennacherib returns to

Nineveh to his death. "David" has once more slain "Goliath." The ideal king is one who, in trusting God and keeping his law, puts to flight all God's enemies.

Josiah is the best king of all in 1–2 Kings, a second Moses to match the second David—the ideal king who does not turn from the law to the right or to the left, according to the stipulations of Deuteronomy 17:20 (cf. 2 Kgs 22:2). This is only the first of several references in 2 Kings 22–23 that link Josiah with the law of Moses in general and with the figure of Moses in particular. His religious reforms are themselves based, of course, on the "book of the law" that is found in 2 Kings 22 and that is clearly meant to be thought of as the book of Deuteronomy, since the phrase "book of the law" is only used in the Pentateuch of Deuteronomy (Deut 28:61; 29:21; 30:10; 31:26; cf. also Josh 1:8; 8:30–35; 23:6; 24:26). His actions against the Bethel cult that is focused on Jeroboam's calves (2 Kgs 23:15–20; cf. 1 Kgs 12–13) equally clearly recalls Moses' own action against the first golden calf, as Josiah burns the high place (along with the Asherah pole) and grinds it to powder (cf. *śrp*, "to burn," and *dqq l'pr*, "to grind to powder," in v. 15, noting also v. 6, and Deut 9:21). After the purification of worship comes the command to celebrate the Passover, according to the stipulations of Deuteronomy (16:1–8, noting esp. v. 6). In celebrating this festival Josiah not only outstrips Hezekiah in faithfulness to God, the authors tell us, but even David himself; for a Passover like this had not been observed since before the days of the judges who led Israel (cf. Josh 5:10–12 for the last mention of Passover in the narrative). Little wonder, then, that having reported the removal of mediums and spiritists (2 Kgs 21:6), household gods (*trpym*; cf. Judg 17:5; 18:14, 17), idols (2 Kgs 21:11, 21) and detestable things in general (1 Kgs 11:5, 7) from Judah and its capital, the authors should conclude their account of Josiah's reforms by telling us that there was simply no king like him when it came to "turning to the Lord" (2 Kgs 23:24–25). He did so, in fact, with all his heart and with all his soul and with all his strength, in accordance with all the law of Moses (cf. Deut 6:5). Never had anyone turned to the Lord as Josiah did, in accordance with all the law. The ideal king is one who does precisely that.

If it is asked, then, what kind of ideal future king the authors of Kings had in mind, the descriptions of the reigns of Solomon, Hezekiah, and Josiah in particular give us our clues. Here are the "types" of the future king that anticipate him and sketch the outlines of his character and rule. Is this king a messianic figure? In terms of the book of Kings taken by itself, one might argue the point. Much depends upon just how firmly one is prepared to draw a distinction between a future hope that is allegedly this-worldly, national and political, on the one hand, and one that is allegedly truly eschatological, in that it concerns "the final age" *per se*, on the other. Mowinckel, for example, distinguishes between an ideal of kingship that belongs to the present (though also looking towards the future) and an expectation of the Messiah as a purely future, eschatological figure. Before the ideal of kingship could become the expectation of a future Messiah, he maintains, it had to be separated from those possibilities that were associated with the next festival and the next king, yet never realized. The gulf between ideal and reality had to become considerable.[12] If this is one's understanding of Messiah, then one would have to admit that the book of Kings of itself is not overtly messianic. Yet whether one can in practice distinguish very easily between ideal king and Messiah along these lines must be open to question. How, precisely, does one tell the difference between a future-oriented, yet presently-grounded ideal of kingship, and a messianic kingship, in a body of texts where the language of myth, with all its implications of ultimacy, is so readily applied to historical kings, and where the future is always described in terms of the past? Given this pronounced blurring of present and future, and the difficulty therefore of telling which it is, precisely, that a particular text concerns, how "overtly" messianic does a book like Kings have to be before it is considered "truly" messianic? How "considerable," indeed, must be the gulf between ideal and reality before we can speak of messianism? It is surely the case that the gulf was *always* thought of as considerable, at least by those who took the language of the ancient royal psalms seriously as referring to tangible reality. Psalm 72, for example, with its "Of Solomon" heading, appears to be a thoroughly "eschatological" psalm in terms of its expectations of the Davidic king. Ultimate justice, the crushing of oppressors, fertility and prosperity, universal and eternal rule, universal blessing—the language is just as extravagant as that of the prophets who looked into the distant future. How easily, then, can past, present and future be distinguished? When the book of Kings itself draws attention to the same gulf between ideal kingship and reality, acknowledging Solomon's many faults while acknowledging ideal elements in his reign that correspond to elements in Psalm 72, is it not then somewhat artificial to differentiate between ideal king and Messiah on the ground that the first is not truly an "eschatological" figure?

1 and 2 Kings in Context

The impossibility of the distinction becomes even more apparent when one remembers that the book of Kings is not in any case intended to be read alone, but in its context; and in this context, the ideal king can hardly be read otherwise than as a messianic figure. The immediate context to which I refer is that of the other prophetic books that are linked with Kings, especially the book of Isaiah—a link that is formalized in the binding together of what are often now called "narrative books" (Joshua–Kings) with what are still called "prophetic books" in one single section of the Hebrew Bible entitled "Prophets." One only has to look at what has happened in these "Latter Prophets" to the figure of Hezekiah, and to a less obvious extent to Josiah, to see the point.[13] Isaiah 36–39 contains, of course, much of the material found in 2 Kings 18–20 (with additions), and it has been convincingly argued[14] that we must see these chapters as they appear in Isaiah as a counterpart to Isaiah 6:1–9:7 [6]. Here a critique of the Davidic dynasty and the ruling king Ahaz (Isa 7) is followed by the promise of a Davidic child (9:1–7 [8:23–9:6]) in whom the promises to David will be realized. This child to whom such great expectations attach is most naturally taken to be Ahaz's son, Hezekiah (cf. Isa 11:1–10; 14:28–32); and in Isaiah 36–39 his reign is duly described, in a way that appears to heighten his piety in relation to both Kings and Chronicles (cf. the prayer of 38:9–20, which is not to be found in the other books; and the omission, as in Chronicles, of any mention of the paying of tribute to the Assyrians that is recorded in 2 Kgs 18:13–16). The positioning of these chapters immediately before the oracles of glorious deliverance and restoration that begin in Isaiah 40, Isaiah's oracle about exile and Hezekiah's response (Isa 39:5–8) leading directly into "Comfort, comfort my people" (Isa 40:1), is crucially important. Childs has noted the way in which, within the book of Isaiah, chapters 40–55 have become detached from any specific historical situation and have become fully eschatological, testifying to Israel's future with God.[15] In this context, he argues, Isaiah 36–39 have assumed the metaphorical role of commentary on the death and rebirth of the nation. We may go still further than this, however, and note the way in which the figure of Hezekiah himself is drawn into this vision of the nation's future by the structuring of the book that makes his reign so central. Isaiah 6:1–9:6

(with the other associated passages mentioned above) imply that Hezekiah is the "second David" who is completely to fulfill God's promises: it is in his lifetime that the anticipated era of universal peace and security will be ushered in. Isaiah 36–39 also make this link between Hezekiah and God's promises. It is not just that the activity of Isaiah in the period of Hezekiah is being presented as the historic occasion for the giving of the words of consolation in Isaiah 40–55.[16] The impression is rather given by the immediate juxtaposition of Isaiah 39:8 ("There will be peace and security in my lifetime") with the beginning of these words of consolation (and indeed the absence of any note of Hezekiah's death and burial, such as is found in this position in Kings) that the promises will indeed come to pass, in some sense, in "Hezekiah's" reign. In other words, it seems that the figure of Hezekiah has himself become detached from any historical moorings, and has become within the literary context of the book of Isaiah just as fully eschatological as Isaiah 40–55. Isaiah 8:23–9:7 [6] also encourages this theological move, of course, because of their portrayal of the future king as one possessing divine attributes, ushering in the reign of God.

The total effect of all these texts within the context of the book of Isaiah as a whole is thus to identify Hezekiah as a paradigmatic king in whose reign the promises were in fact as yet unfulfilled, and who thus points beyond himself to another Davidic monarch to come. This sort of move from present to future is seen equally clearly in the book of Jeremiah in relation to Josiah, who becomes the model (22:15–16) for the Davidic king of the future who will rule over Israel and Judah in righteousness (23:1–8)—an antitype of the wicked Jehoiakim, who burns scrolls rather than obeying their words (Jer 36; contrast 2 Kgs 22:11 ff.).[17] The description in Zechariah 12:10–14:2 of the shepherd who is "pierced," and the fall of Jerusalem and the exile that follow this, is also clearly reminiscent of the later events of Josiah's reign (cf. "Megiddo" in 2 Kgs 23:29 and Zech 12:11; and the description of Josiah's death in 2 Chr 35:23–24). The suggestion of vicarious suffering in Zechariah 13:1 reminds us, indeed, of Isaiah 52:13–53:12; and some have wondered whether this passage, too, also reflects those events.[18] When Kings is read in the context of prophetic writings like these and like Haggai 2:20–23, where Jehoiachin's grandson Zerubbabel becomes the explicit focus of messianic hope, it matters little whether the hope in Kings is overtly messianic of itself or not. As a prophetic text among other prophetic texts, it lends itself naturally to such a reading. The addition to the canon of books like Psalms, where the royal psalms provide an important structuring element in the eschatological shaping of the book;[19] or of 1–2 Chronicles, where Hezekiah is portrayed as the first king since the division of the united kingdom to reunite all Israel under one king and around one temple since the time of David and Solomon, a kingly model for the future and a focus of expectation in relation to the time when God would reestablish his kingdom[20]—such additions serve only to broaden the scope of a messianic hope that is already there.

It is therefore not surprising that, although Hezekiah and Josiah do not appear by name in the New Testament except in the genealogy of Jesus in Matthew 1:1–17 (cf. vv. 10–11), we should hear so many echoes of the Old Testament narratives about their reigns when we read the New Testament.[21] For Jesus' reflection upon his own identity, as well as the thinking of the early Christians about the one they regarded as the Root and Offspring of David (Rev 22:16), was bound to be influenced—as the thinking of the Jewish rabbis about the Messiah in the early centuries AD was clearly influenced (cf., for example, *Sanh.* 94; 98b; 99a; *Ber.* 28b)—by the reading of these narratives in their canonical context. Thus it is that we find, for example, in Jesus' attitude to the ritually "unclean" and in his healing of people after assuring them of divine forgiveness (Mark 2:1–12; 7:1–23), echoes of Hezekiah's attitude to the "unclean" Israelites during his Passover celebration in 2 Chronicles 30:18–20. Jesus cleanses the temple, like both Hezekiah and Josiah (Matt 21:12–13 and parallels; John 2:13–17), looking for a truly reformed religion. He himself is one who, like Josiah, keeps the whole law of Moses and actively promotes its keeping (e.g., Matt 5:17–20; 8:4). There is to be no lasting reform, however, and no immediate deliverance for Jerusalem from her foreign oppressor (Rome). Jesus does not function as a Hezekiah in this respect—at least, not at this time. The city will fall again; the temple will know desecration of Manasseh-like proportions; and there will once more be exile (e.g., Matt 23:37—24:21). Jesus' own fate in the midst of all this judgment is to die, like righteous Josiah (cf. John 19:37), a suffering servant to his people. It is, however, also to be "restored to health" after three days (like Hezekiah; cf. *Ber.* 10b for the rabbinic view that Hezekiah's recovery was a near-resurrection from the dead, comparable to Elisha's miracle in 2 Kgs 4:18–37). There will be a second coming, when Jerusalem and her remnant will once again know salvation. Victory, rather than defeat, will be experienced at Megiddo (=Armageddon, Rev 16:16), as the nations are defeated and Babylon is brought low by the Davidic King (Rev 16–19). The kingdom of God will have fully arrived. The Lamb will sit forever upon his throne (Rev 21–22). Biblically speaking, this is the king towards whom all the other agents of God's kingship in the world point, actualizing and anticipating the rule of God that is ultimately to be ushered in completely by the Lord's Anointed.

4

WHY BARZILLAI OF GILEAD (1 KINGS 2:7)? NARRATIVE ART AND THE HERMENEUTICS OF SUSPICION IN 1 KINGS 1–2

Like the essay in chapter three, this one arose out of my work on the commentary on 1–2 Kings for the New International Biblical Commentary Series, and it too was published in 1995 (this time in the Tyndale Bulletin*). As in the previous case, it clearly reflects the sea change occurring in biblical studies at the time with respect to the reading of biblical narrative, as predominantly historical-critical interests gave way in many circles to predominantly narrative-critical ones, and with that change came a renewed skepticism about the ability (and even the desire) of the authors of biblical narrative to speak truthfully about the past, and a new elevation of the reader of the text over the author of the text as the ultimate creator of meaning. The essay itself rejects as incoherent any systematic program of "suspicious reading" of texts arising from an extreme reader-response ideology, but it argues that at least on occasion suspicion can in fact be invited by the author himself, on the way to arriving at a fuller understanding of authorial intent. The case-study chosen here to illustrate this point is 1 Kings 2:5–9.*

These are interesting times for those who are concerned with the interpretation of biblical texts, particularly Hebrew narrative texts.

Old certainties are under attack. New revolutionaries clamber over the barricades, pronouncing those only recently considered (and considering themselves) as radicals to be, in fact, boringly conservative and quite *passé*.

It seems just a blink of the eye ago, for example, that the average commentator on Kings thought it an important part of his task to tell his readers quite a bit about the sources from which the book might have been constructed and the editors who might successively have worked upon it. Of the existence of such sources and editors there was really no doubt, even if there was much disagreement about the details. It was simply accepted that there was a greater or lesser degree of incoherence in the text—inconsistencies, repetitions, variations in style and language, and so on—features unexpected, it was said, in the work of a single author. Either the person who put Kings together was not a free agent, able to do just as he wished—he was to a greater or lesser extent constrained by the material available to him, and he was unable or unwilling to impose complete consistency upon it. Or (perhaps and) the original work has been expanded by one or more editors, also constrained by what lay before them, they, too, being able to make the text convey their particular message only to a certain extent. What we had in Kings, then, was a composite work, put together over a longer or shorter period of time by a number of authors or editors, its various parts speaking with more or less conflicting voices. Some voices may be louder than others, on such a view; but they are unable entirely to drown out their fellows.

It is hardly surprising, given this general perception of the nature of Kings within the academic community throughout most of the modern period, that scholarly reading of the book *as a book* in this period should generally have ceased. Thus we have had a plentiful supply of commentaries which tell the reader, on the one hand, what individual pieces of Kings might have meant before they were incorporated into the book; or, on the other, which pieces are "original" to the book and which are late additions or glosses.[1] There is no shortage of discussion of the historical and cultural background of the various parts of Kings; of the likely geographical location of the various cities mentioned in the text; of the obscurities of Old Testament flora and fauna.[2] Of the analysis of bits and pieces there has been (and continues to be) no end. Of the reading of a reconstructed narrative of some kind, there has been a little. But of the reading of the book as it stands as a complete story in its Hebrew form (or for that matter its Greek form), there has been, until recently, scarcely any.

It is into the midst of this conservative consensus that the new radicals have charged with their revolutionary yells. Can repetition not be an aspect of literary artistry, they have asked? Can variation in style and language not have many explanations other than difference in authorship? Is not "inconsistent" a word which is often used where terms such as "theologically complex" or "ironic" would do just as well? Is not the problem, in fact, largely that Old Testament scholars, often lacking general competence in matters literary, and approaching the text with inherited presuppositions about its incoherent nature (among other things), have largely found what they expected to find? And so we have had a succession of books and articles in recent times on the narrative art of the Hebrew Bible,[3] work that is perceived by many to have been extraordinarily fruitful in revealing the extent of the skill which has been involved in constructing, not only individual stories, but also whole sections of text and entire books. Incoherence tends to dissolve in the course of such analysis; and models of composition that presuppose frustrated or reluctant authors, not fully in control of their material;

or incompetent editors, intruding their presence sufficiently that we should notice them, but unable fully to impose themselves; or even multiple scribes, each adding their pennyworth without giving much thought to the question of overall coherence—such models are bound to be called into question.

The commentator who feels the force of such questioning is bound to attempt a commentary that differs from many that have preceded it.[4] He will be obliged to make the attempt even if he feels uneasy about the precise direction in which some of the scholars devoted to the newer approaches are moving. I am not personally very impressed, for example, by the way in which both the newer literary critics and the newer historians tend increasingly (and vocally) to divorce narrative texts from the past which the texts often claim to be speaking about.[5] Nor am I impressed by the way in which many scholars also tend increasingly (and quite explicitly) to deify the reader in respect of the text that is being read, whether by making the reader the creator of meaning, or by assigning readers the moral duty at all times of exercising a "hermeneutic of suspicion" in relation to the object of their study.[6] Yet the commentator who is aware of the debate about the relationships between texts and history, and recognizes the sharpness of many of the questions raised in that debate, is bound to approach the task of commentary with literary questions uppermost in the mind first of all. It is inevitable that the attempt to understand the literature *as literature* will precede the attempt to understand it in relation to the past to which it refers. By the same token, the commentator who has listened to the debate about the nature of our biblical texts as literature is bound to approach the task of commentary with heightened sensitivity to the presence of diverse voice, ideological conflict, and the like within the text. Even if a systematic program of suspicious reading is eschewed, there will remain an awareness that it is possible, for example, for authors themselves *to invite* suspicion by the artful way in which they tell their story. It is possible for authors to invite their readers to ponder individual statements in the light of that story as a whole, and through suspicious reflection upon those statements, particularly statements made by certain of their characters, to come to a deeper understanding of what is going on overall. It is possible, then, if this is what is happening in the text, for a hermeneutic of suspicion to be employed, not as a counter-reading strategy, but as a strategy that aims at arriving at a fuller understanding of authorial intent. It is this possibility that I would like to explore in the present paper, taking as my example the story in 1 Kings 1–2, and beginning with the crucially important section of this story in 1 Kings 2:5–9.

1 Kings 2:5–9

To those with an interest in the artistic qualities of a text, rather than simply and naïvely in the text as "telling one how it was," what is immediately striking about this passage is the rather careful way in which it appears to have been constructed—a fact unsurprising to those who generally know the Hebrew text of 1–2 Kings well, and are conscious of the very deliberate way in which its story is told. Three characters are mentioned here. In the middle stands Barzillai of Gilead, whom David commends in relatively few words to Solomon's care. On either side of Barzillai stand Joab and Shimei. Their sins and their hoped-for fates are described at much greater length; indeed, at approximately equal length. They are also described in rather similar terms: note the common emphasis on guilt; on Solomon's need for wisdom in dealing with them; on bringing their grey heads down to Sheol.

Why these three men? And why these three men in this order? For it is not quite the chronological order, so far as the narrative of Samuel is concerned. Joab comes first in that narrative, certainly; but Shimei's cursing of David is narrated in 2 Samuel 16:5–14, whereas we are not told of Barzillai's kindness until 2 Samuel 17:27–29. The question thus arises: is there a particular reason, from the point of view of the narrative of Kings, why 1 Kings 2:5–9 has been structured in the way it has, with faithful Barzillai located in the midst of these villains whom David now wishes to see disposed of? Is there a point? I think there is; but to get to it, we have to give broader consideration in the first instance to what David is saying here, and to the question of how his words are to be read in the light of the preceding story in Samuel (and earlier in 1 Kings) that they recall. And here we return to the hermeneutics of suspicion. Are we supposed to take David's words at face value?

The question is most pointed in relation to what the king has to say about Joab in 1 Kings 2:5. Now it is, of course, quite true that Joab had killed both Abner (2 Sam 3:22–30) and Amasa (2 Sam 20:4–10); and David seems to be saying that in so doing, he had also done something to David himself. 2 Samuel 3:28–29 suggests that, in the case of Abner, Joab had in fact brought the danger of divine retribution on David and his house, through association with the awful deed. Certainly that is how Solomon interprets the situation to Benaiah in 1 Kings 2:31–33. Joab is to be killed so as to clear Solomon and his father's house of the guilt of the innocent blood that Joab shed (v. 31), both Abner's and Amasa's.

This is all well and good; but there are some questions to be asked. Hitherto, David has apparently not felt at all compelled to take any action against Joab of the sort now being contemplated. He has been content simply to state his innocence and to leave the rest to God: "I and my kingdom are forever guiltless for the blood ... May it fall upon the head of Joab" (2 Sam 3:28–29). Notice the somewhat "hands-off" approach being adopted here, in contrast to the rather more proactive stance in 1 Kings 2. We are bound to ask, then: how seriously concerned can David have been about this blood-guilt? Apparently not sufficiently so, that he had hitherto been prepared to rid himself of someone utterly loyal to him, someone who frequently took the initiative on his behalf and for his good (e.g., 2 Sam 14, in the reconciliation of Absalom; 19:1–8, in his rebuke of David after Absalom's death). Joab was, after all, a very useful person to have around, especially when David wanted someone killed without any blame being attached to the king, as in the case of Uriah (2 Sam 11:15)—another instance when David seems quite unconcerned about blood-guilt.

We may wonder, then, about the sincerity of what he has to say to Solomon, particularly when we remember that the circumstances in which Joab carried out these killings were not quite as unambiguous as David's speech here makes them appear. In one sense Joab's killing of Abner was itself blood-vengeance for the death of Joab's brother; and who is to say that he did not sincerely believe that Abner had come to Hebron to spy (2 Sam 3:25), and was thus committing an act of war, and not of peace? The circumstances in which Amasa, so recently the commander of Absalom's rebel forces (2 Sam 17:25), mysteriously fails to collect the men of Judah in time to pursue the rebel Sheba (2 Sam 20:4–5) are even less clear. Is he simply incompetent, or is his delay deliberate? And is Joab really to blame, in view of what he knows of David's character thus far in the narrative, if he interprets David's implicitly critical words in 2 Samuel 20:6 ("Now Sheba the son of Bichri will do us more harm than Absalom") as signalling his desire that Amasa should disappear? Joab had, after all, built a career on having people killed for David's benefit, whether at his express command or not (cf. the killing of Absalom in 2 Sam 18:14–15); and there is certainly no mention of any concern on David's part over Amasa's death before we reach 1 Kings 2:5

(note the deafening silence in 2 Sam 20). All in all, then, it is difficult for the reader who knows the story as it has been told so far to believe that blood-guilt is the real reason why loyal Joab is now, at this very late date, to be done away with. It is difficult indeed to take David's words in 1 Kings 2:5 at face value.

It does not become any easier to do so if we pursue the story of Joab into the latter part of 1 Kings 2. It is here, of course, that we read of the steps taken by Solomon to remove exactly those people mentioned to him by David, plus a couple more for good measure. Adonijah is the first to bite the dust, closely followed by Abiathar and Joab. There is, of course, no evidence that Abiathar and Joab had anything whatever to do with Adonijah's initiative in regard to Abishag, of which we read in 1 Kings 2:12 ff. They are apparently simply pronounced guilty by association. Abiathar is banished to his family estate in Anathoth—treated very leniently, in fact, in comparison with the others in the story. A reason is found for such leniency (v. 26), although it is not a very convincing one.[7] Joab could also have cited a long history with David in mitigation of his crimes, had anyone been concerned to listen. The authors, indeed, themselves remind us of this history with that curious phrase "though not with Absalom" in verse 28. This is very interesting. Why mention Absalom here at all, if not to help us to recall that this is Joab's "first offence" in an otherwise blameless career, from the point of view of loyalty to David? And why give us this reminder at all, in this context, if they are not by the way in which they tell the story inviting us to be skeptical of what their characters are saying?

What really differentiates Abiathar from Joab, of course, is not his history at all, but his importance in Solomon's mind. Solomon is simply not very interested in Abiathar, whereas he is utterly determined to settle with Joab. No doubt that is why Joab, upon hearing what had happened to

Adonijah and Abiathar, flees to the tent of the LORD and takes hold of the horns of the altar (v. 28). He knows that he can expect no mercy: that is why he refuses to come out (v. 30). Perhaps he does not count on Solomon being just as ruthless as he is—prepared even to have someone killed in the place of sanctuary.[8] If so, he has miscalculated. Benaiah is dispatched to the tent; and with a cool obedience to his king which is worthy of Joab at his best (or worst), he strikes him down at the sacred altar (v. 34).

There is, in truth, something of poetic justice in all of this. Joab had lived by the sword, killing (among others) two army commanders who just happened to be his professional rivals; now he dies by the sword, and is immediately replaced by his killer as commander of the army (v. 35). Yet we must ask of Solomon as we asked of David: are we to take the king's rhetoric in verses 31–33 seriously? Is Joab really being killed at this point in Israel's history because of an overwhelming desire to clear David's house of blood-guilt (v. 31)? We have already seen reason to question this line. What are we to make now of Solomon's claim to occupy the high moral ground in relation to Joab, this waxing lyrical about the difference between Joab's house and his own? Again, remember the story. Solomon is a king himself born of a union forged in innocent blood (2 Sam 11–12)—a union made possible, indeed, through the obedience of the very man being hounded in this passage. Are we really supposed to bracket this knowledge out, suspend our disbelief, in fact, as we listen to such Solomonic sermonizing? Or are we being asked precisely to set words and actions alongside each other, and come to our own conclusions about what is going on here?

The Old King and the New King

What I am suggesting is that it is very difficult indeed for anyone who has grasped the story of Samuel–Kings so far to believe in the justification that David and his son are offering for Joab's murder. The way in which the story is told undermines the narrative that these two characters offer us. That is true of the particular passages we have looked at so far; but it is also true of the way in which 1 Kings 1–2 is narrated in general. For it could not be said, I think, that either David or Solomon is presented in a very favorable light throughout.

Here we have the dying king, David, now out of touch with reality, now fully in control, with a curiously ambivalent attitude to oaths and a selective memory. His oath to Bathsheba he stands by; his oath to Shimei he chooses to "interpret," so as to allow Solomon to kill him ("I may not kill him, but you may do so"). The loyalty of Barzillai he remembers, for it costs him nothing to do so; the loyalty of Joab he chooses to forget, because to remember would be to make evident that his conscience about blood-guilt has been found late and conveniently.

Here, on the other hand, we have the new king, Solomon. He, too, takes oaths seriously when it suits him to do so, and interprets them ungenerously otherwise (cf. his murder of Shimei).[9] He, too, has a selective memory, as both his treatment of Abiathar and Joab, and his speech in 1 Kings 2:31–33 reveal. The general impression throughout, indeed, is of a fairly sordid story of power-politics thinly disguised as a morality tale. So tortured are the attempts, however, to convince us that the men who died did so because they deserved it, that we cannot but be aware of their speciousness. We are invited to be suspicious, and to ask what the real reason for David's advice about Joab and the others really is. Why is Joab to be killed now, at precisely this moment in Israel's story?

The clue is to be found, I suggest, not so much in the religious significance of the actions that are described in verses 5–9 of 1 Kings 2, but in their political significance. What is it that we are really being reminded of in these verses? We are being reminded of two occasions when David's attempts at reconciliation between two warring factions in Israel were undermined by Joab's independent activity (on the one hand, reconciliation between Saul's supporters and David; on the other, between Absalom's supporters and David). Is the real issue here, then, not simply that Joab is too dangerous to be allowed to live in Solomon's united kingdom once David is gone? Is that not perhaps the real reason for the timing of the action? Joab is simply too much a man of the Judean past; he has already shown that through his allegiance to Adonijah.[10] Joab is not a man who will be content with Solomon's kingship, and make the government of a united Israel easy. He must therefore be removed; and the issue of blood-guilt becomes simply a convenient justification for his death.

Now if it is indeed concern for "the good of the state" that lies behind David's words in 2:5–6, then we may well have the explanation for why it is that these three men in particular—Joab, Barzillai and Shimei—have been selected for consideration at all, and placed in the order they have. For Shimei, too, has been from the very first, like Joab, a partisan—though this time of the north, and not the south (2 Sam 16:5–14; 19:20). It is, indeed, in the context of a (failed) attempt at national reconciliation (2 Sam 19:9–20:22) that David spares his life—an attempt, we may note, to which neither of the sons of Zeruiah are apparently sympathetic (19:21–23; 20:8–10). Shimei, like Joab, represents an element within the kingdom likely to be hostile to unity under a Davidic king, his implied support for Solomon in 1 Kings 1:8 notwithstanding.[11] It is interesting, then, that between these disruptive elements from Judah and Israel (2:5–6; 2:8–9), hostile to harmony, has been positioned Barzillai from Gilead in Transjordan (2:7): the very model of dutiful service to his king, service which is rewarded in peaceful fellowship around the king's table. Is it possible that the passage has been structured precisely so as to present Solomon with an ideal (peaceful community), and to suggest to him which kind of people from David's past—on both sides of that past—have to be removed if this ideal is to be attained (i.e., those likely to disrupt peaceful community)?[12]

Conclusion

Consciousness of narrative art, I have argued, alerts us to questions which a hermeneutics of suspicion can help us to answer. The art should be the author's, however, and not the reader's; the suspicion should be invited and not imposed. Sensitivity to art and invitation in the case of 1 Kings 1–2 leads us to a rather different reading of the end of the David story and the beginning of the Solomon story than that at which we might otherwise have arrived.

5

IDEOLOGIES, LITERARY AND CRITICAL:
REFLECTIONS ON RECENT
WRITING ON THE HISTORY OF ISRAEL

This third essay from 1995 explores the implications for the study of Israel's history of the "sea change" described in chapter four, as narrative-critical perspectives began to be taken much more seriously in biblical studies. Over the preceding few years I had become intrigued by, and then gradually very irritated by, the increasingly dogmatic and indeed strident voices raised in parts of the Academy, both in print and at academic conferences, concerning the folly of reading very much history relating to ancient Israel out of our biblical texts. Frankly, I considered the arguments advanced by these voices to be exceedingly poor. It seemed, however, that many scholars were intimidated by the force of the rhetoric deployed by some of those who later came to be widely referred to as "minimalists," and that their arguments were not being very much critiqued, at least in public. I took it upon myself, therefore, to enter the fray, choosing a 1994 conference at the University of Edinburgh to do so.[1] The essay itself, in fuller form, was published in the Journal of Biblical Literature *in 1995, and caused quite a stir, eliciting fierce responses in the same volume from Professor Philip Davies and Professor Thomas Thompson, who have remained dialogue partners of mine (if that is the best way of putting it) ever since.*

It was one of the more interesting of the various punishments known to the ancients that a guilty party should be tied by arms and legs to two horses, which might then be sent off jointly at a gallop into the blue beyond. The consequences for the person thus attached to his equine companions were ultimately rather bloody, as each horse turned independently to seek pastures new. Those who care about the integrity of biblical narrative might well ask what it has done in recent times to deserve a similar ghastly fate. Why at this point in the history of our discipline are story and history found, in so much scholarship, to be heading at speed in opposite directions, torn apart with sometimes violent force?

It is a long story. Its later chapters, however, certainly concern, as a major contributor, the growing enthusiasm for "the Bible as literature."[2] The more the emphasis in work on Hebrew narrative has fallen on the creative art of the biblical authors; the more the artistry of the biblical literature *as literature* has been highlighted; the more that this literature has been dated late, and its construction from earlier sources questioned—the more that scholarship has moved in these directions, the more it has also asked whether our biblical narratives are better described not as fictionalized history (the older consensus)[3] but as historicized fiction. *Of course* these narratives give the impression of speaking about the past, it is conceded. A history-like element is an obvious and important feature of this kind of text. This is "realistic narrative": the depiction lifelike, the story lacking in artificiality or heroic elevation. We may grant all that. But why assume that the narrative world thus portrayed has anything to do with the "real" world of the past? Why not regard it as a "fictive world," an ideological construct created by its authors for their own purposes? And why, then, accord these texts a primary place in the reconstruction of the history of Israel? Why not treat them rather as they are, as stories that at most tell us about the Israel within which they came into being, and certainly tell us little or nothing about the Israel of the more distant past? The history of "ancient Israel," if that is the correct term, must in this case be sought not in the biblical stories, but in the artifacts, buildings, and inscriptions the people themselves left behind. It must be sought more widely through attention to such matters as climatic change and population movements. History and story must be kept quite separate.

It is, of course, this perspective that dominates much of the recent writing on the history of Israel. Niels Peter Lemche, for example, claims that "the traditional materials about David cannot be regarded as an attempt to write *history*, as such. Rather, they represent an ideological programmatic composition which defends the assumption of power by the Davidic dynasty."[4] History is played off against ideology. Then again, we hear from the late Gösta Ahlström thus: "Because the authors of the Bible were historiographers and used stylistic patterns to create a 'dogmatic' and, as such, tendentious literature, one may question the reliability of their product."[5] The nature of the literature raises questions about historical reliability. And the same author writes: "Biblical historiography is not a product built on facts. It reflects the narrator's outlook and ideology rather than known facts."[6] Ideology is played off against facts. And again: "The biblical narrators were not really concerned about historical truth. Their goal was not that of a modern historian—the ideal of 'objectivity' had not yet been invented."[7] Ideology is played off against objectivity.

Moving on now to Philip Davies, we find the following:

> Biblical historians assume an "ancient Israel" after the manner of the biblical story, and then seek rationalistic explana-

tions for it, instead of asking themselves what is really there ... Here is where the increasing role of literary criticism ... is making a valuable contribution to historical research, by ... pointing out that the reason why many things are told in the biblical literature, and the way they are told, has virtually everything to do with literary artistry and virtually nothing to do with anything that might have happened.[8]

Literary artistry is played off against historical referentiality. Later on Davies has this to say: "There is no way to judge the distance between the biblical Israel and its historical counterpart *unless the historical counterpart is investigated independently of the biblical literature.*"[9] It is in that investigation, of course, that archaeology plays such a crucial role: archaeological investigation is played off against literary reconstruction.

And lastly, a quotation from Thomas Thompson:

The biblical concepts of a "God of the Fathers," and of a God giving laws by command, are in essence literary concepts observable in story traditions of the Old Testament ... If we do not have corroborative evidence from the real world that such deities and laws existed ... then we can hardly have any form-critical or literary and interpretive grounds for using such materials for historical reconstruction. Such historical conservatism and sobriety is justified by the further observation that such literary motifs ... function admirably both as central literary elements in the multiple variant stories of Israel's constitutional law being given to Moses by God and as redactional efforts associating the patriarchal narratives with the Mosaic traditions.[10]

The story world is different from the real world, and the two must not be confused: story is played off against history.

These are just a few quotations from many that might have been cited, but they suffice to illustrate the general direction in which research into the history of Israel has been moving in the last decade. What these quotations perhaps do not illustrate fully, however, is the extent to which it is not simply the ideologies of the biblical *texts* that are seen as problematic by these authors but the ideologies also of many of their *colleagues* in the Academy as well.

Davies, for example, argues that the entity "ancient Israel" has been created by a discipline (biblical studies) that is "motivated by theology and religious sentiment, not critical scholarship."[11] It is a scholarly construct invented by people with a particular religious ideology;[12] and the disciplines of theology and history may both be the better if traditional biblical scholarship ceases to practice the kind of theologically dictated form of historical criticism that has produced this construct.[13]

Thompson is also concerned to portray the opposition as corrupted by ideology. There is in his mind a clear distinction between what he calls "critical academic scholarship," on the one hand, and "religiously and theologically motivated biblical interpretation," on the other.[14] The latter involves "an ideologically saturated indifference to any history of *Palestine* that does not directly involve the history of Israel in biblical exegesis."[15] It also involves unjustified assumptions such as, for example, that poetry is early and prose late—an assumption that is "a product of a systematic, ideologically motivated scholarly agenda."[16] A critically acceptable history of Israel, asserts Thompson, "cannot be written on the basis of ancient biblical historiography" by writers who are captivated by its story line.[17] We must define history, he states, "as disciplined research rather than as ideologically motivated assertions about the past."[18] Recent publications have indeed shown clearly, he maintains, "that a history of Israel's origins can now be written, in a relatively objective, descriptive manner, once issues relating to the historicity and relevance of later biblical tradition are bracketed."[19]

Ideologies to the left and to the right, then; but mainly, it seems, to the right. Ideologies literary and critical, preventing us from seeing clearly what is and was there. The ancient texts are bad enough, but at least their authors have the excuse of not knowing any better, because "the ideal of objectivity had not yet been invented." Moderns scholars are much more culpable. They knew what the ideal was, but failed to devote themselves to it wholeheartedly, selling their academic inheritance for a mess of religious pottage, preferring to embrace fantasy rather than to swallow hard fact.

Such is the case for the prosecution, then; and an expanding crowd of witnesses can be called in support of it, not all saying exactly the same thing, certainly, but all nevertheless pursuing a similar line in relation to the place of biblical narrative within historical reconstruction, and perhaps justifying the title of "school" or "movement." But does the case that has been made stand up to cross-examination? I, for one, remain unconvinced of much of its logic and certainly unimpressed by much of its tone. In the remainder of the paper I shall try to explain why this is so, by asking and attempting to answer three questions.

What is Historiography?

I begin with an important, central question: What is historiography? What is the nature of the historian's task? This is a question that many of the scholars mentioned above have evidently addressed. Here, for example, is Thompson's view:

> Sound historical research is not a highly speculative discipline, but rather is based on the very conservative methodology and simple hard work of distinguishing what we know from what we do not know, and of testing our syntheses and hypotheses to ensure that they respect the all-important separation of reality from unreality. It is only in this way that history, like any other of the social sciences, can be scientific, progressive and cumulative. To the extent that the social sciences are based on probability and analogy, they are also based on guesswork and prejudice. The heart of historical science ... is the specific and unique observation of what is known ... When researchers go beyond the observable singular, they also go beyond what is known and involve themselves with the theoretical and the hypothetical.[20]

Here we have a very clear statement of method, which I *think* I understand. I hesitate only because it is hard to believe that anything quite so naïve (and confessed to be so by the author[21]) should have issued from the pen of a scholar writing in the last decade of the twentieth century. We live in a culture that is slowly but steadfastly losing faith in the technological age and its high priests, as the confidence, even arrogance, of earlier times has given way to the disillusionment and cynicism of the nineties. We are beginning to count the cost of believing too readily those who claimed to have a handle on objective scientific truth and to possess the ability to manipulate reality at will. We are beginning to understand how what is perceived in the so-called real world is inevitably connected with the knowledge, the prejudices, the ideologies that the person doing the perceiving brings with him or her; and to understand also how the myth of the neutral, uninvolved observer has functioned and continues to function as an ideological tool in the hands of those whose political and economic interests it has served. The "objective" spectator of classical physics has become the "impossible" spectator of the newer physics; and some scientists themselves are becoming much more aware, as a result of the work of scholars such as Jürgen Habermas and Mary Hesse,[22] of the ways in which the great broad theories of science are underdetermined by the facts, and even of how experiments are themselves, from the moment of their conception, shaped by the theories of those conducting them. Scientific theories come and go, argue the philosophers and sociologists of knowledge, partly on the basis of their success in prediction and control of the environment, but partly also on the basis of the interests they serve in a particular culture, whether they are theological and metaphysical, sociological, or simply aesthetic. Scientists cannot, any more than other human beings, escape from this matter of "interests." There is no such thing as value-free academic endeavor. Science, just as much as religion, has its orthodoxies and its heretics; its free thinkers and its inquisitions. Science, just as much as religion, has its liberals and its fundamentalists; those who think, and those who simply act according to the conventional wisdom and rules.

This is the intellectual world in which we now live. This is where we have come to in our pursuit of knowledge about how it is that we know. Yet here we find Thompson writing of a historical science involving at its core "the specific and unique observation of what is known." There is knowledge, hard fact in the universe. It may be directly observed in a way that does not involve probability and analogy, guesswork and prejudice, the theoretical and the hypothetical. History is "direct ... description of events on the basis of sources" rather than "historiographical reconstruction based on ideal models or patterns of what ...

can or must have happened."²³ "History," he later states quite bluntly, "is *Wissenschaft*, not metaphysics."²⁴

This is all quite extraordinary. Which events *are* these that may be directly observed and described by the historian? Where *are* these hard facts that simply "exist," the bedrock upon which everything else may be built? And who *is* this historian who may observe and describe and know without indulging in theorizing and hypothesizing, and especially without indulging in metaphysics? We require to be told. And we also require to be told how anyone so committed to "the observable singular" as Thompson claims to be could possibly have written a book on the early history of Israel that is 489 pages long. For such a definition of the heart of the historian's task really does not give one that much scope.

It is perhaps not surprising, then, that as soon as Thompson moves from criticizing other people to the actual task of history writing, we should almost immediately find him entangled in inconsistency. Having offered some discussion of the origin of the Semites, a discussion that opens with an explicit warning about its highly speculative nature,²⁵ he concludes as follows: "However speculative such reconstructions may be, they clearly suggest that the indigenous population of Palestine has not substantially changed since the neolithic period."²⁶

How that which is highly speculative can suggest anything worthwhile at all to someone so opposed to speculation remains a mystery. But it is by no means the only speculation in the book, if one is working with Thompson's definition of history. For, of course, every time one offers an explanation of a piece of pottery in the ground; every time one correlates an ancient inscription with other information from an archaeological site; every time one makes a connection between population movements and climatic conditions—on every such occasion, one is theorizing and hypothesizing, assessing probability, and using analogy and guesswork. There can be no attempt at understanding the past that does not involve these things. There is no history writing without them. And in the process of doing all these things, one is inevitably bringing one's own worldview to bear, in terms of fundamental beliefs and prejudices, in terms of ideology. One is inevitably engaged not only in *Wissenschaft* but also, quite clearly, in metaphysics.[27]

Others among the scholars mentioned thus far understand very well the inevitable subjectivity that is thus bound up with all historiography. Ahlström acknowledges that in the doing of historiography "there will always be a need for a method that uses reasoning, hypotheses, logic and imagination."[28] He also acknowledges that in this whole process the historiographer "often might be influenced by cultural trends," and he lists some of these: romanticism, positivism, idealism, Marxism, or one's confessional background.[29] Davies presents a most insightful discussion of the nature of historiography which goes even further:

> Historians today (as in classical times) are aware of the elusiveness of "history" in an objective sense. History is a narrative, in which happenings and people are turned into events and characters ... Whenever we try to understand the past we indulge in story-telling ... All story is fiction, and that must include historiography ... Most literary critics would accept that ... literature is ideology. If so, historiography, as a branch of literature, is also ideology ... all historians are inescapably bound to tell a story and not "the facts."[30]

This is very similar in its thrust to some comments of Ernst Axel Knauf:
> We cannot know the past, for the past is gone ... All that we can examine are the present remnants of the past: memories

> and relics, stories and material remains ... relics are as mute as ancient texts if not perceived within an interpretive framework that bestows upon them meaning and significance. Meaning and significance do not exist outside the human mind ... Every history is the creation of a human mind.[31]

Such comments indicate self-understanding in relation to the historian's work just as clearly as Thompson's remarks indicate the opposite. They are consonant with what many historians outside the field of Old Testament studies have said and are saying about the nature of historical knowledge.[32] Historiography is story: it is narrative about the past. Historiography is also ideological literature: narrative about the past that involves, among other things, the selection of material and its interpretation by authors who are intent on persuading themselves or their readership in some way. It is a narrative, moreover, that is underdetermined by the facts in precisely the same way that each broad scientific theory is underdetermined by the facts. All historiography is like this, whether ancient, or medieval, or modern; whether we are thinking of the anonymous authors of ancient conquest accounts;[33] of Thucydides or of Bede;[34] of Gibbon or Macaulay or Michelet or Marx;[35] or whether we are thinking, indeed, of the works of Lemche, Davies, Thompson, and their colleagues, all of whom tell a story so that we who hear it may believe.

A Gulf Fixed: History and Story

But having established this important point about the nature of historiography, here is my second question. If all historiography is story; if all narrative about the past has this story-like quality about it; then why is it that such a gulf is fixed between history and story when these same recent historians of Israel treat the *biblical* narratives about *Israel's* past? Why is the nature of these *particular* narratives as story so problematic? And why, conversely, is history reckoned to be found more objectively in other kinds of data, such as those collected from archaeological digs? It is at this point that we find some interesting contradictions and illogicalities in the recent literature that it is important to ponder.

Ahlström, for example, is apparently ready to concede in some of his writing the necessity of the subjective involvement of the historian, with all his/her own particular philosophical presuppositions, in the construction of history.[36] He is prepared to concede the inevitability of such involvement in the face of archaeological material which is, as he puts it, "mute":

> Archaeological source material can be seen to be "mute," and there is no method for exact dating. It does not tell the whole story by itself. A stone is a stone and a wall is a wall ... because mute sources and texts do not give all the necessary information, there will always be a need for a method that uses reasoning, hypotheses, logic and imagination.[37]

Archaeological remains do not speak for themselves but must be interpreted creatively both by the archaeologist and by the historian. As F. Brandfon writes:

> Once the researcher begins the necessary task of grouping the evidence into typologies of artifacts on the one hand, or charts of comparative stratigraphy on the other, theoretical concerns begin to transform the archaeological evidence into an historical account. In this sense, archaeological evidence,

despite its brute factuality, is no more objective than any other type of evidence.

And again:

> I can "experience" a given ash layer by touching it, seeing it and even tasting it; but this immediate experience is not history until I talk about it or write about it to someone else. The minute I do that, however, I begin to interpret the facts. I have to choose the words which will describe that layer, e.g. "destruction debris" or "burnt debris." This interpretation transforms the individual facts into "general concepts" by grouping them with other facts and other ideas. This transformation is the creative process of historiography.[38]

It is this line that Ahlström sometimes seems ready to pursue. He is, nevertheless, prepared to write elsewhere as follows: "If the meaning of the archaeological evidence is clear, one might say that it gives a more 'neutral' history than the textual material. It is free from the *Tendenz* or evaluation that easily creeps into an author's writings."[39] He is also prepared to speak of archaeological remains speaking by themselves, rather than through the Bible.[40] Suddenly, miraculously even, mute data have found a voice: a value-free, neutral voice that can be trusted. It is presumably partly for this reason that, as Ahlström tells us, his approach has been "to gather not only literary information, but also to a large extent archaeological material, in order to get as close as possible to the actual events."[41] The stories archaeologists tell can apparently be trusted to inform us directly about reality, to reveal to us "the facts." Point of view does not enter into it. Here lies naked truth.

The biblical stories, conversely, often contain description that, according to Ahlström, is "ideological, rather than factual."[42] Biblical historiography "follows an ideological pattern. It is not really concerned with facts."[43] Again: "Much of what was written down was carefully selected by the writer in order to promote his viewpoint ... the biblical writers were not really concerned about historical truth. Their goal was not that of a modern historian."[44] It is not clear, he tells us, how the biblical texts "relate to what history really looked like."[45] It is in consequence of these kinds of considerations that Ahlström concludes that "the archaeology of Palestine will have to become the main source for historiography."[46]

To all of which comments on biblical historiography we may respond briefly as follows. First, that the concept of "what history really looked like" is logically incoherent, as the simple question "looked like to whom?" illustrates. Second, that if selectivity can be traded off quite so simplistically against historical truth, then it is not just biblical historiography, but all historiography, that is unconcerned with historical truth.[47] Third, that if the presence of ideology of itself disqualifies narrative writing as historiography, then Ahlström's own book is not historiography but something else; and fourth, that if the goal of the modern historian is disinterested objectivity, and if this involves the pursuit of an illusion, then we should not blame ancient historiographers for eschewing this goal. We should, rather, praise them for their intelligence.

All historiography involves selection. All historiography is ideological in nature. And the uninvolved, disinterested observer has never existed, whether as Ideal Chronicler or as Ideal Historiographer.[48] Yet Ahlström, for all that he wants to make a few concessions in this general direction, still wants to argue that there is something fundamentally problematic about biblical narrative when it comes to using it in modern historiographical work on Israel—problematic in a way that other, more modern narratives are not. The problem for this reader of Ahlström is to see what, exactly, is the problem.

I have the same difficulty also with other scholars who take a similar line. Lemche, for example, suggests that modern scholars should not simply function as spokesmen [his term] for the biblical writers with regard to the Canaanites, but should rather form their own "unprejudiced opinions of Canaanite life and culture."[49] The presupposition here, of course, is that prejudice, like the plague, is a disease that could not be avoided by our forebears, but that in the modern, enlightened world has been eradicated. Even if the Old Testament authors intended to write history rather than novels, Lemche argues against Baruch Halpern, they "did not possess the necessary methodological tools to write a history which can be compared to the work of the historians of our age, except remotely."[50] In fact, however, Lemche seems quite certain in his own mind that they did intend to write *novels*, quite different in nature from our modern "scholarly reconstructions of the past, the only (or main) goal of which is to describe a historical development 'as it really happened'"; histories that are written, therefore, "without political or moralistic aims."[51] This seems somewhat naïve. Once we are prepared to question either the notion of "what really happened" or the notion that we alone of all mortal beings on earth are in a position to perceive those "happenings" accurately and to form unprejudiced opinions about them, then most of Lemche's case collapses. It remains only to pursue further the question of intentionality: did the biblical authors intend to refer to the past? It is a favorite theme of recent historical work on Israel that they did not.[52] The assertion is frequent. Compelling arguments are, however, in short supply. And compelling arguments are what one requires, in the face of the quite obvious surface claims of the text itself to the contrary. For it is beyond question that the text itself gives the impression of wishing to speak about Israel's past, at least as one important aspect of its overall purpose. That is certainly how the vast majority of its readers throughout the centuries have perceived its intention. Those among the newer historians who care sufficiently about intentionality to make an issue of it have considerable work still to do if they are to convince the rest of us to disregard what we might call "the plain sense of the text" on this matter[53] and to characterize the biblical authors as engaged in a task other than the one they represent themselves as carrying out.

Is there, then, anything else about the biblical texts that makes them fundamentally problematic when it comes to using them in modern historiographical work on Israel? Some scholars seem to think that their sheer *literariness* is an obstacle. It is striking that K. A. D. Smelik's carefully worked out method for approaching the Hebrew Bible as a historical source, for example, seems clearly to presuppose that the more connection there is between the text and its context, the more completely ideology and textual detail explain each other, the more the text approximates to well-known *genre* patterns, the less likely it is that the text is historical.[54] Now it is, of course, the case that we must always ask of individual aspects of the text precisely in which sense they are intended to refer. To speak of Israel's past certainly appears to be one aspect of the overall purpose of many of our biblical narrative texts; but it is not the only aspect.[55] In view of everything we have said so far, however, it seems tendentious in the extreme to adopt a general attitude to texts that is effectively that "the better the story, the less likely it is to be history!"[56]

Then again, many scholars argue that it is precisely the presumed lateness of the biblical narratives in their present form that makes them so problematic. Thompson, for example, speaks of "the disparate origins and nature of the traditions that were brought together as a relatively coherent whole only by the shell of their secondary literary frameworks."[57] Later he picks up this theme as follows: "An understanding of the coherence of the biblical tradition, as arising out [sic] first within intellectual milieu of the Persian period, causes great difficulty in affirming the historicity of the Israel of tradition at all."[58] In relation to the Pentateuch and the Deuteronomistic History in particular he writes: "The coherence of the pentateuch and of the so-called deuteronomistic accounts leading up to the narration of 2 Kings is based neither on plot development nor on theme." Coherence is given to the story only by "a secondary, imposed structure that orders, interprets and gives meaning to the successive narratives of the tradition."[59] What is interesting here is that Thompson is apparently quite prepared to buy into modern literary studies on biblical narrative insofar as they characterize the narrative as story and not history, while at the same time ignoring these same studies insofar as they demonstrate intrinsic coherence rather than incoherence in the narrative. He does, of course, require incoherence for his argument to get off the ground. This perhaps explains the selectivity of his approach. But once in the air, does the argument actually fly? Thompson himself seems to accept elsewhere the fairly obvious truth that what is primary is not necessarily historical and what is secondary not necessarily unhistorical.[60] So even on his own arguments, there is no necessary connection between secondary coherence and nonhistoricality.

What if one were to avoid talk of incoherence and were merely to consider the question of the presumed lateness of the texts *per se*? I leave aside the questions of whether this increasingly popular position in relation to the date of our texts can be substantiated, and in what sense it is true. Let us for the moment simply grant that in their present form at least the texts are late. It remains the case, nevertheless, that one simply could never argue logically from the mere *distance* of a text from the events it describes directly to its *usefulness* as historiography or otherwise.[61] It is amazing that modern scholars, themselves twenty-five hundred years or more distant from the events they seek to describe, should risk advancing such an argument at all—amazing, that is, if they themselves have aspirations to be taken seriously as portrayers of the past and do not wish simply to be regarded as novelists.[62] It is equally surprising, and for similar reasons, to find scholars who would presumably like their own work to be regarded as something other than simply self-referential, maintaining with such force that texts like the biblical texts, written at distance from the events, tell us more about their authors than they do about the past they claim to describe. One can only imagine that the scholars concerned do not fully appreciate the nature of these arguments as extremely sharp double-edged swords.

Ideology and Critical Scholarship

This last point leads rather neatly into my third and final question: If all historiography is story—if all historiography, because it is literature, is also ideology—then why is it that biblical historians of an earlier era are attacked so fiercely in so much of this recent literature precisely because their approach to the history of Israel betrays ideology? And why is this approach contrasted so deliberately with critical (for which we may read "objective") academic scholarship? These are exactly the antitheses, the reader will recall, that are found in the comments from Davies and Thompson cited toward the beginning of this paper. How is the kind of distinction that lies behind them to be maintained? Since I have thus far debated with Thompson more than Davies, and since

I am naturally anxious to be perceived as even-handed, let me at this point pursue mainly the latter.

It is Davies who offers us one of the more insightful analyses in the recent literature of the nature of historiography. "No story ... is ever an innocent representation of the outside world," he tells us. "Literature is a form of persuasive communication, and it cannot help conveying its author." And "all historians are inescapably bound to tell a story and not 'the facts.'"[63] And so on. Any scholarly history of Israel must therefore be a scholarly construct that will convey its author. It could never be otherwise. That is the clear implication of these incisive remarks on what historiography is.

It is all the more puzzling, then, that as we read on in this interesting book, we should find it argued that the notion of "ancient Israel" is fundamentally problematic precisely because it is a "scholarly construct" that straddles literature and history, a construct that, it is claimed, is "neither biblical nor historical."[64] It is equally puzzling to find the contention that scholarly commitment to this nonhistorical construct has meant that "there is no searching for the *real* (historical) ancient Israel"; and the assertion that "biblical historians assume an 'ancient Israel' after the manner of the biblical story, and then seek rationalistic explanations for it, instead of asking themselves what is *really* there."[65] By the time we reach the end of the second chapter of Davies' book, in fact, we have moved a considerable distance away from the insights of the first concerning the necessary subjectivity of all historiography. We find ourselves instead in a world inhabited basically by two sorts of people. There are the misty-eyed theologians, prevented by faith from engaging in "real historical research," content largely to find their own reflection in the muddy pool of biblical literature.[66] And there are the hard-nosed historians, striving to exercise critical scholarship in a hostile environment, anxious only to discover the truth about the past. Ideology characterizes the first group; objectivity the second; and the battle is on for our academic souls.

It is all very puzzling. What sense does it make, exactly, to concede that all literature is ideological in nature and then to criticize other scholars for writing histories of Israel that are reflective of their own ideology? How else could they write? What sense does it make to allow that history is elusive in an objective sense,[67] is inevitably the construct of the historian, and then to criticize others for creating the construct "ancient Israel"? And what possible sense can it make, in the context of all such concessions, to claim that one's own group alone are the guardians of real academic scholarship, and that everyone else is only pretending?[68]

The argument is unclear. It is very difficult indeed to know what to make of it. It seems that all the theoretical concessions in the book about the nature of historiography in general count for very little when it comes to the substantive arguments about which histories of Israel are more valid than which others, which historians are truly scholars and which are not. And we are entitled to ask why this is. Why this tension? Is it simply a slip, unconsciously made by one who is unaware of his own ideology? Or is it part of a more deliberate authorial strategy—part of an elaborate deception whose purpose is to highlight the ideology of others while concealing one's own? Whatever is the case, it is clear that, particularly as those well-versed in the hermeneutics of suspicion, we simply cannot allow such a paradigm unchallenged space. For that would be to allow what is essentially a disagreement about the relative merits of *different* ideologies to parade itself as something quite different. That would be to allow disagreement *among scholars* to be portrayed as if it were warfare between *scholars*, on the one hand, and *obscurantists*, on the other. And that would be to distort reality.

The reality is, of course, that the approach to historiography that Davies advocates with such passion is no less representative of a confessional stance or ideology, is indeed no more free of unverifiable presuppositions, than those other approaches he so vehemently attacks. That which he represents so frequently simply as "real historical research" is in fact a very particular sort of historical research founded squarely on a particular way of looking at the world. When, for example, in the course of a discussion of "what really happened" during the siege of Jerusalem in 701 BC, we find the following statement: "To this Israel [i.e., biblical Israel] happen things that as an historian I do not accept happen in history here or anywhere else";[69] we are encountering a confession of personal faith, lightly disguised as a job description.[70] For historians are not required by contract as historians to make sweeping general statements of this tenor about the nature of reality. If they choose to do so, it is only because they have already embraced a particular philosophy, a particular worldview, which informs their thinking as historians. The surface appeal in this example, of course, is to analogy—that well-known Troeltschian touchstone of proper historical method. But the principle of analogy always has operated and always will operate within the wider context of the background beliefs and experience of the historian concerned.[71] Faith and life are determinative here, as elsewhere. To claim, therefore, that it is "as a historian" that one does not accept this or that claim about reality is to mislead or to be self-deceived. It is not Davies the historian who is speaking here. It is Davies the believer; and he is sharing with us his faith.

What kind of faith is it? What label may we fairly attach to the "school" whose work I have been analyzing above? I believe that we can do no better overall than the tag that Max Miller has suggested.[72] He pronounces the position simply "positivist." Given the great emphasis in much of the literature on scientific objectivity and on "what really happened"; given its dogmatic anti-narrativist stance, its inherent reductionism, and its secular, anti-theological and anti-metaphysical orientation—given all this, the label "positivist" does not seem at all out of place. It is certainly the one used among historians generally as they have endlessly debated the issues raised in this paper in the course of the last several decades. If one wished to supplement this label with another, in order to fill out the picture somewhat, then one could do worse, I think, than "materialist."[73] But "positivist" will do for the moment. The historiography may to some extent be new, at least in the field of Old Testament studies.[74] The philosophy is certainly not.

A particular way of doing history, then, based on a particular philosophy—that is what we have here. On what grounds is this particular approach now to be pronounced the only legitimate one for scholars to embrace? In truth, the grounds are conspicuous by their absence, at least in the literature known to me. What we generally find instead is simple assertion of the "no true scholar" variety. This is unlikely to convince even those who only believe that there are several ways of doing history, and not just one. It is certainly unlikely to convince those many scholars, among whose number I certainly count myself, who positively believe that positivism is intellectually incoherent—incoherent, among other reasons, because if its level of skepticism with regard to some favorite things were applied consistently to everything, there could be no knowledge of anything.[75]

The "favorite thing" of the positivist historians of Israel in this respect, of course, is the biblical text, which is treated with a skepticism quite out of proportion to that which is evident when any of the other data relating to Israel's history are being considered. Those of us who are not true believers in the positivist cause, however, find it difficult to understand why the position which insists that biblical data be verified before being accepted as historically valuable should be considered any more acceptable than the position which insists that these data must be historically valuable even when they are apparently falsified.[76] Both these positions smack of what might itself be considered fundamentalism; and I have yet to hear convincing arguments as to why I should abandon what might be described as the traditional middle ground of scholarship and adopt either. I refer here by "traditional middle ground" to an approach that seeks to build broadly based hypotheses on all the available evidence, textual and otherwise; an approach that certainly does not decide *a priori* which parts of the evidence should be utilized and which ignored; an approach that certainly does not require "proof" before accepting something as true, however provisional that truth might be considered to be; an approach that considers the doing of history to be art, and not science, in what we may now call the old-fashioned and outdated sense of the latter term.[77]

This is, of course, not Davies' approach, on the whole. It does not help his argument, however, that after pages and pages of passionate advocacy of a thoroughly nonbiblical approach to Israel's history, he should in the fifth chapter of his book seek to reoccupy just this middle ground in the case of Ezra and Nehemiah. Suddenly we are told that "it is the profile of the literary Israel which provides the focus." We are advised that it is all right to look for elements of convergence between "the society or societies which may have wished to claim the name 'Israel' for themselves" and "the character of the biblical Israel itself."[78] It is acknowledged that there is a danger in all of this that the author will fall into the methodological trap that he so strenuously criticized earlier in the book, namely, of using the biblical story as a framework for reconstructing history. He is anxious to avoid the charge of switching from skepticism to credulity concerning the biblical literature once it has passed the sixth century BC.[79] Yet anxious as he claims to be, he proceeds anyway, with all the necessary caution, to give these texts a central place in his historical reconstruction of the postexilic period. This is something of a surprise, to say the least. But the reason is clear enough. Without the biblical texts we cannot write any worthwhile account of Israel in the Persian and Hellenistic periods. And without such a history Davies has no foundation for the imaginative and revisionist account of the production of the biblical literature that occupies the second half of his book—his discussion of what he refers to in the title of his fifth chapter as "The Social Context of Biblical Israel." Rather than say nothing, therefore, he seems quite prepared to engage in what can only be described as a methodological back-flip.[80] His skepticism, it seems, extends just as far as it may without threatening the viability of his overall project.

This is selective skepticism with a vengeance. One may well ask why what is considered possible with Ezra and Nehemiah is considered impossible with other biblical texts; and why when Davies adopts in *this* place what is a rather traditional approach to the history of Israel, he is apparently a *bona fide* historian, whereas when others adopt this approach in *other* places, they are not. Davies is, after all, involved in creating "ancient Israel" just as much as they are. Scholarly construction somewhere between text and external data is very much the order of the day.

Those who think only that selective skepticism is a poor foundation upon which to build historical reconstruction are, however, likely to take a very different view of the pictures of Israel that are found in our biblical texts. They will be regarded, certainly, as only some of the portraits of the past among the many that might have been painted. It is clear on any reading of Kings, for example, that its authors do not tell us everything that happened during that part of the Iron Age about which they are writing. They do not even claim to do so. Theirs is, as we know, a highly selective account, in which fairly long periods can be passed over briefly, and periods of a year or less can occupy quite a bit of space. It is a particular view of the past, with its own highlights and its own persuasive appeal; only one portrait of what happened—but if the argument of this paper is at all right, no less valuable for that reason. For that is simply how historiography is. That is simply how historiographers behave. There is no other way of going about the business of representing what has been.[81]

Conclusion

To sum up and to conclude. I do not dispute that biblical historiography is, in at least a very general sense, ideological literature. There is room for further separate discussion about precisely in which sense this is so. It is interesting that there is clearly disagreement among the newer historians of Israel themselves on this point, seemingly arising in part from differing perceptions as to how much narrative coherence is to be found in the text.[82] How far is biblical historiography ideologically unified? And whose ideology is it? These are questions for another time. I do not wish to argue with the general label "ideological." And I certainly do not wish to dispute, either, that ideology has partially shaped the literature of the last century or two on the history of Israel. It is quite clearly the case that it has. What I have wished to dispute in the course of this paper, however, is that ideology of itself renders these biblical and modem texts problematic in a way that the more recent histories of

Israel are not problematic. It is simply in the nature of historiography, I have argued, that it is problematic in just these terms. And to present the matter otherwise is either to display remarkable naïveté about the nature of human knowing and doing, *or* it is quite deliberately to misrepresent reality for the sake of one's own scholarly or other ends. There is a certain irony, indeed, in the situation as it has now become clear to us. Past historians stand accused of naïveté; but the accusers appear unable to avoid the same charge. The biblical authors are painted as ideologues, weaving words to establish David on his rightful throne; but they are painted thus in a story whose authors' aim appears to be to establish their own sole legitimacy as scholars. Confessionalism of a religious sort is attacked in the name of critical enquiry and objectivity; but the noisy ejection of religious commitment through the *front* door of the scholarly house is only a cover for the quieter smuggling in (whether conscious or unconscious) of a quite different form of commitment through the *rear*.

As we enjoy the irony, however, we must not miss what I think is the important moral or political question that arises. It has to do with the kind of scholarly world we wish to inhabit. Is it to be an intellectually narrow world, where a particular set of presuppositions is presented simply as the way things are; where there is only one method of approach to the subject that is thought worthy of respect; where there is only one sort of person who is considered truly a scholar? Or is it to be an intellectually liberal, pluralistic, broad world, where differing beliefs and philosophies are recognized as just that; where differing approaches to the subject, deriving from these beliefs and philosophies, are accepted as valid; where the label "scholar" is not simply hung around the necks of those with whose philosophy and method we happen to agree? My own preference is certainly for the broader of these two worlds. There are, however, certain preconditions of successful community living in that kind of world. Greater epistemological self-awareness on all sides is certainly one; for awareness of one's own presuppositions and predispositions is the first step toward meaningful dialogue with others. The willingness more self-consciously to confess one's presuppositions is another; for then it will be clearer how far any disagreement involves theory and method, and how far it concerns only the interpretation of data. And the willingness, finally, to debate both presuppositions and interpretations, rather than simply to anathematize one's opponent, is clearly another necessity.

Of all those writing recently on the current state of things, it is ultimately Knauf who is the most perceptive in this kind of area. He writes:

> The acknowledgment that facts are theoretical constructs would highly facilitate the discussion between conflicting theories and partially unburden scholars from ignoring their opponents—or from charging them with stupidity, the deficit of knowing enough facts, or ill will, the refusal to acknowledge facts for what they are.

Epistemological self-awareness should, in other words, lead on to humility; and humility should then issue in constructive dialogue. For as Knauf goes on to say: "Only ideologists are always right; scholars know that everything they say is potentially wrong."[83]

6

FOUL SPIRITS, FORNICATION, AND FINANCE: REVELATION 18 FROM AN OLD TESTAMENT PERSPECTIVE

While all the turmoil of 1995 with respect to Bible and historiography was still swirling around me, I set off for the American Academy of Religion/Society of Biblical Literature meeting in Philadelphia, U.S.A.—as the beneficiary of generous financial assistance from the British Academy—with something very different in mind. I had been invited to deliver my first and only conference paper relating directly to New Testament studies, as one participant among several in a section of the conference focusing on the book of Revelation. The paper was published shortly afterwards, in 1996, in the Journal for the Study of the New Testament. *It asks a similar question to the one I asked in 1990 about the book of Lamentations: how easy is it to read history out of this kind of text—in the case of Revelation, an apocalyptic text? The particular case study is Revelation 18. My conclusion is that the kind of material we find in that chapter does not easily lend itself to a historical-critical reading of it.*

That the book of Revelation as a whole has been composed in intimate conversation with the Old Testament is widely acknowledged. It is a book that can scarcely be understood at all without reference to the Old Testament texts to which it constantly and variously alludes. Chapter 18 is no exception. The language and imagery of the chapter is throughout the language and imagery of the Hebrew Scriptures,[1] especially of the particular prophetic passages that are cited.[2] This much is universally acknowledged, and there is no need to rehearse the detail here. But what are the implications of this fact? That is the question at the heart of this paper—a question of particular interest to a reader who knows something about the Old Testament and, especially in relation to our chapter, knows something about Old Testament laments and dirges.[3]

On Reading Revelation: The Old Testament Dimension

It is again widely acknowledged that one of the implications is that we cannot engage in the kind of reading of the chapter that we find in older scholarly works like R. H. Charles' commentary. Charles,[4] following a number of earlier scholars, dated chapter 18 to Vespasian's time, just after the fall of Jerusalem, some 25 years before the time of the author of much of the remainder of Revelation. His rather complicated reading of the chapter depends to a very large extent on an overly literal and pedantic approach to the text that it is difficult indeed to justify. The supposition in verse 2 that the fires of Rome were long extinct and its ruins had become the abode of the unclean was not possible (even in a vision), he argued, for an author writing in AD 95, who looked forward to the destruction of Rome as one of the last acts in the judgment of the world, after which the fires of judgment would never be extinguished (19:3). Moreover, verse 4 presupposes a body of the faithful still alive in Rome, whereas chapter 13 has all the faithful already put to death; and in verses 6–8 we have such an expectation "as would naturally be entertained by a zealous Jew after the destruction of Jerusalem." Charles simply does not take sufficient account of the quite stereotypical nature of lament language, which demonstrably has a long history behind it and cannot easily be pinned down to one particular time and place.[5] In particular, this is not language that is capable of revealing straightforwardly to us the emotions, expectations or psychological profile of the particular authors who have used it.[6] Nor does Charles consider whether it is not hazardous in the extreme to draw his kind of conclusions about sources and redactors from a text that so freely borrows from Old Testament material—material that just as obviously as Revelation 18 mixes its metaphors and is not noted for its attention to logical consistency. It is in fact curious how inconsistent Charles himself is on this question of "inconsistency." His argument in chapter 18, for example, depends on taking some of the language about Babylon's destruction (the language of fire) much more literally than is sensible; and yet he knows quite well that at least some of the remainder is symbolic (cf., e.g., his comments on 18:21, on the language of millstone and sea). Perhaps we are to deduce from this kind of Charlesean inconsistency that the commentary was written by a "Charles School" rather than by an individual.

In this last fault, of course, Charles is joined even by some recent commentators. Verse 14, for example, is still sometimes said not to suit its present context, because it apparently interrupts the third-person description of the merchant's wares and their laments, being addressed to Babylon in the second person.[7] Adela Yarbro Collins, however, notes that the abrupt digression that verse 14 represents is not unique even in the book of Revelation itself.[8] We may add to this the plain fact that in Old Testament texts like the book of Lamentations, sudden switches of person and theme are common, and represent an aspect of the dramatic art of the genre.[9] To the Old Testament scholar, verse 14 certainly does not grant us grounds for speculation about sources, redaction, or indeed corruption.[10] The conclusion that I draw from an example like this, in fact, does not concern the history of the text at all, but rather the influence of the Old Testament on the author. We have here one example among many of the way in which it is not simply Old Testament language and imagery that has shaped Revelation 18, but also the very form and structure of Old Testament texts—the very manner in which they have been composed. This is generally true, but seldom appreciated,[11] as indeed the whole range of influence of the Old Testament on the New Testament is seldom fully appreciated. With regard to Revelation in particular, it is astonishing that as recently as 1985, Elisabeth Schüssler Fiorenza could say of a book so obviously dependent upon the Old Testament that "a thorough study of the use of the Old Testament by the author of Rev. is not available."[12] A few more recent studies have done something to fill the gap.[13] It is undoubtedly the case, however, that in the absence of any overall study, the tendency has been vastly to underestimate the influence on Revelation of every part of the Hebrew canon, whether in content, language, structure, or style.[14]

An Economic Critique of Rome?

This brings me rather neatly, however, to a further implication of the nature of the text we have before us; and it concerns the question of whether and how far we can discover here an economic critique of Rome that accompanies criticism of other kinds. Richard Bauckham has recently argued[15] that the language of harlotry in the chapter suggests that John is accusing Rome of associating with the peoples of her empire for her own economic benefit—that John views the benefits of the Pax Romana as the favors of a prostitute, purchased at a high price. The Pax Romana is in reality a system of economic exploitation of the empire—Rome's subjects give far more to her than she gives to them, though they are too intoxicated/spellbound to see it. The best evidence that John is intent on attacking the concrete political and economic realities of his time in this way, argues Bauckham, is to be found in the list of cargoes in Revelation 18:12–13, for the merchandise in question is generally portrayed in contemporary sources as a feature of the newly conspicuous wealth and extravagance of the rich families of Rome. Moreover, the structure of the chapter gives special prominence to imported wealth in general.[16] We are justified in supposing, therefore, that John wished in his account of the fall of Babylon particularly to highlight the wealth which was to perish with the city.

Now a number of questions must be posed by an Old Testament scholar about such a reading of our chapter. Perhaps the best way to begin my questioning is to refer to George Beasley-Murray, who like Bauckham notes the prominence of merchants in our chapter, but draws a very different conclusion. "The merchants of the earth are given more space than the kings (vv. 11–17), doubtless through the precedent of Ezekiel's song, whose longer list of wares in which Tyre traded inspired John's catalogue in this passage."[17] The same data, in other words, are explained in terms of literary antecedent, rather than in terms of specific authorial intention in respect of Rome. It is not John's desire to address the contemporary situation that explains this specific aspect of the text, but rather the Scriptures which provide the basis for his reflections.[18] And this highlights the general question we must ask about the economic material here: with literature of this sort, how safely may we make Bauckham's kind of deductions? Does the text in truth allow us to do this?

Thus of the list of cargoes we must certainly ask: does this list signify an economic critique of Rome as such, or is it there simply because it is the sort of thing that one finds in biblical laments and dirges? Bauckham seeks to undergird his argument by noting that John's list is not simply modeled on Ezekiel's,[19] and by attempting to demonstrate that the detail ties the list more to the contemporary situation than to the biblical text. I find this demonstration unconvincing. It is clear that some of the cargoes mentioned (e.g. wheat, cattle, sheep) are far from being attacked by Roman writers as extravagances, and that only 13 of the 28 cargoes in fact occur in Pliny's list of the most costly products of nature. Bauckham himself acknowledges that some of the commodities were not expensive (except in quantity), and that there are some surprising omissions (e.g. exotic foodstuffs) if a list of luxuries is intended. He is very hard put to demonstrate at all, in fact, that John saw Rome's wealth as profit from the empire enjoyed *at the expense of the peoples* of the empire. This is, of course, because Revelation 18 does not speak of economic *exploitation* at all.[20] The courtesan under examination here may well enjoy an extravagant lifestyle; but there is no hint in the passage that she does so at the *expense* of her clients, and much evidence that the clients have been more than happy with the exchange of goods. They lament the passing of trade that has been in their own interests. It is true that there is a reference to slaves in verse 13; but it is far from clear to me that Bauckham is right when he says that John's use of a scriptural description of slaves from Ezekiel 27 alongside the common term must mean that he intends a negative comment on the slave trade.[21] It seems just as likely that he intends to direct us to Ezekiel 27 itself—not so much to comment on his contemporary situation as to say to his readers "read Ezekiel if you wish to understand what I am saying here."

This is, of course, the whole problem. Is this material really *intended* to have specific external reference to Rome in terms of economic critique? Or is its primary reference internal, inner-biblical, and its nature such that the sort of reading that Bauckham offers is difficult to sustain? He is undeniably correct when he tells us that John's list of cargoes is not simply modeled on Ezekiel's. There is substantial overlap, however,[22] and where there is not, it is often possible to find another Old Testament passage that may explain the presence of an item in the list just as well, if not better, than its significance in first-century Rome. Perhaps the most interesting example here is the reference to chariots (v. 13). Chariots do not have any place in Ezekiel's list. They do, however, have a very interesting and important place alongside horses in another biblical passage that describes at some length the goods that flow into a center of world power. I refer here to 1 Kings 4—the description of Solomon's imperial glory centered in Jerusalem. Right in the midst of this passage, in 1 Kings 4:26 and 4:28, is found mention of Solomon's many horses and chariots. Commentators have not always noted the negative implication of the reference; but it is tolerably clear that what the author of Kings is doing here is alerting the reader to some of the seeds of Solomon's later apostasy, reminding us of the warning given to the Israelite king in Deuteronomy 17:16. This verse forbids the king of Israel from acquiring "a great number of horses for himself" and forbids him further from making the people "return to Egypt to get more of them." The first part of the prohibition Solomon clearly infringes in 1 Kings 4:26; the second he infringes in 1 Kings 10:26–29, just before we hear of his apostasy. What is interesting about Solomon, of course, is that it is he of all the royal figures in the Old Testament who is most associated with trade with Tyre; and it is Tyrian trade that is the subject of Ezekiel 27:12–24. Solomon is also a king very much associated with slaves, the commodity mentioned alongside horses and chariots at the end of John's list. It is certainly possible to explain the presence of chariots in this list, then, in terms of literary influence and without recourse to the commodities found in first-century Rome. One could certainly not deduce from their presence in Revelation 18 that we are dealing here with specific criticism of Rome's economics, rather than with the sort of general criticism that world powers receive in the Bible as a whole.[23]

That general criticism is much more about religion than it is about economics; or to put it another way, economic sins are only ever a function of idolatry, so far as the Old Testament is concerned, and it is on the idolatry that the emphasis falls, rather than upon the economics. The stereotypical world ruler in the Old Testament is one who has arrogated to himself the prerogatives of divinity, and thinks of himself as a god. The claim to be the provider of prosperity and good to the peoples of the empire is one aspect of his *hubris*, and descriptions of things economic are important, not in themselves, but for what they have to say about the idolatry. For example, Sennacherib, the king of Assyria, is presented to us in precisely this way in 2 Kings 18–19. He makes all sorts of claims that set him in opposition to Yahweh as an alternative deity. He maintains that Yahweh cannot deliver Jerusalem because he is simply one of many powerless national gods (18:33–35), and a duplicitous god at that (19:10–13). Sennacherib, on the other hand, is one who claims to have brought judgment upon Egypt (cf. Isa 19:1–15) and upon the cedars of Lebanon (2 Kgs 19:23—something only Yahweh can truly do, cf. Ps 29:5: Isa 2:12–13; Amos 2:9; Zech 11:1–3). He ascends the heights so that he can look God straight in the face (Heb. *mrwm*, "height" in both v. 22 and v. 23; cf. Ps 73:8; 75:4–5; Isa 14:13–15). Amidst all this we find the claim that it is he, and not Yahweh, who brings or withholds fertility, creating springs and drying up rivers;[24] that it is he who brings economic blessing to all peoples.[25] It is he, and not Yahweh, who is the god of exodus, the true provider of material blessings and life itself. The economics are an aspect of the idolatry. Their description is part of the portrayal of world power opposed to God. They are not important in themselves, but for what they signify, just as Solomon's horses and chariots are not important in themselves, but for what they signify about that king's religious allegiance.

I return to Revelation 18, then, and I ask of this text that draws so heavily on an Old Testament background: is this really the sort of literature that allows us to deduce anything either about John's attitude to Rome's economics or indeed about Rome's economics in themselves?[26] May we with literature of this genre safely make the kind of deductions that Bauckham makes?[27] Much depends on whether we agree with Adela Yarbro Collins, when she asserts, "If idolatry and blasphemy were the only criticisms John had of Rome, his book would have been very different."[28] This is precisely what I think cannot be demonstrated at all,[29] any more than can her allied claim that the book is calling on Christians to withdraw from the economic life of the cities of Asia.[30] My sense of unease with this kind of reading is only heightened by the fact that we are dealing in this passage largely with sea trade—and the sea, of course, has such symbolic significance in the Old Testament texts. The watery chaos is the archetypal enemy of Israel's God, set within its bounds at creation, but always threatening to break out and challenge the divine rule.[31] If one is looking for a reason why sea trade, in particular, finds such a place of prominence in Revelation 18, one does not need to have recourse to the fact that Rome herself was involved in sea trade. The emphasis on the sea is entirely bound up, not with the significance of sea trade to Rome, but with the significance of the sea in general in the Old Testament, with the importance of Ezekiel's prophecy about Tyre as specific background to the chapter,[32] and with the significance of the sea within Revelation itself. The sea is the place from which the beast of Revelation 13:1 came, who is associated with the harlot Babylon who is seated upon many waters (17:1, 7), and the place where, appropriately, the millstone representing Babylon is thrown in chapter (vv. 22–23), as the earth returns to the silence and darkness of the primeval chaos (cf. Jer 4:23–26) that must precede the new creation in which bridegroom and bride, music and light, will be restored.[33] In such a context, it seems to me, great care must be taken when asking questions about the relationship between the text and its supposed historical referents. One wonders whether the lack of interest in economics that Bauckham notes among previous commentators on Revelation is really testimony to their intuitive grasp of this fact, rather than (as he has it) evidence of a preference for theology over concrete history and of a failure to recognize the thoroughly contextualized nature of John's prophetic message.[34]

Does Revelation Concern Rome At All?

Let me now finally just press the kind of critique I am offering here a little further, and ask the question, not simply whether the passage allows us access to John's attitude to Rome's *economics*, but how far it even allows us access to his attitude to *Rome*. Is it, in fact, clearly Rome that is in view in Revelation 18 at all? It is often simply assumed that this is the case, because Rome was the world power of the author's day, with few solid and specific arguments advanced in support of the notion. For example, John Court can assert of the material we have been considering that "the context of the Book does seem to demand the application of this picture to Rome."[35] The intelligent question here, of course, is "which context demands precisely what?" Does the literary context demand the application of this picture to Rome? Does it even *permit* it, *simpliciter*? Josephine Massyngberde Ford and Alan Beagley, among others, have recently argued that Rome is not in fact the focus of the Babylon material, but rather Jerusalem and those associated with Jerusalem in the mind of the author. This case interests me as an Old

Testament scholar precisely because both these interpreters have arrived at their conclusion through a more careful consideration of the Old Testament background to Revelation than has sometimes been evident, giving serious attention to the way in which the Old Testament is used in the book. Beagley explicitly asserts what I think is clearly the case.[36] Most previous studies have taken external considerations too much into account when asking their questions about the enemies in Revelation, and have paid insufficient attention to the internal evidence, particularly the Old Testament background of many of the images used. Both he and Massyngberde Ford go some way towards redressing the imbalance, while not in the end (in my view) quite convincing the reader of the specific case they are seeking to make.

The latter, for example, notes the way in which the harlot in the Old Testament is predominantly faithless Israel, the bride who has broken her covenant promise to her husband (cf. Hos 2:5; 3:3; 4:15; Isa 1:4, 9, 21, where Israel is named Sodom and Gomorrah; Jer 2:20; 5:7; Mic 1:7; Ezek 23, noting the cup in 23:31–34; and especially Ezek 16). Only twice is a non-Israelite nation called a harlot: Isaiah 23:15–18 (Tyre) and Nahum 3:4 (Nineveh).[37] The metaphor is continued at Qumran in relation to Jerusalem and her priesthood, where it is particularly interesting that the Qumran scroll *4QpNah* has accommodated the whole text of Nahum to Jerusalem ("Nineveh"), indicating the way in which even texts that did not originally concern faithless Israel could be read as if they did.[38] Massyngberde Ford also notes the way in which this priesthood is widely associated in Jewish literature with economic activity and with bloodshed.[39] Rome, she notes, is never mentioned in Revelation, but the new Jerusalem is, in antithesis to the Babylon we are discussing; and there is significant use of Jewish temple imagery in the book. Moreover, the phrase "great city" in Revelation 11:8 appears to refer to Jerusalem, and one might therefore well expect it also to refer to Jerusalem in 18:16.[40] So for Massyngberde Ford, it is Jerusalem that in chapter 18 is found in political alliance with the Romans, trading (committing adultery) with the nations; and she provides persuasive detailed exegesis of the chapter along these lines. For example, it is Jerusalem that is recalled by verse 1, alluding to the divine glory leaving the temple and city in Ezekiel, and by verse 2, with its language of religious defilement. It is Jerusalem that fits best the covenant language of verse 5, where the city's sins, rather than her love, have cleaved to God; verses 23–24 are based on Jeremiah 25:10, which is an oracle against Judah and Jerusalem; and so on. Particularly interesting is her treatment of the list of cargoes, many of which, she argues, would have been used for the Jerusalem temple and its services.[41]

Beagley argues in a similar way, noting that when enemies of the church are explicitly referred to in Revelation 1–3, it is the synagogues in Asia Minor and Philadelphia that come into view, rather than the imperial authorities;[42] that in Revelation 4–8 the first four seal visions are strikingly paralleled by Ezekiel 5–7, where Ezekiel utters threats against Jerusalem, the house of Israel and the inhabitants of the land;[43] and that in Revelation 8–11 Jerusalem is clearly the city where the plagues of Egypt are to fall (11:8).[44] The great city is distinguished from the cities of the nations in Revelation 16:19, implying a Jewish city, verse 21 recalls Ezekiel 13:8–16 (concerning Jerusalem).[45] The striking influence of Ezekiel on Revelation 17–18 in general implies that the harlot in these chapters refers to Jerusalem (cf. Ezek 16; 23; also Matt 23:29–38, where Jerusalem, not Rome, is the city which killed the prophets), and the double recompense language of Revelation 18:6 clearly recalls Israel/Judah, not Babylon.[46] The view of Jerusalem found in Revelation is already prepared for, in fact, by the Old Testament prophets, who always denounce contemporary, empirical Jerusalem because of her immorality, injustice, and apostasy, threatening her with destruction, but promising her future glorification. This is precisely the pattern found in Revelation.[47]

The cumulative exegetical case presented by these two scholars is a compelling one; and in fact I think there is even more to be said in support of it, when one is sensitive to the number and nature of Old Testament allusions in our chapter. It is interesting to me, for example, that Massyngberde Ford, in attempting to explain the list of cargoes in Revelation 18:13–14 in terms of the Jerusalem temple, confesses that horses and chariots do seem somewhat incongruous in this context. The answer to this puzzle, however, seems to me to lie clearly in the Old Testament connection between the Jerusalem temple and the figure of Solomon. I argued earlier that chariots may have been added to the list of Ezekiel 27 precisely because of their important place in that other passage, 1 Kings 4, which describes the goods that flow into Jerusalem. It is Solomon who is the Israelite most associated in the Old Testament with Tyrian trade (the subject of Ezek 27:12–24); and what was it, according to 1 Kings 5, that Hiram of Tyre provided Solomon with? Materials for the building of the Jerusalem temple! Then again, both Massyngberde Ford and Beagley draw attention to Revelation 18:24, where it is said that the blood of prophets and saints and everyone slain on the earth was found in Babylon. Both scholars cite Matthew 23:35, where a similar statement is made in reference to Jerusalem.[48] Neither, however, draws support from a textual precedent just as obvious to the student of the Old Testament, a text where another Davidic king based in Jerusalem appears, this time one who was thoroughly apostate rather than just partially so. I refer to Manasseh, the most idolatrous of Judah's kings, and the one who ultimately brought God's judgment down on Judah and caused the people to go into exile. All sorts of charges are laid against Manasseh; but among them is the charge that he shed much innocent blood, until he had filled Jerusalem from one end to another (2 Kgs 21:16). It is difficult to resist the impression that we are not only hearing in Revelation 18 about the old Jerusalem that is to be destroyed and replaced by the new, but also echoes of its old Davidic kings, shortly to be superseded by the son of David who is faithful and true (Rev 19:11). It is certainly intriguing that passages like 18:22–23, with their picture of a city devoid of people and religious festivals, call to mind no book quite so much as the book of Lamentations, set in the period after Jerusalem has fallen and her people are in exile (cf., e.g., Lam 1:1–5; 2:6–10; 5:14–18).[49]

The case for Babylon as Jerusalem, then, is in my view a compelling one. Whether we are to think of a literal, historical Jerusalem, or indeed a particular group of people within a particular historical context is, of course, another question.[50] What I think Massyngberde Ford and Beagley have done is to remind us that it is far from self-evident that reference merely to Rome is intended in the language of Revelation 18. What I think they have themselves failed to see is that the nature of the language as they have described it makes it very difficult to know precisely what kind of external reference is intended *at all*.[51] They think the language suggests that the enemies in the chapter are not, after all, Romans, but Jews. I think, on the other hand, that the language creates very real difficulties in identifying particular enemies and in deducing particular facts about these enemies with anything approaching probability. For this is language brought over from other biblical texts in which it already has a supra-historical quality. It has already transcended particularity, and moved into the realm of the stereotypical, the hyperbolic, the apocalyptic. The enemies of Old Testament texts like the book of Lamentations are no more particular enemies than are the enemies of the various psalms of the Psalter. Sennacherib king of Assyria is as much an archetype of the world power opposed to God as Hezekiah king of Judah is an archetype of the faithful ruler of God's people. And when the language of enemies is used, therefore, in a text like Revelation 18, so heavily influenced by the Old Testament, great caution has to be exercised in moving from the world of the text to the world of the author, and beyond that to the world outside the author's head, as Leonard Thompson has so recently shown particularly in relation to attempts to read Revelation as a response to Domitian's supposed excessive claims to divinity, or to a supposed reign of terror at the end of his period of rule.[52]

Thompson is adamant that we cannot move from the world of the text to the world of the author quite as easily as has often been done in the past, reading social situations straightforwardly out of the texts. The empire-wide political crisis during Domitian's reign that has been assumed to lie in the background of Revelation by many commentators on the book, he argues, arises out of the kind of naïve reading of Roman classical sources as "objective" that all too often accompanies a severely critical attitude to biblical sources. There is in fact no evidence that the cities of Asia knew political unrest, widespread class conflict or economic crisis at this time, or at any other time known to us in the period of Revelation's writing. The empire, especially under Domitian, was beneficial to rich and poor provincials, and there is little evidence that Jews and Christians found much of a problem living in it as such. One certainly cannot assume widespread oppression and persecution. John may urge his readers to see conflicts in their urban setting and to think of Roman society as "the enemy," but those conflicts do not reside in Asian social structures. John rather *encourages* Christians to see themselves in conflict with society—it is part of his vision of the world, not part of the social reality.⁵³ The crisis orientation is a characteristic of the genre of the book, not of the political circumstances occasioning the genre. The presence of "the crisis theme" therefore tells us nothing about the social and political situation of the author's time. Attempts to link the book with upheaval and crisis are thus wrongheaded, as is the attempt to locate it in a particular social class or social/economic status.

A Tale of Two Cities

The problem, it should be stressed, is not that the social world outside the author's head cannot be presumed to exist. It is that the precise way in which analogical, symbolic, liturgical prose refers to that world is in essence uncertain. Reading social situations out of biblical texts like Revelation is therefore a perilous undertaking.⁵⁴ Indeed, it may well be asked what point there is in trying to undertake it at all. The assumption that so often governs exegesis at this point, of course, is that it is the particular that is important, or authentic, or whatever, and that this is especially the concern of the biblical critic. Thus it is not uncommon for commentators on Revelation to be quite well aware of the difficulty of restricting the text to the particular, and to be equally well aware of the universalizing nature of the language. Yet the particular is nevertheless their starting point. Thus Massyngberde Ford says of the beast in Revelation 17 that whatever might be the historical allusions in the description,

> one must not make the mistake of stopping here as if our author's interest were only or primarily centered on the particular event. A particular event is the point of departure, and so we must start with it and take into consideration the universal application.⁵⁵

Likewise, Chris Rowland says of the whole book that,

> the visionary experience, while conditioned by life under Roman dominion, is not determined by it. It is the Beast and Babylon, not Rome and Caesar, which are the vehicles of John's message. As such they have a wider appeal than a narrowly focused political analysis rooted in particular historical events.[56]

I myself certainly would not wish to argue that there is no allusion to Rome in the book of Revelation, no intended application of the imagery to that city and her empire. That would scarcely be credible. Nevertheless, I should prefer to express the matter rather more firmly the other way around; for I do not believe either that a particular event is in any meaningful sense the point of departure for John's writing (at least I find no evidence to support this assertion), nor do I think that it can be demonstrated that John's visionary experience was even conditioned by life under Roman dominion, much less determined by it. The point of departure, and the conditioning factors, of a chapter like Revelation 18 lie in the Old Testament Scriptures that have shaped the worldview, beliefs and even language of the author. The particular is only a function of the universal. I therefore think that a comment such as that by Leon Morris with regard to Revelation is much closer to the mark. Babylon is not Rome, he affirms, "though doubtless to men of the first century there was no better illustration of what Babylon means than contemporary Rome."[57] This is a much better way of putting it; for it is surely typology, not history, which is the key to understanding the picture of the great city in Revelation.[58] Babylon, like Vanity Fair, is infinitely more than any city that might have been its model.[59] If Austin Farrer can say, therefore, that John has no reason for limiting himself in his use of the Old Testament to prophecies against Babylon, "since the Rome he is denouncing is no more Babylon than she is Nineveh or Tyre,"[60] I should prefer to say this: that the Babylon that John is denouncing is no more Rome than any other city of biblical times, or indeed of any time. The particular is not central to a chapter like Revelation 18, even if universals are inevitably particularized by each generation that takes its ancient scriptures seriously.

As an Old Testament scholar I therefore stand much closer, in the end, to writers on Revelation like Jacques Ellul[61] than to many of those other commentators whose approach to the book, to my mind, has been rather too comprehensively forged in the not-so-ancient fires of historical-critical method. The kind of material we find in Revelation 18 simply does not lend itself to this latter manner of reading it. Indeed, in asking particular and historical rather than general and universal questions about the chapter, such reading obscures what it is really about: the ongoing, long-fought battle, spanning the length of the Christian Bible, between God and those political and religious powers that oppose even while sometimes appearing to serve God, and the resolution of that conflict in the coming of the kingdom of God and the new Jerusalem. It is the generalities, rather than the particularities, of the chapter, and indeed the book as a whole, that are important. This is just as well, when it is so clearly the case that the nature of the literature confronts us with many obstacles as we attempt to gain access to anything else.[62]

7

CANONS TO THE LEFT OF HIM:
BREVARD CHILDS, HIS CRITICS, AND THE
FUTURE OF OLD TESTAMENT THEOLOGY

Like the conference paper reproduced in chapter six, this paper dates from 1995.[1] It was then prepared for publication during a period of sabbatical leave in Tübingen, Germany, in 1996, funded by a stipend granted by the Alexander von Humboldt-Stiftung, and it was ultimately published in the Scottish Journal of Theology *in 1997. Brevard Childs was a great influence on many of us graduate students in the Bible during the 1980s when we were writing our Ph.D. dissertations, holding out before us the possibility of remaining theologians even while doing proper justice to all the many truths about the historical nature of the Bible into which we had been inducted during our studies. However, his "canonical method" had been much criticized, and I was keen to discover whether these criticisms were justified. This essay is the eventual product of a voluminous amount of reading and thinking on this topic. I was glad to meet and then correspond with Professor Childs after writing it; he was warmly appreciative.*

It is well known that the seeds from which the modern discipline of Old Testament theology grew are already found in 17th and 18th century discussion of the relationship between Bible and Church, which tended to drive a wedge between the two, regarding canon in historical rather than theological terms; stressing the difference between what is transient and particular in the Bible and what is universal and of abiding significance; and placing the task of deciding which is which upon the shoulders of the individual reader rather than upon the church. Free investigation of the Bible, unfettered by church tradition and theology, was to be the way ahead.² Old Testament theology finds its roots more particularly in the 18th century discussion of the nature of and the relationship between Biblical Theology and Dogmatic Theology, and in particular in Gabler's classic theoretical *statement* of their nature and relationship.³ The first book that may strictly be called an Old Testament theology appeared in 1796: a historical discussion of the ideas found in the Old Testament, with an emphasis on their probable origin and the stages through which Hebrew religious thought had passed, compared and contrasted with the beliefs of other ancient peoples, and evaluated from the point of view of rationalistic religion. Here we find an unreserved acceptance of Gabler's principle that Old Testament theology must in the first instance be a descriptive and historical discipline, freed from dogmatic constraints and resistant to the premature merging of Old Testament and New Testament—a principle that in the succeeding century was accepted by writers across the whole theological spectrum, including those of orthodox and conservative inclination.

It is against this background that the more recent era of the doing of Old Testament theology must be understood—an era in which it has become increasingly and transparently clear just how intransigent a problem has been bequeathed to Old Testament scholars by those early Enlightenment thinkers who first defined the task of the Old Testament theologian in the way they did. The idea that there might be a center to the Old Testament in Eichrodt's sense of the term, for example, has now been thoroughly explored, and found wanting.⁴

Von Rad's proposals regarding Old Testament theology are also far from acceptable—if indeed what he offers us is strictly Old Testament theology at all, rather than simply a history of theological traditions. Ironically, in view of his opposition to the kind of program embodied in Eichrodt's work, he can in fact be criticized along precisely the same lines as Eichrodt, in that he ends up claiming far too much for what is effectively *his* center for the Old Testament, namely salvation history.[5] A similar criticism has been made of the Biblical Theology Movement in its concentration upon the God who acts in history, quite aside from the more general critique that has been offered of that movement's linguistic methods and that has radically undermined the attempt to derive theology from the Old Testament read historically, via its supposedly distinctive ideas. It has increasingly seemed to many Old Testament scholars, in fact, that the whole enterprise of Old Testament theology as defined by the Enlightenment is one that is doomed to failure. No viable and intellectually respectable route from the historical-critical base camp even to the theological uplands, much less the theological summit, can be identified. In the aftermath of the Biblical Theology Movement, there is seemingly no territory in which Old Testament theology can make its home, somewhere between the earthly realm cultivated by criticism and the heavenly realm inhabited by faith.

It is against such a background that we must understand the program outlined by Brevard Childs in various books and articles over the last three decades, most recently in his *Biblical Theology*.[6] It is not easy to summarize this program in a brief space, particularly since it has not retained an unaltered shape over these three decades, but has inevitably been adjusted in the light of further thought and criticism. Let me nevertheless recall its outline, particularly as it relates to the Old Testament. The leading idea is this: that the concept of canon, pushed to one side in the Enlightenment in the name of academic and religious freedom, must be brought back to the center of the agenda in Old Testament studies. For canon does not represent, as many have claimed, an arbitrary and late imposition on the Old Testament texts by religious authorities, alien to and distorting of the essence of the Old Testament. That is a misrepresentation of the reality. Canon is itself a complex historical process within ancient Israel that entailed the collecting, selecting and ordering of texts to serve a normative function as Scripture within the continuing religious community. It is far from being a late development without hermeneutical significance. The notion of canon is intrinsically bound up with the Old Testament texts as we have them, and should be taken seriously by those who study them. It is indeed these Old Testament texts *as we have them* that should be the focus of readerly concern: the final forms of the biblical books that have been recognized as authoritative for the Jewish and Christian faith communities, the forms where these communities claim to find the normative witness to God's revelation. It is the final form that alone bears witness to the full history of revelation, rather than earlier stages of the tradition that may or may not be plausibly recovered by the historical critic. It is, therefore, the final canonical shape of Scripture that must guide our interpretation of the Old Testament books as we reflect upon them theologically. The canon provides the arena in which the struggle for contemporary understanding takes place. It is precisely the disregarding of this canonical shaping by historical-critical interpretation that has in large measure led to the modern hermeneutical impasse. The text is transported into the hypothetical past by destroying the very elements that constitute its canonical shape, the vehicle that has enabled its journey to the present. It is little wonder that having destroyed this essential vehicle, historical critics are then unable to devise a way of relocating the text in any modern religious context. Childs' approach, on the other hand, while not wishing to bypass two hundred years of critical research, nevertheless demands that historical-critical tools be used to illuminate the canonical text as we have it, rather than for some other purpose. He does not deny the theological significance of a depth dimension of the tradition; but features within the tradition that have been subordinated, modified, or placed in the distant background of the text cannot be interpreted apart from the role assigned them in the final form. The task of Old Testament theology, then, is to reflect theologically on this final form of one portion of the Christian canon.[7] It is a distinctively Christian enterprise, which offers us the prospect once again of bridging the gap between Bible and theology.

What are we to make of this program? Where do its strengths and weaknesses lie? And what does it have to say about the way ahead for Old Testament theology? I turn now in the main part of this paper to a critique of Childs' work in the light of the criticisms and modifications that it has received, and my own reaction to these.

Is Canon an Arbitrary and Late Imposition?

Is Childs right, first of all, when he claims that canon does not represent an arbitrary and late imposition on the Old Testament texts, but is rather intrinsically bound up with the Old Testament texts as we have them? Does canon consciousness lie deep within the Old Testament literature itself, and in what sense does it do so? As Francis Watson has rightly pointed out,[8] the traditional critical model of interpretation begins with an assumption about biblical texts that is not visible to the untrained eye but is nonetheless of fundamental importance. It interprets the biblical texts as chance remnants of a previous stage of human history whose meaning is wholly determined by their historical circumstances of origin. It is however quite proper, he insists, to regard the *effects* of a text, which extend beyond their immediate, originating circumstances—which transcend their initial environment and determine in some measure the course and shape of a community extended in space and time—as a property of the object to be described. It is reductionism, he maintains, to insist that canonicity is an extraneous distortion of a more fundamental essence that can be recovered only by historical methods. With this general point I wholeheartedly agree. But the question I wish to press is this: just how deep does canonical consciousness go? I ask the question precisely because I agree with Watson that description of a given object always presupposes a prior construction of that object in terms of a given interpretative paradigm; and I am intrigued, therefore, by the apparent concession to historical-critical method implied in his phrases "extend beyond their immediate, originating circumstances" and "transcend their initial environment." How much do we actually know of the immediate originating circumstances, the initial environment, of our Old Testament texts? How much of what is apparently knowledge is actually speculation born of the necessities of the historical-critical interpretative paradigm itself, which simply assumes without argument that canon is a late and artificial imposition on originally unrelated texts of diverse originating circumstances? If we are to query the dissociation of canonicity and textual essence at all, should we not also reexamine in some depth the assumption about origins? So I ask again: just how deep does canonical consciousness go?

James Barr has addressed this matter in some detail, in a book that is critical of the whole canonical approach.[9] Barr's general view is that biblical faith was not, in its own nature, a scriptural religion. In what we call biblical times, there was as yet no Bible. Old Testament man related to God much more through holy persons and institutions and through a sort of direct personal and oral communication with God, and little or not at all through preexisting written and authoritative holy books. It is not until the 7th century BC that we first come across a book of the Torah (law) and that we first hear of prophetic sayings being collected in a scroll. It was the Deuteronomic movement around the 8th and 7th centuries that first began to make something like a scripture central to the life of Israel; but it is probably only in late times (for example, in Daniel) that we begin to find within the Old Testament itself actual references back, integral to the text and not mere glosses, literary similarities or allusions, but explicit references to a preexisting book as a source requiring to be explained and interpreted. It is only in these last centuries before the coming of Christianity that we find a clearly-defined holy written Torah and other books of profoundly authoritative religious status—much of the rest of what we now call the Old Testament. This change meant a fateful and all-important change in the character of Israelite religion that, Barr argues, has had the consequent effect of leading Christians to misconceive of Christianity also as a scriptural religion. The idea of scripture is a relatively late phenomenon, then, and the idea of canon (in the sense of a precise definition of the scriptures) later still.

Now this is a description of reality which invites a considerable degree of critical comment.[10] How can its central claims be substantiated? It is asserted on several occasions in the course of the argument that they are grounded in the scriptures themselves; that this reading of the past is true to the Bible in a way that others are not. Yet to me, the general contours of the picture that Barr paints here is reminiscent of nothing so much as 19th century German criticism, which likewise portrayed the history of Israel in terms of an early authentic period of faith, particularly symbolized by the prophets, that then gave way to a later regressive period of book-dominated religion, which in turn gave way to a renaissance in early Christianity. And indeed, the reading of the Bible that Barr offers us here turns out on closer inspection inevitably to be very far from the purely inductive reading he claims. It depends at every point on a prior commitment to an overall theory about the history of Israelite religion—the traditional historical-critical theory, in fact, deriving in large measure from Wellhausen. Barr's is certainly not the only way in which to read the texts. Why should we believe, for example, since he himself acknowledges that many of the national-religious traditions of Israel that later became scripture were already central and authoritative—and that Deuteronomy in particular evidences scripture consciousness—that scripture consciousness only began to be an important feature of the life of Israel around the 8th and 7th centuries? This assertion depends partly on prior acceptance of a hypothesis about the book of the law in 2 Kings 22 that is not supported by the book of Kings itself and is certainly not a necessary hypothesis (although it has been a popular one) in terms of the narrative and prophetic texts that Barr cites. It depends partly on a further ungrounded assertion about Israel's authoritative traditions not yet being separable from the general life of all the traditions of the community. It is not at all clear in the midst of all this assertion where the hard evidence lies that necessitates the view that texts later regarded as having special status as scripture were once not so regarded, and already demarcated in respect of other texts that did not have this status. It seems intrinsic in the careful preservation and passing on of prophetic traditions, for example, that these traditions were already regarded at the point of origin as especially important.

One test of this, as Barr rightly points out, is whether there is the kind of cross-referencing between our Old Testament texts, at some fundamental level within these texts, that would suggest that they were formed in the midst of scripture consciousness; and he himself acknowledges that a great deal of cross-referencing is indeed to be found in the Old Testament. Again, however, the theory drives the interpretation of the evidence in a very noticeable way. He insists that it is only *explicit* references back to other Old Testament books as scripture that count as evidence. He dismisses what he calls mere glosses, literary similarities and allusions, or cross-references that suggest only a rather loose relation between books and traditions. Why explicit references should be privileged in this way is unclear, particularly when it is evident that even in the later biblical period, when Barr acknowledges that scriptures do obviously exist, such references are still nonetheless very thin on the ground. Why other sorts of cross-reference should at the same time be so radically downplayed is also unclear. I confess that I no longer know what a "mere" gloss is; but what I increasingly find in working with Old Testament texts is that the level of intertextuality among them is extraordinarily high. It is not a trivial or marginal matter, this reality of cross-referencing. It is, rather, a central matter. It is, for example, an intrinsic feature of the nature of our Old Testament narrative texts that they have come into their present form in relationship with each other and with Torah and prophetic texts, the very form in which they are written inviting reference time and time again to these other scriptural texts. If I may simply write of the narrative text I know best, the book of Kings, it is evident in that book that the whole way in which the story is told is designed to get readers thinking about the broader context of the story in Torah, especially in Deuteronomy; to cause them to reflect on the way in which earlier events and characters in the story of Joshua–Samuel illuminate the events and characters of Kings; and to bring to mind also prophetic perspectives on the story.[11]

For all these reasons, then, I do not find Barr's case for the lateness of scripture-consciousness in Israel convincing. I do not see the evidence for marked discontinuity between the earlier period of biblical faith and the later. Nor, indeed, do I see the evidence for the further marked discontinuity that he suggests between *scripture*-consciousness and *canon*-consciousness.[12] Barr's assertion here is that Torah was never canonized in the sense that the New Testament was canonized. It simply arrived at supreme and authoritative status in the time of Ezra. Nor is it certain that the Prophets were canonized either. Their religious authority in fact predates the recognition of the supremacy of Torah. This prophetic section of the canon was probably not, however, closed early on. Some books in the Writings may well have originally been in the Prophets, initially a catch-all category for any non-Torah book that was holy scripture, yet a fluid category still in the first century AD. The point about Barr's argument, however, is this: even if he is right in his central claim that we cannot talk about a canonization process for the Hebrew Bible similar to that undergone by the New Testament—and this is largely an argument from silence[13]—does this mean that no *canon-consciousness* existed? Is it in fact not implicit in the notion that a certain text is scripture that another text is not? Is this implicit notion not seen precisely in the position attained, however it was attained, by Torah and Prophets? The question I am asking here is not at the moment whether everyone agreed precisely which texts were scripture and which were not. The question I am asking is whether the idea of scripture does not itself imply the idea of limitation, of canon, even if it is not yet conceived that the limits have yet been reached. I believe that it does so imply.[14] The question of when and how the Old Testament canon was formally closed is another matter, which is not immediately relevant to the question of canonical consciousness.[15] This is precisely the point Childs himself makes when discussing his use of the word "canon" in his *Introduction*. He rightly insists that it makes sense to speak of an "open canon," precisely because closure is only one element in the process of canon, and not constitutive of it. That process, he affirms, had already begun in the pre-exilic period.[16] Scripture and canon cannot be sharply distinguished.[17]

My conclusion to the first question I have asked of Childs, then, is this: Childs is right when he claims that canon does not represent an arbitrary and late imposition on the Old Testament texts, but is rather intrinsically bound up with the Old Testament texts as we have them. Canon consciousness does lie deep within the Old Testament literature itself. If I have a criticism of Childs it is that he does not fully perceive the implications of the kinds of arguments that he and I have used in support of this position—a point to which I shall return later.

Which Canon?

Let me turn for the moment, however, to a second question that leads on naturally from the discussion above. Which canon, and indeed which text, so far as the Old Testament books are concerned, should form the basis for the kind of theological reflection that Childs has in mind? The view that Childs himself expresses on this point in the *Introduction* is that it is the final limits of the *Jewish* canon that should be observed by Christian interpreters; and that it is the Masoretic Text that should be regarded as the vehicle both for recovering and for understanding the canonical text of the Old Testament.[18] This is a point of view that has attracted much criticism. Why, it has been asked, should modern Christian interpreters observe the limits of a canon that in all probability did not exist in early Christian times; that, if it did exist, was only one canon among several; and that has, moreover, been the canon of only a minority of Christians throughout the ages? Why should they regard as canonical a text of the Old Testament that clearly represents only one of the Hebrew versions extant in early Christian times, and when the LXX (and other Greek texts) were so widely used both by New Testament and later Christian writers? In the face of such questions, the arguments in the *Introduction* that link the theological determination of the boundaries and text of the Old Testament canon to the historical dominance of a particular Jewish community; that stress that from the Jewish perspective the Greek Bible never had an independent integrity which could contest the Hebrew; and that explain the church's use of Greek and Latin translations as historically valid but theologically irrelevant—these arguments have seemed to many to be weak.

It is interesting, then, that in his more recent *Biblical Theology* we find Childs now speaking rather of "the *search* for the Christian Bible," which is characterized as being part of the task of a Biblical Theology.[19] In this new presentation of his position, we find some significant shifts in emphasis and perspective. In the *Introduction* all the emphasis falls upon the first century AD. It is in the latter part of this century that the canonical text is stabilized, and although there is no conclusive evidence for the date of closing of the third section of the Hebrew canon, this stabilization implies a relatively closed Hebrew canon by the beginning of the Christian era. In the *Biblical Theology*, on the other hand, the emphasis is quite different. The direct literary evidence with its uncertain implications is once again reviewed; but now the emphasis falls upon the very strong indirect evidence that within the circles of Pharisaic Judaism the concept of an established Hebrew canon with a relatively fixed scope of writings and an increasingly stabilized authoritative text of Masoretic type had already emerged in the first century BC. This is, of course, the period before the rise of Christianity; and when Childs goes on to note that it is the scriptures of Pharisaic Judaism with which Jesus and the early Christians identify; that the New Testament does not cite as scripture any book of the Apocrypha or Pseudepigrapha; that 1 Clement and Justin Martyr assume a common scripture between synagogue and church; and that it is only later use of the LXX in the church that erodes the limitations on the scope of the Hebrew canon that rabbinic Judaism had established; then we might well think that what Childs is doing here is simply strengthening his previous position. The Pharisaic canon did exist in early Christian times and was given its status as Christian canon by Jesus and the apostles, their use of texts in translation notwithstanding.

Readers well-versed in Childs will know, however, that the last thing to be expected from him at such a juncture is what might be called the obvious. Argument towards a definite position on such matters is usually only a launching-pad for another foray into dialectic in the service of various kinds of ecumenism. And so it is in this case. Having provided argument that seems to strengthen his first case, he now moves in a different direction. He acknowledges the importance of Christian experience and use in the post-apostolic church's decisions about canon, and he acknowledges too the significance not only of the New Testament's employment of the LXX, but also its *manner* of employment. There has always been diversity within the church regarding the form of the Christian Bible; and this diversity, Childs now affirms, should be respected, although it should not be exaggerated. Just because the outer limits of the Christian canon remained unsettled, or because the role of translations was assessed differently among various groups of Christians, the conclusion cannot be drawn that the church has functioned without a scripture or in deep confusion. The areas of disagreement, in fact, have made little theological or practical difference. A Christian biblical theology in which canon plays a central role does not need to resolve these issues of text and scope before it begins, because the search for the

Christian Bible is not something that will be resolved once-for-all, but something that appears to be constitutive for Christian faith. Biblical theology should, rather, work theologically within the narrow and wider forms of the canon in search for both the truth and catholicity of the biblical witness to the church and the world.

Now at one level it is possible to see the point that Childs is making here. It is not at all clear, for example, what the sum of the theological difference is between the MT and the LXX in the case of any individual Old Testament book, even where the differences in content are marked (e.g. in the case of Jeremiah). The same can be said of the Christian Bible with or without the deutero-canonical books.[20] It could be argued, then, that a canonical approach to Old Testament theology is not really undermined by the kind of difference in perception within the church regarding text and canon that Childs outlines. Yet we must ask whether the new position that he adopts here is actually tenable. It is one thing to state as a matter of description that differences in perception have not come to very much in practice. It is another thing to extrapolate meaningfully from description to method. How exactly does one approach the Old Testament canonically, in terms of the program outlined in the *Introduction* or the *Old Testament Theology*, while at the same time searching for the Christian Bible? Does one not need to have clearly in mind, as one goes about the task, which Old Testament text and canon one is thinking of? The emphasis in Childs' earlier work, it must be remembered, is upon the Old Testament canon as something that is Jewish first, and then Christian. Canonical analysis aims to study in their final form the texts of the Jewish canon in relation to their usage within Israel, as historically and theologically conditioned writings that were accorded a normative function in the life of the community. This finality is expressed both in terms of text and canon. Childs puts it this way: "The canonical approach to Old Testament theology is unequivocal in asserting that the object of theological reflection is the ... Hebrew scriptures which are the received traditions of Israel ... the Christian church accepted the scriptures of the synagogue, as previously shaped ... as part of its own canon."[21] The Old Testament thus functions within Christian scripture as a discrete witness to Jesus Christ precisely in its pre-Christian form.

This position I understand. But I am not at all clear how one puts it together with the newer position, in which a book or a text not part of the Jewish canon might turn out after "searching" to be part of the Christian Bible. How was *such* a book canonically shaped, and by whom? How does *its* final form bear pre-Christian witness to Christ? Is the Old Testament, understood in this new way, any longer a *discrete* witness at all? And what of the issue of text? Has Childs really moved to a position, for example, where he might accept Augustine's view of the LXX; where he is prepared to say that the Holy Spirit might have decided to say something through the translators in Greek that was not said through the prophets in Hebrew? If this is not acceptable, why not? For Augustine's position on *text* rests just as clearly on consensus among the churches—on catholicity—as his position on *canon*.[22] To rephrase an old question: what has Rome to do with Jerusalem? Can the canonical approach really be as ecumenical in respect of both Jews and non-Protestant Christians as Childs now seems to desire? I am not clear myself how it can be; and I am not clear either that Childs himself believes it. For all the ecumenical noises in the opening pages of the *Biblical Theology*, it is striking that when he himself gets down to the task of doing biblical theology, he appears to be working with precisely the older model already mentioned.[23] This is not a biblical theology particularly marked out in any sense by a search for the Christian Bible.

Childs seems to know exactly which Old Testament he is working with, on the whole; and it is largely the same Old Testament as before.[24] I do not see how it could be otherwise, given the way he has developed the argument. And I believe, therefore, that he cannot afford to adopt the rather relaxed attitude to questions of text and canon evidenced in his *Biblical Theology*. In order for his general approach to be well-grounded, Childs is required to defend the notion of a Jewish canon (and text) that is canonical also for the church.

Canonical Intentionality

Now in fact I believe that this can be done, developing many of the arguments that Childs himself presents in his work. There is insufficient space in this article, however, for such a discussion. If we were to grant, however, that the phrase "Old Testament texts as we have them" makes sense as referring to the books of the Jewish canon in their 1st century Masoretic form, we would then have to ask—so what? Childs' answer is as follows. It is the final canonical shape of the Old Testament texts that should provide the focus of exegetical activity, for it alone bears witness to the full history of divine revelation to Israel.[25] As useful as the prehistory (and indeed the posthistory) of the literature may be for interpreting the final form, it is the final form that has been received as authoritative Scripture in both Judaism and Christianity.[26] Old Testament theology, a constructive task as well as a descriptive task, derives from theological reflection upon this body of Old Testament texts as received and shaped, regarding the Old Testament as one discrete part of Christian Scripture. The canon provides the arena in which the struggle for contemporary understanding takes place.[27]

A number of questions have been asked of Childs at this point in the argument, and the first concerns the question of how, in general terms, the final canonical shape of the Old Testament may be thought of as coercing, in some sense, the interpreter of the Old Testament in his exegesis and theological reflection, keeping him within certain bounds and guiding him in certain directions. It is clearly Childs' view that the canonical shape does do this;[28] yet he has been criticized for imprecision in his framing of the argument. On the one hand, he seems to want to depart from the idea of authorial intentionality, or even editorial intentionality, as the norm for interpretation, and to move towards a text-grounded hermeneutical construct. In the *Introduction* he speaks of a "canonical intentionality" that is co-extensive with the meaning of the biblical text and the means by which the tradition was rendered accessible to the future generation.[29] Elsewhere he speaks of the "objective status" of the text, and quite explicitly resists the idea that the main focus of research on the Old Testament should lie in pursuing the motivations and biases of redactors. Logical and literary rules, to which the interpreter must pay attention, are clearly operative within the text itself.[30] So on the one hand Childs has moved away from a traditional critical position. On the other hand, however, he remains resistant to any hermeneutical theory that appears to him to underplay the importance of the intention of the text as an authoritative witness located in history and to over-emphasize the importance of the modern-day interpreter or interpretative community in the construction of meaning. That is the basis of his critique of Ricoeur in the *Introduction*, for example;[31] and it resurfaces in his comments in the *Biblical Theology* on the idea of "the classic" and on Brueggemann's views as to the importance of the canonical interpreter.[32] Nothing must be allowed to compromise the theological appeal to an authoritative canonical text that has been shaped by Israel's witness to a history of divine, redemptive intervention. Childs seeks to stand as usual, then, between two critical poles;

but the ground upon which he seeks to stand has often been regarded as somewhat ill-defined.

How far can Childs' view of canonical shaping and intention be defended? Can texts have communicative intentions that are not wholly related to the intentions of the human authors or editors who produced them? Charles Scalise (briefly), drawing on Ricoeur,[33] and Mark Brett (at length), drawing mainly on Gadamer,[34] have argued persuasively in relation to Childs' work that they can. It is Brett's more extensive treatment that I wish to consider here. Even Hirsch, Brett notes, in his anxiety to defend the role of the author in determining the verbal meaning of a text, has come to accept that, while it is true that later aspects of verbal meaning are fixed by its originating moment in time, that moment has fixed only the *principles* of further extrapolation. These principles will not cover with full determinacy all unforeseen possibilities. That is not to say that future meanings of texts are radically indeterminate. It is only to affirm that they are not exhaustively determined by the author's original consciousness in addressing future readers.

Now Brett questions whether Hirsch really should be speaking of future meanings here rather than of future significance: the text, placed in a new and wider context, takes on new significance and is found to have fresh implications. He further argues that the canonical approach cannot rest upon a theory of intentions to address future readers that are not actually embodied in the text itself. It needs a theory of relatively autonomous texts, from which implications can be drawn that find no justification in the intentions of authors and editors. On the first point I think Brett is quite right. On the second point, I am not so sure. I see the force of its first part, although I am not entirely clear how one assesses the claim that intentions to address future readers are not actually embodied in the text itself. I have more difficulty with the statement about the canonical approach needing a theory of relatively autonomous texts, from which implications can be drawn that find *no* justification in the intentions of authors and editors. For to put it this way, particularly in a context where Hirsch is being criticized, is apparently to suggest allowing a greater gulf to exist between tradent and text than the canonical approach overall would appear to permit.

Childs himself, although concerned that we should concentrate on the communicative intention *in* the text rather than spend time speculating on the prior intentions *behind* it, is most anxious to avoid such a gulf. His view is particularly clear in his *Biblical Theology* where—I suspect in reaction to much of the past debate about this issue—he writes of "the multilayering activity of tradents who were continually at work in the individual testaments bringing the authoritative writings into conformity with a larger canonical intentionality."[35] This is contrasted with simple juxtaposition (the particular example is the four Gospels), where there is no attempt to make the individual books conform to a single redactional pattern, yet the juxtaposition itself causes a strong effect on the reader because of the newer and larger context created. Notice the emphasis here on the *consciousness* of the tradents in relation to the larger canonical intentionality of the Old Testament, an emphasis fully in line with his general emphasis upon canon-consciousness elsewhere. There is no great gulf between tradents and text in Childs, for all he is prepared to allow that the reading of texts in larger contexts has effects on the reader unrelated to single editorial intentionality.

In one sense, of course, this Childsean view does require a "relatively autonomous text." Much depends, however, on what is meant by "relatively autonomous." If we are speaking of a text that has a future-oriented communicative intentionality intrinsically bound up with its tradents, but that is not fully determined in terms of its implications, then I think we are speaking of a text as Childs describes it.[36] My own judgment, however, is that with all its difficulties (and which position in this area of intention and reception, meaning and significance, is without difficulties?) the language of Hirsch is more appropriate for describing such a text than the language of Gadamer,[37] for all that Brett's discussion of Gadamer and Childs is immensely stimulating and helpful. The objectivity of the text as a text speaking authoritatively from the past is more carefully guarded—and that, of course, is crucial to Childs' position. Much depends, of course, on how one reads Gadamer. He could be understood to stress much the same kind of authority of past tradition or "canon" that we find in Childs,[38] his assertions about human finitude and tradition-dependence so undermining the role of critical reason that it is difficult in the end to take seriously his insistence upon the latter's importance.[39] Whether this is the case or not, the kind of dialogue that Gadamer theoretically envisages between text and reader, involving as it does a *conversation* about the truth claims of the text, and occurring as it does in significant detachment from the past, is not in my judgment the kind of dialogue that Childs has in mind at all. That is why, as Brett recognizes,[40] one *does* find in Childs Gadamer's emphasis upon the continuing truth claims of the text, but one does *not* find the emphasis upon the need for the text continually to demonstrate its truthfulness in new situations in the light of modern criticism. For all that Childs wishes to find an appropriate place for reason within the framework of faith; for all that he affirms that the exact nature of the canon's authority must be an object of constant critical reflection within the community of faith, and that reasoned defences must be mounted to criticism from outside it; for all that, as he says in one of his responses to Barr,[41] it is still the "testimony of faith and not reason [that] establishes the canon." So far as the Bible is concerned, then, he could not agree with the Gadamerian view that if an ancient work does not continue to demonstrate its truthfulness we are "not compelled to identify it as classical in his normative sense."[42] The authoritative text speaks to us from the past, appreciative of it or not as we may be. It is this text that coerces us in our reading, its canonical shaping providing larger contexts for interpretation, establishing the semantic level, and presenting us with important structural and material keys for understanding it.[43] I shall return to the matter of what exactly this entails in a moment.

The Final Form, Divine Revelation, and Historical Criticism

Let me go on at present to ask why any reader should accept the coercion in view here. That is the second question which has been addressed to Childs by his critics in relation to this question of the final form. Why should we give in to coercion? Even if it is the case that there is a canonical shape to the Old Testament, produced by a canonical process—so what? Should we not be free to examine earlier stages in the tradition, and indeed to find theological value in these earlier stages? Is it not our responsibility, in fact, to subject the final form of the text to criticism, in terms of its relationship both to the reality which lies behind it and to the reality which lies in front of it, our own reality in the modern world? All this ties in very much to the issues I was raising just a moment ago. The heart of Childs' answer to these questions lies in the idea that it is the final canonical shape of the Old Testament that alone bears witness to the full history of divine revelation to Israel. This is the authoritative, normative text of the Old Testament, so far as Christians are concerned. It is therefore this text, rather than other texts behind it, upon which Old Testament theologians should reflect theologically, taking their stance within the circle of tradition rather than pretending to any objective stance outside it. The task is not to criticize, but to struggle to discern the will of God for the present through the Scriptures, in dependence upon the Holy Spirit.

It is at this point that Childs gets into serious trouble with some of his critics. One may do many things within the academic guild of biblical studies, some of them quite bizarre and extraordinary; but the thing one must never do, the unforgiveable sin in some quarters, is to give even the impression that, ultimately, authoritative tradition is the bedrock of one's scholarly endeavors—that limits are being accepted to freedom, that "objectivity" is being sacrificed to dogma. In this respect, Old Testament studies in the West as we come to the end of the 20th century, for all that we are seeing many changes within the discipline, is still largely and resolutely the child of the Enlightenment. Freedom is the badge of authenticity; and it is a word, therefore, that is often uttered when Childs' work comes up for discussion, a sticker stuck with pride to the bumper of scholarly endeavor. If we may return to Barr just for a moment, for example, we find him clearly arguing that freedom is integral to the historical-critical outlook—freedom to follow critical methods wherever they lead. This freedom is grounded not only in the secular outlook of the Enlightenment, he maintains, but also in the Reformation: the Protestant principle of "the plain sense of Scripture" leads directly to Wellhausen. Childs is essentially a counter-revolutionary, an ideologue who aims to destroy the values of the Enlightenment and drive out its way of dealing with biblical materials.[44]

No one wishes to be seen nowadays to be opposing a freedom-fighter, of course. Freedom is a potent word to scrawl on one's banner. But even at great personal risk we must ask whether the kind of view that Barr is espousing here is really credible. Is the Enlightenment's polarization of authoritative tradition and the freedom of reason at all adequate? With Gadamer and others,[45] I should have thought the answer is clearly "no."

It is certainly quite evident, as Childs himself has pointed out, that all the great giants of biblical study in the last 200 years have worked within certain dogmatic and philosophical traditions. It is equally clear that even those Old Testament theologies within this period that have explicitly striven for descriptiveness have been at the same time thoroughly undergirded with dogma and tradition.[46] As for Old Testament commentaries, only a brief engagement with a selection of series on the same book, in whichever theological camp the series may lie, should be necessary to reveal to the reader the relative weight of dogma and tradition, on the one hand, and the free exercise of critical reason, on the other. The task of writing a "meta-commentary" is in this respect a very interesting and useful one. The reason is plain: description of a given object always presupposes a prior construction of that object in terms of a given interpretative paradigm. To assert that the "freedom to follow critical methods wherever they lead" actually exists in any absolute sense, then, is either to display signs of self-delusion or to suggest a conscious ideological move designed to draw a line, by sleight of hand, around those whom one regards as the scholarly sheep, separating them off from those who are self-evidently the obscurantist goats. Of *course* this "freedom" does not exist; and that is the fact of the matter, no matter how vehemently its existence is asserted, as it has been, for example, in the recent positivist histories of Israel that I have discussed elsewhere.[47] There *is* no objective ground somewhere outside of tradition; and if such does not exist, Childs cannot fairly be criticized for not standing on it. Indeed, his refusal to allow the kind of relativizing of the final form of the text in which scholars like Gottwald indulge is simply a matter of consistency.[48] Whether his continuing rejection of Lindbeck's position is equally justifiable is open to question. It certainly seems on the face of it, as Mark Brett reasserts in a recent review of *Biblical Theology*, that

"Lindbeck's version of Barthian theology represents the closest theological ally of the canonical approach in contemporary hermeneutics,"[49] at least in so far as Lindbeck insists, with Childs, on the indivisibility of the form and the content of revelation.[50] The crucial question appears to be whether Childs' concern is well grounded, that on Lindbeck's view the Bible no longer bears witness to a reality outside the text, namely God. On this point there is disagreement among interpreters of Lindbeck.[51] I do not seek in this context to be a thoroughgoing interpreter of Lindbeck, but only of Childs, which is more than enough. I therefore offer no comment on this dispute. All I require to do here is to note the broad similarity between Lindbeck and Childs in certain respects, and leave it at that.

An important question must now be asked, however. In adopting this kind of stance with regard to the final form of the text, has Childs not now raised some interesting questions about his account of the canonical process? We recall here that the problem as Childs set it up in his *Introduction* was how it might be possible to understand the Old Testament as canonical Scripture and yet make full and consistent use of historical-critical tools;[52] and throughout his work, and in interaction with other scholars about his work, he goes out of his way to accommodate historical-critical perspectives, stressing that they are valid in their own right.[53] There is enormous diversity in the Old Testament, he tells us; canonical intentionality can indeed cut against the grain of original intentions as we can recover them; texts were included within Old Testament books that were simply inherited and made no sense (for example, the servant song passages in Isaiah);[54] and so on. Yet it is equally clear throughout his work that his commitment to the final form itself influences, indeed determines, the descriptions that he allows about the authorship and redaction of Old Testament texts. He will not, for example, allow the historical-critical theory about Deuteronomy which would construe it as a pious fraud created for propaganda reasons, for this raises serious questions about a canonical interpretation that claims that the book was shaped by predominantly religious concerns.[55] For the same reason he dismisses Gottwald, not on the basis of any fundamental disagreement about the facts (whether there was a canonical process or not), but because Gottwald's interpretation of the facts is not consistent with his own.[56] It is clear, then, that the authoritative final form is exercising significant influence on judgments that are being made even about authorship and redaction. Here, as elsewhere, description is no straightforward matter. Freedom is constrained by framework, reason by faith, even if it is acknowledged that faith must mount a reasoned defence for its positions.[57] Objectivity is only "alleged" by historical critics.[58] Historical research counts for something, but historical-critical theories are not simply "givens" presented to the canonical critic to do with what he can, not least because of their frequently fragile basis in what might be termed "evidence."[59]

If historical-critical hypotheses are not simply "givens" presented to the canonical critic, however, then why does Childs so often in his work treat them as just that—as data that must be accommodated? Is the question to which the canonical approach is the answer really a question? How difficult a question is it? It is worth pondering the matter, for there is little evidence that Childs himself has pondered it greatly. He simply takes historical-critical reality in general as a fairly obvious and self-evident starting point. He adjusts it here and there, where it is necessary for him to do so; but somewhat in the manner of Ptolemaic astronomy, the complexity of the theory that results never really causes him to question its fundamental premises. As Scalise points out, he is often preoccupied with the detailed rehearsal and evaluation of the historical-critical state of the question against which his canonical proposal is set, to the extent that sometimes this focus on the reconstruction of tradition even outweighs his efforts to specify both the canonical shape of a biblical book and its larger theological and hermeneutical implications.[60] It is in part this preoccupation, one supposes, that has led him to pay insufficient attention to the massive amount of work carried out in the last two decades that has gone a long way towards undermining the traditional historical-critical approach to the Old Testament texts.[61] On the one hand, particular theories (for example, about the Pentateuch) have been seriously questioned.[62] More seriously, however, the newer literary approaches have steadily been undermining the very notion that the *sort* of theory in question is at all necessary in order to explain the phenomena of the text. If Barr could claim in 1983, for example, that "the plain sense of Scripture" leads directly to Wellhausen,[63] scholars are now not quite so sure. In fact, since Wellhausen himself affirmed that if J and E could not be found in the Joseph story it would seriously call in question his whole theory about the Pentateuch, and since almost everyone now doubts whether they *can* be found there, one would hope that Wellhausen himself, if he were yet with us, would also not be sure. This may, however, be naïve.

My point is this: that Childs describes himself as setting out to reconcile two sovereign nations. His own worldview clearly entails commitment to one, however, and he is often to be found making speeches that subtly or explicitly undermine the other. At the same time, unacknowledged by Childs, *agents provocateurs* from different parts of the world are gradually persuading the community at large that "nation B's" pretensions to sovereign status are just that—pretensions. The observer is forced to ask: why then does Childs persist in speaking of nation B as an equal? Is it simply out of politeness or political niceties? Is it simply habit? Can he really justify it?

He certainly cannot assert at this point in the argument, after all that has gone before, that it is simply self-evident that the Old Testament texts require the sorts of historical-critical theories that he sets on one side of his equation. It is not self-evident to many;[64] and even if it were, that should not logically, on his view of things, make any difference. The nature of the object, we must recall, is not a pure datum, but is precisely what is under discussion. Having taken the stance he has, would Childs not be more consistent to begin, not by assuming a discontinuity between the final form of the text and what might lie behind it, but rather by enquiring whether and how far it is necessary to posit such discontinuity at all? Are there really grounds for conceding, as he is wont to do, that the final form of the text presents a faith very different from the faith of Israel in its historical development?[65] How far is this simply an assumption born of not spending sufficient time with literary critics, watching in their company as perfectly respectable redactors disappear in a puff of smoke, greater and greater appreciation of their genius leading to the certainty of their nonexistence? How far is it a consequence, indeed, of not really believing that canon-consciousness goes very deep at all, assertions to the contrary notwithstanding? I promised towards the beginning of the paper that I would return briefly to this question of canon-consciousness, for I was not convinced that Childs fully perceived the implications of the kinds of arguments that were being used in support of his position. In fact, I think he vastly underestimates the level of intertextuality in the Old Testament, which leads him to posit a far greater gulf between the later and earlier stages of the tradition than is justified. This is a function of his much greater degree of engagement with traditional historical-critical exegesis than with any other kinds of textual reading.

One consequence of his partial starting point within the historical-critical camp is that he makes himself more vulnerable than necessary to attacks from those he is in the process of leaving behind.[66] More seriously, however, from the point of view of those interested in Old Testament theology, it is clearly the case that Childs' lack of literary sensitivity and his over-commitment to particular historical-critical positions can have consequences for his reading of the final form and his theological construal of it. It is not always the case that this is so. Often, Childs' interaction with these positions has no visible effect, in the end, on his exegesis of the canonical text.[67] Consider, however, the case of the book of Jonah, where Childs in the *Introduction* begins by simply accepting without argument the view that the psalm in chapter 2 was inserted into the original by a redactor.[68] As Landes has pointed out, this clearly has an effect on the way Childs understands the whole book, for it leads him to under-emphasize the theme of repentance therein—a theme which, as Landes has shown from a rhetorical-critical standpoint, is of central importance not merely throughout the book of Jonah but also in the wider canonical context.[69] This is an excellent example of the way in which Childs, because of his starting point in historical-critical theory, arrives at a "canonical reading" different from the one at which he would have arrived if he had begun with the text simply as canonical text. A more sensitive reading of the text *as text* in the first instance would have made it clear just how unnecessary the theory was as a starting point at all, and would have led to what is arguably a more satisfactory grasp of its canonical shape.[70]

The Final Form and the Reading Community

I return now, finally, to the question which I left hanging a little while ago. Childs maintains that the final form of the text coerces us in our reading. But how does it do that, exactly? What does working from the final form of the text mean in practice for the doing of Old Testament theology?

Watson has recently expressed the view[71] that the move from the abstract to the concrete in this area is far more problematic than Childs allows. It is one thing to accept that the final form of the text has been shaped for an authoritative role within a communal context; it is another thing to make this abstract notion of an authoritative role concrete. The canon itself, he maintains, does not do this.[72] For Childs the canonical texts are unfailingly helpful in mediating the many-sided will of God to the reader or hearer located within the community of faith. In reality, however, the act of reading or hearing will always be enmeshed in interpretative conflicts about how their authoritative role is to be actualized—as the history of interpretation demonstrates. Childs is operating with a concept of an ideal community of faith to which real communities only occasionally and imperfectly correspond.

Now this is a very interesting section of a wonderfully stimulating book; but I am not entirely sure myself that the analysis in this instance is correct. In the first place, it is clear that Childs fully accepts that the task of interpretation, even for the canonical critic, is by no means straightforward. In response to Roland Murphy's review of the *Introduction*, for example,[73] Childs has this to say:

> There is no claim being made to objectivity. Still to dismiss the analyses as inherently subjective … seriously underestimates the logical and literary rules clearly operative within

a sacred text. Although Murphy is correct when suggesting that there is no complete escape from the ambiguity of interpreting the canonical signs, the nature of the exegetical task emerges as a very different one when the canonical shape is given preeminence.[74]

Elsewhere Childs is quite explicit as to the subjective aspects of interpretation and the importance of the work of the Holy Spirit in the struggle for understanding:

> The modern biblical theologian takes his stance within the testimony of Israel and struggles to discern the will of God. Fully aware of his own frailty, he awaits in anticipation a fresh illumination through God's Spirit, for whom the Bible's frailty is no barrier.[75]

Childs is not unaware of the reality of interpretative conflicts, nor of the location of interpreters within time-bound social realities. His point is that where the final canonical shape of the text is the focus of attention as authoritative Scripture, at least the parameters of any discussion about interpretation are clearly set. Exegetes know *about* which text *in* which context they are disagreeing; and they also recognize the arena in which attempts to resolve their disagreements must take place, in the communal struggle to discern God's will as revealed through Scripture for the present day. The notion of the ideal community of faith in fact arises directly from the idea of an authoritative Scripture through which God speaks to shape the Church—the idea that God calls the Church to live in a certain way, calls them to an ideal. It is an important notion, precisely because it relativizes all existing communities of faith and refuses to allow them and their readings any ultimate autonomy, reminding them of the need continually to search the Scriptures anew and to be sure that they have heard God's voice. Childs is "oblivious to the function of the canonical text as a site of ideological conflict" only in this sense—that he refuses to allow the fact of historical diversity in the reading of Scripture to divert him from the task of deciding which reading he himself believes to be consonant with its canonical shape. In this I believe he is being quite consistent with himself. One may disagree with his reading; but then one will have to argue the case on the basis of rules which have, at least, been agreed by all the participants in the exercise.

Watson's main problem, though, if I understand him correctly, is that he believes that the canon itself does not provide us with enough help even to begin to translate abstract authority into concrete decision-making—that it offers us no hermeneutical guidelines to aid us in understanding how authority translates into practice. If this is his assertion I can only disagree; but I am at the same time not at all clear that he himself believes this. For he grounds his critique of patriarchy in the Old Testament, for example, within the fundamental structure of Old Testament narrative itself, in association with the New Testament claim that Gospel is more fundamental than Law. He refuses to oppose Old Testament to New Testament in addressing this issue, refuses to characterize the latter as superior to the former, in part because such an antithetical approach is the product of an unreflecting *de facto* Marcionism which deprives the gospel narrative of its essential hermeneutical context.[76] And later he says this:

> To see Jesus Christ as the center of a single Christian canon, comprising an Old and a New Testament, is not necessarily

to impose an artificial unity on an irreducibly heterogeneous body of writings ... it is to suggest that hermeneutical criteria might be found which would help to make some sense of the heterogeneity of these writings ... Such criteria would have to be formulated, developed and corrected in the course of an interpretative practice in which one would again seek and expect to find substantive links between the writings of the two testaments.[77]

I deduce from all this that Watson does indeed think, whether in respect of the Old Testament and New Testament taken individually or in respect of the Christian Bible taken as a whole, that the canonical shape of Scripture itself presents us with hermeneutical guidelines for its interpretation, although there is still more to discover about these. There is no great distance, in that case, between Watson and Childs. It may well be the case that Childs does not go as far as he might in demonstrating the ways in which the canonical shape carries with it hermeneutical implications; but he does go some way, particularly in his *Biblical Theology*.[78] In some measure his earlier failure to do this arises from precisely that over-commitment to historical-critical "reality" that I have already mentioned, and its allied under-emphasis upon the intertextuality of the canon.[79] If defence is needed, then it is probably sufficient to say that these are still relatively early days in what is a new way of approaching the discipline, and that Old Testament theology in its resurrected form will take some time yet to find its resurrected feet. As it does so, however, it would be a mistake to imagine that it is beginning from scratch. Many of the hermeneutical guidelines we seek have already been identified by those Christians of previous generations who took the canonical shape of Scripture seriously and were committed, not only to the general notion of Scriptural authority, but also to the notion that Scripture itself guides the reader in how to understand it. That each generation of readers must read Scripture in its own context does not mean that there is such discontinuity with the past that older readings cannot offer help to those who struggle for understanding in the present.

The Future of Old Testament Theology

What, then, of the future of the discipline of Old Testament theology? Where do we go from here? If one is convinced, as I am, that the fundamentals of Childs' approach to Old Testament theology are correct, then the starting point must be the continuation of the sort of exegetical work on the Old Testament texts that seeks to understand them in their final form in interrelationship with the other texts of the Old Testament canon—that seeks to understand their literary artistry and shape and the nature of their intertextuality, and in the process devises precisely the kind of hermeneutical guidelines just mentioned. We need to follow Childs' logic further than he himself has been prepared to do,[80] and to seek in the first instance fresh readings of the text—readings that are consistent with the larger vision of the nature of the material; that allow historical-criticism to tell us something about the nature of the exegetical problem, but not to dictate to us the shape of the exegetical solution;[81] that are aware of the text-critical data, but aware also of the way in which text-critical judgments are entirely bound up with interpretative decisions.[82] It is important to do this not least because starting points, as I have shown, can make a theological difference in the end. The kind of exegesis I am speaking of has not been very common in Old Testament studies, the tendencies on the right having been rationalistic and on the left reductionist, commentators often united only by their disregard for the text that actually lay before them. Yet the sort of theological endeavor on a larger scale we are considering here seems impossible without a concerted effort in this exegetical direction, utilizing all the literary and theological tools at our disposal. Perhaps I am bound to say this, since I have just written a commentary on Kings with this thought in mind;[83] but I do wonder whether the greatest contribution to Christian theology that can be made by Old Testament scholars in the short term is precisely the sort of commentary that seeks to render the text in such a way that it is not, as Childs would put it, "theologically mute."[84]

At the same time, of course, the more general effort to think theologically from an Old Testament point of view within the Christian context must not be sacrificed. There is an enormous amount of work to be done in convincing the skeptical world outside the "ghetto" inside which Old Testament studies all too often now finds itself walled that the Old Testament should indeed be regarded as a fundamental part of Christian Scripture and should be taken with utmost seriousness at a theological rather than a merely historical level. The task of the Old Testament theologian is therefore to persist in his or her efforts to convince others of the continuing importance of the fact that the Old Testament is the Scripture of Jesus and of the early church and the background against which Jesus was read *in* the early church. It is to persuade others that the very narrative and theological fabric of the New Testament is interwoven with that of the Old Testament, in ways sometimes only partially seen by those not deeply aware of the Old Testament background. It is to provide critical input when interpretative paradigms and theological positions are developed which are not consonant with the Christian Bible as a whole, at least for those who care about the place of the Bible in the doing of Christian theology. It is to remind everyone, where reminders are necessary, that "a Christian church without the Old Testament is in constant danger of turning the faith into various forms of gnostic, mystic, or romantic speculation."[85]

The discipline of Old Testament theology thus described clearly has (or at least should have) a future in the Church. Does it have a future in the Academy? There are really two questions disguised here, of course. Can the discipline be academically justified, and will such justification make any difference? That it can be justified I have no doubt. Persuading others of its street credibility may be another matter, in a context where the rationalist-materialist-reductionist paradigm of education still holds so much sway[86] and still seems to many self-evidently to define the territory within which proper academic discourse may occur. Yet in some ways it is much easier to argue now for a legitimate place within the Academy for the kind of discipline I have been describing than it was even ten years ago. Disillusionment with the older paradigm is rife, as more and more scholars within the discipline of Old Testament studies ask themselves whether it makes very much sense for each to construct the text in his own image and then to realize nothing very much can be done with it and few meaningful conversations with others can occur in regard to it.[87] The narrow individualism that is so characteristic of the discipline seems to an increasing number to be intrinsically bound up with its broader irrelevance, and indeed with the incoherent, even self-indulgent nature of much of what is currently taking place.[88] Indeed, the general fragmentation and compartmentalization of theological education into individual disciplines that often have no idea how to speak to each other is also a source of widespread angst. The crisis of modernity is keenly felt, whether it is articulated as such or not. In such a situation, a holistic model with a coherent philosophical base stands every chance of a hearing. It does so in particular to the extent that the enterprise of canonical reading of the Old Testament can be presented as a matter of which method is most appropriate to the material; can be presented as a descriptive exercise rather than a dogmatic one[89]—indeed, to the extent that the facile polarization of reason and dogma can be laid to rest once and for all. It might then be possible to persuade others that intellectual integrity does not demand that they any longer work with a model of the discipline that tends towards fragmentation, when a different model might just as properly be adopted that tends toward integration and indeed towards inter-disciplinarity and user-friendliness.[90] These last two terms are, of course, particularly attractive to many in the current British university context in which I work, not least because of their connotations in terms of "quality assessment" and high university finance. I fear that I am just about cynical enough as to the way in which the world works to believe that if Old Testament theology could indeed be tied so closely to the success of theology in the marketplace, its long-term place within the university would be assured. But that, I hasten to add, is more than halfway a joke, and not truly a part of my vision of the future.

8

THE END OF (ISRAEL'S) HISTORY? A REVIEW ARTICLE ON K. W. WHITELAM'S *THE INVENTION OF ANCIENT ISRAEL*

Like the essay in chapter seven, this one was written in 1996 while I was on sabbatical in Tübingen, Germany, funded by a stipend granted by the Alexander von Humboldt-Stiftung. This sabbatical was largely spent working on the early drafts of what would later become A Biblical History of Israel *(2003). I very much welcomed, therefore, a request from the* Journal of Semitic Studies *to review Keith Whitelam's controversial new book, which alleged not only that "ancient Israel" was an invention of Western scholarship, but also that the invention had been produced in order to achieve "the silencing of Palestinian history" (the subtitle).[1] Whitelam provides us in this book with an excellent, extended example of so much of what is wrong-headed about the so-called "minimalist" approach to the history of Israel, which is the reason my review ultimately became a significant part of the first chapter of* Biblical History. *The original appeared in the* Journal of Semitic Studies *in 1997.*

Two main trends in biblical scholarship that have led us to the present debate about the history of Israel may be identified.[2] First of all, it is the case that recent work on Hebrew narrative that has tended to emphasize the creative art of the biblical authors and the late date of their texts has undermined the confidence of some scholars that the narrative world portrayed therein has very much to do with the "real" world of the past. There has been an increasing tendency, therefore, to marginalize the biblical texts in asking questions about Israel's past, and a corresponding tendency to place greater reliance upon archaeological evidence and anthropological or sociological theory. Over against the artistically formed and "ideologically slanted" texts, these alternative kinds of data have often been represented as providing a much more secure base upon which to build a more "objective" picture of ancient Israel than has hitherto been produced. This leads us on to a second trend in recent publications: the tendency to imply or to claim outright that previous scholarship has itself been compromised by ideology when addressing the matter of Israel's history. A contrast has been drawn between those in the past who, motivated by theology and religious sentiment rather than by critical scholarship, have been overly dependent upon the biblical texts in their construal of the history of Israel, and those in the present who, setting aside the biblical texts, seek to write such a history in a relatively objective and descriptive manner. Thompson, for example, finds among previous scholars "an ideologically saturated indifference to any history of *Palestine* that does not directly involve the history of Israel in biblical exegesis";[3] and he avers that a critically acceptable history of Israel cannot be written on the basis of ancient biblical historiography by writers who are captivated by its story line.[4] These two trends—the increasing marginalization of the biblical texts and the characterization of previous scholarship as compromised by ideology—are perhaps the main distinguishing features of the newer writing on the history of Israel over against the older, which tended to view the biblical narrative texts as essential source material for historiography (albeit that they were not simply historical texts), and was not so much given to bringing scholars' ideology and motivations into scholarly discussion.

The Argument of the Book

The Invention of Ancient Israel may certainly be characterized as an exemplar of the newer historiography rather than of the older, although in this book the kind of argument I have described above is pushed much further than ever before. Following (or perhaps only consistent with) some lines of thought found in Davies,[5] Whitelam now argues that it is not simply the information provided by the biblical texts *about* ancient Israel that is problematic, but the very *idea* of ancient Israel itself, which these texts have put in our mind. Even the newer historians are still writing histories of *Israel*; and this, Whitelam argues, is a mistake. Indeed, it is worse than a mistake; for in thus inventing ancient Israel (whether using biblical texts in practice very much or not), Western scholarship has contributed to the silencing of Palestinian history. Here the *ideological commitments* of scholars are once again a major issue. However, if in other writings of the newer historians these appeared to be relatively harmless commitments with no noticeably important implications outside the discipline of biblical studies, they are certainly not so here. Here ideology is quite deliberately set in the sphere of contemporary politics. Biblical studies as a discipline, it is claimed, has evolved a rhetoric of representation that has dispossessed Palestinians of a land and a past. Biblical scholarship has "collaborated in an act of dispossession, or at the very least, to use Said's phrase, 'passive collaboration' in that act of dispossession."[6]

Chapter 1 prepares the way for the substantive argument, with its discussion of the nature of texts from the past as "partial"; of the way in which the context of modern biblical criticism in the period of European colonialism has led scholarship to impose an inappropriate model (the modern nation state) on the past; and of the need for a history of Palestine divorced from the discipline of biblical studies, which has distorted the past in this search for the nation state in the guise of Israel. Chapter 2 then proceeds to discuss concepts of time and space, vitally important because of the importance of perceptions of the past for shaping identity. Both concepts are ideological constructs to be manipulated in the construction of social identity. For Whitelam, the discourse of biblical studies has professed to remain aloof from the contemporary political situation in Palestine while all along denying time and space to any Palestinian claim to the past. With regard to space, Palestine has been merely the scene of the history of Israel, not a place with Palestinians in it. With regard to time, the history of Palestine has been subject to the tyranny of biblical time and of "prehistoric time,"[7] and has been silenced by these. Palestinian history must rather be granted its own temporal and geographical domain outside the discourse of biblical studies. In reclaiming the temporal and spatial elements for such a regional history, Palestine has to be recognized for its own intrinsic value and not solely as the locus for the origins of European civilization.

Chapters 3 and 4 develop the idea that ancient Israel has been invented. Postmodernist discourses have led to the realization of the essential subjectivity of the academic enterprise, exposing the role of various academic disciplines in the colonial enterprise. This had led to the growing awareness that the search for ancient Israel is not about some disinterested construction of the past but an important question of contemporary identity and power. Each of the three major models of the emergence of Israel, in fact, mirror and are implicated in contemporary struggles for Palestine. They represent a series of imaginative pasts that have been responsible for the silencing of Palestinian history in the name of objective scholarship. The "immigration" and "conquest" models both mirror perceptions of contemporary Palestine at the time of increasing Zionist immigration. Neither model questions the right of Israel to the land or raises the issue of the rights of the dispossessed indigenous population. Both invent ancient Israel in the image of an Israel of their own day, and this at a critical point in the history of the region. Palestinian time and space are completely subsumed by Israel and its claims to the past. The "struggle model" at first sight values more highly the importance of indigenous Palestinian culture and history. In fact, however, in emphasizing the uniqueness of Israel on the basis of its faith over against Canaanite ideology, it sharpens the distinction between Israel and indigenous culture, and again reflects a particular view of modern reality in Palestine. The protracted search for and location of ancient Israel in the Late Bronze–Iron Age transition provides, however, only one of the defining moments in the history of Palestine. The creation of an Israelite state is for biblical scholarship *the* defining moment in the region's history. The "fact" of a large, powerful, sovereign and autonomous Iron Age state founded by David has dominated the discourse of biblical studies throughout this century, and coincides with and helps to enhance the vision and aspirations of many of Israel's modern leaders. Yet this too is an imagined past.

Chapter 5 concentrates in particular on the "newer search" for ancient Israel, which has focused on the failure of the three models mentioned above to deal with the growing body of archaeological data from the region and with the shifts in literary approaches to the Hebrew Bible. A number of these "newer searchers" have in fact argued for the study of ancient *Palestinian* history. Yet in practice these works tend to reinforce the continued search for *Israel*, which remains the focus of attention. For Whitelam, the main problem with the new search is that it depends on an archaeology itself bound by the discourse of biblical studies, especially as it is represented in the work of Israeli archaeologists. Yet the archaeological investigation of the Late Bronze Age–Iron Age transition and the Iron Age 1 period in recent years is itself in reality a narrative—a narrative about possessing the past. It has been couched in terms of objectivity and scientific investigation, which mask the power of representation. Only after the biblically inspired assumption and the political necessity that identifies the settlement shift of the Late Bronze Age–Iron Age transition with Israel has been removed can the discussion proceed to explore the possibilities of giving voice to alternative Palestinian claims to the past. Chapter 6 brings the book to a conclusion, with some brief thoughts on "reclaiming Palestinian history." The shift towards a regional history of Palestine has been obstructed, Whitelam claims, by the lack of an appropriate rhetoric with which to represent this alternative past. The only rhetoric available has been that of a biblical studies in search of ancient Israel. In order to give voice to an alternative Palestinian past, it is vital to construct a rhetoric of Palestinian history. Whitelam outlines such a rhetoric and sketches the areas for future work. Such a rhetoric would remove Israel from center stage, and would provide a much more positive appreciation of the material and cultural achievements of the inhabitants of the region as a whole. It needs an alternative location, however, outside the confines of biblical studies, where a different narrative of the past can be created, thereby helping to restore the voice of an indigenous population that has hitherto been silenced.

Thus is the scholarly ivory tower comprehensively stormed and sacked (from the inside); thus are all those who wished only for a quiet life surrounded by books reminded somewhat forcibly that no scholar can be an island, divorced in body and intellect from the sea of philosophical and political controversy around about. Of *course* it is the case that in all our thinking and doing we are inextricably bound up with the world in which we think and do. Of *course* we cannot help but be shaped by our context, at least in part and no matter if we consciously strive to be aware of that context and its influence upon us. Of *course* it is the case that our ideas and publications may have wider effects than (perhaps) we thought or intended, and sometimes these effects may be felt in the political sphere. No thinking person who believes that openness to criticism and indeed self-criticism are essential aspects of the scholarly endeavor will object to being reminded of all this, nor indeed object to being invited to remember it in respect of such a serious matter as the contemporary situation in Palestine. Every scholar who has been involved in working on the history of Israel will need to listen carefully to what Whitelam is saying, and weigh the value of the many important individual points that he makes.[8] Yet no thinking person will wish, either, to refrain from asking the obvious question: is Whitelam, in fact, persuasive in the overall case that he argues? My own view is that he is wholly unpersuasive on a number of important points, and indeed that a serious objection ought to be registered to some of the things he says—not simply (as Whitelam seems to fear) because they subvert a dominant view, but for the much more important reason that they paint a portrait of the discipline of biblical studies that is at variance with reality. It is this misleading view of reality that is now in the public domain, because of the widespread publicity that the book has attracted. This is itself an effect, intended or otherwise, of an academic publication.

The Bible and the Past

To begin where Whitelam has the greatest point of contact with preceding work, it is a presupposition of this book that we have arrived at a point in scholarship where it is possible to use the biblical texts in constructing Israelite history only with great caution. In fact, their value for the historian lies not in what they have to say about the past in itself, but "in what they reveal of the ideological concerns of their authors, if, and only if, they can be located in time and place."[9] Accounts of the past are, after all, invariably the products of small elites and are in competition with other possible accounts, of which we may have no evidence.[10] Changes in perspective in reading the biblical accounts in particular, affirms Whitelam, have raised serious questions about standard historical-critical assumptions and use of the biblical traditions for historical reconstruction.[11] For example, the work of Gunn and others has opened new vistas on appreciating the literary qualities of the biblical texts, and has served to undermine confidence in standard reconstructions of the history of Israel.[12]

It is, however, unclear to me why the fact that accounts of the past are invariably the products of small elites possessing particular points of view must necessarily mean that they cannot inform us about the past they describe *as well as* about the ideological concerns of the authors. One presumes that Whitelam himself wishes us to believe that what he (as part of an intellectual elite) writes about the past can inform us about that past as well as about his own ideology—although I shall return to this point below. All accounts of the past may be partial (in every sense), but it is by no means clear that partiality of itself is a problem. Then again, it is clearly the case that changes in perspective in reading biblical narrative have raised questions in many minds about standard historical-critical assumptions about and use of biblical traditions, and about standard reconstructions of the history of Israel. No doubt there is much that can be criticized with respect to past method and results when the biblical texts have been utilized in the course of historical enquiry. Whether any of this leads on, however, to the conclusion that the texts ought not now to be regarded as essential data in such historical enquiry, as witnesses to the past they describe rather than simply witnesses to the ideology of their authors, is another matter. The assertion or implication that scholarship has more or less been compelled to this conclusion partly as a result of what we now know about our texts is a commonplace in recent writing about Israel and history. As I have argued elsewhere, however, there are some questions to be asked about such assertions and implications.[13] *Why*, exactly, does the fact that Hebrew narrative is artistically constructed and ideologically shaped mean that it is somehow less worthy of consideration as source material for modern historiographers than other kinds of data from the past? *Why*, exactly, does the fact that the biblical traditions about the pre-monarchic period in their current forms are late (if it is conceded for the sake of argument that this is the case) mean that these are not useful for understanding the emergence or origins of Israel?[14] The points need to be argued. I am all for caution in the use of *all* evidence, including biblical texts, in the construction of Israelite history. It is not particularly cautious, however, to decide in advance what these texts can and cannot inform us about.[15]

Archaeology and the Past

This brings us, however, to archaeology; for like others among the "newer historians," Whitelam sets a considerable amount of store by the evidence of archaeology, over against the evidence of text. It is, in fact, one of the linchpins of his argument that archaeology has demonstrated things to be the case, which in turn demonstrate that the ancient Israel of text and scholar alike is an imagined past. For example, it is above all archaeological data, in combination with newer ways of looking at Hebrew narrative, that have "shown" the various models or theories about the emergence of ancient Israel described in chapter 3 "to be inventions of an imagined ancient past."[16] If some of the newer historians reveal a degree of naïveté about the degree of "objectivity" to be found in archaeological data,[17] however, then Whitelam is certainly much more astute than they. This becomes particularly clear in chapter 5.[18] Here we are told quite directly that archaeology, like literature, provides us with only partial texts, a partiality governed (in part) by political and theological assumptions that determine the design or interpretation of the archaeological projects. The historian will in fact always be faced with partial texts, however extensively archaeological work might be carried out; and archaeology is itself influenced by the ideology of the investigator. These are important points for Whitelam to make in this chapter, for he goes on then to question much of the existing interpretation of the excavation and survey data from Israel, particularly that provided by Israeli scholars, claiming that this itself has played its part in creating Israel's "imagined past." He is in fact resolutely resistant to interpretations of the archaeological data that conflict with the thesis being developed in the book—that ancient Israel is an "imagined" entity. A particularly striking example is provided in this respect by the Merneptah stele.[19] Here we have an early piece of extra-biblical evidence that refers to Israel as a distinguishable entity in Palestine. Leaving aside the question of whether particular interpretations of the stele can be defended, one might have thought that this evidence should at least qualify claims about the "imagined" past;[20] yet this is far from the case. What we find instead is the interesting claim that the stele "represents a particular perception of the past embodying important ideological and political claims on behalf of the Egyptian Pharaoh."[21] The suggestion that it is reasonable to make a correlation between the Israel of the stela and biblical Israel is dismissed in these terms: "The appeal to what is reasonable is part of the rhetoric of objectivity in order to support the dominant construction of Israel's past within the discourse of biblical studies. Any opposing views are by definition unreasonable and to be rejected."[22]

We thus have a rather ambivalent attitude to archaeological data in this book. Where such data appear to conflict with the claims of the biblical text, they are said to "show," or help to show, that something is the case. They represent solid evidence that historical reality looked like this, rather than like that. Where such data appear to be consistent with the claims of the biblical text, however, all the emphasis falls on how little these data can actually tell us. Now we are reminded of the ideological dimension either of the data or of the interpretation. Now we read of "the implications of archaeology or the constructions of the past for contemporary struggles over a contested land,"[23] and of the need to subject to scrutiny and reinterpretation the research results of those archaeologists (particularly Israeli) who work with the belief that ancient Israel existed.[24] It does not seem to me, however, that Whitelam can have it both ways. Either archaeological data in fact do, or they do not, give us the kind of relatively objective picture of the Palestinian past that can be held up beside our ideologically compromised texts and said to "show" that the ancient Israel of Bible and scholars is an imagined entity. If he wishes to say that they do not—that "the historian is faced with partial texts in every sense of the term,"[25] and that archaeological data must be understood in the context of the ideologically-loaded narrative in which it is interpreted—then he must explain why archaeology is in a better position than texts to inform us about a "real" past over against an imagined past; why these particular "partial texts" are to be preferred to others.[26] As things stand, he *might* be taken to be working with a methodology that invests a fairly simple faith in those interpretations of data that happen to coincide with the story that he himself wishes to tell, while choosing to view those interpretations of data that conflict with his storyline with a maximum degree of skepticism and suspicion. He might be taken as occupying a position in which no counter-evidence to his storyline would ever be accepted as compelling: where the implications of such evidence would always be resisted, because it could always be said never to "prove" anything,[27] and in any case to be the product of scholarly minds whose ideology Whitelam did not share.

Ideology and the Past

This is, in fact, the point at which we must address the most troubling aspect of *The Invention of Ancient Israel*: the way in which the question of ideology rather than the question of evidence is placed at the fore, with its various consequences. Here we need to consider two things: on the one hand, the misleading way in which past scholarship is claimed to have "invented" ancient Israel as a consequence of its ideological commitments, thus contributing to the silencing of Palestinian history; and on the other, the way in which Whitelam, while criticizing others for being more influenced by ideology than by evidence, in fact himself sometimes gives the impression that commitment to a point of view, not evidence, is the decisive factor in his argument, and sometimes explicitly makes statements that indicate that this is so.

First of all, the "invention" of ancient Israel. It is repeatedly asserted in this book that the ancient Israel of biblical studies is an "invented" or "imagined" entity, and the discussion proceeds in such a way as to suggest (consistent with Whitelam's general view of texts)[28] that modern histories of Israel tell us more about the context and the beliefs of their authors than about the past they claim to describe. The picture with which we are presented is that of a scholarship with a will to believe in ancient Israel—a will that overrides evidence, which marginalizes scholars who threaten the belief-system,[29] and which in the process offers succour to the Israeli state while contributing to the plight of the Palestinians by silencing their history. It is even claimed on the closing pages of the book that the vested interests involved in this "silencing" are such that the narration of an ancient Palestinian history is not permitted within the discipline of biblical studies, or even within departments of history. The very beginnings of the project of narrating such a history will, indeed, necessarily involve self-reflection among scholars on the development of biblical studies in the context of the colonial enterprise, and this will require "an investigation of the archival materials which exist in order to allow a complete reappraisal of the motives and interests which have been masked in the public writings of the discipline."[30]

In a world dominated by newsgatherers hungry for such things as scandal and conspiracy theories, this sort of writing has its appeal. However, it is appropriate in a context where questions have been raised about the relationship between texts and reality to ask whether *this* particular narrative description has in fact very much to do with the reality it purports to describe. It is certainly the case that many practitioners of biblical studies, even after self-reflection on the development of biblical studies in the context of the colonial enterprise, will not recognize this as the world that they inhabit. They will, rather, wonder whether this world, where there is a need to search through "archival materials" so as to reveal truth which has hitherto been "masked" in public writings, is not more reminiscent of the recent political situation in Eastern Europe than of the current situation in Western universities. Since I am one of these questioning souls, and lest my bafflement be taken simply as proving my blindness to my own ideology, let us move the focus away from ideology and back to evidence.

The assertion is that some scholars have remained marginal voices within the discourse of biblical studies precisely because they have challenged the kind of construction of an "imagined ancient Israel" that Whitelam himself wishes to question. It is certainly the case, however, that other scholars who have been engaged in such challenging are no longer (if they ever were) marginal voices within the discourse, and this includes Whitelam himself. Perhaps other reasons should be sought, therefore, as to why some individuals have remained marginal, other than the mere challenge in itself.[31] The assertion is also that narration of an ancient Palestinian history is not permitted within the discipline of biblical studies, or even within departments of history. I am not aware that this is generally the case, and no evidence is presented that it is. There *is* a claim on the opening pages of the book that Whitelam's original plan to write a two-volume history of Palestine foundered not simply on the size of the task, but on the reality of the "discourse of biblical studies."[32] Again, however, the precise connection between the foundering and the discourse is not clear, and it is actually when Whitelam goes on to speak of the paucity of evidence upon which could be based a history of the kind he wishes to write that one feels that the real reason for his difficulties becomes apparent.[33] It is obviously true that Israel has often been the focus of scholarly interest in Palestine, partly because the bulk of the available evidence has been perceived as concerning Israel; but it is not demonstrably the case that this interest entails denial of permission to narrate Palestinian history differently.[34]

Nor is it demonstrably the case that those who have been engaged in the writing of Israelite history have generally been influenced by ideology rather than by evidence, by a will to believe that has not taken account of evidence. Whitelam himself concedes in respect of his thesis that it is "not easy to make these connections between biblical scholarship and the political context in which it is conducted and by which it is inevitably shaped. For the most part, they are implicit rather than explicit."[35] A reading of the book convinces me that he is quite right: it is indeed not easy. I find his examples generally unconvincing[36] and his reading of some scholars in pursuit of his thesis, in fact, to be highly curious.[37] It is not that individual scholars cannot be criticized for pushing evidence too far or for offering a poor interpretation of it. Some can no doubt be criticized more than others. Nor can it be denied that all authors are to some extent bound up with their context, and that their thinking is shaped in terms of the categories available to them. The crucial question, however, is whether it is generally the case that an ideological perspective of the kind Whitelam describes, *rather than* evidence, can be shown to have driven scholarship or influenced it to a very great degree. I cannot see that this has been demonstrated.[38] The discussion obscures the real issue, in fact, in focusing on the question of ideology. For there *has* demonstrably been a general acceptance among scholars that theories about Israel's past must be accountable to evidence—that if historiography is more than simply the listing of such evidence, nevertheless all historiography must attempt to take account of it. The real disagreement in this whole debate is, in fact, about what *counts* as evidence. Whitelam happens to believe, for reasons that I do not believe to be compelling, that it is not right to bring the biblical texts into conjunction with other evidence in our examination of Israel's ancient past. Scholarship hitherto has generally believed otherwise. To portray that scholarship as not dealing seriously with evidence because of ideological commitments of one kind or another ("imagining the past"), when in fact the real issue is *which* evidence is to be taken seriously, is very much to misrepresent reality.[39]

Biblical Scholars and Politics

If the choice of terms such as "invent" and "imagine" (in preference to terms like "hypothesize") is thus bound to give a false impression of the discipline of biblical studies as it has actually gone about its work, and to present a difference in the *assessment of* evidence as if it were a difference in *attitude to* evidence, what of the claim that the effect of scholarly works on the history of Israel has been succour to the Israeli state, on the one hand, and contribution to the plight of the Palestinians, on the other? Here the line of thought is exceedingly difficult to follow. It is, of course, the case that some Israelis themselves (as Whitelam shows) draw particular connections of a political nature between their ancient past and their present. Yet these connections are by no means inevitable. Nor are these connections commonly made in scholarly literature on the history of Israel. Indeed, Whitelam is at pains to point out the way in which scholars have tried to "stay out of politics." In what sense, then, has Western scholarship succoured modern Israel and contributed to the plight of the Palestinians? By failing to write the ancient Palestinian history that Whitelam himself confesses himself unable currently to write, and that Palestinians themselves (as he notes) have shown no interest in writing?[40] Simply by writing histories of Israel at all? Is he really saying that scholars should not write about ancient Israel, even if that is their interest and even if they think that what they are writing is consistent with the evidence, because others may interpret and use their work for political ends with which they may not agree? Is he suggesting that we should only write such books as do quite the reverse, promoting the Palestinian cause and calling into question the legitimacy of Israel's occupation of the land? Is scholarship really to bring itself so fully and deliberately under the sway of political commitments, abandoning even the attempt at relative objectivity and enlisting itself wholeheartedly in this cause or that?

There are various indications in *The Invention of Ancient Israel* that this is, in fact, what Whitelam thinks. I have already noted above the way in which it appears in his treatment of the archaeological data that the narrative line that he has already chosen in respect of ancient Palestine determines the interpretation offered. I have also cited a particular comment that reveals, it seems to me, an associated general position on the use of reason: "The appeal to what is reasonable is part of the rhetoric of objectivity in order to support the dominant construction of Israel's past within the discourse of biblical studies." Reason, he appears to be claiming, is a servant of the story being told, and not a master to whom the story is in any sense accountable. Similar claims are made elsewhere about the impossibility of objectivity, the necessity of commitment. He cites Said with approval, relating the citation to the "profession" of biblical studies to remain aloof from the contemporary political situation: "There is no neutrality, there can be no neutrality or objectivity about Palestine."[41] He writes of the exposure of "the aura of objectivity which has been projected to cover the collusion of biblical studies in the dispossession of Palestine," and of the postmodernist discourses that have "led to the realization of the essential subjectivity of the academic enterprise exposing the role of various academic disciplines in the colonial enterprise."[42] He affirms that the construction of the past is a political act, and characterizes biblical scholars and archaeologists as seeking to "escape to the haven of objectivity effectively ignoring, or even denying, the context in which they work and the contexts in which their works are received and read."[43] Finally, by way of example, he claims that "history writing should not be merely descriptive, nor is it objective."[44] One is left wondering at the end of all this in what, precisely, Whitelam's critique of other scholars consists, and how, precisely, his own position coheres. Is it simply that these other scholars possess an ideology at all, and that this compromises their scholarship because it leads them inevitably to abandon reason and ignore evidence, whereas Whitelam, unencumbered by ideology, is able to see things more clearly? Sometimes it does seem that this is what he is saying; yet elsewhere he equally clearly suggests that everyone brings ideology to his/her scholarship. Is his position, then, that reason and evidence always and inevitably function at the service of an ideology, a set of commitments, and is his objection that other scholars simply do not share his particular set of commitments, his particular ideology—that they do not support him in the story about Palestine that he wishes to tell? Some of what he says does seem to imply this. So here is a question: is this book really a plea for a more objective picture of Palestinian history, or is it rather a very committed and partisan treatise in favor of the Palestinian cause?[45] I ask the question as someone who certainly has much sympathy with the Palestinian cause (although not, perhaps, as much as Whitelam).[46] I also ask the question, however, as someone who does not think that we have come or ought to have come to the end of histories of Israel. The answer that Whitelam might give to such a question, and that others will also have to make a decision about, is important; for at least some of the arguments that he has deployed in arguing for an end to Israel's history, if accepted as valid, mean an end not only to history but also to scholarship. There is then no longer a broad community of people seeking, even in the midst of their matrix of commitments and beliefs, to be accountable to reason, evidence and truth, and to be in dialogue about such matters with each other. There is only the committed scholar with his/her "rhetoric of objectivity" and his/her will to power. Scholarship has become only an aspect of politics. Each must take a position, and write only such books as come to appropriate conclusions in relation to this position. Even book reviews, in such a world, will come under the rubric of ideology,[47] and it will then become pointless, of course, to raise the kind of questions and objections that I have raised in this one. I hope it has not yet come to that.

9

THE HISTORICAL BOOKS OF
THE OLD TESTAMENT

My 1996 sabbatical in Germany produced one more essay to add to the two already reproduced in chapters seven and eight.[1] *At some point just beforehand, I had been asked by Professor John Barton to write the chapter on the historical books of the Old Testament for the new* Cambridge Companion to Biblical Interpretation, *which was eventually published in 1998. I was very glad to do this, because it gave me the chance to write a "state of the debate" kind of essay with respect to most of the narrative books of the Old Testament, drawing in and summarizing much of my preceding work on history, narrative, and indeed on Brevard Childs. The reader of this volume who reads my essays sequentially will see exactly how this has worked out.*

The biblical books to be considered in this chapter are Joshua, Judges and Ruth; 1–2 Samuel, 1–2 Kings and 1–2 Chronicles; Ezra, Nehemiah and Esther. Together they tell the story of Israel from the point at which the people entered Canaan down to the Persian period, when some Jews had returned to their homeland and others still remained in foreign lands. The state of current research on these books may perhaps best be summarized in the following way. There is a lively debate among interpreters as to whether they are indeed best considered as "historical books" at all, and in which sense they might be best considered so. There is a further debate about the proper or primary task of interpreters in relation to these books. In what follows we shall join these two debates and reflect upon the various issues that arise from them. In this way we shall form a rounded, if somewhat generalized, view of the ways in which our literature is currently being approached.

History or Story?

The phrase "historical books" is a modern term as attached to the books in question, and one that already implies that an interpretative decision has been made about their nature. It might be argued that the phrase "narrative books" would be a better term with which to begin. This is just as clearly a modern label, which in no way corresponds to nomenclature of earlier times. In the Masoretic Hebrew canon, for example, Joshua, Judges, 1–2 Samuel and 1–2 Kings make up the "Former Prophets," while all the remaining books mentioned above form part of the "Writings." If a modern label is sought, however, "narrative" is perhaps a good first choice. It certainly has the merit of enabling us to avoid in the first instance the question of reference—do the books in question "refer" to the real world of the past or not?

In spite of the fact that the phrase "historical books" has been so commonly used in the modern period, indeed, the phrase "narrative books" corresponds at least in a general sense much more closely to how many modern interpreters have in practice thought of this literature. At least in the period during which the historical-critical method has dominated biblical interpretation in the scholarly world, history has not been regarded as something that can straightforwardly be read off the surface of these texts. On the contrary, the task of extracting history from them has been regarded as a more or less arduous quarrying operation. The text in itself has not commonly been regarded as historical. It has been viewed simply as the narrative mine out of which the skilled interpreter may dig nuggets of history. The extent to which individual books in our group have in fact been regarded as allowing a window onto the past has naturally varied widely, depending on various factors—differing preconceptions as to what history looks like, differing assessments of the worth or implications of extra-biblical evidence, and so on. On the whole, however, it would be fair to say that in this period and up until fairly recently the books of the Former Prophets along with Ezra and Nehemiah would have been fairly highly rated in terms of their ability to divulge historical information (Samuel–Kings especially so), while Ruth and Esther would not have scored so well, and 1–2 Chronicles would have received mixed reviews.

Historical-Critical Reading

It is one of the interesting ironies of this period of historical-critical domination that although interpreters were thus aware that they were dealing with books that were not simply historical, and indeed sometimes (in many minds) not historical at all, yet the vast majority of the effort in interpretation went into the task, not of interpreting the narratives as narratives, but in extracting therefrom such data of a historical kind as was thought possible. Thus in the case of 1–2 Kings, for example, it is not difficult to find interpreters in this period hypothesizing about the original source material used by the editors of Kings or the various levels of editing that might exist in the text, or writing about the historical and cultural background against which various parts of Kings might be read.[2] It is somewhat more difficult in the period before the 1980s to find readings of the book as it stands *as narrative*.

The explanation of this fact lies not simply in an obsession with history that rendered scholarship virtually blind to other aspects of the texts that were the object of their study. It lies also in a deep-seated and in large measure unexamined assumption that the historical books, although in a very general sense narrative rather than history, were not truly *narrative literature*. That is, when historical critics looked at the historical books, they did not generally see works of impressive narrative art. They saw relatively incoherent and self-contradictory collections of material, put into some kind of narrative order by their editors, but not in a very convincing manner. These were books that suggested to scholars that their creators were not free agents, but rather those to a greater or lesser extent constrained by the material available to them and unable or unwilling to impose complete consistency upon it. In a real sense, the only coherence to be found in these books was the coherence provided by the historical timeline. There was nothing else there to interpret but the historical process to which the texts bore witness.

Narrative-Critical Reading

Such an unexamined assumption could not long stand critical scrutiny once a sufficient number of interpreters had taken time to step back from their subject matter and look at it afresh. Thus it is that the pendulum has in the past two decades swung away from historical-critical approaches to the historical books, and towards literary approaches—interpretation that takes its starting point from the narrative shape of the texts, and may not even move beyond this to ask historical questions at all. As momentum has moved behind the pendulum, in fact, historical-critical methodology has been pushed on to the defensive. Historical critics are no longer able to make the sorts of assumptions they once made about texts like Joshua or Kings, safe in the knowledge that because such assumptions were widely shared they would in all probability remain unchallenged. On the contrary, challenge is all around, and debate is fierce. If in the older paradigm it was generally accepted, for example, that repetition in a text was an indication of composite sources or redaction, now it is asked whether repetition cannot itself be an aspect of literary artistry. If variation in style and language was likewise widely regarded as a sign that more than one hand had been at work on a text, now it is asked whether such variation cannot have many explanations other than difference in authorship (e.g. in the construction of the various "regnal formulae" of the books of Kings). And if it was often claimed that texts were replete with "inconsistencies" that must perforce indicate the presence of more than one mind active in their construction, now it is asked whether "inconsistent" has not been a word often used in historical-critical scholarship where terms such as "theologically complex" or "ironic" would do just as well[3] (e.g. in discussion of the interesting 2 Kings 17:24–41).[4]

A Disappearing Past?

In such a manner, then, has the focus of scholarly interest in the interpretation of the historical books of the Old Testament shifted markedly in the past two decades.[5] If we have now arrived at a time in which their nature as narrative is much better understood, however, we find ourselves at the same time and for obvious reasons in an interpretative era in which their nature as historical books is even more widely questioned than previously. For if the history in the historical books was previously found underneath the narrative, as it were, in those remnants of texts which could be salvaged from the narrative through historical-critical means; and if we are now told that in fact there is no access of this kind to the depths of the text, such that salvage is possible; what then of history? If an artistically constructed narrative is what we have, and we may no longer exploit incoherence in pursuit of the earlier layers of text that offer up the buried treasure that is historical fact, in what sense may we consider the historical books "historical" at all? Thus it is that the narrative studies of the recent decades of biblical interpretation have played their part in producing a much greater degree of skepticism about the historicality of these biblical narratives and an increasing reluctance among biblical exegetes to move beyond the story to anything recognizable in the modern context as history. We may observe the trend at its most marked in a scholar like Philip Davies, who is quite ready to oppose biblical story and history, claiming that "the reason why many things are told in the biblical literature, and the way they are told, has virtually everything to do with literary artistry and virtually nothing to do with anything that might have happened."[6] Narrative studies are judged from this perspective as having serious implications in terms of the use of narrative texts as a window on the ancient past.

Such a point of view has gathered numerous adherents in recent work on both the biblical texts and the history of Israel, in the latter of which there is a noticeable tendency to regard the historical books as much more problematic for historians than hitherto. It is not just Ruth, Esther and Chronicles that are now treated with a high degree of skepticism when scholars ask historical questions about Israel. Already in 1986 J. M. Miller and J. H. Hayes[7] displayed a marked reluctance to offer historical reconstructions of the pre-monarchic period because of perceived difficulties in using Joshua and Judges for this purpose, and even in the case of the Samuel traditions they were somewhat tentative. This book is commonly perceived as something of a watershed among scholars currently interested in the history of Israel, some of whom have even more doubts about biblical tradition than Miller and Hayes.[8] It is of course not only narrative studies that have brought about the current state of affairs. The perspective of archaeology on ancient Palestine has also been important, and broader philosophical and cultural currents have played their part. In particular, it is unsurprising that in a postmodern context in which biblical scholarship shows signs of becoming as obsessed with ideology as it was previously obsessed with history we should find that even where the biblical texts are regarded as offering testimony to a real past, that testimony is widely perceived, because of its ideological nature, as offering little help to modern scholars in reconstructing that real past. Yet it cannot be doubted that, of all the factors that have combined to create the interpretative context in which our historical books are now read and in which the term "historical" as attached to these books has become ever more problematic, it is the new interest in the narrative character of these texts that has been the most important.

In which direction discussion of this matter of history and story will proceed remains to be seen. Certainly there are manifest indications of intellectual incoherence at the very heart of much of the current interpretative endeavor in this area, which might suggest that it cannot long continue on the path it has chosen without collapsing with exhaustion brought on by internal contradiction. Much of what has been written in the area of the ideology of the biblical texts in particular is difficult to take with much seriousness, since it apparently asks its readers to believe that biblical narratives alone are to be disqualified from consideration as referents to a real past on the grounds of ideology, other narratives (including those of modern scholars) remaining untouched by difficulty. For those who share some residual vestige of concern for truth and rationality, this kind of argumentation is unlikely to hold out much long-term attraction. Yet one of the difficulties about the interpretation of the historical books of the Old Testament in the present climate is precisely that truth and rationality are not necessarily any longer held by interpreters as self-evident goods. These things too can be portrayed as simply the tools of the ideologue,[9] and indeed ideology can be claimed as being virtually all that in any case exists. One cannot be sure, therefore, that intellectual incoherence will indeed in the end be eschewed and rationality embraced. For those who do wish to embrace it and to move ahead some interesting questions remain. Is it really the case that artistically constructed narratives cannot also and at the same time refer to a real past? What precisely is the difference between narrative and historiography in any case? Is not modern historiography itself both ideologically-loaded and also (if well-written) artistically-shaped narrative? Does archaeology, in particular, not require a narrative in which its mute data can be located and thus interpreted? Whence should come that narrative—from the imaginations of modern scholars, perhaps informed by (inevitably ideologically loaded) extra-biblical texts? Why should such a narrative not be informed by the only comprehensive account of the history of Israel that we possess, namely by the biblical account? These are some of the broader questions that interpreters of the historical books of the Old Testament are now discussing and debating. It is on the answers given to such questions that the continued viability of the label "historical" for the books we are considering will depend.

Texts or Readers?

Mention of ideology brings us now to our second main area of debate concerning the historical books: the matter of interpretative responsibilities. It would fairly characterize the historical-critical school of interpretation if we were to say that proponents of that school see their primary task as to understand and to expatiate upon Old Testament historical texts in their own terms and within their own context. They mean by this, of course, the original context, historically speaking—or perhaps we should rather say original *contexts*, to allow for the idea of successive redaction. Thus if 1 Samuel 8, for example, characterizes Israelite kingship as something that arose out of the initiative of the people of Israel and represented a rejection of Israel's God, then the primary and important thing is not what this means in the context of the Old Testament or perhaps the Christian Bible as a whole, nor what significance this has for the reader. The important thing is what the passage tells us about the institution of the monarchy in Israel, its development, and the attitude of various ancient Israelite parties thereto. If 1 Kings 14:21–4 is found criticizing the religion of Judah in the time of King Rehoboam, then the important thing is likewise to locate the passage within the development of Israelite religion, drawing conclusions about what religion actually looked like "on the ground" during the pre-exilic period, how far the "Deuteronomistic" perspective that now dominates a book like Kings represents an early or a later perspective, and so on. History is again the key to the whole interpretative process. The primary task of the interpreter is to use that key to open doors on meaning.

A question has lately been addressed to interpreters adopting such a stance, however. Why should our interpretation of the text be confined by the alleged communicative intentions of its author(s) or editor(s) in writing it or editing it in their historical contexts? It is a question asked from two very different points of view, but by scholars who nevertheless have in common that they do not agree with historical critics in their view of primary interpretative responsibility.

The Freedom of the Reader

On the one side are those who wish to know why the primary interpretative task should be defined in terms of clarifying the perspectives of those Israelites who were, after all, only a very few of those capable of offering a perspective on life in Israel during the periods described by our historical books. What we have in these books are ideologically-loaded pictures of the past produced by an intellectual elite (since it is always such people who produce literature), all of them Israelites and all of them (probably) men. It is the perspective of those who had the power to transmit their vision of society, and in the process to suppress or contextualize other, perhaps different visions. What of the perspectives of the marginalized? How might Israelite women, or indeed Philistine or Moabite men, have told the story? How might Israelites holding religious convictions quite different from those of the orthodox Yahwists whose vision the Bible now passes on? The stories of such people are surely just as valid and just as important, if not more so, as the story told by the biblical authors. Thus it is that much of the newer work on the historical books has not taken as its task the elucidation of the texts-as-intended-by-their-authors. The goal has rather been to reach behind authorial meanings and intentions and to give expression to alternative visions. The text becomes simply a springboard for interpretation, rather than its foundation. Sometimes, indeed, the text provides little more than a starting point for hostile criticism of the biblical tradition, which may then be left behind as the interpreter moves on to higher things.

Let us take as an example the question of the nature of Israelite religion in the pre-exilic period. The idea that the "Deuteronomists" (the authors of Joshua–Kings) have distorted reality with regard to Israelite religion in this period is not new, and is already found in traditional historical criticism. The basis for the historical-critical analysis, however, is the perceived presence of differing perspectives on certain matters in the historical books themselves (as well as elsewhere). Certain texts appear to speak in terms different from the book of Deuteronomy and other passages influenced by Deuteronomy on matters such as the centralization of the Israelite cult. In more recent writing on Israelite religion, on the other hand, interpretation is not necessarily constrained by what texts actually have to say. These texts, after all, even if they differ somewhat from one another on specifics, still represent only a very limited number of perspectives on the past. The interpretative horses come, as it were, from a similar ideological stable. Recent interpretation feels itself free, therefore, to move beyond and behind texts in pursuit of alternative points of view. The case of the goddess Asherah well illustrates the difference between the older and newer approaches. Previous scholarship was generally content to accept on the basis of widespread biblical testimony that whatever else might be true about Israelite religion, it was certainly true that basic distinctions existed even in the earlier periods between "Israelite" and "Canaanite" religion, not least in attitudes to female deities. It is now argued, however, that worship of Asherah, who is referred to or alluded to frequently in the historical books along with cultic objects apparently associated with her, was far from incompatible with authentic worship of Yahweh. Where the Deuteronomists criticize the Asherah-inclusive religion of Rehoboam's time because it was conducted according to the abominations of all the peoples which Yahweh had dispossessed before the Israelites, for example, it is now maintained rather that it was "in harmony with its time, no more and no less."[10] Worship of Asherah was far from being an alien element in Israelite religion—a corruption of original purity. She was worshipped by the Israelites from the earliest times, and even had a place in the Jerusalem temple.[11] Particularly on the basis of extra-biblical inscriptions we may now say that Asherah was the female consort of Yahweh in Israelite religion in much the same way that the goddess Athirat/Ashratu is found in special relationship to the chief deity of whichever other ancient Near Eastern culture she appears in.

The important thing to notice about this position is just how little it is grounded in anything that might be considered in the conventional way as evidence. Archaeologists may or may not have uncovered data suggesting that some Israelites in certain places and at certain times regarded Asherah as Yahweh's consort.[12] Even if they have, this would not prove that the religion of Israel was syncretistic in origin and in essence. There is, in fact, no hard evidence that establishes that the worship of Asherah was an indigenous and original feature of Israelite religion. Nor is there any evidence that demonstrates that Asherah found a place in the Jerusalem temple before the time of Manasseh, and even then the evidence is only that of the biblical text itself (2 Kgs 21:7), which forthrightly condemns what is seen as an innovation. It is not then *evidence*, textual or otherwise, that is driving this vision of the Israelite past. The fuel that powers this scholarly construction may be suspected to lie, in fact, much more clearly in the present—in the desire of scholarly interpreters influenced by the religious or secular Western culture in which most of them live and work to find a past which is congenial to their present. An ancient world of religious pluralism, and in particular an ancient world in which it turns out after all that Israel had a female goddess, represents such a congenial world, whether to those who think monotheism dangerous or the Judaeo-Christian God a little too resolutely male.

It is always an aspect of the interpretation of texts, of course, that interpreters bring their world with them to the text. That is inevitably so. In the historical-critical past, however, there was at least a theoretical acceptance that interpreters should not simply absorb the biblical narrative texts (or any others) into their world, reading their own dreams and visions into it. The text had its own integrity, and that integrity had to be respected in the interpretative process, with due attention to what the text itself was saying. What is problematic in much recent interpretation of biblical texts, including biblical narrative texts, is that with the general move away from the notion that the communicative intentions of author(s) or editor(s) are centrally important to the interpretative task—that what the text itself is saying is centrally important—we have arrived in an interpretative era in which the distinction between text and interpreter has become blurred. For those who care not in the end whether the voices of the "marginalized" that they claim to hear behind the biblical texts represent simply the externalized figment of their own imagination—whether the past that they claim to find behind the texts is simply a reflection of and validation for what is important to them in the present—this is not a problem. It is at least a question, however, whether those who adopt such a stance are engaged in an activity that may reasonably be called *biblical* interpretation at all, rather than something else. It is certainly sometimes the impression of the reader of such interpreters than he or she is finding out considerably more about the interpreter than about the Old Testament.

The Constraints of the Canon

In contrast to this kind of recent response to historical-critical methodology we may consider now the response of an interpreter like Brevard Childs. Childs certainly does not wish to argue for readerly freedom in relation to textual meanings. He is, on the other hand, no happier than those who argue thus with the idea that the primary task of the biblical interpreter is to offer interpretation of texts in their original historical context(s). That is not the way in which to arrive at the true communicative intention of biblical texts, narrative or otherwise. It is the canonical context of a text, rather than its historical context, that should be regarded as decisive in its interpretation.

Childs' central contention is that the concept of canon, pushed to one side in the Enlightenment in the name of academic and religious freedom, must be brought back to the center of the agenda in Old Testament studies. Canon does not represent, as many have claimed, an arbitrary and late imposition on the Old Testament texts by religious authorities, alien to and distorting of the essence of the Old Testament and without hermeneutical significance. Canon is rather a complex historical process within ancient Israel that entailed the collecting, selecting and ordering of texts to serve a normative function as Scripture within the continuing religious community. It is intrinsically bound up with the Old Testament texts as we have them, and should be taken seriously by those who study them. It is indeed these Old Testament texts *as we have them* that should be the focus of readerly concern. It is precisely the disregarding of canonical shaping by historical-critical interpretation that has in large measure led to the modern hermeneutical impasse. The text is transported into the hypothetical past by destroying the very elements that constitute its canonical shape, the vehicle which has enabled its journey to the present. It is little wonder that having destroyed this essential vehicle, historical critics are then unable to devise a way of relocating the text in any modern religious context. Childs' approach, on the other hand, while not wishing to bypass two hundred years of critical research, nevertheless demands that historical-critical tools be used to illuminate the canonical text as we have it, rather than for some other purpose. He does not deny the theological significance of a depth dimension of the tradition; but features within the tradition that have been subordinated, modified or placed in the distant background of the text cannot be interpreted apart from the role assigned them in the final form.

Here, then, is an approach that clearly insists on the primacy of the text rather than the reader. To that extent Childs lines up with traditional historical criticism. Where Childs parts ways with such criticism, however, is in his understanding of the primary context in which texts are to be read. The primary context is itself textual, rather than historical. We may illustrate the difference in terms of the approach taken to the historical books by returning to the example of 1 Samuel 7–12.

Historical criticism understood its primary task in relation to such a section of text as involving such things as elucidating the origin and development of monarchy in Israel and the attitude of various ancient Israelite parties thereto. It was this kind of matter that the biblical interpreter had above all a duty to investigate and explain. Much has therefore been written, for example, on whether chapter 8 is later than chapter 9, where a noticeably warmer welcome to kingship is perceived. If so, perhaps chapter 8 represents an Israelite perspective on monarchy from a later (exilic or postexilic) time when monarchy had been found wanting, and chapter 9 represents an earlier, more optimistic view. In opposition to this view some have argued that there was already in the beginning a difference in perspective over monarchy in Israel, some Israelites thinking it a necessary and right development and others believing it to be in tension with some fundamental Israelite principles. Our two chapters simply preserve side by side the two viewpoints in the debate.

Childs does not object in principle to this kind of historical reading of 1 Samuel 7–12. On the contrary, it is this kind of reading that provides us with the "depth dimension" of the tradition. Whatever various Israelite authors might have meant to say about the monarchy when they first wrote their pieces of text about it, however, these meanings are not determinative when it comes to modern biblical interpretation of 1 Samuel. Childs sees his task as an interpreter as lying rather in presenting a theological reflection on the Old Testament king that does justice to the peculiar canonical shaping of the biblical literature.[13] The canonical process has given the anti-monarchical source preeminence, bracketing the earlier pro-monarchical source at both beginning and end. We must recognize, therefore, that the dominant note sounded by our text is that of prophetic warning. Yet the message of the pro-monarchical source in its new context must still also be heard—that the establishment of the kingdom, although arising out of unbelief, is not to be regarded as a purely secular act. Israel cannot move from judge to king in the manner described in 1 Samuel 7–12; yet kingship becomes part of God's plan for Israel in David, whose career (canonically speaking) adumbrates Israel's messianic hope.

Thus does Childs' interpretation of 1 Samuel 7–12 and indeed the historical books overall differ markedly from that both of historical critics and of those interpreters who stress the freedom of the reader. The interpreter is not free from constraint. The constraint is not ultimately that of authorial meanings in historical contexts, however, but that of canonical shaping. It is in the elucidation of texts in their canonical context that the primary responsibility of the biblical interpreter consists.

How far Childs' stance on interpretation will be widely adopted remains to be seen. Doubts have been expressed about the coherence of his notion of canon, both in terms of the depth of "canonical consciousness" within the Old Testament texts and in terms of the concept of canon itself. It has further been asked whether texts can really have communicative intentions that are not wholly related to the intentions of the human authors or editors who produced them, and why these intentions (if they exist), rather than others, must form the basis of the interpretative task.[14] My own view is that Childs can be adequately defended in all these areas. Whether one considers that the program which he outlines is entirely satisfactory as it stands, however, will depend not simply on convincing responses being given in these areas of concern, but also on one's convictions about the long-term viability or otherwise of the historical-critical method. For what is striking about Childs is the way in which he characteristically takes historical-critical reality as a fairly obvious and self-evident starting point for his interpretative work. He pays far from sufficient attention to the massive amount of work carried out in the last two decades that has gone some way toward undermining the very historical-critical approach that he presupposes. Narrative studies have affected scholarly approaches to 1 Samuel 7–12, for example, just as much as other sections of the historical books, and whether there is any need to see the kind of tension between the chapters that historical critics have exploited must now be considered open to question.[15] If the foundations are questioned, however, then so of course must the superstructure. It may be, then, that those who are otherwise attracted by a canonical approach to the historical books of the Old Testament will wish to begin the interpretative process at a more fundamental level than Childs has done—with the texts themselves, rather than with historical-critical theories concerning them.

10

IN THE STABLE WITH THE DWARVES: TESTIMONY, INTERPRETATION, FAITH, AND THE HISTORY OF ISRAEL

In 1997, I emigrated to Canada, resigning from my Senior Lectureship at the University of Edinburgh and taking up a new position as the Marshall Sheppard Professor of Biblical Studies at Regent College in Vancouver. In 1998 I was invited back to Europe, however, to participate in a panel on Hebrew Bible and History at the 16th Congress of the International Organization of the Societies for Old Testament Study in Oslo, Norway. It is the paper prepared for that conference that became this essay, which was originally published in 2000 in the Congress Volume. *The panel was an interesting experience, not least because the panel members were seated in a line at the front of a large lecture hall with myself at one extreme (the right), Professor Thomas Thompson at the other (the left), and other colleagues who were clearly regarded as the centrist "voices of reason" in the debate in the middle. Structure communicates meaning, and provides insight, indeed, into authorial intent (in this case, I believe, Professor Lester Grabbe's)! The reality is that in all sorts of ways I had no disagreement at all with those "in the center"—all of us reasonable people together, in my opinion. The paper itself develops my thinking on historiography in general, and on historiography relating to ancient Israel in particular, especially in dialogue with many of the critics of my 1995*

JBL essay. It stands now as a window into what was at the time a work still in progress—eventually much of the content found its way in revised form into A Biblical History of Israel *(2003). I remain quite satisfied with the essay, including the guiding metaphor borrowed from C. S. Lewis to describe those who are sufficiently confused, epistemologically-speaking, to think that a reality ignored or denied is a reality that does not exist.*

The writer C. S. Lewis, near the end of the last of his children's stories known as the Narnia Chronicles,[1] pictures for us the eschatological end of everything, when the world of Narnia has been made anew and the old things have passed away. Even though the new world clearly exists, there are nevertheless some to be found—the dwarves—who refuse to acknowledge it. They have been let down earlier in the story, discovering that the god-figure whom they had been worshipping as Aslan the lion is in fact a donkey merely disguised as a lion. Having been taken in once, they are not about to be fooled a second time. Disappointment thus gives way to cynicism and self-interest; and that is why, as Aslan in reality appears, the dwarves are to be found huddled in an inward-looking group, in a stable that no longer really exists, complaining about the darkness and the smell. They are not about to be taken in again—not even by reality. And so all attempts at testimony to the reality outside the group founder on the rock of dwarvish solidarity one with the other—on the shared commitment to cynicism and skepticism. Even Aslan himself cannot shake their worldview. His low growl in their ears is interpreted simply as another attempt to trick them into faith; the glorious banquet he provides for them is experienced as animal fodder and dirty water. But in a curious way they are satisfied with their lot. "At any rate," they remind each other, "there's no Humbug here. We haven't let anyone take us in. The Dwarfs are for the Dwarfs."[2]

The story nicely illustrates the issues at the heart of the current debate over the Hebrew Bible and the history of Israel. For centuries the Bible has been widely held to define reality for its readers, including historical reality. It has more recently been discovered, to put this statement in its mildest form, that matters are a good deal more complex than hitherto suspected. This has led most readers of the Hebrew Bible, at least in the scholarly world (and that is all I am concerned about in this paper), to some degree of modification in their views about the relationship of the Bible to history. It has quite recently led significant numbers to doubt whether whole sections of the Bible give us access to history at all, and a few to the opinion that the Bible as a whole is more of an obstacle to the historian than an aid. So it is that we have journeyed from implicit trust in, to explicit distrust of, the Bible as providing access to Israel's past. Scholars who tend towards such principled distrust sometimes perceive themselves as the champions of truth and justice over against the forces of obscurantism and oppression. Their distrust is addressed not just towards the Bible, but often towards those who differ in their attitude to and use of the Bible, who are characterized as motivated more by religious or political commitments than by the pursuit of truth and justice. In brief, like the dwarves, these scholars are against humbug—historical humbug, whether found in the Bible or among the Bible's interpreters. They are determined not to be taken in; and so they take a maximally suspicious stance in respect of both. The dwarves are for the dwarves, and most assuredly against anyone who is not to be found in their stable.

Is this attitude of principled suspicion toward the Hebrew Bible in particular, with regard to history, justified or indeed sensible? My own view, already expressed in my 1995 *JBL* article on this topic,[3] is that it is not at all justified, or sensible. Clarifications are immediately in order at this point, given the misunderstandings that have arisen in some quarters about the argument of that essay.

Clarifications

I have not taken my stand against some of the more recent developments in writing on the history of Israel primarily because of my theology. I do not in fact hold a view of the Bible as Scripture that requires me to defend its historicity against all comers and in contradiction to what can otherwise be said to be facts. I do not hold a view of the Bible as Scripture that commits me to treating it, as historical source, differently from any other historical source;[4] nor a view that commits me to what has been called "maximal conservatism" on historical matters.[5] I find it puzzling that my previous arguments in respect of the approach and attitude of some scholars writing recently on the history of Israel should have been read by some as implying such a view.[6] I should have thought it perfectly clear that I was mainly opposing them on the grounds of epistemology and logic. I welcome, in any case, the opportunity to restate my position here in fuller terms, and to clear up any possible misunderstanding. I do not oppose the marginalization of the Hebrew Bible in the task of writing the history of Israel because I am a Christian and revere these texts as part of Christian Scripture. I oppose this move on the grounds of epistemology and logic—because I do not regard the position adopted as well argued or, indeed, intellectually coherent.

Nor am I unaware, as some seem to imagine,[7] that in opposing this kind of position I am also raising questions about various aspects of Enlightenment historical method that have resulted by degrees in the position I am now criticizing. I am perfectly aware of doing this, and happy to raise these questions for consideration. Nothing should be sacrosanct in the pursuit of truth—not even method. It is, in fact, the perceived sanctity of method that has for too long stifled debate in biblical studies (if not elsewhere) about the truly important question that should lie at the heart of any discussion about the history of Israel. How do we know what we claim to know about the reality of the past? It is a fundamental question, and yet often not articulated and itself debated by those writing about the history of Israel. All too often it is a question that in my view has been at least partially repressed and avoided for fear that it might complicate too greatly our ability to get on with our work. Here is the game known as historical enquiry. Here are the rules of the game. This is how one must play. If it is objected that perhaps some of the rules do not make particular sense, or that some aspects of the game are not worth playing, then the response is often, not debate on these points, but naked reassertion. We have always played the game this way; at least, we have done so since proper historical scholarship began in the 19th century. It is simply how modern scholarship is. If you do not like it, find a game of your own. In fact, if you do not like it, you are a fundamentalist, or some such undesirable.[8] So the game is saved, to be enjoyed by all its participants; but it is saved by avoiding fundamental questions about its viability.[9] The danger of adopting this strategy is, of course, that a detachment from reality may begin to set in. The game goes on, but does anyone know any longer whether it has any connection with the world outside itself? The rules are upheld, but are they rules that allow or prohibit us from seeing reality more broadly? Are they rules, in fact, that in the end simply leave us in epistemological darkness, beyond the reach of any evidence that might invade our comfort zone, unsettle our ideology, spoil the game?

This leads on to a third initial clarification that I feel it necessary to make, which will lead on to the substance of this current paper. For reasons that are again not entirely clear to me, I have been perceived as giving "the impression that the biblical text is unproblematic"[10] with regard to the history of Israel. This is again certainly not my position. My position is, rather, that the Hebrew Bible is indeed problematic for the historian, but that it is no more essentially problematic as a window onto the past than any other kinds of material available to him or her. The problem, in so far as we have a problem, lies not with the Bible over against other allegedly more objective, more trustworthy, more factual witnesses to the past. The problem lies rather with the historian, faced only and ever with witness to, and interpretation of, the past rather than with the past itself (which is gone, and never existed as a single entity to be discovered in any case), but required by his profession nevertheless to weave a meaningful story about it out of the data available to him. The very business of writing history is problematic. It is this far more fundamental problem upon which, in my view, much scholarship on the history of Israel has failed to reflect in sufficient depth. It is aware of the problem of the *Hebrew Bible* and history. Of the problem of history more generally it is seemingly partially or wholly unaware. Only thus is it possible to explain why it is so often the case in recent discussion that it is the problem of the Hebrew Bible that has loomed so large, while the problems presented by other data are either ignored completely or minimalized. Indeed, the perception of just how problematic the Hebrew Bible is has in large measure arisen because scholars are so prone to compare it with other data that they regard as giving virtually unmediated or at least minimally mediated access to naked fact.[11] My impression is that many do this in all innocence, entirely unaware that they are thus making unargued assumptions that have already predetermined the results of their study of the texts. To that extent, I assert, much recent scholarship is indeed unaware of the epistemological problems involved in writing history, even where epistemology is otherwise mentioned or discussed.¹² It has a narrow idea of the nature of the problem we confront, and indeed a narrow view of reality as it seeks to confront it.¹³ To that extent—ironically in view of its frequent assaults on others for being insufficiently critical—it is itself somewhat naïve and uncritical, and indeed often involves itself in self-contradiction and incoherence. That is the thrust of my criticism of it in my *JBL* article.

Knowing About the Past

I hope that it is now clear what I have hitherto argued and why. In this paper I return to the argument and seek to develop it. I ask again: is the attitude of principled suspicion toward the Hebrew Bible with regard to history that is now so commonly found in writing on the history of Israel justified, or indeed sensible? I begin by returning to that other, fundamental question mentioned a moment ago: how do we know what we claim to know about the reality of the past? I assert the following in response to this question: we know it, to the extent that we know it at all, primarily through the testimony of others about it. Testimony lies at the heart of our access to the past. There is the testimony of people(s) from the past about their own past, communicated in oral and written forms. There is the testimony of people(s) from the past about the past of other peoples, also communicated in oral and written forms. There is also the testimony of figures from the present about the past, whether the past of their own peoples or of others—figures like archaeologists, who make certain claims about what they have found and what it means in respect of what has happened previously. It is such testimony that gives us access to the past, to the extent that anything does. There is no way of doing any historiography that does not involve testimony. Even if I am the very person who digs up an artifact from the Palestinian soil, I am still entirely dependent upon the testimony of others who have gone before me in trying to make sense of its significance, in trying to decide how I shall add my testimony to theirs.[14] Testimony, storytelling if you like, is central to our quest to know the past; and therefore interpretation is unavoidable as well. All testimony about the past is also interpretation of the past. It has its ideology or theology; it has its presuppositions and its point of view; it has its narrative structure; and (if at all interesting to listen to or to read) it has its narrative art, its rhetoric.[15] We cannot avoid testimony, and we cannot avoid interpretation.[16] We also cannot avoid faith. I began this paragraph by using the language of knowledge: how do we know what we claim to know about the past? In truth, however, this is a concession to the view of what we are about as historians from which I wish to distance myself. What we call knowledge of the past is more accurately described as faith in the testimony, in the interpretations of the past offered by others. We consider the gathered testimonies at our disposal; we reflect on the various interpretations offered; and we decide in various ways and to various extents to invest faith in these, to make these testimonies and interpretations our own. If our faith is very strong, or we are simply not conscious of what we are doing, then we tend to call our faith knowledge; but it is a dangerous term to use, since it too easily leads us into self-delusion, or deludes others who listen to us or read our books, as to the truth of the matter. It is this delusion, indeed, that seems to me to lie at the heart of the problem, so far as much of our recent (and not so recent) writing on the history of Israel is concerned. I shall return to consider it in due course.

We "know" what we claim to know about the past, then, by listening to testimony, to interpretation, and by making choices about whom to believe.[17] What sense does it make, then, in our pursuit of knowledge of the history of Israel, to adopt a principled distrust of major sections of, or even the totality of the Hebrew Bible? In this literature we evidently have, among other sorts of texts, testimonies about (interpretations of) Israel's past in narrative form.[18] To tell us about this past is certainly not the only purpose of these narratives; it is arguably not even their main purpose. Yet so far as can be deduced from the texts themselves, it is clearly one of their purposes.[19] Whether it were one of their purposes or not, they might indeed still succeed in doing it.[20] How is it, then, that we have come to a place where a principled avoidance of the Hebrew Bible as a whole by historians of Israel can be advocated by some, and many more have come to regard entire sections of this Bible as being of little usefulness in getting at historical truth?

Verification or Falsification?

As we review the literature, it is evident that one of the reasons scholars have for their doubts is that it is difficult, if not impossible, to verify so much of biblical tradition; and without verification, it is asserted or implied, we cannot have great confidence in the material as source material for the doing of historiography. Thus Miller and Hayes, to take one example, are concerned about the general lack of what they call "non-biblical control evidence" throughout Genesis–Samuel and into 1 Kings. They do not think that one can presume the historical reliability of the Genesis–Joshua narrative in the absence of it; they are extremely hesitant about using the Samuel narrative in writing about Saul because of lack of external verification of the truth of the kernel of the stories there; and they would clearly prefer to have the same kind of verification in the case of David.[21] In the absence of such verification, which they regard as essential to the task of properly writing a critical historiography, they are to be found either not attempting to say anything (in the case of Genesis–Joshua) or virtually apologizing for what they are indeed attempting to say.[22] Soggin, the author of the other watershed history of Israel dating from the 1980s, is just as unwilling in general to presume historical reference in biblical accounts without external verification.[23] Both histories are indeed regarded as *watershed* histories in part precisely because they apply the verification principle to the extent that they do. If some more recent scholarship has found them deficient, it is not because they are thought to have gone too far in this direction, but because they are considered not to have gone far enough. External verification for the Davidic and Solomonic periods, it is claimed, is just as absent as for the earlier periods, and indeed is also far more sparse than hitherto suspected for the period of the later monarchy. Since it is well known that we are struggling somewhat for verification in the postexilic period as well, it is unsurprising that a number of scholars are calling for what they see as simple consistency in the approach adopted to the Hebrew Bible and history. If Genesis through to sections of 1 Samuel is not to be considered primary source material at least partly for the reason that verification is not available, why treat any differently the remainder of 1 Samuel through to 2 Kings and into Ezra–Nehemiah? Thus it is made to seem inevitable that any truly critical scholar will adopt a principled suspicion of the whole Hebrew Bible in respect of historical work; and conversely, that those who partially or generally adopt the biblical story-line in writing their histories of Israel are, to the extent that they do this, religiously-motivated obscurantists rather than critical scholars.

It is my view, on the other hand, that this headlong rush to skepticism is a result, not of being more purely critical, but rather of being insufficiently critical. Criticism is indeed widely employed; but it is not employed in respect of the sacred cow at the heart of the matter—the verification principle itself. Why should verification be a prerequisite for our acceptance of a tradition as valuable in respect of historical reality?

Why should not ancient historical texts rather be given the benefit of the doubt in regard to their statements about the past unless there are compelling reasons to consider them unreliable in these statements and with due regard (of course) to their literary and ideological features? In short, why should we adopt a verification rather than a falsification principle—why should the onus be on the texts to "prove" themselves valuable in respect of history, rather than on those who question their value to "prove" them false? I have raised these questions before. I have still not received, in my view, an adequate answer to them. It cannot be, as many seem to assume, that verification is necessary because of the merely general *possibility* that any given biblical text is not in fact reliable as historiography.[24] I grant the possibility in any given case; but the individual case still must be examined in order to come to an individual decision about it. I do not therefore see how the general possibility leads on logically to the methodological stance just described.[25]

I use the inverted commas around "prove" in any case advisedly, for it is not at all clear whether the notion of verification or "proof" under consideration here is at all coherent. How exactly is verification thought to be possible? Suppose that we have an archaeological datum which is consistent with the claims of a biblical text about the past. Does this "verify" that the text is historically accurate? This is certainly the kind of thing that used to be argued. Yet that piece of data, even if a written text, is still itself only another testimony to the past; it does not "prove" that the event to which the text refers happened. Non-written data are even less precise and more ambiguous.[26] How many testimonies are needed, then, before verification happens? And for whom does it happen—for everyone, or only for some? Recent discussion on the history of Israel has clearly suggested that the answer is indeed "only for some." One person's sufficiency of data is another's insufficiency, or even another's forgery.[27] This raises the interesting question as to how far verification lies in the eye of the beholder, and whether it is not one's primary attitude to the texts in the first instance that is far more decisive in terms of one's approach to the history of Israel than the discovery of this or that piece of external data.[28] This very question then thrusts us back to our opening questions on the point of method, and indeed sharpens them. Why, exactly, is verification commonly regarded as so central to the historiographical task, especially when it is so unclear in what it consists? To this question we may add another that sharpens the point still further. How much history, ancient or otherwise, would we know about, if the verification principle were consistently applied to all testimony about it? The answer is clearly "very little"—which is precisely why those who employ the principle, whether historians in general or of Israel in particular, only do it selectively, choosing their targets for rigorous skepticism most carefully.[29] That delusion that I mentioned earlier—the delusion that we possess knowledge unmediated by faith—is indeed only possible if skepticism is directed at certain testimonies about, and interpretations of, the past, and not at others.[30] Method that holds verification to be centrally important can only ever be method that is partially (in every sense) followed through. The more consistently the method is applied, the more it collapses in upon itself, until the point is reached where it is realized that nothing can truly be known at all. It is one of the remarkable (if also tragi-comic) aspects of recent writing on the history of Israel that a number of its practitioners seem to imagine that it is an advance in knowledge as a result of empirical research that has led to the end of "ancient Israel," when in fact it is only an advance in ignorance as a result of the quasi-consistent application of the verification principle.[31]

I continue to reserve further comments on the delusion to which I refer, however, for a moment. In summary of this section of my argument, I simply affirm that I can see no reason why any text offering testimony about the past, including the Hebrew Bible, should be bracketed out of our historical discussions until it has passed some obscure "verification test."[32]

Specific "Rules" of Evidence

There is a second, connected reason, however, why scholars have increasingly expressed doubts about whole sections of the biblical tradition. It is not just that the Bible has "failed" in its own terms to verify itself. It is also because so much of the biblical literature is now widely considered intrinsically deficient in its very ability to testify about the past that it claims to reflect. Here we have to do with an accumulated inheritance of rules about which kinds of testimony really count, so far as the historian is concerned, and which kinds of testimony do not count as much or at all. These rules have apparently been designed, like the rules of textual criticism (for example), to make life easier for the historian, on the one hand, by absolving him from thought in specific instances; and, on the other hand, to reduce the subjectivity otherwise inevitably involved in deciding between witnesses to the past. We may list the most influential of these rules, as appropriated, comprehended and used by historians of Israel in particular, as follows. First, eyewitness or otherwise contemporaneous accounts are to be preferred on principle to later accounts.[33] Secondly, accounts that are not so ideological, or not ideological at all, in nature are to be preferred to accounts that are ideological in nature.[34] Thirdly and finally, accounts that fit our preconceptions about what is normal, possible, and so on, are to be preferred to accounts that do not fit such preconceptions.[35] These rules have, of course, been in operation for some time, and as such have been applied for some time to smaller or greater sections of biblical tradition. What has changed in recent times is not the rules, but the extent to which the biblical text is seen as unsatisfactory in respect of them. Scholars have found in the Bible fewer of the kinds of traditions that score highly in respect of their granting of direct access to the past (e.g. eyewitness or early sources), and more and more of the kinds that do not score highly. Thus once again there has seemed a certain inevitability about the marginalization of the Bible by historians, as the places where "history" might be found therein have been by degrees eliminated. And again, this perceived inevitability has led also to the perception that those who insist on finding history, say, in the books of Samuel are simply committed to being conservative and are not properly critical scholars.

Once again, however, the interesting question is: who is it that is really being critical? For the rules I have just enunciated are by no means self-evidently "true." The claims that are made about them (taken together and labelled as rules of "scientific method") in terms of their capacity to lead us into all truth, or at least to enable us to pronounce upon the probability that something did or did not happen in the past, are inflated. I leave aside for the purposes of the present discussion the question of whether scholars are in fact are correct to see the Bible as more problematic than before in respect of the rules. There is certainly an interesting question here, for those who believe in verification, as to the status of many of the scholarly hypotheses about the dating of biblical texts in particular, and as to the defensibility of any rejection of the Bible as testimony to Israel's past on the basis of these unverified hypotheses. I leave this question aside, however,[36] and press the more radical question about the rules themselves, which I consider highly problematic. There is no good reason at all to believe that eyewitnesses are, any less than later reporters of events, interpreters of those events, nor any reason to assume on principle that their testimony is going to be more or less trustworthy.[37] There is, indeed, no reason to believe that earlier accounts are generally more reliable than later accounts,[38] even *if* the literary coherence of the latter can plausibly be argued to be a late feature in their development.[39] Certainly most modern historians do not believe this, or they would not write their own books on history.[40] Nor is there reason to believe that there is any account of the past anywhere (including the archaeologist's account)[41] that is not ideological in nature, and thus in principle to be trusted more than others[42]; nor indeed to believe in any case that an ideological account cannot also be a historically accurate account.[43] There is no good reason, finally, to believe that just because a testimony does not violate our sense of what is normal and possible, it is more likely to be true than one that does, nor that an account that describes the unique or unusual is for that reason to be suspected of unreliability.[44]

In sum, there is no way that "rules" of evidence can prejudge whether particular testimonies are in fact worthy of faith or not. It is an illusion to think that they can. There is no intellectually defensible way of avoiding, in the particular case, the inevitable consideration of all testimonies together, weighing them up on their own terms and in comparison with each other and asking how far they are each likely (or not) to be in relationship to the events to which they refer. In that respect historical criticism is indeed directly analogous to textual criticism, but not in the way that was once supposed. There is no way, in either case, in which the application of a general set of "rules" to any particular case of itself settles very much. All that the so-called "rules" do is to provide a helpful background in terms of generalities, an accumulated wisdom that may or may not help in the resolution of any particular case. In the final analysis there is no substitute for the judgment of the individual reader of the testimonies in coming to some resolution in each particular case—in deciding in which testimonies to invest faith (as to "better" text or historical event), in deciding which reading makes better "sense." All this being the case, there is once again no good reason to marginalize the testimony of the Hebrew Bible in our pursuit of the history of Israel.[45] There is every reason, in fact, to place its testimony at the heart of our deliberations.

Faith and Knowledge

We "know" what we claim to know about the past, I have suggested, by listening to testimony, to interpretation, and by exercising faith. There is no good reason, I have further argued, to think that any testimony and interpretation should be required to "verify" itself in some way before being listened to. Nor is there any good reason to think that any testimony and interpretation can be prejudged either positively or negatively by "method" rather than being listened to on its own terms. The only rational course of action for the person interested in the reality of history is, in fact, to consider all the testimony and interpretation available to him or her and to make his/her best judgments on a case by case basis about whether and how far it is to be believed.[46]

I would characterize this as a position of epistemological openness to past reality. It is the position that I adopt in respect of reality in general, and which would be widely recognized, I trust, as rational in that regard.[47] To illustrate this point, let me return briefly to verification and rules of evidence. I asked earlier how much knowledge we would have of past reality if the verification principle were consistently applied to testimony about it. The answer was "very little." Now I ask: how much knowledge of reality in general would we possess if we truly and consistently functioned in this suspicious manner, demanding of all and sundry that they validate their testimony to us before we accepted its veracity? Again, the answer is "very little." We generally regard it, indeed, as a sign of emotional or mental imbalance if people ordinarily inhabit a culture of distrust in testimony at the level of principle, and most of us outside mental institutions do not in fact inhabit such a universe. It is true, of course, as the old joke goes, that just because we are paranoid, this does not mean that someone is not out to get us. Suspicion may sometimes, or often, be justified. Yet we recognize that healthy people generally place trust in the testimony of others, reserving suspicion for those who have given grounds for it. The adoption of a thoroughgoing hermeneutic of suspicion is not considered sensible in terms of our apprehension of general reality. Nor is the adoption of a "method" in respect of testimony about present reality considered sensible either. We do not always, if we are intelligent, critical people, invest faith in eyewitnesses as opposed to those people who testify to us secondarily, nor vice versa. Indeed, if we characteristically believe one sort of person rather than another, (for example, consistently accepting "insider" accounts of reality over against "outsider" accounts), then we are considered, not intelligent, but prejudiced. Reality is more complex than is allowed for by method. We do not, therefore, if we are intelligent, critical people, allow method overly to influence us in seeking to apprehend it.

Whether it is historical reality, then, or present reality, or indeed textual reality,[48] epistemological openness (I assert) is the only rational stance in respect of the reality that is beyond us. With regard to the history of Israel in particular, it is thus in my view the most rational thing in the world to approach the Hebrew Bible with an *openness* of mind in respect of the major testimony it bears to Israel's past, acknowledging that we have to *bear* in mind the other important reasons for which these texts have been handed down in the form they have been handed down. It is in my view an historiographical virtue, not a vice, having identified what that testimony is, to employ it fundamentally in any modern retelling of the history of Israel, whether or not other testimonies are available to us to consider alongside it (although certainly *along with* such other testimonies as *are* available to us), looking for coherence and incoherence among the testimonies and making our assessment of how far each reflects reality. It is to my mind absurd to adopt any other approach.[49]

Any other approach, in fact, is not truly epistemologically open. It is, rather, an approach that is only selectively open. It is to that extent an irrational approach.[50] This is indeed how I would characterize the approach adopted in some of the recent scholarship on the history of Israel of which I am critical. It is open to receive testimony about Israel's past predominantly or entirely from non-biblical sources, and generally exercises a high level of trust in these sources. It is predominantly or entirely closed to testimony from the Bible itself, generally exercising a high level of distrust in these sources. The main reason for this selectivity, so far as I can determine it, is precisely the delusion about knowledge that I mentioned earlier.[51] In spite of all their claims to the contrary, and indeed all their claims about others misrepresenting their views, significant numbers of historians of Israel seem to believe deep in their souls that the attainment of historical knowledge, beyond testimony and interpretation and without faith, is possible. At least, they appear to believe that some types of testimony and interpretation communicate knowledge more directly, and with less investment of faith, than others.[52] Not only is attainment of such knowledge thought possible, indeed, it is commonly regarded as having been achieved. Sometimes statements to this effect are explicit. Towards the end of his response to my 1995 *JBL* article, in which he claims that I thoroughly misrepresent him, Thomas Thompson reasserts precisely the kind of position for which I criticize him in the article, when he says: "There is no more 'ancient Israel.' History no longer has room for it. This we do know. And now, as one of the first conclusions of this new knowledge, 'biblical Israel' was in its origin a Jewish concept."[53] "Knowledge" of the past is obtained somehow, and held over against the construct "ancient Israel," which previous scholars have created in considerable dependence on the Hebrew Bible, and over against the Hebrew Bible itself, which is evidently thought of as providing us with something other than knowledge of this past.[54] The explicit statement of this kind of position is not so common, however, as the implicit adoption of it. Knowledge is simply assumed to have been accumulated in various ways. This knowledge can then be used as a yardstick against which to measure biblical testimony and come to some judgment upon it, or indeed as a basis upon which to build a "scientific" history in complete independence of it.[55]

Yet whence, exactly, did the knowledge under consideration spring, in the light of which the Bible's testimony is now to be assessed? Here, as when observing an accomplished magician, it is important to watch carefully for the sleight of hand. For the reality is that this so-called knowledge is really faith in disguise. When Thompson says, "There is no more 'ancient Israel' ... This we do know"; *he* actually knows nothing of the kind, and "we" certainly do not. *He* simply believes it strongly, and "we" are drawn into the faith statement to offer some community support for the faith expressed. What he "knows," he "knows" because he has decided to invest faith in certain testimonies about the past rather than others, the most notable of the "others" being the testimony of the Hebrew Bible. The grounds upon which this epistemological privileging of non-biblical testimony can be defended are, however, entirely unclear. The wisdom of it is equally unclear. For the delusion that one possesses knowledge when one is only exercising faith is ever prone to lead on to a refusal to exercise faith when there are good grounds for doing so. We claim that we already know, and on that basis we close ourselves off from testimony that challenges our already preconceived knowledge.[56] "Knowledge" becomes the wall that we build around ourselves to protect ourselves from reality, whether individually or as a group. It becomes the excuse for narrowness of vision and intolerance of other points of view. It is, when manifest in this way, an obstacle rather than a means to the apprehension of reality. We may hold the opinion that we are enlightened, but in truth we inhabit epistemological darkness. It is one of the ultimate ironies, indeed, that when Enlightenment scholarship gets to this point, it is essentially no different from the fundamentalist religion that it so profoundly despises.[57] It is closed in on itself, unable and unwilling to hear voices from the outside. It is an irrational approach to reality indeed.

On Tolerance and Intolerance

I conclude this section of the paper with some further comments on tolerance and intolerance. I have sometimes been challenged when in dialogue about matters historical to say whether, on my view of the way in which history should be approached, there is any way of saying that one history of Israel is better than another. Is it not the case, on my view, that any story about the past is as good as any other? I am glad to be able to clarify here that I certainly do not believe that any story about the past is as good as any other, any more than I believe that any reading of a text is as good as any other. There are histories that in my view do a good job of weaving testimonies about the past together to make a coherent story, and histories that do not. There are histories that in my view do better justice than others to the various testimonies and interpretations upon which we depend for access to the past. There are histories, indeed, that in my view falsify the past in all sorts of ways (i.e., do not deal convincingly or at all with "the evidence" as I see it). I do not believe, in other words, that the past is simply an indeterminate mess out of which one can make anything one wishes. We are constrained by testimony and interpretation in our reading of it, if we are as attentive as we should be to that testimony and interpretation. However, I also do not believe, on the other hand, that history is one objectively observable story which has one empirically verifiable "correct" interpretation. It is not simply that we have such a relatively small amount of data to go on in respect of the ancient past, and therefore must "fill in" thousands of gaps in the narrative of the past according to our own view of the world's story. That in itself, it is true, would lead us to different renderings of the story, each of which might be argued to be consonant with the "facts." More seriously, however, even if in some inconceivable world we had access to all the millions and millions of "facts" of history—every conversation, every action by every person, every "event"—we would still be found rendering the story in different ways, selecting and shaping the "past" in respect of the themes that we wished to develop. It is not lack of data that is our problem. Greater amounts of data would not improve matters. There is an inevitably subjective aspect to all our storytelling about the past, connected with the reality of our own contingency as mortal beings, which means that our stories will always be different from each other even if we all accept as a fundamental principle that we should be epistemologically open to testimony and interpretation, accountable to "the facts." It is thus a logical (and I would say moral) consequence of epistemological openness to the reality of the past that we should also be maximally tolerant of each other as we each render the past, listening with respect to each other's stories as we attempt to tell our own. In short, intellectual humility and charity, informed by a pluralist perspective, comprise the entailment of epistemological openness. This is not because any rendering of the past is as good as any other. It is because we (should) recognize that what we call "good" has a considerable amount to do with judgments about matters other than what constitutes the "data" to be accommodated, and that those judgments are themselves a matter of debate and indeed choice.[58]

An Example: Davies and Provan on Sennacherib's Invasion of Judah

I am moving in due course to my conclusion. It will be helpful, however, to illustrate with an example what I take to be the difference in approach to the matter of Hebrew Bible and history between myself and those who hold the more skeptical view of the biblical texts with which I have been engaging above. My chosen example is the invasion of Judah by the Assyrian king Sennacherib around the year 701 BC. Accounts of this invasion are found in 2 Kings 18:13–19:37; 2 Chronicles 32:1–23; Isaiah 36–37 and in the Rassam Cylinder Inscription of the Assyrian king (700 BC)—an account repeated almost verbatim in all the later descriptions of Sennacherib's reign, including the Taylor and Oriental Institute Prisms.[59] There is some archaeological evidence that seems to touch on the detail of the events described by these texts, but it is not directly relevant to our present enquiry.[60] The Kings account opens with a passage not found in the other biblical passages (2 Kgs 18:13–16) that tells us of Hezekiah's initial and unsuccessful attempt, after Sennacherib had taken "all the fortified cities of Judah," to buy off the Assyrian king. Thereafter the Kings and Isaiah accounts proceed in tandem, telling of Hezekiah's refusal to surrender Jerusalem to the besieging Assyrians; his consultation with the prophet Isaiah and Isaiah's promise of deliverance for the city; his later prayer and Isaiah's response to that prayer; the eventual miraculous deliverance of Jerusalem through an angel; and Sennacherib's death. Chronicles provides us with a much shorter account, not only omitting any reference to the attempted payment, but also abbreviating the account in other ways (particularly by omitting Isaiah's prophecies). Some details are nevertheless added (e.g. the building works of 2 Chr 32:3–5 and the speech of 2 Chr 32:7–8). The Assyrian account, in those places where it concerns Judah in particular rather than Palestine in general, also does not mention any initial payment by Hezekiah after the fall of his cities. It moves straight from description of their fall to description of the siege of Jerusalem. It does not explicitly tell us the circumstances in which the siege ended, although it implies that Hezekiah at this point did agree to pay tribute, which he is then described as sending to Assyria after Sennacherib had departed from Judah.

Epistemological openness leads me in the first instance to read all these accounts with great seriousness as apparently offering testimony to the past, and further consideration does not lead me to the conclusion that I should revise my opinion. I recognize, of course, that each of the accounts is an ideological account of the past—it could not be otherwise. I shall not rehearse the ideologies of the three biblical accounts as they become apparent to us through consideration of the individual passages and their wider literary contexts. It is unlikely that any reader of this paper requires such a rehearsal.[61] For reasons that will become clear in a moment, however, I do wish to comment briefly on the ideology of the Assyrian text as it, too, is evidenced in the text itself and on the basis of broader considerations. As Younger has underlined,[62] all Assyrian royal inscriptions cater to preconceived ideological requirements in the way that they are structured. Their stereotypical nature instills in the readers a sense of anticipation of the obvious outcome of the campaign described, and hence of the relentless efficacy of the Assyrian king's actions as he seeks to reinstate (what is from the Assyrian point of view) order, righteousness and life. They are concerned to exalt the reputation of the king concerned, to glorify the gods of Assyria, especially Ashur, and to encourage loyalty and submission among his subjects. This presumably is why such inscriptions are not noted for any frank admission of failure, even where the readers of other, non-Assyrian texts might reasonably deduce that failure has occurred. Any reader of this particular Sennacherib text who is interested in history will have to take these broader realities into account, in just the same way that the ideologies of the biblical texts require to be taken into account.

I repeat, nevertheless, that further consideration of our four texts, helping me as it does to understand them as ideological texts, does not lead me to the conclusion that I should generally revise my opinion of them as testimonies to the past. It reminds me that each is indeed a *story* about the past, and that I must be alert for features of each that perhaps have more to do with the particular requirements of the story than with anything else. It does not compel me to any generalized attitude of suspicion or distrust, however. It compels me only to caution on a case by case basis. We move, then, to the detail. Which kind of story do our four ancient stories allow us to construct about Sennacherib's invasion of Palestine?

Let me suggest the following outline reading. Hezekiah had prepared himself well for the expected invasion, not least in making a preemptive strike against Philistine territory associated with Gaza, whose king Sillibel (we deduce from Sennacherib's own account of the campaign) remained loyal to Assyria throughout the revolt, and in imprisoning the similarly loyal king Padi of Ekron.[63] All this may imply that Hezekiah was one of the moving forces of the revolt. This may in turn help to explain the opening of the Kings account (2 Kgs 18:13–16). Hezekiah offered renewed tribute, the text claims, if the Assyrian king would withdraw.[64] Sennacherib, however, chose, while Jerusalem's gates remained closed to him, to continue to regard Hezekiah as a rebel. An army was thus sent from Lachish to Jerusalem, in order to persuade Hezekiah fully to surrender (2 Kgs 18:17 ff.).[65] We might plausibly suggest that it was because of Hezekiah's prominence as an instigator of the revolt that Sennacherib was so insistent. All the biblical accounts and Sennacherib's own account agree, in any case, that Jerusalem ended up being besieged by an Assyrian army because Hezekiah was perceived as not submitting to Assyrian overlordship. At some point during the campaign, Kings, Isaiah and the Assyrian records also agree, an Egyptian army appeared on the scene. The Assyrian text describes its appearance, and the ensuing battle, before it describes the siege of Jerusalem. It does not clearly intend in so doing to be strictly chronological, however (the arrangement of the text may be according to topic), whereas Kings and Isaiah do clearly imply that the Egyptian advance occurred after the siege had begun, and this perspective is thus the one that I weave into my account. Sennacherib claims to have defeated this Egyptian force at Eltekeh, and we have no reason to disbelieve him. It may be that it was after this Assyrian victory that Hezekiah, in an attempt to buy more time, released Padi of Ekron, whom Sennacherib claims to have "made" come from Jerusalem and to have reestablished on his throne. Whether this is the case or not, Sennacherib does not claim to have taken Jerusalem at any point, nor even to have received tribute from Hezekiah in the immediate aftermath of the siege. He tells us only that after his return to Nineveh, whose occasion he does not describe, Hezekiah sent tribute. The silence on this matter of the conclusion of Sennacherib's assault on Hezekiah, when compared to what Sennacherib says in his inscription about other kings in the region, begs some explanation, and our biblical sources give us some hints in the direction of such, when they tell us of a mysterious reversal suffered by the Assyrians while Jerusalem lay at their mercy.[66] It is entirely plausible that Hezekiah subsequently decided to reaffirm his vassalship to Assyria by sending tribute on to Nineveh, as Sennacherib claims.[67] 2 Kings 18:13–16 suggests that he had wished to settle things in this manner in the first place; and in the aftermath of Sennacherib's campaign Hezekiah was evidently very isolated, with much of his territory annexed by Ashdod, Ekron and Gaza, and significant portions of his army having deserted him.

This is, of course, only an outline reading. Much more could be said in explication of it. The main point to be made about it in this context, however, is that it is a particular sort of reading. It takes the biblical and other data equally seriously as testimony, while recognizing the perspectival nature, rhetorical features, and ideology of each testimony, and seeking to take intelligent account of these. It recognizes the possibility that any testimony may mislead, yet it takes a positive attitude to testimony, open to the possibility that the reading that is based upon it may be falsified, but resistant to any foolish demand that it should be verified.

With this reading I now wish to contrast another: the reading of Philip Davies, in his book *In Search of Ancient Israel*,[68] to which I have previously referred in my *JBL* article and elsewhere.[69] Davies takes the Assyrian invasion as a particular example in the course of his argument about the folly of looking for any "ancient Israel." He is prepared to allow that *behind* our extant accounts there does lie a historical reality. A vassal king of Judah rebelled against the king of Assyria, and the Assyrians in response devastated Judah, depriving Hezekiah of virtually all his kingdom except Jerusalem. Jerusalem was not captured, but Hezekiah paid a large tribute, and afterwards remained a vassal of Assyria without the power of rebellion. This is "what happened" in the history of Palestine. The biblical story, on the other hand, tells us of a victory by the God of Israel over the Assyrian king which left Judah ever after free of Assyrian control—for such control is never referred to again. Why this story is as it is can in the last analysis be explained only if we recognize that it is not simply giving us a different version of a historical event, but is rather telling us a story of something that is not historical. The analogy that Davies offers is that of Shakespeare's *Julius Caesar*, where things happen because of the play's own dramatic logic. Whatever any historical Brutus may or may not have done does not either explain the actions of Shakespeare's character of that name nor make this character into a historical figure.

Davies thus provides an excellent example of precisely the kind of approach to the matter of history that I have already criticized. As he comes to consider the biblical text, he apparently already knows "what really happened" in that part of the history of Palestine that concerns the Assyrian invasion of Judah; and this is then contrasted in particular with what the biblical story has to tell us (although also, to some extent, with the Assyrian story as well). Where does this knowledge of "what happened" come from? Closer attention to the argument reveals that it originates in what is described as a "reasonable guess."[70] How we get in the course of a few lines from this "reasonable guess" to the kind of solid "what really happened" that may be contrasted with what the ancient texts say is unclear. It is particularly unclear because the description of "what happened" is itself partly based upon these same ancient (biblical and Assyrian) texts. It is, in fact, a new story derived from the ancient stories, taking on a mysterious solidity that they apparently lack for reasons that are not fully spelled out. At least part of the solution to the mystery, however, lies in this statement: "The events are described as they are because Israel is involved. And to this Israel happen things that as an historian I do not accept happen in history here or anywhere else."[71] The reference is clearly to the idea of supernatural deliverance through "the angel." Davies, "as an historian," does not accept that such things happen in history. How he knows this "as an historian," is, however, something of a mystery. He may well choose, as Davies the non-theist, to differ with the theological interpretation of the biblical writers with respect to the events they are describing. What is it, however, that drives him as Davies the historian to think that the Assyrians could not have suffered an unexpected reversal that caused their withdrawal from Palestine? Even as an historian deeply committed to the rules of historical method he would only be permitted to consider such an eventuality, by analogy, improbable. If that were what he were arguing, then I would press him further to explain why I should believe that it did not happen in this specific case, improbable or not. In fact, however, there is no *argument* here at all—only a statement of belief accompanied by the customary appeal to community support for the faith expressed ("as an historian"). We are left to decide why we should accept Davies' assertion as to what cannot happen over against the testimony of the texts as to what did happen.

Reasonable guesses and general prejudices aside, whence otherwise does Davies derive his "knowledge" of the past against which the biblical text can be measured? The answer appears to be: from the Assyrian account of the invasion and its aftermath. Only thus is it possible to understand his assertion that the biblical story tells us that Judah was ever afterwards free of Assyrian control, whereas the "facts" were otherwise. Here we find that classical combination of maximal suspicion of the biblical text and maximal naïveté with regard to other sources of information about which I was so critical earlier—a naïveté most puzzling in view of Davies' own general awareness of the ideological nature of the Assyrian texts.[72] It is in truth by no means clear why, if the biblical text were indeed in conflict with the Assyrian text with regard to its testimony, we should think that the latter provides us with access to the facts and the former only to the minds of the biblical authors. In fact, however, the assertion that the texts are in conflict is in any case mistaken. Davies himself allows that the biblical text does not actually say (but only "implies") that Judah was ever after the Sennacherib invasion free of Assyrian control; and non-reference to the Assyrians cannot of itself be taken to indicate that this is what is implied, in a text that is selective in the first place (especially regarding Assyria) about what it records. The conflict is imagined. Even if it existed, however, we should at least require an *argument* as to why we should favor one account over the other. An assertion would not—should not—be considered sufficient.

The difference between the two approaches should now be clear. I am inclined in the first instance to listen to the varied testimony that we possess about the Assyrian invasion of Judah and to try to form a broad judgment about the course of events that might lie behind the testimony. I am much more inclined to form these judgments in the first instance on the basis of ancient claims about the past than on the basis of modern "reasonable guesses" about it. I am indeed much more interested in listening to claims about what did happen than in listening to guesses about what must have happened, for the simple reason that I am vastly more interested in finding out about the past than about the present. I am not unaware of the inevitable ideological nature of all the ancient testimony to which I am listening. Each of the four texts that testify do so within their larger literary and sociological contexts, and with some intention to persuade and to influence. It is precisely because I am aware of this, however, that I do not succumb to the temptation to think of one or other of my accounts as providing me with more or less unmediated "knowledge" of the past in contrast to the others. Davies certainly seems to imagine that the Assyrian text grants him some degree of knowledge of this kind—as if it were not really an ideological text at all, in the same sense that our biblical texts are. I find no reason to see any distinction of this kind. I grant, then, that all four texts are ideological. I do not, however, adopt a fundamentally suspicious attitude in respect of any of them, but rather an open attitude. It may be that I shall find specific reasons to think that one or other of them is unreliable or deficient in their testifying; but I await specific reasons, and do not fall back on general prejudice. It is indeed prejudice, and not reason, that I see as lying at the heart of the alternative approach—a lack of openness to data that precludes the acquisition of knowledge that is not already known. Thus it is that the pursuit of "how it really was" results only in the projection of a narrow present view of reality onto the past—"how we truly expected or needed it to be."[73] It is not the first time in the history of the history of Israel that this has happened. That history demonstrates more than adequately the general truth, in fact, that we either respect and appropriate the testimony of the past—recognizing the forms in which it is cast and allowing it to challenge us even while we engage in critical thinking about it—or we are doomed, while believing that we alone possess objectivity regarding the past and can start afresh in accurately describing it, to create highly individualistic fantasies out of the poverty of our own very limited individual experience and imagination, and to have them masquerade as representations of the world outside our minds.

A final quotation from Davies, in a different publication, enables me to bring this section of my paper to a close: "It is only in religious language that to believe is good and to doubt bad; for a historian, to doubt is good and to believe is bad!"[74]

I think, on the other hand, that whether practicing religion or historiography, or indeed simply living life, it is necessary and good both to believe and to doubt as it seems sensible and appropriate so to do.[75] I find Paul Ricoeur's approach to hermeneutics, in fact, much more persuasive than Davies' apparent approach, in that the former (unlike some of those biblical scholars indebted to him) incorporates a hermeneutic of suspicion into his reading without allowing suspicion to dominate, and indeed balances it with a hermeneutic of belief: "Hermeneutics seems to me to be animated by this double motivation: willingness to suspect, willingness to listen; vow of rigor, vow of obedience."[76]

Conclusion

I began this paper with the picture of the dwarves in the stable. They were happy to be without humbug; determined not to be taken in. They considered themselves enlightened. The reality was that their enlightenment was darkness, and that, through misplaced commitment, they had put themselves beyond ever discovering that this was so. As the lion Aslan himself put it, in reality they inhabited the prison of their own minds, "so afraid of being taken in that they cannot be taken out."[77] This is the fate, it seems, of all who are so convinced that they possess knowledge that they are unprepared any longer to hear testimony and interpretation; unwilling any longer to exercise faith; committed ideologically, if inconsistently, to doubt. It is certainly possible, taking such a stance, to construct very plausible and comforting accounts of reality, historical and otherwise. It is certainly possible that these accounts will find group affirmation. Whether they actually correspond to reality outside one's own head, or outside one's group, is another matter. Without openness to complex reality itself, there is no possibility of ever finding out. Without such openness, indeed, all that one is ever going to discover is "facts" that confirm one's own first-articulated worldview. It is an unhappy position in which to find oneself, if one has any aspirations after truth. By all means, therefore, let us embrace criticism, and let us use it in the manner of Ricoeur to deconstruct idolatry and dogmatism. But let us ensure in embracing it that we do not fall into the trap of being so obsessed with criticism of the Bible that we fail to be sufficiently critical of everything else, including our own prejudices and presuppositions, and thus end up simply with new idolatries and dogmatisms to replace the old. I doubt whether the dwarves required great faith in Aslan in order to hear his voice. They only needed, in the first instance, to match their skepticism respecting him with due skepticism regarding their own beliefs.

11

TO HIGHLIGHT ALL OUR IDOLS:
WORSHIPPING GOD IN NIETZSCHE'S WORLD

In 1999, I was invited to take part in the North Park Symposium at North Park Theological Seminary in Chicago, U.S.A. The Symposium takes place each Fall, bringing together eight to ten national and international scholars, representing various relevant disciplines, to focus attention on a theological topic important for the life of the Church. In 1999 the topic was "Idolatry and the Understanding of God," and I was very glad to participate, offering this paper on idolatry in the Old Testament. My "way in" to this topic is through the genuinely prophetic work of Friedrich Nietzsche, who foresaw with astonishing clarity, already in the nineteenth century, both the nihilism and also the idolatry (including the worship of the nation-state) that would follow in the West from the belief that God is dead. Whether we stand inside or outside of the Church, I argue in this essay, we presently live in Nietzsche's world, which the Old Testament (it turns out) powerfully addresses. The essay was originally published along with the other conference papers in the journal Ex Auditu *in 2000.*

The title of this article plays on that of Friedrich Nietzsche's book *The Twilight of the Idols* (1888), for Nietzsche is undoubtedly one of the great predictors and shapers of the world in which we now live. It was Nietzsche who so famously proclaimed in his book *The Gay*

Science (1882) that God was dead. In a world shaped by Enlightenment and scientific thought, there was simply no place for God; and with his death came also the collapse of all religious and philosophical absolutes—the collapse of the metaphysical and theological foundations of Western culture and specifically of traditional morality. The death of God means that there is no longer any truth that can claim absoluteness, universality, and eternity. What we call "truth" is only a mobile army of metaphors, metonyms, and anthropomorphisms—nothing more than the invention of fixed conventions for merely practical purposes. There are no facts, only interpretations; there is no Truth, although there are many truths. In the same way, the death of God means that there is no universal morality applicable indiscriminately to all human beings. There is only a series of moralities in an order of rank, ranging from the noble to the plebeian. Some moralities are more appropriate for dominating and leading social roles, and some for subordinate roles. What counts as a preferable and legitimate action depends upon the kind of person one is. Nietzsche challenges, for example, the idea that such things as exploitation, domination, and injury to the weak are universally objectionable behaviours.

Nietzsche was well aware of many of the likely consequences of this death of God. He foresaw a point in the future when its reality would dawn widely on Western culture, leading to widespread nihilism—a pervasive sense of purposelessness and meaninglessness. He also foresaw that most people would be unable to accept the intrinsic meaninglessness of existence, but would seek alternative absolutes to God as a way of investing life with meaning. He thought that the emerging nationalism of his own day represented one such surrogate god, in which the nation state would be invested with transcendent value and purpose. The slaughter of rivals and the conquest of the earth would follow, even while people proclaimed universal brotherhood, democracy, and socialism. Yet for all this, he himself was enthusiastically in favour of God's demise, for he held the God of the Judaeo-Christian tradition, along with assorted philosophers, largely responsible for much that is wrong with the world.

From the time of his first book (*The Birth of Tragedy Out of the Spirit of Music*, 1872), it is clear that he idolized ancient pre-Socratic Greece, identifying a strongly instinctual, wild, amoral, "Dionysian" energy within pre-Socratic Greek culture that he saw as an essentially creative and healthy force. Surveying the history of Western culture since the time of the Greeks, Nietzsche lamented that this "Dionysian," creative energy had been submerged and weakened as it became overshadowed by the forces of logical order and stiff sobriety, represented (e.g.) by Socrates, Plato, and the Christians. There is at the heart of all life, including human life untainted by philosophy and religion, a "will to power"—an instinct for growth and durability, expressed in the pouring out of creative energy and in such noble things as pride, competition, and autonomy. It is in the self-expression of such things by those who are strong, healthy, powerful and overflowing with life that the point of life resides.

Christianity, however, privileges soul over body, mind over senses, duty over desire, reality over appearance, and the timeless over the temporal. The world of experience is not, for the Christian, the only or the most important world that we inhabit. Christianity also opposes the "master morality" with a "slave morality," exalting such things as charity, humility, and obedience. For Nietzsche, these things are symptoms of a declining life, a life in distress. His writings aim at redirecting people's attention to their inherent freedom in the presently-existing world, and away from all escapist, pain-relieving, heavenly otherworlds. His hero is not Jesus, but historical characters like Caesar and Napoleon and fictional ones like Zarathustra (*Thus Spoke Zarathustra, A Book for All and None*, 1883–85)—a solitary, reflective, strong-willed, sage-like voice of self-mastery, who envisions a mode of psychologically healthier being beyond the common human condition, which Nietzsche refers to as "superhuman" (*übermenschlich*). *Thus Spoke Zarathustra* is, in effect, Nietzsche's manifesto of personal self-overcoming. His most famous attack on Christianity is found in *The Antichrist, Curse on Christianity* (1888), where he expresses his disgust over the way noble values in Roman Society were "corrupted" by the rise of Christianity, and tries to show that Christianity is a religion for weak and unhealthy people, whose general historical effect has been to undermine the healthy qualities of the more noble cultures. Nietzsche's profound hope was that Dionysus, the god of life's exuberance, would replace Jesus, the god of the heavenly otherworld, as the premier cultural standard for future millennia.

We live in Nietzsche's world. It is a world in which for many people God is, for all practical purposes, dead. The nihilism which follows from that belief is certainly a feature of the culture, as is the idolatry that follows from it. People have indeed transferred their allegiance to other gods, including (as Nietzsche rather eerily prophesied) the nation state. We live in a world in which there is no Truth, but only truths; no facts, but only interpretations; and no right and wrong beyond what the group or the individual assert to be right and wrong. There is an evident Nietzschean hostility to the Judaeo-Christian tradition; and this is very much connected with a Nietzschean commitment to the self—the fundamental idolatry at the heart of Nietzsche's world. We are all worshippers now of Dionysus, the god of life's exuberance. Self-expression, self-fulfillment, and self-actualization lie at the heart of our cultural agenda, as we tread the path towards superhuman status. The Nietzsche Center website advertises itself in these terms: "The Ultimate Nietzsche

Site that presents comprehensive study of Nietzsche's incredible philosophies and his usefulness in tremendous self-empowerment."

The fact that Nietzsche was a hopeless egomaniac who ended his life in madness probably brought on by syphilis does not seem to function as much of a cautionary element here. It was only shortly before losing his mind, in fact, that he wrote his final book, entitled (ironically, as it turns out) *Ecce Homo, How One Becomes What One Is* (1888). This intellectual autobiography opens with three sections revealingly headed "why I am so wise," "why I am so clever," and "why I write such good books." The concluding section of the book is headed "why I am a destiny." Thus ends the sermon of the self-confessed "follower of the philosopher Dionysus."

How are Christians to live their lives, confronted with this Nietzschean world that has indeed destroyed the privilege of soul over body, mind over senses, duty over desire, reality over appearance, and the timeless over the temporal? I suggest that we must do two things. We must first of all be very clear-headed about biblical truth on the matter of God and the gods, and embrace that biblical truth as our own.[1] Second, we must be very careful in reflecting on our modern world to call idols by their names and to avoid their worship, even as we seek to worship and to obey the living God. This paper seeks to address both matters.

Biblical Truth on God and the "Gods"

We begin with the opening verses of Exodus 20:

> Then God spoke all these words, saying, "I am the LORD your God, who brought you out of the land of Egypt, out of the house of slavery. You shall have no other gods before Me. You shall not make for yourself an idol, or any likeness

of what is in heaven above or on the earth beneath or in the water under the earth. You shall not worship them or serve them; for I, the LORD your God, am a jealous God.

This is the obvious text with which to begin, if one is intent on addressing the topic of "idolatry and understanding God" from a biblical, and in my case predominantly Old Testament, perspective. The people of God have been in Egypt, enduring harsh oppression at the hands of a human being who is considered within his cultural and religious context to be a god—the pharaoh of Egypt, son of the sun-god Re and becoming, after death, the god Osiris. This god-king has required servanthood from Israel—a harsh, oppressive slavery, ruthlessly imposed (Exod 1–2, cf. 20:2). The consequence of the oppression has been a remembering (2:23–25). Another God has entered the story, who remembers his covenant with Abraham, Isaac and Jacob, and he has contested the sovereignty of Pharaoh over his world. He has entered Israel's story mysteriously, as a voice speaking from a burning bush; as an angel appearing, yet not seen (3:1–6). He has come as One who is known as God of the patriarchs. Yet his name is unknown, and its meaning cannot be pinned down—"I am who I am; I will be what I will be" (3:14). It is not so much a name as a statement of intent, suggesting freedom of choice and unhindered power beyond all human power to contain, to objectify, and to control.

The Battle of the Gods and the Ten Commandments

That is indeed how the story of the Exodus works out. By the time that we reach the foot of Mount Sinai and hear the commandments, we have read of an almighty, cosmic battle between the god of Egypt and the God of the burning bush. The battle proves beyond doubt that what is assumed of the God of Abraham in the opening chapters is indeed true—that we are dealing here with the only true God, who has ultimate power over both creation and history, and that other gods are not truly gods at all, albeit that they are often regarded as such. Ten plagues suffice to make the point that God who has addressed Moses, and not Pharaoh or any other Egyptian god, is God of fertility and blessing, and in the end God of life and death (note 12:12). The events at the Sea confirm his identity, as creation is replayed in the divine control of the watery chaos and the divine judgment on the forces of darkness, and all God's enemies are dismissed as the Spirit-wind sweeps across the earth (cf. Gen 1:1–10 and Exod 14:21–29). God who promised to deliver his people from the Egyptians—to shape history in terms of his own will, rather than permit it to be shaped by Egyptian gods (Exod 3:7–12)—has proved able to deliver on his promises, for he is the true and living God who creates and redeems and blesses.

The people of God were thus first formed in the midst of a battle between gods; between God and the gods. It is of little surprise, then, as they and we arrive at Mount Sinai to hear from God what it means to be his people—to receive the ten "words" of the desert, in place of the ten plagues of Egypt—that the first and most fundamental theme should be that of true worship. "I am the LORD your God, who brought you out of the land of Egypt, out of the house of slavery": the reality of the redeemer God confronts them, along with the reality of their previous condition when governed by a god who inflicted upon them brutality, exploitation and death. "You shall have no other gods before me" is the central imperative of the whole encounter. Other gods exist who vie for Israel's loyalty; but Israel is to remain true to what she has discovered about God (or rather, what God has "uncovered" to Israel), and not to prefer other gods to the living God. "You shall not make for yourself an idol, or any likeness of what is in heaven above or on the earth beneath or in the water under the earth. You shall not worship them or serve them." With these words the focus moves to an associated matter, the construction of representations of deity for the purposes of worship. And then a particular reason for the opening commandments, grounded in the character of the redeeming God, is provided: "For I, the LORD your God, am a jealous God." God is intolerant of rivals, and will not allow any other god beside him, nor indeed any threat to those who worship him (which is why Israel's enemies are sometimes objects of God's jealous wrath, e.g. Nah 1:2–3; Zeph 1:18). He is jealous of his right to be worshipped exclusively.

Walter Brueggemann nicely sums up the significance of the first three commandments:

> The first three commands ... assert the oddity of Yahweh, who has no utilitarian value and who cannot be recruited or used for any social or human agenda. The God who commands Israel is an end to be honored and obeyed, and not a means to be used and exploited. If it is correct ... that an imageless quality is Yahweh's distinctive characteristic, then we may see in the prohibition of images an assertion of the unfettered character of Yahweh, who will not be captured, contained, assigned or managed by anyone or anything, for any purpose.[2]

The first three commandments are not unconnected, of course, to the remaining seven, for our vision of God is always related to our vision of humanness and society. God, who will not be treated as an object to be exploited, demands that we do not treat our neighbor as such.

God, who insists on being addressed as "Thou" rather than "It," and will not allow himself to be grasped and seized by mortal beings, also insists that we do not disregard our neighbor as a person and sets limits on our grasping and seizing of what that neighbor needs. The Sabbath is the central symbol of the difference between the good society ordained by God and the oppressive society ordained by the gods. For the world created by God has at its heart a seventh day of rest, in which there is space for all creatures to remember that life is more than work, and the universe more than an object to be manipulated in pursuit of gain. The world of Pharaoh, on the other hand, is one in which there is no rest but only feverish productivity (Exod 1–2). As Brueggemann once again rightly observes, the Sabbath command looks to "a human community ... peaceably engaged in neighbor-respecting life that is not madly engaged in production and consumption, but one that knows a limit to such activity and so has at the center of its life an enactment of peaceableness that bespeaks the settled rule of Yahweh." We are presented with an "alternative to the exploitative ways of the world that begin in self-serving idolatry and end in destructive covetousness."[3]

The vision of God involves a vision of society; the worship of God involves a particular view of social relations.[4] The interconnectedness of these things is a fundamental assumption of the Old Testament writers, which explains why the worship of the gods is connected so frequently in Old Testament tradition with a false view of society and of social relations, and indeed with social breakdown, injustice and bloodshed. Worship and ethics are but two sides of the same coin, so far as the Old Testament is concerned. The best narrative example of this connectedness is surely 1 Kings 21, where the abandonment of God inevitably leads on to the abandonment of righteousness. In a society given over to idol-worship, covetousness leads on to false testimony, murder and theft. Abrogation of the opening commandments leads on to abrogation of various of the later ones as well.

The Nature of Idolatry

Already implicit in this discussion of Exodus 20 is a particular view of what idolatry is. It is not the mere representation of God in terms of created things in the sky, on the earth, or in the sea—although such representation is indeed considered intrinsically problematic and as bound to lead people astray (e.g. Deut 4:15–19), since God cannot be represented by any created thing (with a single exception, to which we shall return). More than this, idolatry is the worship of any gods in the place of the living God, for these gods are themselves, of necessity, creatures and not God—creations of God, misused in attracting excessive devotion or trust from mortal beings, or creations of the human imagination. The gods themselves are idols from a biblical point of view. As 1 Chronicles 16:25–26 puts it: "For great is the Lord, and greatly to be praised; He is to be revered above all gods. For all the gods of the peoples are idols, but the Lord made the heavens" (cf. Deut 32:16–21; 1 Chr 10:9; Isa 45:20–21; 48:5 for the same connection between gods and idols). At root, idolatry is about blurring or obscuring the distinction between the living God who creates and the creation that he has created.

Old Testament texts address the matter in various ways, reflecting the variety of ways in which the blurring or obscuring can or might occur. Often the emphasis falls on the representations of gods themselves, assailed and mocked along with those who are foolish enough to worship artifacts that they themselves have created (e.g. Isa 44:9–20; Jer 10:1–10; Hos 13:2). Idols are mute, dumb entities, like scarecrows in a field (Jer 10:5); they have no breath in them (Jer 10:14). They are merely the work of human hands—wood and stone (Deut 4:28;

28:64; 2 Kgs 19:18; Ezek 20:32; Dan 5:23), silver and gold (Isa 2:20). To worship them is folly beyond reason. Sometimes the emphasis falls on the spiritual powers themselves that the physical artifacts of wood and stone represent. Whether these be truly existent powers or merely imagined ones, their power to seduce and to corrupt is recognized. Thus Hosea speaks of the "spirit of whoredom" that has led Israel astray in her idolatry (Hos 4:12; 5:4), and Zechariah suggestively juxtaposes "idols" with "unclean spirit" (Zech 13:2). The paradox of idols is that, though they are simply creatures of no ultimate power in themselves, yet they become powerful when they are worshipped as gods and they represent a doorway to spiritual corruption. The apostle Paul captures the paradox well in 1 Corinthians 8:4 and 10:20, when he first affirms that no idol really exists, and that the many so-called gods and lords are not really so, only later to acknowledge that idolatry invokes genuinely existing, albeit demonic, spiritual forces. This link between demons and the "gods" of the Old Testament is also suggested elsewhere in the New Testament.[5]

Sometimes, finally, emphasis falls on the way that the distinction between God and creation can be blurred or obscured by inappropriate human devotion to or dependence on other human beings. Ezekiel 16:1–34, for example, provides us with a graphic and disturbing metaphorical account of Israel's history as the LORD God's "wife," who turned to adultery with Egypt, Assyria, and Chaldea. Here the most common and well-developed metaphor in the Old Testament for idolatry—the metaphor of sexual unfaithfulness to a husband—is apparently employed in connection with political alliances with other nations. Idolatry itself is sexual sin in a book like Hosea, albeit already linked with the question of which "lover" more successfully satisfies the material needs of his wife (e.g. Hos 2:1–13). In the background probably lie the claims of Canaanite fertility gods and goddesses to guarantee the fecundity of the earth, and the ritualistic fertility practices associated with their worship. Ezekiel uses this metaphor in respect not only of material well-being but also of political security. A similar idea may be found in Jeremiah 2:1–3:5 (esp. v. 18), and it is certainly found in a passage like Isaiah 31:1–3, where it is clear that military reliance on Egypt is akin to abandoning the true God and treating the Egyptians as if they were divine, leading to the reminder, "the Egyptians are human, and not God" (v. 3). Egypt in particular often appears in the Old Testament as a place of both economic and political/military temptation for the people of God. It is a richly fertile and very powerful country to which the Israelites characteristically wish to return (e.g. Exod 14:10–12; 16:2–3, ironically, in view of their recent oppression there), and which they are often tempted to imitate (e.g. Deut 17:14–20). Above all, Egypt embodies the temptation to turn to idolatrous superpowers rather than to God in times of trouble (e.g. Isa 30:1–5; Jer 42–43; Ezek 23). This is a blurring of the line between God and creation, suggestive that the claims of Pharaoh to divinity are true after all and that the Exodus was a mistake.

Idolatry, then, is more than merely the practice of a certain type of ritualistic religion. It is a matter of the whole orientation of a person's (or nation's) being, as it impinges on social, economic and political life. The living God is not to be confused with any creature; the unseen God who speaks from the fire cannot therefore in general be represented by any created thing. That is why biblical tradition knows of an ark of the covenant that is the divine king's footstool and cherubim that are his throne, but does not know of any representation of God himself. That is why biblical tradition sets its face against the religion of so many historical Israelites, who did not share the biblical authors' perspective on what true worship entailed. That is why biblical tradition is so careful, when faced with misunderstandings about the precise significance of religious symbols in ancient Israel, to ensure that we know that the misunderstandings were dealt with (e.g. 1 Sam 4–6, where the ark is carried onto the battlefield in much the same way that an idol would have been [note the Philistines' reaction in 4:7–8] in an attempt to ensure victory; and 2 Kgs 18:4, where the serpent Nehushtan has evidently become an object of devotion).

The Image of God

It is in the light of all this voluminous material insisting upon the distinction between God and creation, however, that we must now consider a remarkable fact. The Old Testament does allow one exception to its general objection to God being imaged in something that is created. It allows that human beings, male and female, are created in the image and likeness of God (Gen 1:26–27) and are granted authority to rule over creation as representatives of God. The Hebrew word is *ṣelem*—precisely the word used of the representations of the gods in Numbers 33:52, Amos 5:26, 2 Kings 11:18, and Ezekiel 7:20; 23:14. It is, however, not simply Genesis 1 that presents the creation of humankind in a way that evokes the construction of idols. Genesis 2 is also narrated in a suggestive way. The human creature Adam is formed from the ground (*'ădamah*), out of the clay, and shaped and fashioned by God, who then breathes the breath of life into his creation and sets it in a garden by a river. The echoes of other ancient Near Eastern texts abound, in which we read about representations of the gods endowed with life by the priests, informed by them that they were to join Ea, father of the gods, in celestial splendor, and led forth by them to a garden by the river to symbolize their new power; or about kings who set up their images in far-flung reaches of their empires to symbolize their ownership of territory and their authority over it.

The biblical religious tradition is resolutely aniconic (i.e. lacks "icons" or images used in worship). Even linguistic representation of God is handled with great caution, lest the impression be given that God might be fully captured in human language. (Note, e.g., the complex and tortured description of God in Ezek 1, especially vv. 26–28, as the prophet strives to avoid telling us what was "there," resorting instead to accumulated similitudes.) But, even though resolutely aniconic, we find the astonishing claim in it that human beings represent God, are made in his image and likeness. Psalm 8 famously picks up the theme without using precisely the same vocabulary: human beings are made "a little lower than God" and are crowned with the two divine attributes of glory and honor (Ps 8:5; cf. Ps 96:1–9, precisely in a passage that contrasts the true God with idols!). If there is some created thing that can image God, then, it is the human being—not an inanimate object, and not just any animate creature either, but one who is set apart from the rest of creation:

> Against the canopy of space and the topography of earth—beating, swarming and lumbering with fertile and fantastic life—Adam stands in unique relationship with God … No stone or wood chiseled into a godling's image, "the Adam" in two … is an animated, walking, talking and relating mediation of the essence, will and work of the sovereign creator God. As living image of the living God, Adam bears a relationship to God like that of child to parent.[6]

An awesome dignity is thus ascribed to humankind in the opening chapters of Genesis; however, it is the source, not only of great wonderment (as expressed in Ps 8), but also of powerful temptation. Here we come to the final aspect of idolatry—and surely the fundamental one—that must be mentioned in any review of the Old Testament treatment of this theme. We must reckon, at the heart of the human condition, with the worship of the self. Genesis 3 describes its inception and its progress. The human eye is first distracted from the true reality of God's character (Gen 3:1). It is suggested, and believed, that God is not after all generously "for" his creatures ("you may freely eat of every tree," 2:15–16), but rather unreasonably restrictive of their freedom ("Did God say, you shall not eat of any tree?" 3:1). The temptation is to take control of the situation and to fulfill human potential in doing so. Delegated, representative divinity is not enough when the real thing is at hand ("you will be like God," 3:5). Thus the fruit of the tree is taken, as the human pair seek to grasp equality with God by becoming autonomous moral beings. Essentially they have come to believe that the image of God in human beings is something to be worshipped rather than to be received as a gift and used for service. They engage in self-worship, in pursuit of self-advancement.

The Old Testament is replete with other examples of this idolatry of the self. It is something found in particular among foreign kings and emperors, whose official ideologies, as we know from various ancient Near Eastern sources, characteristically blurred any distinction between themselves and the gods. A well-known example is provided by the Assyrian king Assur-Nasir-Pal:

> And now at the commands of the great gods, my sovereignty, my dominion, and my power, are manifesting themselves: I am regal, I am lordly, I am exalted, I am mighty, I am honored, I am glorified, I am preeminent, I am powerful, I am valiant, I am lion-brave, and I am heroic. (I), Assur-Nasir-Pal,

the mighty king, the king of Assyria, chosen of Sin, favourite of Anu, beloved of Adad, mighty one among the gods.[7]

Aside from the Exodus material already mentioned, notable biblical passages touching on the theme include Isaiah 14:3–21, 2 Kings 18:17–19:37, Ezekiel 28:1–10 and Daniel 3–4. Isaiah 14 exults over the downfall of the king of Babylon, one who said in his heart, "I will ascend to heaven; I will raise my throne above the stars of God; ... I will make myself like the Most High" (vv. 13–14). Second Kings 18–19 presents us with an Assyrian emperor, Sennacherib, who suggests that the LORD God cannot deliver Jerusalem because he is merely one of many powerless gods (18:33–35), and a deceitful one at that (19:10), while portraying himself (Sennacherib) as the true provider of material blessings and life itself, and indeed as the provider of a new Exodus for Israel to a "promised land" (18:31–32; cf. Deut 8:7–9). Invited to turn his back on his deceitful and powerless god, and so save himself from the fate of all those other kings who went to their doom clinging to their idols, Hezekiah of Judah offers a memorable prayer (19:14–19) in which it is reaffirmed that the God enthroned between the cherubim, who has taken Israel for his special people, is not merely one god among many, but God alone. That all earthly kingdoms should know the difference between God and the gods, Hezekiah asks that Jerusalem be delivered from the Assyrian's hand. Isaiah's reply (19:21–34) makes clear just how much exception the living God takes to Sennacherib's pretensions to divinity.

Ezekiel 28:1–10 addresses the prince of Tyre, who has said, "I am a god; I sit in the seat of the gods, in the heart of the seas" (v. 2), but in reality is mortal and destined to die at the hands of foreigners because of his pride (cf. Ps 82). Finally, Daniel 3–4 tells us of Nebuchadnezzar of Babylon—a king who imagines that he has, in defeating Judah, defeated Judah's God, and symbolically places his vessels from the Jerusalem temple in the treasury of his gods (Dan 1:1–3). His sense of godlike control is revealed in his construction of a massive golden image on the plain of Dura, and in the subsequent demand for political and religious allegiance (Dan 3). Three Jewish exiles refuse to bow down, intent on avoiding confusion between an idol and the living God. After their escape from royal power, Nebuchadnezzar himself receives an object lesson in reality (Dan 4), as he is cut down while flourishing, driven out among the animals, and made to eat grass for seven "times," until he realizes the truth of his existence as king: that Heaven rules (v. 26).

It is doubtless because of this tendency among foreign kings and states to self-divinization that Deuteronomy 17:14–20 instructs Israel in respect of her own kingship that the king should not be a foreigner, should not imitate foreigners, and should have constant recourse to the law of Moses lest he forget that he rules under God. The temptation to be like the other nations was, after all, a strong one (1 Sam 8), the temptation to make "might ... their god" (Hab 1:11).

The Destructiveness of Idolatry

In all the material that we have reviewed so far, there is a powerful sense, not only of the fundamental wrongness of idolatry, but also of its enormous destructiveness. It is not only that the worship of the creation rather than the Creator is an affront to God and a perversion of the true nature of things, although it is both. It is also that in worshipping idols rather than God we mortals do damage to ourselves, to each other, and to the world in which we live. To turn from God to idols is to embrace a lie—a lie about how things are. The serpent speaks in Genesis 3 with a forked tongue. He promises that in turning away from the living God the human pair's eyes will be opened, and they are—but only to see that they are naked. He promises that they will become like God, and they do—but it is very much to their disadvantage, as they are excluded from the tree of life, as good as dead. Their half-step towards divinity brings only alienation and separation from God, for they have believed a lie (cf. also Amos 2:4; Hos 4:12).

The consequences are profound, for alienation from God and the worship of false gods brings in its wake a loss of any true sense of what it means to be a human being. We are fated always to become like that which we worship, as our moral and religious compass swings to its magnetic pole. To go after false idols is to become false (2 Kgs 17:15); to worship the works of human hands is to become like them (Ps 115:8). When we forget who God truly is, it is but a short step to forgetting who we are and who our neighbor is. It is inevitable, from a biblical perspective, that a disintegration and a dehumanization take place in the aftermath of a departure from the one God who alone gives us both an integration point, as we worship him with all our heart and soul and might (Deut 6:4–5), and a proper sense of who we are.

The book of Genesis pictures the process for us, as the human pair, created to be one flesh, naked but not ashamed (2:24–25), are found divided, at odds with each other, and concealed from each other (3:7). Chapter 4 tells us of the alienation of brother from brother, accompanied by death and exile, and of neighbor from neighbor. Even humankind's many achievements of culture in his knowledgeable adulthood cannot disguise the slow but remorseless breakdown of community (4:17–22). Sophistication and technological expertise increase. There is cultural excellence in the arts, but sophistication, expertise, and excellence are quite compatible with barbarism in a world that shuts the living God outside.

The book of Daniel presents this world to us even more graphically as one that is governed by beasts. It is a world turned upside down, in which the dominion that human beings should exercise over the animals (Gen 1:26–30) is currently being exercised by beastly world empires that ravage and destroy it (e.g. Dan 7). The idolatry of the self has been transposed into the idolatry of the state. We are very far away, now, from the society produced by true worship as described in Exod 20. In this world of beasts, indeed, to live the life of the true worshipper is ultimately impossible without spectacular divine intervention (Dan 3, 6), for the blood of the righteous is regularly spilt in such a world (cf. the constant emphasis on the link between idolatry and bloodshed, e.g. 1 Kgs 21:17–26; 2 Kgs 17:15–17; 21:1–9, 16). The various psalms of lament in the Psalter also speak to this theme, as they represent the enemies of the psalmist as wild animals and describe the dehumanizing effects on the suffering righteous (e.g. Ps 22, esp. vv. 6, 12–13, 16, 20–21). The figure of Nebuchadnezzar in Daniel represents, it is true, the possibility of a turn from idolatry to true worship among the beasts of this present age. He, thinking himself a god, becomes a beast for a while in order to learn what it means to be a man (Dan 4:25). When his reason returns to him as a man, he worships the Most High God (4:34–37). There is the possibility of transformation, even in the present, in response to the prayers of God's people that the nations should be judged before God so that they should "know that they are only human" (Ps 9:19–20). Yet there is also a stark recognition in the book of Daniel that universal transformation will not take place until beastly rule passes away and is replaced by the human rule of the future—when one "like a human being" will come with the clouds of heaven and receive a dominion that is everlasting and shall not pass away (Dan 7:13–14).

Idolatry has drastic consequences for human beings and for the creation they are supposed to govern and care for on behalf of the Creator. The exaltation of the created as the divine, the making of the gods in the image of men and women or animals, the substitution of anything at all that is less than God for God, relying on it in place of God—all this can only lead to disaster. We hope as idolaters for freedom and the fulfillment of our potential, for gains in wealth and power and happiness. The world of idols is, however, a world of demonic oppression and confounded hopes that robs and disables, dehumanizes and destroys. This is why idolatry, like sin in general in the Old Testament, is often described not so much as the infraction of a divine commandment, as the committing of an act of cosmic insanity. "Even the stork in the heavens knows its times, and the turtledove, swallow and crane observe the time of their coming"; but Israel, apparently, is too stupid to know when the time has come to repent of idolatry (Jer. 8:7). "The ox knows its owner, and the donkey its master's crib"; but Israel in her perversity does not know the living God (Isa 1:3). God's appeal to his people is to reason it all out (Isa 1:18)—to come to their senses. It is not by accident that it is when Nebuchadnezzar's reason returns to him that he praises God, recognizing that "all his works are truth, and his ways are justice" (Dan 4:37). The first lie of the serpent goes deep, however, and reason is not easy to come by. The living God remains for the most part on the outside of human life, therefore, throughout biblical tradition, while the idols are firmly established within. As the apostle Paul puts it most aptly in Rom 1:18–32, the embrace of the lie leads to the darkening of the mind, which in turns leads to idolatry and all kinds of wickedness. The depth of the human tragedy is that we are, it seems, quite incapable even of enlightened self-interest. We cannot see that false gods that cannot create, or bless, or love, or redeem, can do us no good. Nor can we see that God, in jealously and fiercely opposing idols, and indeed any attempt to make the created into the divine, is actively pursuing our good.

The Idols of the Modern World

Idolatry is, of course, not simply a matter of ancient history. It is, on the contrary, alive and well and living in North America. It is part of the culture, it is present in the Church, and it is deeply rooted in our individual hearts. If its presence is not perceived, it is only because the central myths of our culture, which Christians themselves often internalize quite uncritically, do not *allow* for its existence. We live in a society that commonly prides itself on being secular, in which, as David Lyon says, "the warp and woof of social life contains little explicit reference to religion (at least as conventionally defined), and is held together only by rational contract and bureaucratic rules."[8] Secular outlooks and practices largely dominate the realms of business, government, education, and so on; life is routinely understood without the benefit of explicit religious interpretation, at least in public space. Indeed most people for most of each day are expected to conform themselves to "criteria which have no religious sanction and which may in fact be inimical to Christian teaching and practice,"[9] such as efficiency, productivity and profitability.

Idolatry cannot in principle exist in the secular society; for the secular society has no God at its heart whose reality makes other objects of worship into idols. It is their daily Christian participation in such society, in all its overwhelming public self-evidentness, that no doubt renders idols at least partially invisible even to Christian individuals who worship the living God in their private lives, and to Christian congregations who hold onto God in the marginalized space that is left by modernity to religious groups and institutions. For idolatry does, of course, exist *in fact* in the so-called secular society. Secularization has a constant, ever-present companion, named by sociologists as sacralization—the development by which "people, things, events and processes are bestowed with 'sacred' status, even as the tide of Christian influence ebbs from Western societies."[10] It is a new name for a very old reality.

Nation and State

Sacralization is the process by which created things become central to life, invoking religious-like awe and submission, and modern society has produced any number of examples of it. We may begin, as Lyon himself does, with the concepts of state and nation. The modern state has taken to itself the sacred status once reserved for monarchs. Its citizens have often looked to it as the provider and ordainer of their lives, and have gladly made sacrifices of themselves to it. The nation, in whose interest the state often claims to act, has had a similar status, and has throughout the nineteenth and twentieth centuries called for the sacrifice of self and others in pursuit of its interests. Religion itself has frequently been co-opted to help invest both nation and state with a sacred quality. Even in countries officially atheist, like the Soviet Union, to do one's duty as a patriot was to perform a sacred task. As Hegel once put it, "the State is the march of God through the world"; and many others have implied as much, in their advocacy of politics as the only means of redemption available to us, and in their justification, in terms of necessary sacrifice, of all the bloodshed and oppression that such idolatry has produced.[11]

The state in such thinking ceases to be a gift from God, but becomes instead an idol that supplies us with all blessings, and to which we look for the fulfillment of our many material needs. Christian thinking about such matters, in contrast, begins with the separation of the creation from the Creator, of human rule from divine rule; with the remembrance of Pharaoh, Sennacherib, and Nebuchadnezzar; and with the radical idea of Jesus that there is a distinction between those things that may rightly be rendered unto Caesar and those things that may not (Matt 22:21; cf. Acts 5:27–32). Conscious resistance to the rhetoric of the state's mythmakers is perhaps the first step towards clearing our heads sufficiently that we can think and reason as Christians, rather than simply as North Americans,[12] and come to accurate perception of the idols of power.

Money and Material Possessions

A second and related object of sacralization is money and the material possessions to which it gives access. Here we confront the idols of mammon (Matt 6:24)—the idolatrous elevation of money and material things, which leads on to sins such as covetousness (named as a form of idolatry in Eph 5:5; Col 3:5). Karl Marx assailed this idolatry in these terms:

> Money is the Jealous God of Israel before whom no other god may exist ... Money is the general, self-sufficient value of everything. Hence it has robbed the whole world, the human world as well as nature, of its proper worth. Money is the alienated essence of man's labor and life, and this alien essence dominates him as he worships it.[13]

Yet it is not only the capitalist economic system attacked by Marx that has idolatry at its heart, and so dehumanizes what is human. In truth, modern economic ideologies ranging across the entire political spectrum have at their core a utopianism which promises ever-increasing material prosperity. They all buy into the myth of progress via economic growth, facilitated by science and technology as means of control. Beneath the economic systems in themselves, as different as they may be in their strategies for reaching utopia, lies fundamental agreement that utopia exists, and that its essence is material wellbeing. As Herbert Schlossberg puts it, "materialism, coupled with the productivity of machinery and electronics, has brought us the universal expectation of More."[14] Set in opposition to this approach to life are numerous biblical texts, of which a few are these: "One's life does not consist in the abundance of possessions" (Luke 12:15); "keep your lives free from the love of money, and be content with what you have" (Heb 13:5); and "a love of money is a root of all kinds of evil" (1 Tim 6:10). The Christian view of the world does not make economics coterminous with life (the Sabbath is one great symbol of this truth), nor does it confuse wealth with moral worth, nor promote greed as a virtue. It certainly does not consider creation as humanity's own possession, to be endlessly manipulated and exploited in its own interest, but rather as the possession of the Creator, who allows us to look after it for a while and to enjoy his blessing in doing so. As Schlossberg again notes, this biblical view of wealth "seems odd only because we have adopted as normal a way of life that is hopelessly unable to produce what it promises and has demonstrated that inability to almost everyone."[15] In fact, it is the worship of the idol that is "odd," indeed insane, when one realizes that it cannot deliver well-being, but only mars human life in its often oppressive demands on our time and energy as workers, and in its production within us of unrest and discontent. Destruction is the end of such worship; for "insatiable greed placing infinite claims on finite resources can have no other end."[16]

Perhaps the first step towards defiance of the idols of mammon is once again conscious resistance to rhetoric and mythmaking—on this occasion, the rhetoric of advertisers, in whose world "mundane products take on magical powers and promise to shape new character, reinforcing the primal subtext of capitalism: one is what one owns/consumes."[17]

Human Sexuality

A third object of sacralization is human sexuality. As in the case of devotion to power and money, devotion to sexual activity is not exactly an unprecedented feature of human behaviour. The *Babylonian Talmud* already suggests that this was the real reason for the otherwise incomprehensible Israelite worship of nonexistent gods: "Rabbi Judah said in the name of Rav, 'The Israelites knew that the idols were nonentities, and they engaged in idolatry only in order to allow themselves to perform forbidden sexual relations publicly'" (*b. Sanh.* 63b). The apostle Paul similarly links abandonment of the true God to illicit sexual activity in particular, before moving on to other consequential sins (Rom 1:18–32). In the modern period, with the erosion of the Christian worldview and the advances in technology that have allowed the widespread and fairly reliable severing of sex from procreation, sexual expression has become at the same time a common leisure activity and "a crucial element in the autonomous individual's quest for self-fulfillment"[18]—a means of liberation and the attainment of meaning. The repression of sexual feelings is widely believed to be an innately bad thing. The acting out of those feelings in harmony with nature is thought to be one of the absolutely necessary prerequisites of the happy and fulfilled life. The quest allows for the dissolution of whichever social ties inhibit it, the sacrifice of whatever stands in its way, and it insists on the acquisition of ever more esoteric knowledge in pursuit of the ultimately ecstatic experience.

Anyone who doubts that sex is religion in our culture need only spend a few moments perusing the magazines at the supermarket exit, or watching any one of our daytime chat shows on television. The best recent film evidence is provided by the movie *Pleasantville*. A black and white sitcom based around a 1950s American town is infiltrated by two modern teenagers, one of whom proceeds to set the inhabitants of the town "free" from their captivity and to give them color, largely through seduction and the dissemination of information about sex. The lie is a powerful one, constantly insisted upon in our visual media in particular, and blinding to the reality, which is that sex as an idol is just as destructive as any other, bringing people into self-absorbed captivity and inflicting colossal, ruinous damage both on individuals and society at large. Christian thinking about sexual expression begins in a different place, understanding it as a gift of God to those who are bound in lifelong covenant commitment to one another, as God himself is bound to his people. Sex is not religion, and ultimate meaning and significance are not found in sexual expression, but in relationship to God and neighbor, which embraces sexual expression as only one tiny, if wonderful, aspect.

The Idolatry of the Self

One could go on for pages enumerating and exploring the various aspects of idolatry in modern society, but space forbids.[19] It only remains at this point to underline the fact that the fundamental idolatry described by the Bible lies also at the heart of the varied modern idolatries: the idolatry of the self. The self is set at the center of existence as a god; ultimate significance is found in godlike individual autonomy, self-set goals and boundaries. The sacred is defined in the first instance in relation to the self. The shadow of Nietzsche looms large. Self-expression and self-actualization are important themes in this religion and evident in every corner of society, from the advice columns of newspapers and magazines through to schools, in which sometimes the point no longer seems to be to learn things but to "find oneself" and to be the best person that one can be. We are constantly urged, in fact, to believe in ourselves and to better ourselves—in our individual choices and actions, and in accordance with our personal ambition, to make and to remake ourselves in our own image, or in some other human image of perfection. We are invited to pursue the body beautiful, to take control of our personal health and fitness, to invent our own value and belief systems, with a view to gaining personal fulfillment. We are given ever-increasing permission to ignore and if necessary to dispense with whatever and whoever stands in our way in this quest, be it life in the womb, children, husbands and wives, the poor, foreigners, or the aged. The destiny and direction of whole nations has come to rest at election time on the "feel-good" factor in the population at large. Production of good feelings about the self, unrelated to any moral framework, has apparently become one of the ultimate goals of society, if the behaviour of many politicians, teachers, and psychologists is any measure of this.[20]

The cult of self-worship is in good health as the twentieth century comes to a close, and is perhaps more widely practiced, indeed, than at any point in its long and distinguished history.[21] Yet it is a destructive way of being. As Lyon remarks, "having the autonomous self as the sacred center of cultural gravity extorts a heavy price in competitiveness, isolation and rootlessness."[22] There is no larger story in which the individual story can be located and comprehended, no larger moral universe in which the moral being can find direction, purpose and fellowship, and indeed in which moral evil can be inhibited and restrained. There is only a constant striving to live out a lie—the lie that all things lie within our grasp, if only we reach far enough and wide enough, and with sufficient advice and technique—and the constant disappointment and despair, and devastation wrought on others, that accompanies our failure. The narcissistic society is not the good society, but a deeply dysfunctional and wicked one. Idols cannot liberate; they bring only oppression. Christian thinking begins, on the other hand, with a larger story than the individual story, and with a much larger moral universe that has the only true God at its center, whose worship is perfect freedom—including freedom from the need to believe that we are gods, and that we possess the power to attain salvation by our own exertions.

The Iconoclastic Imperative

The old gods are still with us. They have simply changed their clothes so that they merge more easily into the modern crowd. They still claim to provide meaning to life, to explain the universe, and to provide the basis for personal security. They still demand wholehearted commitment from their worshippers. Christians ought to be free of them; for a truly Christian view of the world provides the basis for such freedom:

> Christian freedoms stems from the separation of the creation and Creator; from the repudiation of a demiurge that binds man to the ground of his being; from the rejection of determinisms and the affirmation of responsibility; and from the limitations on Caesar, the declaration that he is a creature, and the removal of the divine status that he continually seeks to acquire.[23]

Indeed, Christian faith can only be true to itself if it is iconoclastic—if it is actively involved in the unmasking of idols. The Church

> partakes in the real, continuing historical struggle against the baals, the false deities, the mythological personifications of the forces of nature or of the nation ... The mythological deities, which claim men's belief and worship and service, today have different names—Life-Force, *Volk*, Progress, Dialectical Process, and so on [we might add here, "the Free Market"]—but they are just as real, or as unreal, as the gods of the nations of the Fertile Crescent ... Christian faith continues the struggle against mythology, against the secular myths that men have set up, believing vainly in their power to realize the golden future which they predict. The witness of history shows that they are but idols, powerless to save.[24]

Four things should be said about the Christian and iconoclasm as we move towards the close of this paper.

A Dangerous Game

First, the unmasking of idols will always be received badly by society at large. People do not appreciate it when things that they hold to be sacred, gods that they revere, are portrayed as and persuasively argued to be mere creatures of the worshipper, lacking in substance and benefit, or (worse) the conduits of demonic power. To threaten the position of the gods is to threaten the security of the worshipper, as the apostle Paul found out in Ephesus (Acts 19:23–41); and this will inevitably cause "no little disturbance ... concerning the Way" (19:23). In a society that has come to think of the individual himself as a god, to dispute another person's interpretation of the universe and the ethics that follow from it has come to be regarded as tantamount to blasphemy. False gods cannot be named as such, for truth is only ever personal. If it is true for me, then who are you to say otherwise? To set out to unmask idols will only ever bring pain, then, especially in a culture that has learned to tolerate a very wide range of things, but remains highly intolerant of truth claims. One person's idolatry is always another person's worship, one person's abomination always another's god.

A Noble Venture

Yet secondly, the unmasking of idols is clearly a good thing, and an expression at its best only of our love for our neighbor as well as for the true God. For if idolatry is the investment of trust and hope in that which is unworthy of them and incapable of rewarding them, and will in the short or long term only destroy the worshipper and her community or society, then it can hardly be moral behaviour to refuse to tell the truth of the matter. Only a culture that has elevated tolerance above goodness and love could possibly believe this. The unmasking of idols is not simply a Christian duty because of our love for the true God, who alone is worthy of our religious devotion. It is also a Christian duty because of our love for those who do not worship the true God, but only those things which are entirely unworthy of such devotion:

> The fight of faith to which we are committed is not a fight against man. It is not a question of destroying him, of convincing him that he is wrong. It is a fight for his freedom. Reinserted into a sacred, a prisoner of his myths, he is completely alienated in his neoreligions—this brave "modern man." Every religion is both necessary and alienating. To smash these idols, to desacralize these mysteries, to assert the

falseness of these religions is to undertake the one, finally indispensable liberation of the person of our times.[25]

On Beginning at Home

Thirdly, if Christian iconoclasm is to have any integrity, and indeed to approach the non-Christian world with an attitude of humility and love rather than one of arrogance and imperialism—for we are not called to be imperialists any more than relativists—then it must begin at home. There must be a frank admission that the people of God have themselves always shown a propensity to idolatry, almost from the moment of their creation, whether in their desire to construct images (Exod 32:1–6) or to return to Egypt (Exod 14:10–14; 16:1–3; etc.). We have always possessed a memory of idolatry's oppression that is notoriously short. Paul warns the church in Corinth not to imitate these ancestors (1 Cor 10:1–14), and John concludes his first letter with this admonition: "Little children, keep yourself from idols" (1 John 5:21). Yet only a moment's reflection will persuade us of the many ways in which the Christian Church is caught up in the idolatries of the moment in North America.

The nation state is very close to many a Christian heart in this part of the world, for example; faith, flag and country are closely identified with each other. Among those who are more prone to sanctify the nation than the state—and who often actually demonize the state—work and family often become dominating idols. Economic performance is seen, within the Church as much as outside it, as a very important measure of individual and societal worth, and the health, happiness, and security of the nuclear family is assumed to be an ultimate good that justifies all human enterprise, including the acquisition and disposal of material resources. It is arguable, indeed, that it is above all love of the nuclear family that fuels the fires of materialism in the West, including Western Christians, among whom materialism is rampant.[26] Capitalism is often routinely baptized as self-evidently Christian, and other economic systems routinely excommunicated as not. Belief in endless progress, facilitated by scientific and technological control and sound management principles, abounds. So deeply internalized is this thinking that modern Christians sometimes find it all too natural to think of the Church itself in terms of business and management models—planning growth, programming success, and managing change.[27] The professionalization of ministry is one obvious aspect of this importation into the Christian worldview of modern secular thinking—the pastor as chief executive officer of the company, trained as an expert in problem-solving and management, and thus gaining respectability in a world and in a church that no longer thinks in a truly Christian way, even about the church.[28]

The fact of the matter is, then, that the Church itself often displays before the world, not true religion, but only a lightly Christianized version of the world's own most deeply held prejudices about the nature of reality. Idols are established within the temple, and chief among them is the self. Do you want to "find yourself" and to be the best person that you can be? Come to Jesus! Do you covet the feel-good factor? Come to Jesus! Do you desire personal health and fitness, success in business, more effective therapy than your last analyst offered you? Ditto. The Church can be found in North America in as many forms as there are consumers to make demands of it. The narcissistic Church has developed to meet the narcissistic culture, and the two have become great friends. God is constructed in the human image, a pale reflection of our sad, self-absorbed selves, and a panacea for all our perceived problems. If Christian iconoclasm is to have any integrity, it must begin at home. The idols of religion and of the religious must be cast down, before the idolatry of the culture can be addressed.[29]

On Beginning with the Self

With regard to the self as it thus encounters religion, some wise words from Martin Buber are relevant:

> A modern philosopher supposes that every man necessarily believes either in God or in "idols," that is, in some sort of finite good—his nation, his art, power, knowledge, the amassing of money, the "ever new subjugation of women"—which has become for him an absolute value and has set itself up between him and God; it is only necessary to demonstrate to him the conditioned nature of this good, in order to "shatter" the idol, and the diverted religious act will automatically return to the fitting object. This conception presupposes that man's relation to the finite goods he has "idolized" is of the same nature as his relation to God, and differs only in its object: for only with this presupposition could the mere substitution of the true for the false object save the erring man. But a man's relation to the "special something" that usurps the throne of the supreme value of his life, and supplants eternity, rests always on experiencing and using an *It*, a thing, an object of enjoyment. For only this kind of relation can bar the view to God—it is the impenetrable world of *It*; but the relation which involves the saying of the *Thou* opens up this view ever anew. He who is dominated by the idol that he wishes to win, to hold, and to keep—possessed by a desire for possession—has no way to God but that of turning, which is a change not only of goal but also of the nature of his movement. The man who is possessed is saved by being

wakened and educated to solidarity of relation, not by being led in his state of possession towards God. If a man remains in this state what does it mean when he calls no longer on the name of a demon or of a being demonically distorted for him, but on the name of God? ... Do you suppose that the man to whom the nation is a god, in whose service he would like to enlist everything (for in the nation's image he exalts his own image), need only be given a feeling of disgust—and he would see the truth? And what does it mean that a man is said to treat money, embodied non-being, "as if it were God?" What has the lust of grabbing and of laying up treasure in common with the joy in the presence of the Present One? Can the servant of Mammon say Thou to his money? And how is he to behave towards God when he does not understand how to say Thou? He cannot serve two masters—not even one after the other; he must first learn to serve in a different way. He who has been converted by this substitution of object now "holds" a phantom that he calls God. But God, the eternal presence, does not permit Himself to be held. Woe to the man so possessed that he thinks he possesses God![30]

There is little point in inveighing against the idols of Church and culture if we are not prepared to face the very personal reality of idolatry as it touches the question of our own place in the universe. All other idols may pass away, but if we ourselves stand yet at the center of things, we are idolaters still, and all we touch turns to idolatrous gold. Buber rightly notes, then, that the heart of the matter, so far as the abolition of idolatry is concerned, is the transformation of the human heart, so that it "learns to serve differently." In Christian terms, there must be an individual turning to the Father "from whom are all things and for whom we exist" (1 Cor 8:6); to the Son who is the only perfect image of the invisible God, through whom are all things and through whom we exist (Col 1:15; 1 Cor 8:6); and to the Spirit, who guides us into all truth (John 16:13). It is in bowing before the true God, in all God's freedom, and in acknowledging reality (in particular, that we cannot "possess" or control the living God), that idols begin truly to be displaced. It is in acknowledging the centrality of the ultimate icon, the Son of Man Jesus, to human history and to our individual history that God's image in us begins to be restored and other images begin to fade:

> It is necessary, if we are going to truly live a Christian life, and not just use the word Christian to disguise our narcissistic and promethean attempts at spirituality without worshipping God and without being addressed by God, it is necessary to return to Square One and adore God and listen to God. Given our sin-damaged memories that render us vulnerable to every latest edition of journalistic spirituality, daily reorientation in the truth revealed in Jesus and attested in Scripture is required. And given our ancient predisposition for reducing every scrap of divine revelation that we come across into a piece of moral/spiritual technology that we can use to get on in the world, and eventually to get on without God, a daily return to a condition of not-knowing and non-achievement is required.[31]

Indeed so. Amen.

12

ON "SEEING" THE TREES WHILE MISSING THE FOREST: THE WISDOM OF CHARACTERS AND READERS IN 2 SAMUEL AND 1 KINGS

The year 2000 saw the publication of a Festschrift in honor of Professor Ron Clements, who was in charge of the university department in which I found my first academic appointment, as a temporary lecturer at King's College, London. Ron was an incredibly supportive senior colleague at that stage in my career, and I shall always be grateful to him for helping to launch me on an upward trajectory—not least by giving me my first post-Ph.D.-thesis book contract (a commentary on Lamentations in the New Century Bible series). I was delighted, then, to be able to write this essay for his Festschrift, returning to an area of long-term interest for me: how far does traditional historical-critical endeavor help us to read Old Testament narrative texts well, and how far does it hinder us from doing so? The reader will notice, when comparing this essay to the first, found in chapter one, that a decade of thinking about this question "from the inside" (as it were) had by this point led me to some fairly serious (and here strongly stated) doubts about the usefulness of historical-critical hypotheses regarding the "original" shape of biblical texts—although not at all to doubts about the importance of reading texts with attention to their historicality. She will also notice re-emerging here my (associated) long-term interest in epistemology: how do we know things? This essay was based on my inaugural professorial lecture at Regent College, as the first footnote in the original location indicates.[1]

It is one of the more remarkable features of human behavior that we are often to be found believing things beyond all reason and in the face of impressive evidence to the contrary. We recognize the reality readily enough in the case of the "end-times" specialist who continues to believe that the end is nigh, even though he has been wrong on all 47 previous occasions that he has prophesied it. We scoff, indeed, at the political enthusiast who maintains that his party's program will usher in Utopia, in spite of the evidence of all previous periods in power. We even possess a sophisticated vocabulary with which to describe such a phenomenon, whereby belief is not readily swayed by counter-evidence, nor apt to be awed by mere facts. Psychologists refer to "cognitive dissonance." Sociologists, thinking more corporately, write of the "sociology of knowledge"—the way in which we know what we know in community, reinforcing each other's point of view and understanding of the world more by what we *assume* than by what we *argue* to be true, and creating an atmosphere in which dissent seems unimaginable, where a difference of perspective is named "mental illness" or even "sin." Human beings knew all about this phenomenon, however, long before the rise of the social sciences, and communicated this knowledge through stories. They told, for example, of the emperor and his new clothes: of the emperor, vain and gullible enough to think himself resplendent, when in fact he is parading through the streets of the city naked; of the crowd, their sense of self and security bound up with the king, unwilling to rock the royal boat by allowing their minds to register what their eyes are seeing; and of the child in his integrity and innocence, puzzled by the madness that he sees around him, and foolish enough to state the obvious. The emperor has no clothes! We are, as this story reminds us, resolutely tribal beings. We live in groups; we know things as part of a tradition; we are apt to get swept along in crowds. Without the still, small voice to alert us to our self-deception, we are prone to perish in groups as well, charging lemming-like over the cliffs of history, muttering, as we hit the water, "but everyone else believed it too."

As in life, so we find in biblical scholarship the same "mob momentum" that tends to sweep everyone along with it, making direction and purpose seem inevitable, a matter almost of destiny. It happens at both ends of the theological spectrum. It is a feature of the kind of conservative scholarship that tends to confuse its own traditional understanding of the truth with the truth itself, seeing no possibility of a distinction between these two things, and marginalizing all dissent. It is a feature, likewise, of the kind of non-conservative scholarship that, with a magician's sleight of hand, turns the tentative outcomes of intellectual inquiry into "the assured results of scholarship," beyond doubt and question, and likewise marginalizes dissent. The latter case is particularly interesting, involving as it usually does an appeal to "consensus" (a term generally preferred over "crowd mentality"). The word implies agreement about objective fact among a variety of free-thinking individuals who have studied the matter in depth, without prejudice or preconception, and now pronounce themselves satisfied that the matter is really so. Yet the reality is that all learning is inevitably guided by conscious or subconscious expectations; that all knowledge is modification of previous knowledge; that everyone stands in a tradition while doing their supposedly "free" thinking. In other words, in spite of the rhetoric of the Enlightenment that opposes reason and tradition, biblical scholars—like everyone else—are all still governed and led by tradition even as they reason. They know as part of group, part of a crowd, they are inducted into that particular crowd's reading tradition, and it is from that basis that they may (or may not) go on then to think their own thoughts. Consensus may not in reality be the *result* of the exercise of free thought by individual scholars at all, so much as something that exists *before* freedom of thought is ever conceived of. It is the consensus of the crowd watching the naked emperor.

The history of non-conservative biblical scholarship over the past 150 years illustrates this reality. Relatively few scholars have dared to distance themselves entirely from such great originators of tradition as Wellhausen or Gunkel or the like, preferring to bow in their direction even if their feet are at the same time moving off on their own path. When individuals have made moves that tend to undermine the authority of these giants, the broader community of scholars has often managed, by acts of quite remarkable cognitive dissonance, to ignore the individual contribution, and to go on articulating the truth of the interpretative tradition in any case. They may adjust it a little here and there; they may absorb this or that detail into it; but they are most reluctant to believe that any modern thinker can actually *replace* the apostles and saints of the nineteenth and early twentieth centuries. It is one thing, after all, to allow sparrows and swallows in under the roof of the scholarly temple. It is another thing to allow moles in under the foundations. The consequence, at the extreme, is that theories are held in blatant contradiction to the facts, or at least with little or no grounding in evidence—interpretative paradigms that survive on the faith of the community that believes in their veracity, and on little else.

To put this in another way: just as crowd mentality in general can disable people from seeing clearly the reality of the *world* that truly exists, so also crowd mentality in biblical scholarship in particular can disable readers from seeing clearly the reality of the *text* that truly exists. There may be a missing of the forest due to over-concentration on the trees. This general argument might be supported with any number of particular cases from the history of biblical interpretation, and could be directed against all varieties of readers. The example chosen for consideration here, however, is a particular 20th century reading tradition in regard to 2 Samuel and 1 Kings—the tradition that places at the center of its concern a "Succession" or "Court Narrative" and a "Deuteronomistic History." Both hypotheses have had their share of criticism, some of it quite fundamental criticism, over the course of the years since they were first articulated, yet both they, and the reading tradition that rests upon them, survive. This endurance, I believe, has much more to do with the faith of the community of readers than with anything else; and indeed, the reading that this faith produces is in my view deeply flawed. The text itself is in fact not clearly seen at all, for attention is focused elsewhere, and in the wrong place.

Sources and Redaction in Samuel–Kings

To begin with the hypotheses themselves:[2] where does the imagined Succession Narrative end? Does it end in 1 Kings 1–2, and if it does, has the ending been adjusted by pro-Solomonic redactors in order to whitewash Solomon and perhaps David? This view has indeed been advocated. Alternatives have also been advanced, however. Is the entire work as it stands anti-Solomonic, and perhaps anti-Davidic as well? Where, in either case, does the document begin? Can it really begin with 2 Samuel 9, when David's request for survivors of the house of Saul in that chapter presupposes the death of Ishbosheth in the opening chapters of 2 Samuel? Then again, can it really begin even with 2 Samuel 2, when other aspects of the story in chapters 9–20 presuppose, not only the stories of Ishbosheth and Abner, but also the story of David as far back as 1 Samuel 18–20? Moreover, is it really a "Succession Narrative" at all, whether in its shorter or longer form? The difficulties with this label are well known, even if they have not prevented many from continuing to refer to the hypothetical work in this way. Not the least of the problems is that the legitimate successor around whom the story allegedly revolves (Solomon) is a shadowy figure at best in the book of Samuel, and emphatically the product of the adulterous relationship between David and Bathsheba; and that 1 Kings 1 (even if part of the document) provides no clear signal to the reader of his legitimacy. Are we dealing, then, with a "Court History," beginning perhaps in 2 Samuel 13? The question then arises, of course, as to whether 2 Samuel 13–20 is any more viable as a self-contained document than the others suggested, particularly given these chapters' links with passages elsewhere in Samuel.

So the discussion goes on. It might have been supposed that by this stage there should be some general feeling of unease about a method of dealing with our texts that could produce such wildly disparate accounts of their origin and meaning, but this is apparently not the case. As Gillian Keys has recently observed, Rost's thesis has dominated scholarly thinking on 2 Samuel for some time now, and even though his ideas have been challenged and questioned, as she reminds us, "they still form the pivotal point of every argument." It was Rost who, as she puts it, "*authoritatively* established the view that 2 Samuel 9–20 and 1 Kings 1–2 was a single literary unit."[3] That is to say, people may disagree about this or that aspect of Rost's thesis, and cumulatively this may add up to the questioning of the whole idea, but somehow the thesis survives as the baseline from which the discussion moves on, the presentation of the matter that sets the parameters. We cannot agree on where this hypothetical source document behind our text begins, or where it ends, or even what it is really about. We do not know who wrote it, or anything about the circumstances of its production. But we all "know" that it exists, that there is a "literary unit" there somewhere, for we have been told authoritatively that it is so. It is part of the fundamental structure of our community discourse, and apparently beyond criticism. Thus it is that even when quite authoritative little boys or girls point at the emperor and cry "naked," their voices are apt to go unheard. As long ago as 1981, for example, Peter Ackroyd wondered aloud whether the Succession Narrative hypothesis was in danger of becoming an article of faith for the crowd—a matter of "critical orthodoxy." His conclusion is worth quoting:

> If our reading and response are to be with fullest effect, we must not be hindered by restrictions imposed by artificial and hypothetical categorizing of the text; and one such may appear to have been the supposition that there is an identifiable unit to be described as the 'succession narrative,' when, in reality, such a unit is to be seen rather as the product of too narrow reading and too great a desire to find uniformity where there is in reality diversity and richness. A less rigid reading may open up a wider perspective.[4]

In spite of this, and in spite of a broad sea change in the Academy in our approach to Hebrew narrative texts that might have been expected to allow the less rigid reading of which Ackroyd speaks, we have not in fact seen a general move away from such thinking about "units of text" such as he describes here. There has been no general move towards a more holistic approach, in which 2 Samuel 9–20 and 1 Kings 1–2, for example, are thought of simply as "a part of the story of David and

Solomon," and no further label is attached to them. There has been no general move away from the neat simplicities of redactional theory and towards the treatment of the text as a complex unity, the ambiguities in the text about David or Solomon taken as cues for interpretation of the text as we find it rather than for holy war among redaction critics.[5] The paradigm survives, more or less intact.[6] We still see the publication of dissertations such as that written by Keys, for example, which take issue with Rost only in the end to offer yet another modification of his theory.[7] I cite this example not in any sense to blame Keys: graduate students have to play by the rules of the game in which they find themselves. I cite it to illustrate rather that old rules still apply, and that orthodoxy is (as ever) resilient in the face of criticism. It does not need to face criticism, indeed, so long as it can keep on producing disciples who know the creed.

What of the Deuteronomistic History? Here too we are dealing with a work whose existence is characteristically simply presupposed, as if we all just "knew" of its existence—as if it were currently sitting in a library somewhere and could be compared with the biblical texts that we actually possess. The novice simply would not guess from reading scholarly work in this area that we have to do here with an intellectual construct rather than a solid reality. Nor would she guess the extent to which the construct is so vulnerable to critical scrutiny. Yet there is no agreement in this case, either, as to the original extent of this hypothetical work. Was it perhaps originally a pre-exilic work, reaching only as far as Hezekiah or Josiah? Might it rather have been an exilic work, taking in the whole story from Deuteronomy to the fall of Jerusalem? Discussions about the coherence (or not) of its theology are interminable—discussions forced upon the perceptive reader by the evident fact that particular books of the so-called History tend to display much greater theological subtlety and complexity than any description of "standard" Deuteronomistic theology ever captures. In the manner of pre-Copernican astronomy, wildly improbable solutions are then proposed for this problem, involving differing groups of Deuteronomists with differing perspectives reworking the text within a few years of each other, rather in the manner of pro- and anti-Solomonic redactors.

All this contributes to our difficulty in talking about "Deuteronomists" even moderately coherently. Why should we assume that such people existed at all? The answer, seemingly, is that the biblical texts imply as much, since they have been shaped by a relatively uniform ideological perspective on the world that has some connection with Deuteronomy. But is there not evidence in the texts, in fact, that the ideological perspectives therein are not entirely uniform, and sometimes far from being so? Then, the reply comes, the textual evidence is to be disregarded, or at most it is to be understood as implying that the Deuteronomists had broad interests and worked over a long period of time. It is worth reflecting on just how seriously one ought to take such a selective approach to what the texts "imply." It is also worth asking just how broad "Deuteronomistic interests" can be before the idea of "Deuteronomists" begins to lose any coherent sense. It is certainly important to note the extreme difficulty that scholars have had when they have tried to put any flesh on these skeletal and shadowy figures who are said to lie behind books like Kings and to be so crucial to their understanding. Some say Levites or priests; some, prophets; some, the wise men of the Jerusalem court. "Who do *you* say that they are?" seems the next reasonable and biblical question. All of the above, perhaps? A "Deuteronomistic School" to which people of varying traditions belonged? At this point, however, the question sharpens as to whether the Deuteronomistic Hypothesis is being kept alive more by the faith of the scholarly community than by the quality of the arguments. It is, after all, very difficult to know what to make of a "school" that seems to have no unified ideological perspective and no plausible social location. Is the hypothesis, then, the presupposition of scholarly inquiry or its result? Is it *necessary* to posit "Deuteronomists" with a "Deuteronomistic theology" at all, when thinking about the Former Prophets? And yet the paradigm continues unscathed. The enduring hold which the Deuteronomistic theory retains on scholarship is well demonstrated in the fact that even among scholars who are now more interested in reading the Old Testament books in their final form (which is presumably, on any theory of composition, a *post-Deuteronomistic* form) than in speculating about the history of their composition, terms like "Deuteronomistic theology" and "Deuteronomistic History" should still be so widely used. It seems that the construct, once embedded in the mind, is difficult to dislodge.

Both the "Deuteronomistic History hypothesis" and the "Succession Narrative hypothesis" thus seem strangely immune from the many and varied criticisms to which they have been subjected, apparently having the capacity endlessly to change shape without in general giving rise to the suspicion that they are not the same entities as they were when their scholarly journeys began. Perhaps it is because of the respect in which the founding fathers, Noth and Rost, are held—authority figures of great stature, and the sort of people whose perspectives must be validated if we are not to feel generally insecure about our modern tradition of reading. Whatever the reason, the community continues simply to "know" that it makes sense to talk of a Succession Narrative or something like it, and to speak of a Deuteronomistic History. All the criticism of the past decades has made little difference to this "knowledge." It is the wisdom that the reader brings to the text. Presupposed, unquestioned, it is simply "there." It survives even where those same readers know in part or all of their minds that it is unlikely to correspond to reality.

One's assessment as to whether any of this matters will depend upon one's beliefs about texts and about truth. We are no longer living in times in which everyone believes that texts have meanings independent of their readers or that truth exists "out there" to be grasped. It is possible in these times, confronted by the tale of the emperor, to object to the suggestion that the crowd had a problem. Perhaps some of them sincerely did think that the emperor was wearing clothes. If so, that is all that matters—that they had a perspective, and it was sincerely held as their own. Perhaps it is true that many of the crowd knew that he was naked; but even then, we could not say that they were wrong to act as they did. Did the crowd not have the right to react to the king as they did, forbidding reality to impinge on their community values or interfere with their fun? On this kind of view, there would be no sense to any critique of scholarship in terms of dogged persistence in a particular perspective in the absence of, or contrary to, evidence. If biblical scholarship is mainly about playing with texts and making a living and a reputation out of them where we can, then my observations thus far are beside the point. Assuming, however, that most readers of this paper still imagine that truth does matter and that there is more to reading than shaping the text in our own image, I can continue. My assertion is this: that the reading that the faith described above produces in respect of Samuel–Kings is deeply flawed. The commitment to and focus upon hypothetical entities behind the text, and the filtering of the textual data through that lens, have disabled readers from seeing what the actual text that exists is saying. The "trees" of scholarly theory, which although only constructs are clearly "seen" by the reader, in fact lead to blindness with regard to the complex forest of the text as it exists. In the remainder of this paper, I should like to illustrate that this is so by referring to one overarching theme in 2 Samuel and 1 Kings that has clearly received insufficiently perceptive treatment among scholars—precisely because, I believe, theories about composition have so dominated in the readers' minds that they have been unable or unwilling to see the theme clearly. To return to Ackroyd, we have been "hindered by restrictions imposed by artificial and hypothetical categorizing of the text," and this has resulted in a "too narrow reading [of the text] ... a too great a desire to find uniformity where there is in reality diversity and richness." A less rigid reading, I suggest, "opens up a wider perspective."

Having alluded to the questionable wisdom that readers have brought *to* the text, then, I now turn to the wisdom of the characters *in* the text, wishing to suggest that in reality the question "what is wisdom and who possesses it?" is one that dominates 2 Samuel 13–1 Kings 11.[8] I shall conclude by suggesting that the coherence that is thus found in 2 Samuel and 1 Kings, once a particular interpretative paradigm regarding the history of the text is set aside and the text is read in itself, in turn provides us with further reason to question whether that paradigm corresponds to the reality. In short, I shall be arguing that hypothesizing in terms of a "Deuteronomistic History" or a "Succession Narrative" is not only unhelpful in reading Samuel–Kings, but in fact that reading Samuel–Kings in the first instance without reference to these hypotheses itself renders them even less plausible than they were to begin with. The coherence of the picture that emerges is itself evidence against the idea of a self-contained Succession Narrative, and indeed against any narrow notion of what Deuteronomistic theology might have been.

The Wisdom Theme in 2 Samuel and 1 Kings

It is one of many extraordinary aspects of exegetical work on the book of Kings in the last fifty years that exegetes, on the whole, have shown themselves quite unwilling to read the first 11 chapters as if they followed each other consecutively. They have been unwilling in particular to do the obvious and read chapter 3 as if it followed chapter 2. The reason is clear enough: most scholars "know" that these chapters do not belong together, because they "know" about the compositional history of the text. "Knowing" this, they tend to think of 1 Kings 1–2 as providing an ending and 1 Kings 3 as representing a fresh beginning.[9] This perception lies at the root then of what we might call the dominant perception of Solomon's reign in Kings. It is a reign usually divided into two fairly self-contained parts: an earlier period, in which Solomon was obedient to God and was blessed by God; and a later period, in which he was disobedient to God and God's judgment fell upon him. A further step in the process is then to criticize this representation of Solomon as being artificial and schematic, and indeed simplistic theologically. We thus move by degrees from a theory about the genesis of the text to a particular reading of the text that leads on to critical judgments on the text. What are we to make of this line of argument?

The Wisdom of Solomon

I have argued elsewhere,[10] and I shall not repeat it at length here, that the popular reading of Solomon I have just described in fact represents an entirely shallow understanding of the Solomon story. The Solomon of many exegetes has little to do with the Solomon of the biblical text. The Solomon of the *text* is a king who, even at the zenith of blessing, invites divine cursing in various ways—a questionable character right from the beginning of his reign. Here we must note in particular the obvious textual fact that Kings does not present Solomon's reign as beginning in 1 Kings 3, as modern scholarship characteristically does, but rather as beginning in 1 Kings 2:12. It is in chapter 2 that we read of the early days of the reign, during which Solomon enacts the advice of his father David and rids himself of his enemies; and here we come to our first consideration of the wisdom theme in Samuel–Kings. David urges Solomon to "act according to his wisdom" in getting rid of Joab son of Zeruiah (v. 6), and he refers to this wisdom again in advocating the removal of Shimei son of Gera (v. 9). The emphasis is upon subtlety: Solomon must not act rashly, but use his brain, and find some justification for removing these people from the scene. The word used for wisdom is, however, Heb. *ḥokmah*, exactly as in chapter 3 and elsewhere in the Solomon story. Its usage here, in a chapter that is highly ambiguous about the rights and wrongs of the executions and banishments described in it, raising questions both about the quality of the wisdom that is being described and about the character of David and his successor, must surely influence our understanding of its usage later.

Read in this context, 1 Kings 3 clearly presents Solomon as a king aware of the deficiency of his previous wisdom, and addressing God about this fact. The emphasis of the whole section 3:4–15 falls upon wisdom as a supernatural gift from God, rather than as something that is innate (as it is implicitly in chapter 2), or acquired by patient hard work, utilizing careful observation and self-discipline (as it is explicitly in much of Proverbs and in 1 Kgs 4:29–34).[11] It is wisdom from above, not below. A "wise and discerning heart" is granted by God, which will enable Solomon to govern his people and to distinguish between right and wrong (3:9)—a veiled allusion to the events of chapter 2 by a God who expresses pleasure that the king has not sought long life, wealth, nor the death of his enemies (3:10–11), and then grants him long life and wealth but specifically not the death of enemies (3:13–14). The whole implication is that Solomon has recognized, and that God is confirming, that the "wisdom" of chapter 2 was of a highly unenlightened, self-serving kind that must now be replaced with a higher wisdom in order that the king may rule justly and well over his subjects (3:9, 11). The fear of the LORD is truly the beginning of wisdom (as elsewhere in the Old Testament, e.g. Job 28:28; Ps 111:10; Prov 15:33). The latter part of chapter 3 then illustrates the difference that the new wisdom makes, as Solomon uses his sword, not for arguably unjust executions, but to threaten execution in order to achieve justice. The glory of Solomon's wisdom is then further celebrated in 1 Kings 4, with questions asked about it in chapters 9–10, just before the collapse into apostasy in chapter 11. Ultimately, the Solomon story, from chapters 2–11, is exploring these questions: what is the source and the nature of true wisdom, and can wisdom truly be wisdom that does not issue in obedience to divine Torah? I believe that this is quite easily seen, once we are dealing with the text as we have it rather than with hypothetical entities of dubious extent and nature that may once have lain behind it. It is only such theorizing, and associated theorizing about the Deuteronomists and their theology, that has disabled us from seeing the reality. Our inherited expectations about the extent of the text and the theology of its authors have led us off the right track. Such theorizing has had, among others, this consequence: that it has produced a two-dimensional Solomon vastly less interesting and colorful than the Solomon who actually inhabits the text in all his complexity and ambiguity—the Solomon of the scholar rather than the Solomon of the artist.

As 1 Kings 3–11 has its immediate and proper background in 1 Kings 2, so the entire Solomon story of 1 Kings 2–11 has its own background in the David story that precedes it. Here, too, we find the wisdom theme explored, as part of a presentation of King David that likewise portrays him as an ambiguous and complex character from whom the reader is invited to learn. And here too, theory *about* the text has disabled perceptive reading *of* the text.

We begin in 1 Kings 1. Here we find the king from whom Solomon takes his first example—a dying king, now out of touch with reality, now fully in control, with a curiously ambivalent attitude toward oaths and a selective memory. The chapter opens with the story of David and Abishag—a beautiful woman whom we are told David does not "know" sexually. The days in which David took possession of Bathsheba are now far behind; and Adonijah sees his chance, in the midst of the king's impotence, to gain power. David's lack of knowledge is not confined to the matter of sex, however. As the chapter progresses we discover that he is also lacking in knowledge about Adonijah's coup. Verse 18 has Bathsheba herself, whom David had clearly "known," addressing him thus: "Adonijah has become king, and you my lord the king, do not *know* about it." We ourselves need to know the preceding story to get the whole point here. This is the king, apparently, who had previously had the reputation of possessing "wisdom like that of the angel of God [to know] everything that happens in the land/on the earth"—at least that is what the wise woman of 2 Samuel 14 has to say (v. 20). A declining king indeed, who now does not "know" things or people, even though they live in his own house! We are thus directed still further back in our story, if we wish to discover the full extent of our wisdom theme—to the wisdom of David that provides the background for the description of the wisdom of his son. What manner of wisdom is this?

The Wisdom of David

In exploring this question we are by no means lacking in already existing resources, upon which I shall now in turn build in outlining the overall picture as I see it.[12] It has been noted before that one of the themes that runs throughout 2 Samuel 9–20 and 1 Kings 1–2 is that "the role of the king involves a keen discernment that helps him judge between good and evil ... almost a superhuman knowledge like that of the angel of God."[13] This is a theme that comes before the reader again in 1 Kings 3, as Solomon's endowment with divine wisdom is put to the test in the case of the two mothers who claim the one child. The David who responds to the challenge to display such wisdom in 2 Samuel is a complex character, like his son—a king for whose interpretation the reader himself feels in need of divine wisdom, plumbing the depths of David's actions and his motivations. How are we to explain his actions and words when his first son by Bathsheba dies, or his inaction in the case of the rape of Tamar? The narrative leaves such matters unclear. What *is* clear, however, is that David after 2 Samuel 11–12 is a divided man with a divided family, who in the later years of his reign fosters division in his kingdom in pursuit of power, foreshadowing in his own person the divided kingdom of his grandson's day. What kind of wisdom is it that produces the results that are the story of David in 2 Samuel 13–20? Is David truly a wise man? Or are the words of the wise woman of Tekoa that I just cited simple flattery, more evocative of Davidic ideology than of Davidic reality?

Several features of chapter 14 certainly give us further pause for thought. For one thing, it is the *woman* who is clearly in control of the situation, manipulating the king so that he moves by stages to the place in which she needs him to be. David, allegedly possessing the wisdom of a messenger of God, does not even get to first base when confronted by this wise messenger of Joab, who disarms him through disguise and deception, shocks him with direct speech, and finally praises him, in order to give him the chance to get over the painful surprise.[14] Even though David has previously suffered a similar manipulation through story at the hands of Nathan in 2 Samuel 12, he has not the first idea where the woman's story is leading, and he is caught in the same trap—slow learner more than swift-comprehending angel. His sole moment of insight in the story is the stunning deduction in verse 19 that perhaps Joab might be involved somewhere in the affair—a response which must raise a smile in the reader who has followed the speeches of the woman to this point, in all their depth, and eloquence, and artistry. "Speak," says David in verse 12, and the wise woman weaves her spell. "Speak," says the woman in verse 18; and David, befogged and confessing that she knows much more than he, offers his dim perception of reality in the midst of illusion. It is for this amazing feat of discernment that David is then lauded by the woman for possessing divine wisdom. We are justified in asking whether we should take her words as ironic,[15] particularly in view of two other factors. First, the woman's double comparison of David to an angel recalls two other texts. Both the Philistine Achish (1 Sam 29:9) and later the Saulide Mephibosheth (2 Sam 19:27) make similar statements to David. In both cases these statements by characters in the narrative are undermined by the narrative itself. David is not as angel-white as Achish thinks, nor is angelic wisdom much in evidence in the king's erratic decisions about Saul's property. He fails to discover whether it is Ziba or Mephibosheth who is lying, and contents himself with dividing Saul's estates between them—effectively *dividing* between good and evil, rather than *divining* between good and evil, as Solomon later manages (1 Kgs 3).[16] In context, the words of the Tekoan woman in 2 Samuel 14 thus indeed sound with "unavoidably ironic tones. All three situations underline in various ways how far off the mark are such servile statements about David, who is either a deceiver or a dupe at the point in the story when such comparisons are made ... David only *appears* to be wise 'like … a messenger of God.'"[17]

A second factor influencing our reading here is what has just happened in chapter 13. For the woman from Tekoa is not the only wise person to appear in the story as a foil to David. In chapter 13 we have met Jonadab, Amnon's friend: a wise man, anxious to help this son of the king who, like his father, desires to possess a woman. He, too, contrives a story for David. He knows only too well how to manipulate the allegedly all-knowing king; and his plan to facilitate the rape of Tamar duly succeeds. At the end of the chapter, too, Jonadab reappears as someone who again knows vastly more than David about what is going on in David's own kingdom. David simply believes what he is told: Absalom has killed all the king's sons. Jonadab knows differently: only Amnon is dead. How he knows is never made clear: perhaps his wisdom partly resides in knowing when to stick with his friends, and when to keep quiet about plots to have them murdered. The main point is this, however: that David knows nowhere near as much in these stories as the other wise people around him. His ignorance here foreshadows his ignorance in 1 Kings 1, when he is unaware of what is happening at the feast of another of his sons. By the same token, Jonadab's manipulation of the king foreshadows the manipulation in 1 Kings 1 by Nathan and Bathsheba, both of whom "know" of a Davidic oath from the past that the biblical narrator does not otherwise mention, and manage to convince David to remember it too.[18]

Fokkelman has summed up quite excellently the movement of the narrative in 2 Samuel 13–14. A combination of illusion and reality holds the texts in this section of the book together:

> The illusion: David thinks that he is visiting an ailing Amnon, that he is sending his sons to a feast, and that he is

hearing a widow pleading for her son. The reality: Amnon, full of energy, is on the way to gratifying his sexual appetite, Absalom kills his brother, and Joab tries to arrange a reconciliation.[19]

As Fokkelman goes on to suggest, David, blinded by his ego, repudiates the unity of life and people, dividing Bathsheba from Uriah, divorcing himself from God, dividing his family against itself. From that point onwards the world that is presented to him becomes steadily less reliable, fragmented, and difficult to put together. As David has abused people around him mercilessly, now he is abused. His sons manipulate him, using him for their own crimes.[20] Yet David knows little throughout of what is really happening.

The play on the nature of wisdom and who possesses it does not stop with 2 Samuel 14. The theme of "the overturning of the king's counsel" is central to chapters 15–17, the story of the decline of Ahithophel forming a meditation on the divine destruction of human plans.[21] In both the stories in 2 Samuel–1 Kings, in fact, in which the king's counsellors are central figures during crucial turns in the monarchy, the particular counsel chosen by the king leads to disaster for that king—Absalom here in Samuel, and Rehoboam in 1 Kings 12.[22] What is striking about 2 Samuel 16–17 in particular is first of all the remarkable statement in 16:23 that both David and Absalom (but not the narrator) regarded the counsel of Ahithophel as equivalent to a word from God. The narrator himself at first appears to lend some weight to the equivalence of Ahithophel and a prophetic oracle, since Ahithophel's advice to Absalom in 16:21 leads on to the fulfillment of Nathan's prediction of 12:11 about David's wives. It becomes clear in 17:14, however, that Absalom and David are guilty of a misperception, for God is perfectly well prepared to frustrate even the good counsel of Ahithophel in order to carry out his plans. Indeed, the very point appears to be this: "whether good or bad, wise or foolish, merely human advice lacks the providential status and epistemological guarantees that result from seeking out or inquiring of the LORD."[23] The way the story is told makes it clear that it is indeed to be the word of God, and not the counsel of men, that carries out God's curse upon the house of David. Human wisdom, of itself, is not up to the task.

We follow our theme, finally, into 2 Samuel 18–20. We have already met Ziba and Mephibosheth, but here we also meet Barzillai—someone who refuses David's offer of patronage because of his great age, and the fact (among others) that he is unable to tell the difference between good and evil (19:35). It may be that this is at one level simply a statement about his inability to enjoy life at the royal court. It is difficult in the context of the story as we have read it, however, not also to see in Barzillai's words the implication that service in the royal court, as an extension of the crown, involves the keen discernment claimed for David earlier in the story,[24] and that old age does not necessarily bring improvement to this ability to discern that kings and their courtiers require. It is this sad reality that 1 Kings 1 goes on to illustrate with its picture of the aged David, never very *good* at discerning things, now utterly *unable* to do it. We are thus faced with the irony that Barzillai, in questioning his own ability to discern and in refusing a place at court, shows considerably more wisdom than the aged David, still on the throne yet unable to know anything of what is around him. It is perhaps no surprise in this context that it is not even his own wisdom that David eventually deploys on his death bed, when advising Solomon to deal decisively with his enemies. David had never proved himself so decisive. This is very much wisdom learned from someone else—the last wise person mentioned in 2 Samuel, and the last foil to the wise king David. I refer to the wise woman from Abel beth-maacah in 2 Samuel 20, who saves her city by having the rebel Sheba executed. The political wisdom that David requires of his son is the wisdom of this resourceful woman, much more than it is the wisdom of the angel of God. It is the wisdom also of the doomed counsellor Ahithophel in 2 Samuel 17—the wisdom that seeks blessing through the death of the enemy—rather than the wisdom of 1 Kings 3, which looks for better ways of governing the people.

A Questionable Wisdom

What manner of wisdom is this wisdom of David, then, that provides the background for the description of the wisdom of Solomon? It is a highly questionable kind of wisdom, I believe. It is not just the waning David of 1 Kings 1–2 who does not know good and evil, and who hands on a dubious view of wisdom to his son. The David of the entire preceding Samuel narrative is a king whose mind is darkened as he lives his life under divine judgment, "under the curse."[25] Under these circumstances his wisdom is of no avail as he faces his troubles. He is no match for Jonadab or the Tekoan woman, he comes off badly in comparison to Barzillai, and he fails to convince us of his wisdom in regard to Saul's family. On the one occasion in the story that the failure of another's wisdom redounds to David's advantage, the narrator pointedly tells us that it was not David who truly engineered it, but God.[26] It is not that we are to think, of course, that the wisdom of the other characters in the story is necessarily beyond question either. The wisdom that in 2 Samuel 13 facilitates rape, or that in chapter 14 eases Absalom's return and rebellion, or that in chapters 16–17 advocates the humiliation or execution of David—this is not intended to be wisdom of which the reader should think well. It is not just Davidic wisdom that is under a cloud in 2 Samuel, therefore, but the very notion of human wisdom *at all*, as it seeks to function in independence of the divine will.

The whole David story from 2 Samuel 12 onwards therefore helps to prepare us for Solomon's vision at Gibeon in 1 Kings 3 and what comes afterwards. If one way of looking at the David story of the latter part of 2 Samuel is to see it as the tale of a king divided against himself because he is divided from God, and therefore fostering division in his family and his land; then one way of looking at the beginning of the Solomon story is to see it as the tale of a king putting his father's later example behind him, learning once again what it is to be a man after God's own heart, and being able therefore to govern a united kingdom once again with justice. If the theme of 2 Samuel 9–1 Kings 2 is "that which has been divided cannot be reunited, unless one has the wisdom of the angel of Yhwh,"[27] then Solomon's early and later reigns *both* illustrate that truth. The early Solomon illustrates it positively and the later Solomon negatively; for it is as the later Solomon himself forgets that the fear of the Lord is the beginning of wisdom—that wisdom can only truly be wise when it springs from worship and obedience—that the kingdom is once more divided. Solomon, like his father, begins under divine blessing and ends under divine curse. I would therefore want to affirm these words of Ackerman, near the end of his article: "The Court History is a critique of the wisdom of the wise."[28] It is important, however, to make this qualification: that in the light of the Kings sequel to Samuel, we can see that it is in fact a critique of a *particular* sort of wisdom only—wisdom that is not rooted in God and the divine Torah. We find the same two wisdoms, of course, in the New Testament, and a similar critique of one and praise of the other. There is wisdom from below that is vain philosophy, and there is wisdom from above that we must embrace if we are to think and act in accordance with the divine will.

Conclusion

It is to my mind fairly evident that 2 Samuel–1 Kings as a whole text addresses the theme of wisdom in much the way I have described it. It is only inherited assumptions brought to the text without much reflection from outside it that are capable of dulling our wits sufficiently to miss the point. It is because these assumptions have been so widely held, indeed, that the kind of holistic reading of the wisdom theme in both Samuel and Kings that I have attempted here has not generally been pursued, even though various scholars over the years have touched in different ways on the theme in Samuel in offering revisions of Rost's position. The Rost paradigm had already set boundaries in their minds as to what their task should be. It is also quite clear, in my view, that the sort of cross-referencing and allusion that we find throughout this section of text, as the authors invite us through the way in which they tell the story to ponder a particular section of text in the light of the whole, is in fact a feature of the entire David and Solomon story, and beyond that of the whole narrative of the Former Prophets. If this is so, and the level of interwovenness of our narrative texts is thus vastly greater than was ever suspected by traditional source or redaction critics, then it can readily be seen how the very constructs that have rendered readers just as blind as David to the reality around them will increasingly come under pressure. If it was difficult enough under the old rules of the game to talk convincingly about a Succession Narrative or a Court History, partly because Rost's claims (and indeed other claims after him) about the self-contained nature of his literary unit could not be sustained, how much more difficult will it continue to be under the new. That is not to say that the attempt will not be made; for the power of the constructs themselves, and the will of the crowd to believe in them, or at least to use words that imply that they do, should not be underestimated.[29] It would be comforting to think that the time must surely come when exegetes begin to question whether it is worth holding on to words and concepts that have long since lost their meaning—and that indeed run the risk of distorting their reading of the text—just because they happen to be words and concepts found in the official dictionary of critical orthodoxy. If I really thought this, however, I would surely be guilty of the naïveté of the boy who thought he saw the emperor clearly, when he was merely under-educated in the sociology of knowledge.

13

THE TERRORS OF THE NIGHT:
LOVE, SEX, AND POWER IN SONG OF SONGS 3

It was not just the Clements Festschrift described above (chapter twelve) that appeared during 2000, but also a Festschrift in honor of my predecessor in the Marshall Sheppard Chair of Biblical Studies at Regent College, Professor Bruce Waltke. I did not know Bruce very well at the time, but I was delighted nevertheless to be asked to contribute an essay to the collection. I had been working for some time on the NIV Application Commentary on Ecclesiastes and Song of Songs, the offer of which had appealed to me purely because of the difficulty that Christian readers have had all through history in integrating these books, in their "plain sense," into their reading of Scripture and into their theology and practice. The commentary was eventually published in 2001. One of the major interpretive questions facing the reader of Song of Songs is whether there are two main speakers in the poems, or three. To this day I cannot see that the two-person theory, albeit that this is the majority theory throughout the ages, makes good sense of the text. This essay was one of the products of my efforts to explain my reasons, developing as it does the idea that Solomon in the Song represents "the dark side" of male attitudes and behavior toward women, while the shepherd-figure (a second male figure) represents an ideal. It is linked to the preceding essay both by its interest in biblical wisdom (the overall theme that unified both Festschrift volumes)—in the present case, wisdom con-

cerning love—and by its interest in offering coherent readings of biblical texts where such have not been attempted successfully before.

In the last twenty-five years, biblical scholarship has gone from having a fixed (and often obsessive) interest in the *parts* that make up our biblical texts to having a gradual, but inexorable, renewed and widespread interest in the way the parts contribute to the *whole*. Although rigorous inquiry into the nature of even the smallest part of a text is important for gaining a full understanding of it, it has been more clearly seen that our comprehension of the part itself is intrinsically bound up with our understanding of the whole to which it contributes. The common idea that one can arrive at an entirely objective account of what various sections of text once meant in isolation from each other, and what they mean independently of the interpreter's preunderstanding, has been largely discredited. One consequence of this shift in perspective has been that biblical scholars are now prepared to revisit many texts previously characterized (and often caricatured) as having little internal coherence. Where scholars once assumed incoherence, they are now open to finding coherence.

This article is offered as such a second look at the two parts of Song of Songs 3:1–11 and also as an evaluation of the way in which this two-part passage contributes to our understanding of the whole "way of wisdom" that Scripture reveals regarding male-female relationships. For although this biblical book is described in its heading as *the Song*, modern commentators commonly identify it as an anthology of love lyrics more or less loosely associated with each other.[1] Scholarship has allowed for little true coherence between the parts, beyond the most general thematic and linguistic links. Certainly the widespread perception of chapter 3 in particular is that only the loosest, if any, connection exists between its two sections, verses 1–5 and verses 6–11. Roland Murphy presents the common view in writing thus of vv. 6–11: "These verses describe a procession of 'Solomon,' which has nothing to do with the episode of the woman's search in verses 1–5."[2]

The juxtaposition of the two sections, or "poems," in chapter 3 is thus understood to be merely fortuitous. The interpreter is to make nothing of it.[3] Yet here I will contend that as we grasp the connection between the two parts, we will both understand Song of Songs as a whole more clearly and comprehend more precisely what it says about being truly human. Indeed, as we see the relationship among the parts of the chapter, the whole Song, and the Scriptures in their entirety, we shall begin more fully to understand our need to move, with God's help, beyond the fragmentation of our humanness and toward a restoration to wholeness. But before we can draw out the far-reaching implications of such a reading, we will need to engage in some detailed exegetical analysis of the language and syntax of Song 3.

The Chapter as a Whole

We begin our reconsideration of Song 3 with an exegetical review of its opening five verses.[4] Here we read of a bed (*miškāḇ*) upon which a woman lies and upon which she seeks "the one [her] heart loves" (v. 1). This phrase is repeated in verses 2, 3 and 4, and in its repetition it communicates the intensity of the longing. This woman is most naturally understood as the one who has already spoken in the opening chapters (1:2–7, 12–14, 16; 2:1, 3–13, 15–17), not least because the warning she offers to the daughters of Jerusalem in 3:5 is also found in 2:7. The man she seeks is also most naturally understood as the lover who is addressed or spoken of in these earlier passages and who speaks himself in 1:8–11, 15, 17; 2:2, 14.

The wording of the opening verses of chapter 3 implies, however, that what is described is a dream rather than an everyday reality (as we are also in a dream in 5:2–8; cf. Dan 2:28–29), and that 3:2 is intended not to tell us what happened *next* (as the NIV's "I will get up now" implies) but rather to describe what this woman said to herself and did during the dream; that is, she does not look first for the man while in the bed and then later while in the city. She looks for the man *only* while in the bed, saying to herself in her dream, "let me arise ... [and] search" (v. 2). Verses 1–2 have identical reports of failure that refer to the same, dreamt search; the first part of verse 2 simply expands upon the first part of verse 1. The city in which she searches is not identified, and given that we are in dreamland, we should probably not seek to identify it. But if one does seek a "location," then Jerusalem is the obvious candidate, given the mention of that city in verse 5. In the midst of her own frantic "rounds" of the city (*sbb*, v. 2; "go about the city," NIV) and of her failure to "find" her beloved (*mṣ'*, vv. 1–2), the woman is "found" (*mṣ'*, v. 3) by watchmen as they "make their rounds" of the city (*sbb*, v. 3)—watchmen who are likewise the shadowy figures of dreams. They neither challenge the woman about her unusual presence in the city at night-time (cf. 5:7) nor answer her question. The shadows of the night simply flit past as the desperate woman moves through the streets; and then suddenly (no details are provided), she finds her man (v. 4).

Her anxiety is communicated in what happens next. She grasps hold of him (*'ḥz*), refusing to let him go (*rph* in the Hiph'il; "to leave alone, forsake"), and escorts him to her mother's house and then to her mother's bedroom (*ḥeder*, as in 1:4). Now they are reunited in intimacy once again. Whether the dream bed is the same as the real bed of 3:1 is not made clear, but it is unlikely given the previous reference to the woman's presence in the king's chambers (1:4). Perhaps in the dream-world the maternal home is symbolic of the security and safety for which the woman yearns—the security and safety of younger days.[5] And so the mother, we may imagine, embraces both her daughter and her daughter's lover and hides them away in her inner chamber, with all its associations with the womb ("the room of the one who conceived me," v. 4). A frightening separation has been overcome, and the lovers lie together under parental protection and blessing.

The alarming power of love that is also displayed in the opening chapters (e.g., 2:5–7) has once again been demonstrated. This is a love that can invade even the realm of the unconscious, and it brings with it unsettling thoughts. It is no surprise, therefore, that the warning that follows the embrace in 2:6–7 should also follow the embrace in 3:4–5. The daughters of Jerusalem, we are told, should be wary of stirring up love until the time is right.[6] The power of love is far beyond their control, and it drives one to dream crazy dreams, if not to enact them.

It is with these opening five verses that verses 6–11 and their "procession of Solomon" allegedly have nothing to do. Yet even a cursory reading of the chapter reveals that there are connections between the two parts, connections that invite further reflection. Both parts tell us of things that happen during the night (note the unusual plural *ballêlôt* in vv. 1, 8) and things involving a bed (*miškāḇ*, v. 1; *miṭṭāh*, v. 7, NIV's "carriage"), and both place a mother in a prominent position (*'ēm*, vv. 4, 11). Further reflection in turns reveals (I shall argue), that it is far from clear whether any real Solomonic procession (usually thought of as a wedding procession) can be found in the passage at all. Once the idea of the wedding procession is banished from the mind—and once we resist all the questionable interpretations of individual verses that follow from this false premise—the two parts of chapter 3 appear to have more in common than one might at first think. For the text does not concern, as some commentators believe, the pilgrimage of a princess across the desert from Egypt (or some other distant land) in a heavily defended and very expensive sedan chair.[7] It concerns instead the heavily defended bed of the wealthy Solomon, who has all things at his disposal (including women) and possesses no neurotic fear of losing a unique beloved (in contrast to 3:1–4). Yet despite all he has, he knows nothing of intimacy and fulfillment.

We begin with the *'appiryôn* that Solomon made (v. 9), which, in spite of the highly misleading definite article in NIV ("the carriage"), is not to be presumed to be identical with the carriage (representing a different word, *miṭṭāh*) about which the NIV tells us in v. 7. The word *'appiryôn* is unique in the Old Testament, and its precise derivation is problematic;[8] but the description of it in verses 9–10 clearly suggests a stationary structure (or part of one) rather than a portable structure. First, its interior or middle (*tôkô*) is said to be "paved with love" (v. 10; "lovingly inlaid," NIV). The verb *rṣp* does not otherwise appear in the Old Testament, but the noun *riṣpāh* does, and it always refers to the paved floor of a temple or palace (2 Chr 7:3; Esth 1:6; Ezek 40:17–18). The associated noun *marṣepet* appears in 2 Kgs 16:17 of a stone pavement in the temple in Jerusalem (cf. *riṣpāh*, "glowing stone," in 1 Kgs 19:6 and Isa 6:6). These words never appear in the context of the inlaid interiors of movable objects, which would not actually move very far if encumbered by many stones. Therefore, even if (as I shall argue below) the "paving" is metaphorical rather than literal, the word is clearly associated with large, permanent structures rather than smaller, movable ones.

Second, the word *'ammûd* (NIV translates the plural form as "posts," v. 10) always refers to large pillars of a size and strength sufficient to support a building, except where it refers to a column of smoke. It is used, for example, of the pillars in Solomon's palace (1 Kgs 7:2–6) and in Ezekiel's temple (Ezek 42:6) as well as of the prominent bronze pillars, Jakin and Boaz, that stood before the Jerusalem temple (1 Kgs 7:15–22). It is also used of the movable tabernacle's pillars (e.g., Exod 27:10–11); but this structure was also a large one that could not simply be lifted up *in toto* and carried across the wilderness. The point is that the word *'ammûḏ* never refers to the kind of smaller "post" that might be found on an allegedly movable *'appiryôn*. If such hypothetical posts were indeed fashioned out of silver, they would also add considerable weight to such a structure. The same is true of the gold mentioned in verse 10, whatever the unique noun *rĕpîḏāh* ("base," NIV) refers to. The verb *rpd* has already appeared in Song 2:5 in reference to the refreshment or support that fruit gives. It seems natural, therefore, to understand the *rĕpîḏāh* as something that supports the pillars (cf. Job 17:13; 41:30 [MT 41:22], where the verb refers to something spread out on the ground), and thus as the floor or as the foundation or base of the structure.

As we add all this detail together, we begin to see that the overall impression is not of a carriage at all, but of a large, fixed structure constructed (at least to a significant extent) of wood, with supporting silver pillars and a gold base or floor. The associations are above all with Solomon's major building works as described in 1 Kings 5–10. The two main building materials mentioned in 1–2 Kings are indeed wood from Lebanon (1 Kgs 5:6–10; 7:1–12) and gold (1 Kgs 6:19–22, 30–35; 10:16–21), which can even be used for flooring (1 Kgs 6:30).

It is not surprising, then, that some commentators have understood this passage as alluding to Solomon's throne hall (1 Kgs 7:7; cf. 10:18–20 for the impressive throne),[9] taking the seat of Song 3:10, upholstered with expensive purple cloth, as the throne. Certainly one can interpret the description of verses 9–10 as a visual movement from a vast hall dominated by wood, presumably including a wooden ceiling, down past the great silver pillars to a golden floor, and at last arriving at the centerpiece of the whole scene—the throne that sits on a specially paved area (a mosaic of other precious stones, perhaps?) in the middle of the hall (cf. 2 Kgs 16:17, the analogous setting of the great Sea in the temple on a paved area). At least one of the suggested derivations for *'appiryôn* (from the Egyptian for "house" or "great house") would fit this scenario.

I agree that *'appiryôn* most likely refers to a room within Solomon's palace, which was known as the Palace of the Forest of Lebanon because of the abundant use of wood from Lebanon in its construction. It is important to note, however, the highly metaphorical language used in the second part of verse 10. The centerpiece is not a regular throne (*kissē*, as in 1 Kgs 7:7; 10:18–20) but literally "a chariot" (*merkāb*, Lev 15:9; 1 Kgs 4:26); and the "middle" is not paved in the normal way with stone but with love. In the context of the Song, this last reference to love (*'ahăbāh*, as in Song 2:4–5, 7)—a troubling reference for those commentators who approach chapter 3 too literally—is much more likely a reference to acts of physical love than to the loving construction of a pavement or mosaic. The chariot is therefore, in my view, best thought of as a bed and not as a throne. It is the finely upholstered "vehicle" upon which the king travels, as it were, on his journey of sexual delight. The daughters of Jerusalem (the king's many wives and concubines as well as other women; cf. 1 Kgs 11:3; Song 6:8) pave his way, as it were, by lying with the king in the center of his *'appiryôn*, his bedchamber. These are the people who provide the "stones" that enable the ongoing royal journey. There is, therefore, "movement" in verses 9–10 of our section: it is the movement, however, not of a sedan chair or carriage but of the "chariot" upon which the king rides to meet the dawn.

It is now clear that this "chariot" within the *'appiryôn*—and not the *'appiryôn* itself—is the *miṭṭāh* of v. 7. *Miṭṭāh* is a regular word for bed or couch, a common item of furniture in the Old Testament that is found in, among other places, a bedroom.[10] Beds can sometimes be lifted up and moved, of course (e.g., 1 Sam 19:13–16), depending upon their mode of construction; and *miṭṭāh* is therefore used also of a funeral bier (2 Sam 3:31). There is no justification elsewhere in the Old Testament, however, for understanding the word as referring to a carriage or sedan chair. It is a bed, and it only "moves" in Song 3 because it is, metaphorically, a chariot.

It is not inappropriate, given the context of such fictive movement, to refer to the sixty warriors associated with the bed as "escorting" it (NIV), so long as it is remembered that they are said simply to be *sābîb lāh*, "around it" (v. 7; cf. *sbb* in vv. 2–3). The soldiers are the most striking feature of the scene, and thus they attract detailed comment from our observer. They are "warriors from the warriors of Israel" (*gibbôrîm ... miggibbôrê yiśrā'ēl*, v. 7; "warriors, the noblest of Israel;' NIV)—an elite guard, similar to David's bodyguards (e.g., 2 Sam. 23:8–39), but twice as many in number.[11] They are all men who are "held fast by the sword" (*'ăḥuzê ḥereb*, v. 8; "wearing the sword," NIV), devoted to and possessed by their profession (cf. *'ḥz* in v. 4, "I held him"). They are battle-hardened and ready for action (note the repetition of "sword" in v. 8, emphasizing military readiness). It is a heavily guarded bed, this "chariot" of Solomon. He goes into "battle" with good men around him to protect him from the "terrors of the night" (v. 8)—if it is indeed Solomon's protection that they are concerned with.

This raises the question, however, of what this section of chapter 3 is really about. It is very difficult to read it in the Hebrew, stripped of all the interpretative translation that has confused fictive with real motion, without thinking that we are dealing with satire. Here is the great Solomon, driving around in his pretentious chariot-bed. He is the mighty Solomon, yet he needs sixty elite warriors to stand around his "chariot" and help get him safely through the night. In truth he cuts a rather pathetic figure, inhabiting a lonely world of materialism and sexual conquest—for conquest is implied by the military overtones of verses 7–8. The charioteer Solomon rides roughshod over the daughters of Jerusalem, on a road paved with sexual acts. Perhaps their terror, rather than his, is alluded to in verse 8: the guards are stationed both to keep the women in and to keep intruders out.

In this light, it is intriguing that the language of verse 6—which seems partly designed to evoke the picture of clouds of myrrh and incense rising up from the bed—is at the same time very much the language of temple and sacrifice. The NIV's "perfumed" is *qṭr* in the Pu'al, a verb that regularly means in the Pi'el "to make sacrifices smoke." Myrrh can be an ingredient of sacred oil (e.g., Exod 30:23), and frankincense (*lĕbônāh*) is heavily associated with sacrifice (e.g., Lev 2:1–2; 5:11). The Hebrew feminine noun *'ăbāqāh*, "spices," is unique, but a masculine noun from the same root refers figuratively on one occasion to the clouds (or dust) under God's feet (Nah 1:3). Smoke (*'āšān*) is itself associated with the divine presence in verses like Exodus 19:18 and Isaiah 6:4, and also Joel 2:30 [MT 3:3], which gives us the only other occurrence of *tîmărôt 'āšān*, "billows of smoke." The related *tîmōrôt* actually designates ornamental palm figures in the Solomonic temple.[12] Finally, the feminine participle *'ōlāh*, "coming up," is identical in form to the feminine noun *'ōlāh*, "burnt offering," and the verb *'lh* is often used of offering up a sacrifice.

A good case can thus be made for taking Song 3:6 as an allusion to the sacrificial female victim who lies upon the "altar" that is Solomon's bed. This is the force of the question, "Who is this coming up from the desert?" with its feminine pronoun *zōṯ*, "this?" It is a woman who "comes up"; but she is not moving laterally across a (real) desert in the direction of Jerusalem, as has sometimes been argued. She is, rather, rising up from the royal bed in the way that smoke rises up into the sky when sacrifices are burnt. We might translate verse 6 this way: "Who is this, ascending from the wilderness like a column of smoke, burned with myrrh and frankincense made from the dust of the merchant?" There is, again, movement, but on this occasion it is the movement of the sacrificial victim upward and not (at least in the first instance) of the royal "chariot" forward. It is in fact this initial "movement" in verse 6 that first draws the attention of the observer to the chariot-bed in verse 7. Perhaps we are meant to imagine a watchman standing on a city wall, looking out intently into the wilderness and perceiving in the distance what looks like a column of smoke. As he watches, the smoke clears and he sees, for the first time (*hinnêh*, "look!"—emphasizing the dramatic discovery), the detail of the "chariot." The situation is analogous to that in 2 Kings 9:14–29, where a watchman sees troops approaching in the distance and is gradually able to make out Jehu, son of Nimshi, driving his chariot. So it is possible that, in the end, the "column of smoke" has a double function, suggesting both sacrifice and the dust cloud stirred up by the royal entourage as (in the mind's eye) it approaches the one observing it.[13]

The characterization of the royal bed as a "wilderness" is, of course, a clever touch, for the wilderness, or "steppe," in the Old Testament is uncultivated and unsettled land; it is an uncivilized place often described as harsh and infertile, and it is regarded as a place of danger, evil, and death.[14] It is the antithesis of the garden in Eden (Isa 51:3).[15] To name the royal bed a wilderness is to offer an understanding of it that, we presume, is very different from Solomon's understanding, given all his wealth and cultured sophistication. It is also to contrast most forcibly the lovemaking that happens there with the lovemaking that happens elsewhere in the Song, which is so routinely associated with fertility and abundant vegetation (e.g., Song 1:13–17; 2:1–13).

If Song 3:6–11 is thus a dark and bitter satire concerning Solomon and his string of sacrificial female victims, then the point of the juxtaposition of verses 1–5 and verses 6–11, already suggested in the contrast just mentioned between the royal bed and other beds, becomes clearer. The first part of our chapter concerns an individual woman who is in love with an individual man and who initiates an anxious search for him. She is certainly not an unwilling sacrificial victim in this relationship—although Song 1:4, 12, which set her in intimate proximity to the king, have previously implied that she has indeed been one of *his* victims, as a member of the royal harem. She is not, in this relationship, simply a stepping stone on the man's road toward sexual utopia. She is an initiator; she knows no terrors of the night, but instead steps out bravely into the darkness to find her man. Her fear is not that she will be required to spend time with him; her fear is that she will not be able to spend such time. Hers is a vulnerable bed, unguarded by any military force; and her lover can leave it when he wishes. It is not surrounded (*sbb*) by warriors who are "grasped" (*'ḥz*) by their swords. She herself must therefore "go around" (*sbb*) looking for her lover, risking the encounter with the guards who make their rounds of the city (*sbb*), and she herself must "grasp" him (*'ḥz*). Yet in the midst of the vulnerability there is intimacy and joy, offered and overseen by the woman's mother, who provides her ordinary bedchamber (with all its associations with fertility) for the lovers. There is, on the other hand, no true intimacy experienced in the wilderness, the extraordinary royal bedchamber. It is not even clear that there is Solomonic joy. We do read that Solomon rejoiced on his wedding day, when his mother, too, was involved in the proceedings (v. 11); but that wedding day, for all we know, may be far in the past. The "crown" of verse 11 maybe only a sad reminder of better days—once symbolic of joy but now symbolic only of the royal power to command and of the unequal terms upon which Solomon meets women in his bed.[16] There is certainly no clear evidence elsewhere in verses 6–11 that a wedding is currently being celebrated, and no overall emphasis throughout the passage on joy.

The juxtaposition of the two sections of Song 3 thus seems far from fortuitous; on the contrary, the two parts fit well together as aspects of one whole whose purpose is to present, for the reader's consideration, two contrasting types of male-female relationship. The two kinds of relationship are already in view in Song 1–2, although their precise nature is less clear in those chapters. We do hear, however, of the relationship between the woman and her lover, who address each other and enter freely into love and sexual intimacy in joyful abandonment, without reservation or shame; and we do hear also of the relationship between the woman and the king, a third party to the loving couple who has power over the woman because she is a member of the royal harem. In Song of Songs generally, in fact, Solomon explicitly appears only in this third person mode, whether it be in Song 1:4, 12; 3:6–11; or 8:10–12. This last passage is part of another entire chapter of the Song that is also best read as contrasting two male-female relationships: the relationship between the woman and her lover versus the kind of relationship more commonly experienced by women in the ancient world, one in which the male had dominance and power over the female. In this situation, the woman did not necessarily enter the relationship by choice; she was often only a pawn in a man's game that had to do with legal contracts, money, and the collection of objects of pleasure. In Song 8, the woman proclaims her resistance to Solomon, the famous collector of women

(vv. 11–12), and to the brothers who claim rights of disposal of her in marriage (vv. 8–9).[17]

There are thus clear indications that we have in Song of Songs three main characters (the woman, her lover, and the king) rather than merely two (the woman and her lover, who is the king)—an insight derived ultimately from the medieval Spanish exegete Abraham ibn Ezra, who first distinguished the "king" in the Song from the "shepherd" of the opening chapter. When one understands this, it is a relatively easy matter to go on to articulate a coherent reading of the whole Song. Different versions of such a reading have been proposed, but I understand the movement of the Song in the following way: The woman, already a member of the king's harem, expresses her continuing love for her lover (and, implicitly, her disdain for the king), and her lover reciprocates (chs. 1–2). The contrast between king and lover is forcibly underlined in chapter 3, where both the woman's determination to overcome threats to her relationship with her lover and her negative view of the royal bed and its owner are clear.[18] The threats to and the depths of the relationship are evidenced in chapters 4–5, where the language and the imagery speak of a committed, marital-like relationship between the man and the woman;[19] chapters 6–7 portray in further detail the nature of this relationship. Chapter 8 provides a strong closing statement of the woman's passion for her lover and her resistance to those other males who claim possession of her, whether they are her brothers or the king. The Song thus reveals itself to be a stirring tale of fidelity to first love in the face of power and of all the temptations of the royal court. It is a poetic account of one ancient couple's insistence that sexual intimacy should be bound up with freedom and love rather than with coercion and domination.

The Song and the Biblical Whole

Just as Song 3 (when read as a whole) both illuminates and is illuminated by the broader context of the whole Song of which it is a part, so also it illuminates and is illuminated by the still broader context that is, for the Christian reader who seeks to walk in "the way of wisdom," provided by the Bible as a whole. First we think of the other biblical materials concerning Solomon, which make for interesting reading; for the memory of King Solomon that was kept alive in Israel after his death was not always flattering. He was remembered as a wise king, yet he was also portrayed as one whose wisdom was not always used for honorable ends (cf. 1 Kgs 2:13–46, where he snatches every opportunity to remove threats to his sovereignty over Israel). Toward the end of his reign, his wisdom had degenerated considerably into a self-indulgent game of words (1 Kgs 10:1–13).[20] He was known as a king who was committed to worshipping and obeying God, yet questions about his integrity have persisted. During his reign, he defied in increasing measure the Mosaic law concerning kingship (Deut 17:14–20), as he accumulated first horses (1 Kgs 4:26, 28), then large amounts of gold (1 Kgs 9:10–28), and finally large numbers of women (1 Kgs 11:1–3). Eventually his accumulated individual indiscretions turned to outright apostasy (1 Kgs 11:4–8).

He was in many ways an ideal king ruling over an ideal kingdom, but the ideal and the reality were always in some degree of tension, and eventually the reality was much less than ideal. This was true to such an extent that some rabbis of a much later time spoke of Solomon in the same breath as such notorious kings of Israel as Manasseh (2 Kgs 21). Already in the book of Ecclesiastes, the negative memory of Solomon provides the necessary backdrop against which Qohelet can enact his "Solomonic" quest for gain (Eccl 1:12–2:26).[21] Here "Solomon" is presented as one who initially finds, as he strives for profit from his labor, that wisdom's achievements are limited; he then discovers that pleasure is also a cul-de-sac. He was one who set out in a godlike way to transform his environment and, thereby, to facilitate his enjoyment of life, by building houses, vineyards, gardens, and "parks" (*pardēs* in Eccl 2:5, as in Song 4:13) and by filling this earthly paradise with slaves, herds and flocks, hoards of treasure, and women. All this did not, however, bring him any advantage. He was not able to burst through the limitations of mortality and frailty and somehow get ahead in the game of life.

It is in the context of 1 Kings 1–11 and Ecclesiastes 1:12–2:26, which themselves direct us back, in particular, to the story of creation and fall in Genesis 1–3 and the following chapters, that we must first of all understand chapter 3 of Song of Songs. From the biblical story we are to learn that at the heart of the human problem lies a refusal to live life within the confines that God has ordained for mortal beings, even though this may involve living in a paradise where joy abounds. From the beginning, human beings have chosen to transgress these God-given boundaries in search of something more, turning the life that comes as a gift to be enjoyed into capital that might fund imperial plans for exploitation and expansion. The more power we have, the more we become intent on creating our own paradise to supplant the kingdom of God—which is why kings like Solomon, more than any other sort of human being in the Old Testament, are portrayed as grasping after godlikeness and seeking to fashion reality after their own liking. They have at their disposal the resources to make a credible attempt at equivalence with the gods. Yet their lives are blatant representations of what the Bible presents as the characteristic set of human choices, and these choices have enormous repercussions for other people as well as for the aspirants to godhood. For if I, as a human being, grasp after divinity and regard myself (rather than God) as the center of the universe, it is inevitable that I will no longer view my fellow human beings as my equals, made in the image of God, toward whom I have a duty of love and respect. Instead I will see them as those whose interests must be repressed in favor of my own, and whose value can be measured only in terms of their value to me.

The narrative of Genesis 1–6 shows us all too clearly how the progression works. Rebellion against God leads to alienation between the man and the woman. They were created to be one flesh, naked but not ashamed (2:24–25); but now they are divided, at odds with each other, and concealed from one another (3:7). These humans, at least, stay together and build community; but in Genesis 4:1–16 we read of an alienation of brother from brother that has serious consequences (death for one and exile for the other). Here we have the complete breakdown of community, and the alienation progresses even further, outward from the center of the family circle: neighbor and neighbor are divided and alienated (4:23–24), and the community slides into complete chaos and anarchy (6:11–13). Even humankind's many achievements of culture (cities, music, etc.; 4:17–22) cannot disguise this slow but remorseless breakdown of community; sophistication, we are shown, is quite compatible with barbarism. Some people are valued only when they serve the interests of the others, as is suggested in 5:28–31, where a father welcomes a new son into the world (Noah), not so much as a son, but more so as a worker who will release his father from the toil imposed upon Adam's descendants (5:29).

When we first hear of a man being married to more than one wife (4:19–24), it is in this context of broken-down communities. This man, Lamech, is not a man of character (he boasts to his two wives of the elevenfold and entirely disproportionate retribution visited on another man, 4:23–24), which makes the readers question the rightness of his polygamy. His taking two wives is a striking departure from the creation ideal articulated in 2:23–24, where it is clear that the marriage relationship should involve one man and one woman. That polygamy became accepted by many Israelites does not, of course, mean it was ever intended by God (any more than was the case with divorce; cf. Mal 2:16; Mark 10:2–9).

In this broader context, the juxtaposition of Song 3:1–4 and 3:6–11, separated by the warning about love's dangers in 3:5, may be more fully appreciated. The first passage focuses our attention on a woman's desires, hopes, and fears; and it reminds us that she is not an object to be possessed, nor a number to be called, but a person to be encountered. In the world of her dreams, at least, she is able to pursue the man of her choice, grasp hold of him, and enjoy the deepest intimacy with him. We, as readers, are exhorted to respect that dream and not to hinder its achievement (just as the watchmen do not, on this occasion, prevent its consummation). The world of love is a dangerous one, however, and in 3:6–11 we see its dark side. Here a king who has sought to build paradise sits in a chariot-bed that is, ironically, a desert. He is the polygamist par excellence, adding ludicrous numbers of women to his collection of objects, and the damage both to these women and to himself is plain. The women are victims sacrificed on his altar; he himself cuts a pathetic figure, surrounded by his elite troops and his luxurious furnishings as he waits for his next "offering." The mutuality of the garden in Eden, so desperately sought by the woman in 3:1–4, is entirely lacking here. There remains only power and objectification.

So it has often been for women throughout history, whether in biblical times or later. The male lust for divinity has had terrible consequences for women, as the enormous social costs of idolatry have been passed on, especially to those who have lacked independence and power. Women have typically been the property of men, traded between them without the slightest consideration for the women's desires and with the shared assumption that the matter is somewhat akin to horse trading—the money earned, the status gained, and the breeding potential being the main concerns. Outside the realm of law, including marriage law, women have been vulnerable before a deeply rooted male compulsion toward sexual conquest and domination, and they have frequently been the victims of the abuse of power. Song of Songs gives us a glimpse of life through the perspective of one of these victims: one of many women collected by Solomon (and men of his kind) for his pleasure, who were to him (and men like him) merely "a breast or two," to use the casual and offensive words of Eccl 2:8.[22]

Conclusion: The Bible and Human Wholeness

By putting a description of a woman's dream alongside a description of the typical female life, Song of Songs—in concert with those other voices that make up the chorus that is Scripture—calls us beyond merely acknowledging the all-too-common reality of our distorted male-female relationships and onward in pursuit of a different vision. For the Song rejects common reality as either inevitable or normative, and looks beyond it to a different way of being, one in which persons are taken seriously first of all as persons, whether men or women, and in which joyous mutuality of relationship is the norm. Although the Song reminds us not to be romantic about a world in which coercion and violence often mark human affairs, it nevertheless lauds romance. While it reminds us that sexual activity is not itself intimacy and can even express estrangement, it nevertheless praises sexual intimacy. And in its presentation of ideal love, which we constantly fail to achieve both individually and societally, Song of Songs summons us to repent and to determine to live differently before God and our fellow human beings. It exhorts us to place the erotic in the context of all that is wholesome and most deeply human, and to resolve not to allow our sexuality to wreak havoc on human life by escaping its proper time and place.

The Song calls us beyond repentance, however, to healing: to face the darkness within us, to understand it, and to have dispelled it by God's light in due time. When we read of the woman's dream in Song 3, we are reminded that God did not make the world the way it is, and that he does not ask us to pretend that he did (nor does he commend us when we do). Even if the false gods of the cosmos, whether human or not, are apt to regard women only as somewhat anonymous means to their own ends, we know this is certainly not how the living God regards women (or any of his creatures). On the contrary, the Bible teaches us that God made us as creatures who possess freedom of will. Each of us is precious to God as an individual, and God desires to have each of us in a right and good relationship with him. God is not interested in relating to human beings coercively (although in the end all mortal beings must reckon with his power if they will not embrace his love), and his relationship with each of us is highly personal, not anonymous. None of us is merely a means to his ends. We are ends in ourselves.

So it is that in the book of Hosea, for example, God speaks of wooing his bride, Israel, back from her sinful ways and restoring that one-to-one relationship that she previously had with him (Hos 2:14–23). In the Gospels, we find that when Jesus comes among his people he likewise invites, rather than forces, those to whom he speaks to pursue a relationship with him. Above all, it is clear that those who yearn for the divine Lover and pursue him will indeed find him, just as the woman finds the man in Song 3:1–4 (cf. Matt 7:7–11). It is striking to note how often throughout the Gospels Jesus is found relating to women in ways that would have been offensive to many first-century Jewish men, but that testify to God's equal love and esteem for women and men.[23] Since God's relating to us should always be the largest context within which we work out our relationships to each other, it should be especially clear to those who know the Gospels which of the two kinds of male-female relationship described in Song 3 we should pursue. Only as we pursue relationships of joyful mutuality, rather than those of oppression and coercion, shall we testify truly about who God is.

14

"ALL THESE I HAVE KEPT SINCE I WAS A BOY" (LUKE 18:21): CREATION, COVENANT, AND THE COMMANDMENTS OF GOD

In 2001, I was invited back to the North Park Symposium (see chapter eleven), on this occasion focused on the topic of "Biblical Ethics." My own paper concerned the right and the wrong ways, the helpful and the unhelpful ways, of reading the Old Testament ethically from a Christian point of view. It was written in the midst of growing ethical confusion in North American church circles, with certain Reformed groups arguing for the desirability of a theocratic state deriving not only ethics but also law from the Old Testament; many Christians at the other end of the spectrum seeing no place at all for the Old Testament in forming a Christian ethic (and certainly not any law); and a huge number of quite puzzled and disquieted people in between. This ethical confusion has not lessened in the intervening years, and I believe that the essay still has some important things to say in addressing this state of affairs. It was originally published along with the other North Park Symposium papers in Ex Auditu *in 2002.*

An interesting religious custom was described to me during an Old Testament Ethics class in the Fall of 2000—how new or old it is, I do not know. It is allegedly the habit of some Christian folk in at least one part of the U.S.A. to place in their front yard replica stelae inscribed with the Ten Commandments. This is apparently intended to accomplish for the yard that which the bumper sticker or the fish accomplishes for the sanctified motor vehicle: it marks it off as Christian territory. The implicit belief underlying the practice seems to be that the Ten Commandments represent some kind of distinctively Christian summation of what is important in life—a digest of the basic rules of the human game, now abandoned in large measure by the surrounding culture, but boldly proclaimed in public view by the Christian householder. Here, at least, God's standards will be adhered to. The belief itself still frequently finds expression also among post-Christian people of an older generation, who may not have much practical faith to speak of, but when asked about the guidelines according to which they should live their lives will often make reference to the Ten Commandments as their moral compass. "These, at least, have I kept since I was a boy"—and it would be better for society in general if everyone else still did the same. There is indeed an entire intellectual stream within conservative, Calvinist Protestantism in the U.S.A., commonly referred to as Theonomy, that holds not only to the centrality of the Ten Commandments for Christian faith and life, but also to the centrality of much of the remainder of Old Testament law, since "until heaven and earth disappear, not the smallest letter, not the least stroke of a pen, will by any means disappear from the law until everything is accomplished" (Matt 5:18). In such a way of thinking, it is not just the Ten Commandments that represent God's timeless absolutes for the ordering of human existence, but whatever else in Old Testament law has not been specifically rescinded by Jesus or the writers of the New Testament. The Ten Commandments rightly belong in the Christian front yard, and much else besides. They belong not only in the front yard, in fact, but in every other public space as well—for as God is God of the whole universe, so also God's law should be the standard not only for personal life, but also for public life.[1]

The Old Testament as Scripture

In favor of such an approach to the Old Testament, it can be said that it at least takes these ancient Scriptures seriously as Scriptures, which is not something that can be said with any confidence about vast reaches of the remainder of the twenty-first century Christian church. In Western culture, in particular, the word "old" does not have particularly positive connotations. "Old" entities are likely to be marginalized or disposed of in favor of what is new. Perhaps this has something to do with the declining use of the Old Testament in churches, for declining use there certainly seems to be accompanied by a declining authority in matters of faith and life. The very idea that one might turn to the Old Testament for guidance on *ethical* matters, as a Christian, is one that is scarcely countenanced by many. It is the New Testament that guides the Christian on the pathway through life—a New Testament that has itself left the Old Testament behind.

It is the impossibility of this stance of which Theonomists and those of similar views remind us. Any casual reading of the New Testament will in fact reveal to us the centrality of the Old Testament to the thinking of both Jesus and the apostles on a whole range of issues, including ethical issues. For Jesus himself, the Old Testament Scriptures represented God's authoritative revelation of himself, his own character, and also of the pattern for human conduct. Time and again in the course of his teaching and disputes he prefaces what he is about to say with statements such as "It is written" (e.g., Mark 14:27; Matt 11:10). Time and again he bases his teaching or arguments on the Old Testament (e.g., Mark 12:28–31 [virtually quoting Deut 6:4–5 and Lev 19:18]; Mark 7:9–13 [quoting Exod 20:12; 21:17]); and as we have already seen, he explicitly says in the Sermon on the Mount that these same Old Testament Scriptures have a lasting validity (Matt 5:17–20). The Old Testament was fundamental to Jesus. He did, of course, frequently interpret the Old Testament in ways that his contemporaries did not like, and the Gospels do tell us that in certain respects the Old Testament is no longer binding on followers of Jesus. But that is not the same thing as saying that Jesus left the Old Testament behind as a whole. He certainly did not.

It is unsurprising that we find the same perspective among the apostles. The Apostle Paul, for example, often applies the Ten Commandments to the various ethical situations with which he is confronted in the churches (Rom 7:7; 13:9; Eph 6:2–3); and taking his lead from Jesus, he applies Leviticus 19:18 to what is left untouched by these commandments (Rom 13:9; Gal 5:14). In other places, too, he depends directly upon the Old Testament for ethical guidance (e.g., the injunction that two or three witnesses are necessary to establish a matter, 2 Cor 13:1, quoting Deut 19:15). Second Timothy 3:16 may or may not have been written by Paul himself, but it certainly reflects his attitude and the attitude of the whole New Testament to the Old Testament—"All Scripture is inspired by God and profitable for teaching, for reproof, for correction and for training in righteousness."

It does not appear to be open to followers of Christ, then, to dispense with the Old Testament and to retain only the New as our ethical guide. It is a suggestion that would have amazed the apostles themselves, given that none of them thought that they were in the process of composing a replacement set of Scriptures for the church, rather than merely exegetical reflections on the Scriptures of the church.

And yet, the question remains as to how, exactly, Christians are to read the Old Testament for ethical guidance. Which is the appropriate way to go? Is the Old Testament law truly to be taken over into the modern Christian context in the large measure advocated by the Theonomists? Are the Ten Commandments that lie at the heart of that law indeed to be regarded as timeless moral absolutes that encapsulate the essence of the good life? As we read on in Matthew's Gospel, beyond Matthew 5:18, we find some scriptural reason to ask further questions even about the latter (and therefore also about the former, one assumes). For in due course, we read of Jesus' encounter with the rich young ruler, recorded for us in all three Synoptic Gospels (Matt 19:16–30; Mark 10:17–31; Luke 18:18–30). Here is a man who has kept the commandments, but he is also a man who has fallen short of the kingdom of God. He has kept the commandments, but his Christian discipleship is deficient—for he has failed in generosity to the poor. This raises a very interesting question about the nature of the Ten Commandments in respect of the kingdom of God that Jesus has come to inaugurate. It does not, after all, appear that these commandments, which fail to enjoin generosity, can be quintessentially (or at least exhaustively) Christian; it does not, after all, appear that we can have in these commandments a synopsis of the Christian life. But more than that, the story of the rich young ruler raises an interesting question about the nature of the Ten Commandments in respect to the remainder of the *Old Testament*. For other sections of the Old Testament, if not the commandments, *do* enjoin or commend generosity to the poor (e.g., Ps 112:5; Prov 11:25; 22:9), and it is surely this kind of scriptural material that lies in the background of Jesus' instruction to the rich young ruler to "sell everything you have and give it to the poor" (Luke 18:22). The question is this, then: are the

Ten Commandments rightly regarded as expressing the quintessence of what the *Old Testament* has to say about the virtuous life? Or has much of the Christian debate about the Old Testament and ethics gone awry right from the beginning by failing to understand what the Old Testament truly has to say about such an issue—by failing to set the commandments, and indeed Old Testament law more generally, within a much wider Old Testament scriptural context, and to understand them in that context? It is to reflection on such matters that the present paper will devote itself, moving toward an answer to this question: how *should* Christian readers read the Old Testament, when it is ethical guidance that they are seeking from these Scriptures? How is the word of truth, in this area, rightly to be interpreted?

The Covenant and the Law of Moses

The Ten Commandments do not float above the realm of history, nor are they devoid of literary connections. They are historically located, and they have a literary context, or rather, two literary contexts. They are found in Exodus 20:1–17, in the midst of the Exodus narrative and just prior to the so-called covenant law code of Exodus 20:18–23:19, and in the long prologue to the legal prescriptions of Deuteronomy, in Deuteronomy 5:1–21. Good exegetical practice demands that their historical and their literary locatedness must play their part in determining their meaning and significance.

Analysis of the commandments in context reveals, first of all, that they are clearly marked off from the surrounding "commands, decrees, and laws," as Deuteronomy 5:31 and 6:1 describe them. These ten "words" (the literal translation from the Hebrew, reflected also in the Greek-inspired term for the commandments ("Decalogue"), are words spoken directly to the people of Israel by God, who proclaimed them "in a loud voice to your whole assembly there on the mountain" (Deut 5:22). They are to be distinguished from the many other words from God that were passed on to the people through the mediation of Moses, who was delegated by the fearful people to "go near and listen to all that the LORD our God says," beyond the ten words (Deut 5:27; cf. Exod 20:19). The form of the Ten Commandments is correspondingly different from that of the other "commands, decrees, and laws." The other legal material in both Exodus and Deuteronomy is largely casuistic in form: it relates to particular cases, to which particular instructions apply and attached to which are often particular penalties. We may note, for example, Exodus 21:2 and Deuteronomy 13:1–3:

> If you buy a Hebrew servant, he is to serve you for six years. But in the seventh year, he shall go free, without paying anything.

> If a prophet, or one who foretells by dreams, appears among you and announces to you a miraculous sign or wonder, and if the sign or wonder of which he has spoken takes place, and he says, "Let us follow other gods" (gods you have not known) "and let us worship them," you must not listen to the words of that prophet or dreamer.

The Ten Commandments are, by contrast, apodictic in form. They are generalized rules of behavior, usually employing "you shall not" language (the exception is the sixth commandment) rather than "if" language, which have no particular penalties prescribed for the persons who disobey them. The words that God himself speaks thus have a different shape to the words that Moses speaks on God's behalf. They are marked off from their literary context not merely by the content of the passages in which they occur, but by their very form. It is not surprising, then, that the remainder of the Old Testament tradition should also regard the ten words as "marked off" from the remainder of Old Testament law and should return to these words on numerous occasions as foundational words for community life—as principles of conduct that stand above and behind all the specific guidelines given by God through Moses to enable stable community life to continue. So it is that we find the opening lines of the Decalogue alluded to in Psalm 81:9–10:

> You shall have no foreign god among you; you shall not bow down to an alien god. I am the LORD your God, who brought you up out of Egypt.

We find the seventh, eighth and ninth commandments alluded to in Psalm 50:18–20:

> When you see a thief, you join with him; you throw in your lot with adulterers. You use your mouth for evil and harness your tongue to deceit. You speak continually against your brother and slander your own mother's son.

Hosea 4:1–2 describes eighth-century Israel in similar terms:

> There is no faithfulness, no love, no acknowledgment of God in the land. There is only cursing, lying and murder, stealing and adultery; they break all bounds, and bloodshed follows bloodshed.

Jeremiah 7:9 sets a later Israel against the background of the same "ten words," just as 1 Kings 21:1–16 echoes their content in cataloguing the earlier sins of Ahab and Jezebel.

That the Ten Commandments are distinct in significant ways from much of the rest of Old Testament law, then, is already clear enough. To our observations thus far, however, we may now add the following (or rather, draw out an implication in the preceding discussion): that the Ten Commandments clearly portray *ideals* of behavior for the community of God's people in a way that much of the remainder of Old Testament law does not obviously portray such ideals. Much of the remainder of Old Testament law (where it is not concerned with ritual rather than ethical matters—ritual matters that do not directly concern us in this paper) focuses on dealing with a community in which relationships have already broken down, and persons have already damaged others by their wicked behavior. It is not concerned with inculcating ideals, but with limiting the damage already caused by behavior that falls well short of the ideal, and with providing some kind of recompense to the victim, or some kind of sanction for the perpetrator.

For example, Deuteronomy 22:23–29 provides us with a number of rules about illicit sexual conduct. Since betrothal is tantamount to marriage in ancient Israelite society, it is regarded as a case of adultery if the betrothal contract is breached through sexual intercourse between the betrothed woman and an outsider. The man in both cases where betrothal is involved (vv. 23–27) is therefore put to death, but the woman is not put to death if the act took place in the country (and thus no one knows whether or not she, as *unwilling victim*, cried out for help, vv. 25–27). She is only executed if she failed to cry out for help in a town (and is thus presumed to have consented, vv. 23–24).

It is not much of a choice that is offered to the woman in the town, if she truly did *not* consent to the act: the death penalty on the one hand (because she kept quiet in the face of the assault), or, on the other hand the risk of further violence or death at the hands of the assailant (because of her attempts at noisy resistance to rape). The final case (vv. 28–29) underlines, though, that these are not laws drawn up with the rights of women particularly in mind, or with more than certain aspects of her interests in view. For the rape of an unbetrothed, unmarried woman the fine for the man is only fifty shekels of silver. The woman, however, suffers not only the trauma of rape but the further trauma of having to live with the man who raped her. We may note that the fine is paid to the father to compensate him for the damage to his property, and not to the woman. The woman has no say in the matter, not being a legal person under Israelite law.

We are not reading in this passage about Old Testament ideals with respect to male-female relations. We are a long way here, in fact, from the vision of Genesis 1–2, which speaks of mutuality and intimacy in marriage between two people who are both made in God's image, and from the vision of the Song of Songs, which exegetes the Genesis reality. We are also a long way from the ideal reflected in the tenth commandment, which forbids the coveting of persons or property that belong to the neighbor—in this case, to the prospective groom or to the father. Deuteronomy 22:23–29 is not about ideals at all. It is about dealing with wickedness, in concrete societal circumstances, in ways that at least mitigate some aspects of the consequences of wickedness: the unbetrothed woman is at least guaranteed a home and sustenance, rather than being cast out to fend for herself in a society in which this was virtually impossible for a woman. It is also about providing at least some deterrent to men who are tempted to abuse women, by threatening the prospective perpetrator with either the death penalty or lifelong responsibility for his actions. But it is not about ideals of behavior.

Thus far it is evident, then, that the Decalogue does stand apart from much of the remainder of Old Testament law, offering principles of conduct that come directly from the mouth of God rather than guidance mediated through Moses as to how to handle specific cases of moral and legal infraction. Yet the question remains: is the Decalogue to be regarded as an *exhaustive* account of the morally upright life? Granted that it provides us with important principles of conduct, is it to be regarded as articulating all the principles that truly matter? The answer to this question certainly appears to be "no." It is not just that specific moral principles that are thought to be important elsewhere in the Old Testament do not come to expression in the Decalogue, thus revealing its non-exhaustive nature (although this is true, as the already-mentioned example of generosity to the poor illustrates). More than this, however, it should be noted that the form of the Ten Commandments is predominantly negative. Various activities are selected for prohibition: the worship of other gods, the making of images, misusing God's name, working on the Sabbath, murder, adultery, stealing, giving false testimony, and coveting that which belongs to one's neighbor. Important as it may be that one should avoid such activities, it is difficult to see how the good life can truly be defined only in terms of negatives. Here are some things that one should *not* do; but what is it that one should *do*?

To ask the question is immediately to see that the Ten Commandments cannot represent a summation of all that is important about the ethical life; and indeed, the more predominant note struck by the Old Testament is positive and not negative. For example, Hosea 6:6 expresses God's heart in this way: "For I desire mercy, not sacrifice, and acknowledgment of God rather than burnt offerings." Here the negatives are juxtaposed with positives: God does not desire sacrifice/burnt offerings, but he does desire mercy towards one's neighbor and acknowledgment of himself. Similarly, Micah 6:8 speaks in these terms: "He has showed you, O man, what is good. And what does the Lord require of you? To act justly and to love mercy, and to walk humbly with your God." Leviticus 19:18 famously combines another pair of negatives and positives: "Do not seek revenge or bear a grudge against one of your people, but love your neighbor as yourself." Finally by way of example, the Decalogue in Deuteronomy 5 is closely followed by the Shema of Deuteronomy 6:4–5, which sets the larger context within which the Decalogue is to be observed: "Hear, O Israel: The Lord our God, the Lord is one. Love the Lord your God with all your heart and with all your soul and with all your strength." God is one, and the human vocation is to love God with every aspect of one's being, responding in unity of being to the unity of God. The various specific commandments that also come from God are to be understood and obeyed within this larger context.

Seen within this larger context, the Ten Commandments are revealed to contain, not an exhaustive summation of the godly life, but rather only selected examples of the kinds of things that loving God and one's neighbor involves, and then only in terms (mainly) of negatives to be avoided rather than positives to be embraced. Not everyone will in fact possess manservants or maidservants, or oxen, donkeys and other animals; not everyone will find himself hosting a sojourner within the gates (Deut 5:12–14). Not everyone can express love for God and neighbor, therefore, by ensuring that these fellow creatures rest on the Sabbath. This commandment has particular people of power in mind. In contrast, everyone can seek to refrain from stealing (Deut 5:19), but from an Old Testament perspective, one's duty to one's neighbor is not in fact exhausted by refraining from stealing. It also involves seeing that justice is done to that neighbor and that generosity is extended to him. There is more to that which is good than can be expressed in an injunction not to act in a certain way. There is a larger vision of life within which negative injunctions must be understood and embraced.

It is thus apparent that the Ten Commandments are themselves somewhat like the case law of the Old Testament after all, in the sense that all the material we have been reviewing thus far must be read as a selective rendering of principles of conduct that lie behind it, designed to show by way of example what it means in practice to love God and neighbor, or to act justly, to love mercy, and to walk humbly with God. The Ten Commandments do this in the expression of what we might call "second-order principles"—selected ideals for behavior that mark out in a general (though not exhaustive) way the religious and ethical territory, as it were, within which the Israelite is to live. Loving God and neighbor certainly means refraining (mainly) from these specific activities, even if it means much more than this. The biblical case laws also reflect, but in a different way, what it means for a community to take seriously the love of God and of neighbor. They, too, are presumably selective—we cannot possibly have recorded in the Old Testament all the cases that ever came before a legal authority in Israel. Rather, we are provided with a number of these that reveal to the reader the various ways in which a particular community dealt with the reality of community life when it came into conflict with the ethical vision—the ways in which the attempt was made to approximate to the ethical vision in specific cases.

Such is the nature of covenant law in the Old Testament then, but we are not finished with what the Old Testament has to say about ethics just because we are finished with covenant law. Just as the Decalogue has a larger context within the law that is important for its proper understanding, so also covenant law has a larger context within Old Testament creation theology, and it is important that we examine that context too if we are to gain a clear understanding of what an "Old Testament ethics" truly looks like.

Creation and Ethics

It is an intriguing fact about the Old Testament, which has often been obscured by an overemphasis on covenant as *the* governing and organizing theme of these Scriptures, that it clearly does not root its ethical vision only in the law that was given to Israel at Sinai, but also in the created order, which in different ways is itself thought to "declare the glory of God ... proclaim the work of his hands" (Ps 19:1). No great gulf is set, in fact, between covenant and creation as contexts within which the will of God may be ascertained and the right pathway through life identified.

We may begin here with the Prophets, who are correctly regarded by Jewish tradition as the great interpreters of the covenant, and yet nonetheless are also found to place covenant and creation in close connection to each other. Amos 1–2 provides an excellent example. The opening chapter records a number of oracles against foreign nations, each of which shares a common structure. They begin with the formulaic "For three sins ... even for four, I will not turn back my wrath" before proceeding to describe the crimes of each nation in question and to announce divine judgment. The series builds to a crescendo with the surprising introduction into it, first of Judah (Amos 2:4–5) and then of Israel (Amos 2:6–16). The basis for Amos' condemnation of Israel and Judah is, unsurprisingly, their rejection of "the law of the Lord" and "his decrees" (2:4). The other nations, however, are just as roundly condemned for wrongdoing, even though they were never given any law at Mount Sinai. It is simply presupposed that they know the difference between right and wrong and therefore know very well that their war-crimes (for that is the focus of Amos' indictment) are wicked. Whether knowledge has been gained at Mount Sinai or simply from conscience or a sense of common humanity, genuine knowledge of ethical principles is assumed to be prevalent.

Even when dealing with *Israel's* sins, though, the prophets can move easily between covenant and creation as bases for ethical standards and judgments. There is throughout the prophetic corpus a profound sense that there is an order in nature itself that is worthy of imitation by human beings, whether Israelites or not. Thus Isaiah 1:3 observes, "The ox knows his master, the donkey his owner's manger, but Israel does not know, my people do not understand." Jeremiah 8:7 notes, "Even the stork in the sky knows her appointed seasons, and the dove, the swift and the thrush observe the time of their migration. But my people do not know the requirements of the LORD." Other creatures know their place in the universe and adapt themselves to its true nature. Israel, on the other hand, has no understanding of a similar kind—even though Israel possesses Torah. Sin, in this way of thinking, is not so much the breaking of a commandment as the embrace of cosmic nonsense—a refusal to be sane—and the requirements of the law are understood as nothing other than the requirements for sensible living within the cosmos (since the God who creates the cosmos and the God who makes covenant are one and the same). Amos 6:12 reflects on Israel's sins, for example, which are at the same time an expression of insanity: "Do horses run on the rocky crags? Does one plow there with oxen? But you have turned justice into poison and the fruit of righteousness into bitterness."

Moral norms are built into the nature of things, and not just into the law given at Mount Sinai. Indeed, a considerable number of the references to sin that are found in the prophetic writings are not strictly speaking based on the law at all. The prophets can be found assailing drunkenness, political error, and pride, for example—none of these attacks relating to the law, but depending on ethical ideals deriving from other sources.

A similar perspective on ethics can be found in the biblical wisdom literature, especially Proverbs and Job. Here the language of covenant and law is entirely lacking. In these books we are in fact not in the world of special revelation and mighty acts of God in Israel's history at all, but much more in the world of what we might call natural theology (God's general revelation) and pragmatic religion. And knowledge of God here is derived from the ordinary things of life, and from the experience of those who are older and wiser in the ways of the world—from within the created order, as it continues to function in its normal and harmonious ways. The good life that stands as the goal of the wise person in Proverbs is a long life characterized by good health, an abundance of friends and children, and sufficient possessions to get through life without too much hardship. It is toward the attainment of this good that Proverbs seeks to guide its readers, and certain things stand out as the means by which the good life is achieved and the bad life avoided. The good life is bound up with such things as obedience to parents, (e.g., 13:24; 20:30; 23:13–14); self-control in speech (e.g., 13:3; 25:11–12, 23; 29:20); self-control in subordinating the passions (e.g., anger in 14:29–30; 16:32; 29:11); marrying the right person (18:22; 19:13–14; 21:9, 19); generosity (14:31; 21:26; 25:21–22), and the absence of excessive wealth (30:7–9). The bad life is associated with sexual misconduct (5:1–6, 20–23); drunkenness (23:19–21, 29–35); laziness (6:10–11; 10:4–5; 26:14–16); misuse of the tongue (6:16–19; 10:18; 18:6–8); and other dark realities (e.g., pride in 15:25–26; 16:5; greed in 15:27; 28:25; 29:4). The person who follows the path to the good life is wise, and the one who does not is a fool—because tradition, experience, and observation of the way in which the world works clearly suggest the right way in which to go. Even the ant knows something about this (6:6).

The book of Job also has the good life as its backdrop and goal, even though Job himself does not see much of it during the greater part of the book. The book opens with a picture of a man experiencing the life in all its fullness that is described in the book of Proverbs. It presents us with a man who is renowned for fearing the LORD (cf. Prov 9:10) and who is consequently blessed by God. The question, however, is whether Job's righteousness would survive hardship—whether it is only self-serving and self-interested. A period of extreme difficulty for Job follows, in which his moral integrity is tested, and in the end, as at the beginning, we find that Job is blessed in life because he is indeed righteous. The particular interest of the book from our point of view lies in how Job's righteousness is described, and here chapter 31 is most helpful. In this chapter Job himself provides us with a long list of sins that he considers he has not committed, and at least two things are striking about this list. First, it is a list that reflects Job's ethical ideals, and those ideals far transcend the requirements of the law, even with respect to the Ten Commandments. The Decalogue forbids adultery, for example, but Job claims not even to have looked lustfully at a girl (31:1). The Decalogue forbids stealing, but Job claims to have done much more for his neighbor than avoiding stealing from him (31:16–23):

> If I have denied the desires of the poor or let the eyes of the widow grow weary, if I have kept my bread to myself, not sharing it with the fatherless—but from my youth I reared him as would a father, and from my birth I guided the widow—if I have seen anyone perishing for lack of clothing,

or a needy man without a garment, and his heart did not bless me for warming him with the fleece from my sheep, if I have raised my hand against the fatherless, knowing that I had influence in court, then let my arm fall from the shoulder, let it be broken off at the joint. For I dreaded destruction from God, and for fear of his splendor I could not do such things.

Reverence for God has led Job to radical love for his neighbor; and this involves actions beyond those specified by the law. Examples such as these demonstrate beyond doubt the truth of our earlier contentions: that even the Decalogue does not exhaustively represent the ethical ideals articulated in the Old Testament, and that indeed, the negative commands of the Decalogue are themselves only partial expressions of yet higher ideals that come to expression elsewhere in the Old Testament.

The second thing that is striking about Job 31 is found in verses 13–15. For the most part the chapter does not reveal to us where its moral norms are grounded, if it is not in the law given at Mount Sinai. However, Job claims through his rhetorical question in verse 13 always to have ensured that his male and female slaves received justice when they have a grievance against him. The notion that slaves might legitimately have a grievance against a master is itself remarkable enough, but the ground that Job provides for treating them well in this way is even more astonishing (v. 15): "Did not he who made me in the womb make them? Did not the same one form us both within our mothers?" It is the common origin of both master and slave in God's creative activity that provides the imperative that Job should treat his slaves well, and allow them even to bring a complaint against him. One is reminded of the insistence in Genesis 1 that all human beings are made in the image of God, and indeed of the exegesis in Genesis 9:6 of this reality in terms of the inherent sacrosanctity of human beings: God will demand an accounting from a human being who has shed human blood. What we find here is a creation ethic that lies beneath and behind any covenant ethic that is expressed in the Old Testament, and which to some extent must be understood as making the latter relative. It is precisely this kind of ethic that already comes to expression in the prophetic corpus as the prophets preach the God of all creation to an Israelite community that has too narrow a view of God and of ethics, and has in particular forgotten that there may well be a considerable *gap* between law and ethics—between what God has proclaimed and permitted at Sinai, on the one hand, and what may be the ideals of God's kingdom on the other. The prophet Malachi is on this track, for example, when he reminds his readers, even though he must know that divorce is permitted by Mosaic law, that divorce is nonetheless hateful to God (Mal 2:13–16):

> Another thing you do: You flood the LORD's altar with tears. You weep and wail because he no longer pays attention to your offerings or accepts them with pleasure from your hands. You ask, "Why?" It is because the LORD is acting as the witness between you and the wife of your youth, because you have broken faith with her, though she is your partner, the wife of your marriage covenant. Has not the LORD made them one? In flesh and spirit they are his. And why one? Because he was seeking godly offspring. So guard yourself in your spirit, and do not break faith with the wife of your youth. "I hate divorce," says the LORD God of Israel, "and I hate a man's covering himself with violence as well as with

his garment," says the LORD Almighty. So guard yourself in your spirit, and do not break faith.

This grounding of covenant ethics within the larger framework of creation ethics is not surprising, of course, when it is remembered that Israel is only called out by God to be a special people in the Old Testament so that God will in the end bring blessing to the whole of creation. Abraham is brought from Ur, in response to the disasters of Genesis 1–11, specifically so that "all peoples on earth will be blessed through you" (Gen 12:3), and the covenant that is made with him is made for this very long term purpose. The subsequent covenant at Sinai with all of Abraham's descendants retains this universalist perspective (Exod 19:6): "Although the whole earth is mine, you will be for me a kingdom of priests and a holy nation." It is the task of priests to mediate God's blessing to others. Since it is thus the one God who created the universe who now calls out a people and makes covenant with them in order to bless the whole of creation, we would not expect to read covenant ethics outside of the context of creation ethics and without an eye to the larger story. Nor do our biblical writers encourage us to do so.

"He Has Showed You, O Man, What is Good"

What does this review of Old Testament texts touching on ethics suggest to us about how Christian readers should read the Old Testament, when it is ethical guidance that they are seeking from these Scriptures? It suggests above all that we must read individual Old Testament texts within their broader biblical context.

The largest context is set by the theological theme of creation. God has created all things for right relationships with himself and among themselves, such that all creation knows his blessing (Gen 1–2), and right relationships involve a whole number of things, from a human point of view, that all of God's human creatures are called to embrace. A right relationship with God involves, for example, worship and trust in divine goodness. It is indeed in a distrust in divine goodness that we find the first humans step away from God and into moral darkness, as Adam and Eve chose to accept the serpent's characterization of God as a God of unreasonable prohibition ("You must not eat from any tree," Gen 3:1) in place of an accurate characterization of God as a God of generosity and freedom ("You are free to eat from any tree," Gen 2:16). It is the God of generosity and freedom who is truly the God of creation, however, and he calls his image-bearers to be like him in relating to their fellow human beings and to the creation over which they have been given dominion. The first step in reading Old Testament texts ethically, then, is to locate them within this largest creation context and to ask: how does this text relate to the creation will of God and to God's desire that all his image-bearers should be like him—should act justly, love mercy, and walk humbly with God? It is within this creation context that covenant law can then be understood; it is law that partly reflects God's creation will for all people, including Israelites, but partly (perhaps even largely) does not. For covenant law does more than simply reflect ideals of human behavior in a God-created world. It is also designed to enable Israel, specifically as Israel, to function well within the world that she inhabits—a world in which she is to be a distinctive people in order to fulfill God's purposes, and a world in which moral darkness continually presses in upon human community and threatens to extinguish the light. Covenant law thus requires to be read through the lens of creation theology, if its relevance to the wider, non-Israelite world is to be established.

I suggest that this is precisely the kind of reading of the Old Testament that we find widely practiced in the New Testament. In the Sermon on the Mount, for example, Jesus first describes to his listeners the shape of the blessed life, which involves positively embraced actions and attitudes rather than abstinence from action (e.g., showing mercy; making peace), before going on to teach them that various of the provisions of the Old Testament law, including two of the (negative) Ten Commandments, are not to be read as exhausting one's ethical responsibility to one's neighbor (Matt 5:1–48). Creation theology is specifically invoked in Matthew 5:43–48 with respect to loving one's enemy (cf. Prov 25:21) and is later introduced to explain the teaching in Matthew 5:31–32 about divorce (Matt 19:3–12: "Moses permitted you to divorce your wives because your hearts were hard. But it was not this way from the beginning"; cf. Mal 2:10–16). Job 31, with its own creation perspective, lies in the background of Matthew 5:27–30. There is a wider context within which specific texts are to be read, if they are to be understood properly. We have already seen the same move in the story of the rich young ruler, and we find it throughout the Gospels (e.g. Matt 23:23–24; Mark 2:23–28; 3:1–6; Luke 13:10–17).

The early church adopted the same approach to its Old Testament reading, recognizing in the aftermath of Jesus' death and resurrection, and in the new situation that these events created, that still further questions required to be asked about the relationship between creation and covenant. Those aspects of Old Testament law that appeared to be specifically Israelite (Jewish) now increasingly come under scrutiny and are regarded as irrelevant to Christians (and especially Gentile Christians), since the period of history in which it was important for Jews to be distinct from Gentiles is now over, and all should be one in Christ. So it is that food laws, for example, come to be regarded as redundant for Christians, since there is a more fundamental theology about food that now, in the era of oneness in Christ, reasserts itself (1 Tim 4:3–5): "They forbid people to marry and order them to abstain from certain foods, which God created to be received with thanksgiving by those who believe and who know the truth. For everything God created is good, and nothing is to be rejected if it is received with thanksgiving, because it is consecrated by the word of God and prayer."

At the same time, though, those aspects of Old Testament law that express something more than that which is specifically Israelite are retained in the New Testament and are regarded as undergirding Christian ethics. We have already noted the appearance of the Ten Commandments in various places in the New Testament, illustrating some of the things that loving God and neighbor mean in the New Testament period as in the Old. Another good example would be the way in which Old Testament laws touching on homosexual practice are alluded to in New Testament teaching on this topic (1 Cor 6:9–10; 1 Tim 1:10; cf. Lev 18:22 and Lev 20:13), illustrating that even some of what is often called "purity law" was actually regarded as having a strongly ethical component. Finally, we may note the way in which the early church, thinking of itself as the same people of God as of old, applied to itself the Old Testament's economic ethics. There is the same concern in both testaments for the poor and needy (1 John 3:17) and the same ideal of equality among God's people, both economically (2 Cor 8:13–15) and indeed socially (Jas 2:1–7). If the ideal is fellowship, sharing, and making sure that there is no one who is poor among you (Deut 15:4), then what we find in the early chapters of Acts is a body breaking bread and practicing community of goods, making sure that there was indeed no poor among them.

There is thus in the New Testament both a "yes" and a "no" to Old Testament covenant law, as it is read through the lenses of both creation and new creation. Christian readers of modern times should adopt the same approach in reading the Old Testament ethically.

Conclusion

What are we to say, then, to those who were introduced in my opening paragraph, with their serious attachment to the law of Moses? We should certainly commend the seriousness with which they take the Old Testament Scriptures. We should encourage them (and ourselves), however, to take them more seriously yet by setting covenant law more fully within the entire biblical context and understanding its nature more fully as a result. There is no question but that we shall derive a considerable amount of help, not only for our personal but also for our public lives, by reflecting on covenant law, as the Theonomists claim; but the precise implications of what we learn, both for our personal and for our public lives, will only be grasped by taking seriously both the creation and new creation contexts within which Old Testament covenant law sits. As for those who do not go the whole way with the Theonomists but still hold the Ten Commandments in high regard, this is good! But do not identify the Ten Commandments with the complete will of God, and if you must display them in your front yard, at least lay out beside them all your worldly possessions, so that the poor can take them away after they have read the biblical text.

15

THE LAND IS MINE AND YOU ARE ONLY TENANTS (LEVITICUS 25:23): EARTH-KEEPING AND PEOPLE-KEEPING IN THE OLD TESTAMENT

In 2006, a conference was held in Vancouver, jointly sponsored by Regent College and A Rocha, a remarkable Christian environmental organization working all over the world (http://www.arocha.org) that has strong Regent College connections. The theme of the conference was "Keeping Earth in Common: A Just Faith for a Whole World." Christian faith (or at least some forms of it) has been much blamed in the last several decades for fostering an anthropocentric attitude toward creation that is unhelpful (to put it mildly) in the context of our current concerns about the state of our world. I wrote this essay originally as a paper to be delivered to the conference, exploring the question, not so much whether Christians have been guilty as charged in respect of their attitude to and behavior toward nonhuman creation, but whether the Bible itself (and specifically the Old Testament) steers people in such directions. I believe that it clearly does not. The essay was originally published in 2006 in the excellent but not widely known in-house Regent College journal, Crux.

What kind of story is the biblical story? Does it help us with earth-keeping and people-keeping, or hinder us in these endeavors? It is commonly alleged nowadays that it *hinders*—that people who have taken the Bible story as their governing story have a woeful record of looking after the earth and have often not treated human beings very well either. This is not the place to explore the full truthfulness of such claims about what Christians have sometimes done or not done, historically. There is certainly some truth to be found in such critiques, but there is also much ignorance and propaganda. More to the point is whether the biblical narrative itself has *required* such Christians to act negligently or badly (where they *have* so acted), or whether the biblical narrative itself presents a quite different vision of the world from the one pursued by these badly-behaved Christians, perhaps sometimes misunderstood and misconstrued by its readers. I would certainly want to argue the latter: that the problem lies—where there has been a problem—not with the Bible, but only with certain very inadequate readings of the Bible. In fact, the biblical story in itself provides us with important resources—Christians would say, *ultimately* important resources, provided by God himself—in our quest to be both earth-keepers and people-keepers, and indeed to understand the interrelationship between these two. I want to show some ways in which this is so, focusing on the Old Testament Scriptures, and within these Scriptures primarily on the early chapters of Genesis. This is not only because of the importance of the early chapters of Genesis to a Christian worldview, but also because of the practical matter of the space available for this presentation. Towards the end of the paper I shall nevertheless begin to branch out to some extent into the remainder of the Old Testament, so that we get a fuller picture of biblical teaching. My tendency, incidentally, will be to say more about earth-keeping than people-keeping. This is not because I think that the first is more important than the second, but only because I think

Christians have more often understood the imperatives surrounding the second than those surrounding the first.

The Cosmos has a Creator

Fundamental to the biblical vision of the world are the opening chapters of Genesis. It is here that we first learn to call the thing that we are involved in day by day "Creation" rather than "Nature." *In the beginning God created*, proclaims Genesis 1—a God who is personal and moral, and has tremendous interest in what he has created and what is for its good. Before he creates, there is only *tohu wabohu* (Gen 1:2), a Hebrew phrase referring to the formlessness and emptiness of the cosmos. *In* his creating God *both* provides the "form," giving the cosmos a particular structure and shape, *and* makes an empty place full—full of life. This terra-forming, first, finds light separated from darkness, the heavens from the earth, the earth from the seas, and the earth is given a particular character as a plant-producing place. The earth is made habitable. This shaped but empty place is then, secondly, provided with inhabitants for each of its spheres—luminaries for the heavens, birds and sea creatures for air and the seas, and land creatures for the earth. In this speaking of creation into being, the distribution of God's words perhaps already indicates a certain hierarchy of importance in creation, or at least a certain focus of interest—there is much more to be said on the sixth day (over 80 Hebrew words) than on the first (2 Hebrew words). The spotlight in Genesis 1 falls upon the earth rather than upon the heavens; and on the earth, it falls upon the land creatures above all other creatures. Among the land creatures, it falls upon the human creatures especially—those who are said to have been made in God's own image and likeness. What Genesis 1 suggests by identifying the fashioning of human creatures in this way as a *crucial moment* of God's creation, Genesis 2 also suggests by making human beings the *center* of God's creation, in which plants and herbs cannot appear before there are people to work the ground (Gen 2:5), and indeed we do not hear of trees, animals, and birds until after human creation has been accomplished (2:9, 19–20). The interest of both passages has little to do with chronology, but everything to do with different strategies for emphasizing the importance of human beings in the context of creation.

Is Biblical Creation Theology Destructively Anthropocentric?

Now this conviction about the importance of human beings in creation has brought the Bible into disrepute in some quarters in recent times, as the impact of such beings on the remainder of creation has become an important matter of debate. Many will know of the famous essay dating from the late 1960s by Lynn White, "The Historical Roots of our Ecologic Crisis." Claiming to describe what it is that Christianity has told people historically about their relations with their environment, he writes as follows:

> By gradual stages a loving and all-powerful God had created light and darkness, the heavenly bodies, the earth and its plants, animals, birds and fishes. Finally, God had created Adam and, as an afterthought, Eve to keep man from being lonely. Man named all the animals, thus establishing his dominance over them. God planned all of this explicitly for man's benefit and rule: no item in the physical creation had any purpose save to serve man's purposes. And, although man's body is made of clay, he is not simply part of nature: he is made in God's image. Especially in its Western form,

Christianity is the most anthropocentric religion the world has seen.[1]

Now I cannot here enter into a discussion of whether White is entirely correct in his description of what Christianity has taught, but it is certainly true that I have met or read about Christians who hold more or less the view of the world that White outlines, and who have come to hold as a result a quite instrumentalist and pragmatic view of the rest of creation in relation to themselves. White himself identifies as a spokesman for this Christian tradition Ronald Reagan, when he was Governor of California. The future American President said, it is alleged, of one the great outstanding features of his state, "When you've seen one redwood tree, you've seen them all." Some Christians, we must admit, hold a view of Christian faith that does not have much place in it for earth-keeping. But is this true of the biblical story that allegedly informs the Christian worldview? Far from it!

Beings in Creation Each Have Their Own Purpose

In the first place, although it is true that Genesis 1 describes the fashioning of human beings as a crucial moment of creation, this does *not* of itself imply that "no item in the physical creation had any purpose save to serve man's purposes." One of the recurring refrains of Genesis 1, in fact, is that all creatures were created "according to their kinds"—distinct from each other, in an ordered environment. As Gordon Wenham puts it in his Genesis commentary, "there is a givenness about time and space which God has ordered by his own decree."[2] This "givenness" is all part of the "goodness" of things, and it implies a God-given usefulness and dignity in the case of each individual member of the various families of creation—including plants and trees—that is not dependent upon human beings, even though humans have their own role to play within the cosmos. All creatures are God's creatures, whatever their "kinds"; and the story of God does not simply involve humans, as Job discovers at the end of his long dispute with God in Job 38–41, where he learns just how far that story concerns nonhuman creation and how little it revolves around him. Indeed, human beings are themselves resolutely part of the creation in Genesis 1 and 2. They do not have a day of creation to themselves, but share the sixth day with the other land creatures. The emphasis lies on the commonality that exists between the humans and the rest of the animal creation. Genesis 2 underlines this commonality, by telling us that humans are indeed "produced" from the earth in the same way as the other animals (Gen 2:7; 2:19). Humans are humus. We are made out of soil, "from the dust of the ground," and given life by God who breathes into us the breath of life (Heb. *nišmat ḥayyim*, 2:7), which is what makes a person "a living being" (Heb. *nepeš ḥayyāh*, 2:7). In these respects we are no different from the other animals. Genesis 1:20 uses the same phrase, "living being," of the sea creatures, and 2:19 uses it of the land animals and birds, while 7:22 speaks of the flood as destroying everything that had the breath of life in its nostrils (*nišmat-rûaḥ ḥayyim*). Notice further Psalm 104:30—"When you send your Spirit, they [i.e. all creatures] are created, and you renew the face of the earth." Human beings, in Genesis 2, are only one subset of God's "living beings," into whom God has breathed the breath of life, and they are just as fragile as all those creatures are. They have a limited period of life, and they are vulnerable to threats on every side (Ps 104:29; Job 34:14). Metaphors of dust and grass most frequently describe them (e.g. Gen 2; Job 4:19, Ps 103:13–17). We are wonderfully created as humans, then (see further Ps 139:13–16 and Job 10:8–12), but no more so than other creatures. In none of this material would we find a foundation for White's claim that "no item in the physical creation had any purpose save to serve man's purposes." Created beings all have their own purposes and destinies under God, biblically-speaking, independently of their relationships with humans, as a psalm like Psalm 104 beautifully reminds us (the following extract taken from vv. 10–23):

> He makes springs pour water into the ravines; it flows between the mountains.
> They give water to all the beasts of the field; the wild donkeys quench their thirst.
> The birds of the air nest by the waters; they sing among the branches.
> He waters the mountains from his upper chambers; the earth is satisfied by the fruit of his work.
> He makes grass grow for the cattle, and plants for man to cultivate—bringing forth food from the earth: wine that gladdens the heart of man, oil to make his face shine, and bread that sustains his heart …
> The moon marks off the seasons, and the sun knows when to go down.
> You bring darkness, it becomes night, and all the beasts of the forest prowl.
> The lions roar for their prey and seek their food from God.
> The sun rises, and they steal away; they return and lie down in their dens.
> Then man goes out to his work, to his labor until evening (see further Ps 147:8–9).

The Bible itself, then, does not appear supportive of White's alleged "Christian axiom that nature has no reason for existence save to serve man."[3] The conclusion to the creation week in Genesis 1:1–2:4 occurs, indeed, not on the sixth day with the creation of human beings, but on the seventh when God "rested." It is this Sabbath rest, not the creation of humanity, which completes creation and brings its days to the perfect biblical number of seven. This Sabbath rest was later observed weekly in Israel, on which day it was again the *commonality* of all creatures that was emphasized, not the utility of some in respect of others (Exodus 20:8–11):

> Remember the Sabbath day by keeping it holy. Six days you shall labor and do all your work, but the seventh day is a Sabbath to the LORD your God. On it you shall not do any work, neither you, nor your son or daughter, nor your manservant or maidservant, *nor your animals*, nor the alien within your gates. For in six days the LORD made the heavens and the earth, the sea, and all that is in them, but he rested on the seventh day. Therefore the LORD blessed the Sabbath day and made it holy.

The Cosmos Was Not Created For Human Benefit

What are we to make, secondly, of the notion that "God planned all of this [creation] explicitly for man's benefit and rule"? A nonhuman being might have its own purpose, but yet at the same time have a purpose beyond that and higher than that, in terms of servicing the needs of human beings. Here we must first of all deal with two of White's other statements, which are somewhat misleading—at least if we are tempted to confuse what the Bible actually says with what some Christians have made it say historically.

"Naming" Does Not Imply Exerting Authority

White states that "man named all the animals, thus establishing his dominance over them." It cannot be established from Genesis 2, however, that the naming of the animals has anything to do with establishing dominance over them. Although the naming of someone in the Old Testament is in fact often done by a person who has authority over another (e.g. a parent), it should be obvious that we cannot deduce from this fact that there is an intrinsic link between naming and asserting authority. The case of Hagar's naming of God in Genesis 16:13 stands as an evident counter-example: "She gave this name to the LORD who spoke to her: 'You are the God who sees me.'" Furthermore, the context of the naming of the animals in Genesis tells against any idea of authority being exercised in this *particular* naming. At this point in the story, a search is being made among the other creatures that God has made to see if any of these is suitable as the kind of soul mate required by "the earthling"—*'ādām* made from *'ădāmāh*, "ground." These are creatures in many ways like the earthling—"living creatures," as we have seen, who themselves derive from the ground (*'ădāmāh*, Gen 2:7 and 2:19). Many of these derive, like the earthling, from the sixth day of creation. There is a commonality between human and animal creation that at least suggests the possibility that Adam *might* find his deepest needs and aspirations for society among these other animals. The emphasis of the passage lies on kinship and community. I see nothing in it that implies that the naming has anything to do with asserting authority. It is just that the earthling is the one who possesses language, like God.

The Bearers of the Image of God are Not Transcendent Over Nature

This brings me directly to the second of White's statements that I want to comment on: "Although man's body is made of clay, he is not simply part of nature: he is made in God's image." He goes on to say that "man shares, in great measure, God's transcendence of nature,"[4] and to suggest that it is this belief in human transcendence that has led on to our modern sense of superiority over nature, our contempt for it, and our willingness to exploit it. To this I would only say that if this is what interpreters of the book of Genesis have deduced from it, then they have not been very careful readers of the book, and/or they have perhaps not been sufficiently careful, when reading, to allow the text to critique whichever version of Greek philosophy has been *influencing* their reading at the time. For Genesis does not encourage us for a moment to believe that our human status as beings made in God's image results in our not being truly part of nature, but somehow transcendent over it. In Genesis, it is as resolutely mortal, creation-bound persons that we are *also* God's image-bearers. No part of us is "naturally" transcendent, in the sense that it is immortal and divine. It is true that Greek-influenced Christians throughout the ages have indeed spoken in ways that have suggested otherwise, passing down through the ages a dualism of soul and body in which there is a clear distinction between the earth-bound and the heaven-bound. It is true that this anthropology can all too easily be conscripted to serve in an overall theology of Gnostic tendency that is dismissive of the earthly sphere as only the temporary prison of the precious divine "spark" that is destined to fly back to God. The Hebrew Genesis, on the other hand, holds that humans are created by God as *whole* people. The human being of Genesis 2:7 does not *have* a soul, but rather *is* a soul (Gen. 2:7; *nepeš ḥayyāh*, "a living being"); (s)he is not a collection of "parts," some heavenly and some earthly, but an *integral* being. This is why Christians, when they are thinking rightly and remembering that they are not Greek philosophers, believe in the resurrection of the body, rather than simply in the survival of the soul—although right thinking about bodies has not necessarily been a defining activity of the church throughout all the ages.

Now clearly human beings, while certainly not "sharing, in great measure, God's transcendence of nature" as White would have it, *are* from a biblical point of view made in the "image and likeness" of God (Gen 1:27). We *do* resemble God in some ways that other creatures do not, and various suggestions have been made about what it is that we might share that thus makes us somewhat "divine"—reason, perhaps, or personality, or free will, or self-consciousness, or intelligence. But as important as any of these aspects of humanness might be as reflections of God's nature and character, they must not be allowed to overshadow what is certainly an important implication of the "image and likeness" language here, which is that human beings are created to be *representatives* of God on earth. That is to say: as important as it is to understand what the language of image and likeness means in terms of our *nature* as human beings, it is just as important to understand what it means in terms of our *vocation*. In the ancient world, kings placed statues (images) of themselves in chosen territories in order to lay claim to that territory—the statue represented the king in his claim to sovereignty over the territory. The king himself, in the common oriental view, was made *in the divine image* as God's representative on earth—both Egyptian and Assyrian texts describe the king as the image of God in this way. This is a particular example of the more general ancient Near East thinking that the images of gods placed in temples were representations of them—mediators of their person and presence. Genesis 2:7 in fact clearly recalls in the mind of the reader who has read Genesis 1 the ceremonies of the ancient Near East that invested such "images" with divine "life" and *enabled* them to function as representations of the gods in their temples. In Genesis, the human creature is formed from the ground out of the clay and shaped and fashioned by God, who then breathes the breath of life into his creation and sets it in a garden by a river. This echoes texts from outside Israel in which we read about representations of the gods being endowed with life by the priests, informed by them that they were to join Ea, father of the gods, in celestial splendour, and led forth by them to a garden by the river to symbolize their new power. The presence of the deity in the statue was magically effected through a ceremony called the "Opening of the Mouth." It is not as autonomous beings that humans are "made in God's image and likeness," then, but as mediators of God's person and presence to the rest of creation. Humans function as representative, delegated government. Such persons, we assume, would only be justified in adopting (as White puts it) a superior attitude in respect of nature, or in expressing contempt for it, or in exploiting it, if this were in line with the will of God who delegated to the person that government; and this does not appear to be the kind of God we are dealing with in the Bible.

Human Rule, But Not Sole Human Benefit

This brings us back to consider, then, White's statement that "God planned all of this [creation] explicitly for man's benefit and rule." It is undeniable that in Genesis 1:26–28 human beings *are* told to rule and to subdue the rest of creation—they are presented as kings within their domain.[5] The verb for "rule" in Genesis 1:26 and 1:28 is *rādāh*, and it is allied in 1:28 with *kābaš*, "trample," "subdue." These are both verbs which echo the Old Testament language about kingship and military conquest. *Kābaš* is used elsewhere in the Old Testament to mean "to enslave" (Jer 34:11); "to rape/sexually assault" (Esth 7:8); "to trample underfoot" (Zech 9:15). We read of the land (Heb. *'ereṣ*, the word used for "earth" in Gen 1:28) actually being "subdued" before God and/or his people in Numbers 32:22, 29 and Joshua 18:1; and we hear of David "subduing" all the nations in 2 Samuel 8:11. To use *kābaš* is to use the language of conquest, usually military conquest; and of its common consequence, which was enslavement. *Rādāh* represents the language of government. It is used elsewhere in the Old Testament of kings governing their subjects (e.g. 1 Kgs 4:24); of Israel ruling over those who had previously oppressed them (Isa 14:2); of the upright ruling over the wicked (Ps 49:14); of priests ruling at the direction of the false prophets (Jer 5:31); of shepherds ruling the people (Ezek 34:4). It is often associated, as in this last passage, with ideas of force or harshness, and indeed slavery (e.g. in 1 Kgs 5:16, where the officers "ruled over" the forced laborers). The language used of human rule over the earth in Genesis 1, then, is fierce—even disturbingly graphic—language. It is perhaps unsurprising that some have taken it to legitimate aggressive, exploitative and rapacious human actions with regard to the rest of creation, while others have wondered whether we now need a text rather different from the Genesis text: "Do not fill the earth, be kind to it, and live in harmony with other creatures." However, we must insist here on a basic rule in the interpretation of any text, including biblical texts: that words mean what they mean in a *context*. In the first place, the vocation of kings *in the context of the ancient world* did not involve only ruling and subduing, but also looking after the welfare of their subjects and ensuring justice for all (for an Old Testament illustration of this reality, see Ps 72). To denote human beings as "kings" over the earth by using the language of kingship to describe them is therefore not of itself to imply that these rulers have permission to exploit and ravage the earth. This is especially the case *in a literary context* where it is made entirely clear that the kingship of which we are thinking when we speak of human rule over the earth is derived from the one God who is alone truly King. As Psalm 24:1 will later say: "The earth is the Lord's, and everything in it." Genesis does not have in view absolute and unfettered power that can be used as human beings will, with no moral restraint. Humankind's responsibility is rather to exercise "dominion" *on behalf of* the God in whose world they live—a just, peaceable dominion, of the sort that is described for us in a psalm like Psalm 72. Genesis 2 makes it clear what this actually looks like in relation to the rest of creation, when it exegetes "dominion" in terms of earth-keeping. The world is portrayed in that chapter as a garden—an enclosed parkland, in which human beings live in harmony with their kin (the animals) and with God, who walks in the garden in the cool of the evening. Here the language noticeably shifts from the language of kings to the language of priest, and we find the earthling placed in God's parkland "to work it and take care of it," literally to "serve it and keep/guard it" (Heb. *'ābad* and *šamar*). This is religious language that underlines the importance and sacred nature of the task—it is worship and conservation—and also reminds us of the connection between the garden and the tabernacle or temple. Note in particular Numbers 3:7–8: "They are to perform [*šamar*] duties for him and for the whole community at the Tent of Meeting by doing the work [*'ābad*] of the tabernacle. They are to take care of [*šamar*] all the furnishings of the Tent of Meeting, fulfilling the obligations of the Israelites by doing the work [*'ābad*] of the tabernacle.

The dominion given to human beings is evidently not a *lording it over* the rest of creation—it is sacrificial *looking after* creation. It is part of our createdness in God's image that we should imitate him in his creativity and in his providential care for creatures. This is not to negate the importance of the hard-edged language of Genesis 1. In the course of fulfilling the human vocation, ruling and subduing in a forceful way *will* be required of us along with caring and tending—there is no romantic view of creation-gardening here, in which planting alone, and without weeding, will suffice. It is of course all too easy to allow hard-edged concern for creation to dissipate into the kind of mushy and naïve, often anti-technological, sentimentality about "Nature," of the kind that we see more and more all around us. "Nature" is not, however, the benevolent deity that many would have us believe she is, as the millions of people who struggle with her all over the world would bitterly testify. It does require governance. Genesis 1 and 2 capture the necessary balance, which is also the balance of just government elsewhere in the Old Testament when human society alone is more in view.

In summation of this section of the paper, then, and in response to Lynn White's critique: God did plan creation with human rule in mind, as an aspect of the human role in creation as image-bearer, but the Bible resists the idea that he planned creation "explicitly for man's benefit." On the contrary, the biblical view is that human dominion, rightly exercised, is for the benefit of all creation. The ruling king of Genesis 1 and Psalm 8 is at the same time the priestly servant of Genesis 2, a steward of God's world accountable always and in every respect to the Owner of the Garden, the Creator. In the Genesis story itself, our earliest extended picture of what this looks like is provided by Noah, "portrayed as uniquely righteous in 6:9 ... [and] also the arch-conservationist who built an ark to preserve all kinds of life from being destroyed in the flood."[6]

People-Keeping in the Early Chapters of Genesis

To this point in the paper, having allowed Lynn White to set the agenda, I have been trying to show how the biblical creation story, far from encouraging a casual or negative attitude towards nonhuman creation, in fact provides a substantial foundation for what we might call an ecological theology. A loving and all-powerful God has created this cosmos that we inhabit, and our very purpose as we live here is bound up with the care of creation, which belongs to God and not to us. If, as White suggests, Christianity is the most anthropocentric religion the world has seen, it is only so in this sense: that it has a very high view of what human beings are and can achieve, and holds them centrally responsible for how things work out in the world in which they have been placed. This is true of how we treat nonhuman creation; and of course it is equally true of how we treat our fellow human beings. This brings us to the second theme of my paper: the theme of people-keeping.

Here too I would like to begin with Lynn White's characterization of Christian faith. "By gradual stages a loving and all-powerful God had created light and darkness, the heavenly bodies, the earth and its plants, animals, birds and fishes. Finally, God had created Adam and, as an afterthought, Eve to keep man from being lonely." This is indeed a version of Christian faith espoused by some Christians throughout history and down into present times. In this version of Christianity, the individual man stands apart not only from nonhuman creation, but essentially also from that part of human creation that is female. The woman is not intrinsically bound up with the man in terms of the achievement of his destiny, any more than the animals are. She merely comes along for the ride to provide the man with some comfort on the way. Some of the Church Fathers even doubted if her company was much to be desired if male company were available instead.

Again, however, we must question whether this view is well-rooted in the biblical creation story. Genesis 1:27 suggests to the contrary that the human beings who are called to the task of exercising dominion over the earth are both male and female. They are both *together* created in the image and likeness of God and jointly commissioned to their task. At the heart of human stewardship of the earth on God's behalf, then, stands human *community*—a co-operating, co-dependent unity. Dominion over the world is not to be exercised by one person, but by humankind corporately in sexual differentiation and togetherness. Nothing is said here of any sequencing in the way that males and females are created, nor of any theological significance that might be derived from such sequencing. Genesis 2 does then introduce "sequencing," although it does not make anything of it—which is unsurprising in a section of Genesis where it is generally obvious that the order of events in the creation process is not a pressing concern of the authors.[7] The woman does "come after" the man in this story (if indeed it is appropriate to refer to the 'ādām creature prior to 2:22 as a "man," since no sexual differentiation has yet taken place in the story), but the important point to notice is that the "man" himself is not yet a properly-created human being in 2:7–20, but only becomes so with the creation of the woman. When God finished each of the days of creation in Genesis 1, and completed the making of all the individual elements of each day, he saw that everything was "good"—including the creation of 'ādām, "human beings." In Genesis 2:18, however, we find 'ādām in a state of "not good": "It is not good for the man to be alone. I will make a helper suitable for him." Human beings are *intrinsically* both male and female—that is the reality that is "good." It is a communal reality. It is the human nature that humans are social beings. In Genesis 2:18 we are not yet there. And when we do get there in Genesis 2:22–23, we find the name first used to refer to the earthling (*'ādām*) throughout the story is different than the word for "man" (*'îš*) that is used in v. 23, when the man is spoken of in relation to the woman (*'iššah*). The close similarity of these nouns underlines the close connection between the persons, who are indeed to consider themselves as "one flesh" (Gen 2:24), in a figurative sense sharing the same body. An "afterthought" the woman is not.

The model used to envision human community in this passage is, of course, marriage, but we find here only a particular expression of a more general biblical view, that at the heart of the created order when it is functioning properly stands, not a just human individual, but a just human society. People-keeping and earth-keeping walk hand in hand, and the people-keeping is characterized not by hierarchy, but by mutuality—mutually just and loving relationships, in which the nature of the "other" as God's image-bearer is taken deeply seriously. This is a radical, important idea in the context of the ancient world in which the Genesis story was first told. In the ideology of the ancient Near East in general, it was kings and kings alone (with occasional exceptions) who were said to be made in the divine image. The focal point of the language appears to be Egypt, where, beginning in the New Kingdom, there are numerous examples of the king described as the image of a particular god. The pharaoh was described in these terms because he was believed to be the earthly manifestation of the deity, and thus he functioned on earth exactly as the image functioned in the temple. Other human beings, in standard ancient Near Eastern mythology, were created as the servants of the gods to keep them supplied with food. In the Atrahasis Epic of Old Babylon, for example, we are told that "the toil of the gods was great, the work was heavy, the distress was much," so the gods invented humanity to do the work.[8] Ancient Near Eastern culture was therefore resolutely hierarchical, and ordinary human beings were very much subordinate to the kings and their nobles as well as to the gods more generally. They were gods on earth, as their inscriptions often tell us. Contrary to this ideology, Genesis 1 claims that all human beings (and indeed both male and female human beings) are made in God's image. There is ruling and subduing to be done (as kings often do in their kingdoms), but it is the ruling and subduing of creation by humans beings in general. We have in Genesis, then, the democratization of an older and different idea, leading to the apparently uniquely Israelite notion that all persons, not just the king, occupy a preeminent place in the created order. Moreover, human beings are not created for the benefit of the gods in Genesis 1, and certainly not to supply the gods—including the king—with food. Rather, God provides food for all his creatures, including his human creatures—an abundant supply of food that implicitly enables rest from labor once a week on the Sabbath. The dignity of every human person is thus established. There are no gods in the created order, except those "images of God" who are, in fact, all human beings. There is only one God, and all his human creatures are on the same level in terms of worth and dignity, and in terms of the blessedness of life that they should enjoy under God. This view of human beings involves thus a fundamentally egalitarian, communal view of things that is quite out of step with Ancient Near Eastern ideology and much political and religious ideology since. The various ways in which it is out of step are apparent already in the remainder of the Old Testament story, as we shall shortly see.

Earth-keeping and people-keeping, characterized by mutual love and justice, walk hand in hand in Genesis. The integral connection between the two is signaled clearly in Genesis 3 and subsequent chapters, where dysfunction enters into the human relationships as a result of the human attempt to exercise moral autonomy in respect of God.

The man and the woman enter into a struggle for dominance, and one of their children murders his brother. Human society spirals downwards morally from this point onwards even as it develops economically and culturally; injustice rather than justice rules. The earth has been a blessed place hitherto; now cursing enters the scene. One result is that the work in the garden, which is already an aspect of the human vocation, comes to involve more pain than it had before, since the ground is cursed by God (Gen 3:17–19) and this means that much harder work will now be required to grow enough edible plants to survive. Dysfunction in the human community leads to dysfunction in the relationship between human beings and nonhuman creation. Ultimately, in Genesis 6, we find the earth "corrupt"—ruined, spoiled—and filled with violence, instead of being filled with God's creatures (Gen 6:11; cf. Gen 1:22, 28). God "sees" that "all flesh" have in fact corrupted their ways (6:12)—and by "all flesh" is meant humans *and* animals.[9] The point is not that the animals themselves are morally accountable. Rather, animal creation is caught up in the corruption, because where there is human dysfunction there is also dysfunction in the whole organic system that is creation. The consequence is that a great Flood will "ruin" an earth (Heb. šāḥat, NIV's "destroy" in Gen 6:13) that has already been "ruined" by its inhabitants (Heb. šāḥat three times in vv. 11–12—NIV's "corrupt/corrupted"). There will be an "uncreation," as the waters positioned within their boundaries by God at the beginning of time break back into the inhabited areas of the earth. Noah and his extended family are spared, however, along with animal-creation-in-miniature, and a covenant is eventually made (Gen 9:8–17) that again involves not only the *human* survivors but "all life on the earth." We could not have a more graphic illustration of the biblical conviction that a human society in which it is not acknowledged that I *am* my brother's keeper (Gen 4:9) cannot stand, and that in its falling it brings down the rest of creation that depends upon it for governance. People-keeping and earth-keeping go hand in hand.

People-Keeping and Earth-Keeping in Ancient Israel

To this point I have largely confined myself to what the book of Genesis has to say about these two themes and their connectedness. As we move towards the conclusion of this paper, however, I should like to say a few words about how these themes play out in the remainder of the Old Testament, as we turn from the story of creation to the story of Israel—with which nation, the Bible teaches us, God's plans in the world were directly bound up for a considerable part of human history. It was in Israel that the truth about God and the world was to be kept alive until the Messiah should come and the cosmos should be redeemed. Israelite society was to reflect, as much as it *could* given the reality of its situation in the ancient, fallen world, just people-keeping and earth-keeping. As a nation Israel itself had experienced at its birth in Egypt the counter-vision of the cosmos as it was legitimated by Near Eastern mythology in its ancient context. They had suffered under a "god" and had been required to work endlessly for that pharaoh-god as his slaves—a deity regarded in Egyptian religion as responsible for the fertility and well-being of his land, yet suffering horrendous ecological disaster in the plagues of Egypt as a result of his refusal to acknowledge the true and living god. It was in Egypt that Israel was considered in the biblical tradition to have come to know the LORD in fundamentally important ways, sharpened, perhaps, by way of contrast. It is the memory of being slaves in Egypt that seems to inform so much of biblical ethics. In Deuteronomy 17:14–20, for example, we find some guidelines in respect of kingship in Israel, should it ever come about. We notice in this passage a firm emphasis upon the indigenous character of such a king—he needs to be someone who understands Israelite tradition from the inside, and who understands therefore that an Israelite king cannot function like an Egyptian pharaoh. We note further that he must be obedient to God's law, particularly so that his heart may not be lifted up above his brethren—he is not allowed to become arrogant, either in respect of his neighbors or in respect of God. He is a commoner-king, not a king of the Egyptian sort—a king who serves as much as he rules. So it is that in the Old Testament vision of true kingship, we find the primary emphasis lying upon the provision of justice, especially for the weak and vulnerable, as in the opening verses of Psalm 72 (vv. 1–4):

> Endow the king with your justice, O God, the royal son
>   with your righteousness.
> He will judge your people in righteousness, your afflicted
>   ones with justice.
> The mountains will bring prosperity to the people, the hills
>   the fruit of righteousness.
> He will defend the afflicted among the people and save the
>   children of the needy; he will crush the oppressor.

It was the kind of king represented by the pharaoh, on the other hand, that true worshippers of the LORD in Israel feared, as the prophet Samuel makes clear in 1 Samuel 8—a king appointed out of a popular desire to have done with God's kingship and to institute a monarchy that the people could call their own. Such a king, warns Samuel, would organize society around his own needs and once again oppress the people. This was of course the kind of king that Israel often had, historically. King Ahab stands as a good example (1 Kgs 16–22). Here was a king who had lost touch with the true God, embracing the fertility religion of his wife Jezebel. He consequently lost touch with himself and his proper role in society, and brought disaster on Israelite society, symbolized and summed up in his treatment of Naboth in 1 Kings 21. It was not only kings who were capable of this loss of memory and the consequent abuse of their fellow image-bearers. The lament psalms are full of complaints about the ways in which the wicked generally oppress people. Psalm 73:4–9 graphically describes their lives:

> They have no struggles; their bodies are healthy and strong.
> They are free from the burdens common to man; they are
>   not plagued by human ills.
> Therefore pride is their necklace; they clothe themselves
>   with violence.
> From their callous hearts comes iniquity; the evil conceits
>   of their minds know no limits.
> They scoff, and speak with malice; in their arrogance they
>   threaten oppression.
> Their mouths lay claim to heaven, and their tongues take
>   possession of the earth.

The responsibility that *all* persons have to love their neighbors as themselves, conversely, is everywhere assumed in the Old Testament. It is explicitly stated in Leviticus 19:18, in the context of a number of examples of what this might mean (Lev 19:10–18):

> When you reap the harvest of your land, do not reap to the very edges of your field or gather the gleanings of your harvest. Do not go over your vineyard a second time or pick up the grapes that have fallen. Leave them for the poor and

the alien. I am the LORD your God. Do not steal. Do not lie. Do not deceive one another. Do not swear falsely by my name and so profane the name of your God. I am the LORD. Do not defraud your neighbor or rob him. Do not hold back the wages of a hired man overnight. Do not curse the deaf or put a stumbling block in front of the blind, but fear your God. I am the LORD. Do not pervert justice; do not show partiality to the poor or favoritism to the great, but judge your neighbor fairly. Do not go about spreading slander among your people. Do not do anything that endangers your neighbor's life. I am the LORD. Do not hate your brother in your heart. Rebuke your neighbor frankly so you will not share in his guilt. Do not seek revenge or bear a grudge against one of your people, but love your neighbor as yourself. I am the LORD.

Implicit in all this is the idea that your neighbor is, like yourself, an image-bearer—a person created by the same God as you. In Job 31:13–15 this is explicit:

> If I have denied justice to my menservants and maidservants when they had a grievance against me, what will I do when God confronts me? What will I answer when called to account? Did not he who made me in the womb make them? Did not the same one form us both within our mothers?

In Job's society there is social hierarchy—there are masters and there are slaves. Yet still Job recognizes a moral imperative towards justice in respect of his slaves, because in the end each of them is, as he is, a person created by God.

One of the things bound up with "keeping people" in ancient Israel in such good ways was the issue of how land was dealt with. If our biblical texts regard the earth as a whole as being the Lord's (Ps 24:1), it is equally true that they regard the small part of the earth occupied by Israel in the same way. This land, too, was a gift from God—not something that Israel owned by inalienable right, because of her own activity in possessing it (e.g. Deut 8:7–10; 11:10–12; 26:9), and certainly not something earned through virtue (9:4–5). It was something that could be lost if the nation of Israel failed to act justly within it (e.g. Hos 12:9; Amos 7:17). More than this, injustice itself—human communal dysfunction—is regarded in the prophets as intrinsically involving trouble the rest of creation. Hosea 4:1–3 starkly describes the entire, ailing reality of Israel in the 8th century BC:

> There is no faithfulness, no love, no acknowledgment of
>   God in the land.
> There is only cursing, lying and murder, stealing and adultery;
>   they break all bounds, and bloodshed follows bloodshed.
> Because of this the land mourns, and all who live in it waste
>   away; the beasts of the field and the birds of the air and
>   the fish of the sea are dying.

Communal dysfunction impacts the land itself, disabling earth-keepers from keeping it properly. One reason is that human violence can directly impact the land. Deuteronomy 20:19, for example, recognizes the way in which war, even in ancient times, was disastrous for the rest of creation, and urges combatants to try to limit the damage—partly for pragmatic reasons, but partly just because trees, in this case, do not deserve to be caught up in the conflict:

> When you lay siege to a city for a long time, fighting against it to capture it, do not destroy its trees by putting an axe to them, because you can eat their fruit. Do not cut them down. Are the trees of the field people, that you should besiege them?

Another reason that communal dysfunction impacts the land itself is that it distorts the relationship between earth-keepers and the earth, placing it disproportionately in the hands of those who do not care for God's laws, and certainly do not accept that "the land is mine and you are only tenants" (Lev 25:23). The land is a gift of God that has been by God's command distributed equitably to the people of Israel (Josh 13–22). It is a basic principle in the Old Testament that land is in fact to stay with the family to whom it has been given (Lev 25:23–24). Various rules about the redemption of land exist to ensure that this is so (as illustrated, for example, in the book of Ruth). As we saw in Leviticus 19, there are also rules about allowing the poor to benefit from the land, because they too have a part in it. That such a view of things was often set aside in ancient Israel by those who stood to gain most from doing so is evidenced by such passages as Isaiah 5:8–10 ("Woe to you who add house to house and join field to field till no space is left and you live alone in the land"), and Micah 2:1–5 ("They covet fields and seize them, and houses, and take them. They defraud a man of his home, a fellowman of his inheritance"). The book of Micah in particular paints a stark picture of systemic societal dysfunction in the Israel of his day, as wealth was accumulated in the hands of a few with the support not only of the judicial system but also of the religious authorities. God is not interested in religion that acts as a cloak for deceit and as a comfort for those embroiled in injustice and oppression, claims Micah, even if it is orthodox and conservative religion, or indeed, we might add, evangelical religion. As Micah 6:6–8 famously muses:

> With what shall I come before the LORD and bow down before the exalted God? Shall I come before him with burnt offerings, with calves a year old? Will the LORD be pleased with thousands of rams, with ten thousand rivers of oil? Shall I offer my firstborn for my transgression, the fruit of my body for the sin of my soul? He has showed you, O man, what is good. And what does the LORD require of you? To act justly and to love mercy and to walk humbly with your God.

It is more than a great pity—it is indeed a scandalous thing—that this Old Testament "ethics of land" has so often been spiritualized away in the Christian ethics of our modern period, to such an extent that it is not easy for many modern Christians to understand the kind of easy connection made by Micah in his preaching between religion and social justice, between private morality and social responsibility. To the extent that this disconnect exists, there is a gulf fixed not only between the Bible and its modern readers, but also between these modern readers and Christians of earlier generations like Bishop Ambrose of Milan, who strikes modern Western people as more Marxist than Christian:

> When you give to the poor, you give not of your own, but simply return what is his, for you have usurped that which

is common and has been given for the common use of all. The land belongs to all, not to the rich; and yet those who are deprived of its use are many more than those who enjoy it.[10]

The world has been made for all, and a few of you rich try to keep it for yourselves. For not only the ownership of the land, but even the sky, the air, and the sea, a few rich people claim for themselves ... Do the angels divide the space in heaven, as you do when you set up property marks on earth?[11]

Conclusion

Much more could be said. I hope that I have said enough, however, to communicate the way in which the Old Testament looks at the whole matter of people-keeping and earth-keeping. You and I are made in the image of God. We have responsibility to look after other image-bearers; we also have a responsibility to look after the garden in which we have been set. "A Just Faith for a Whole World" involves taking both aspects of our vocation seriously. The Old Testament well understands that in a fallen world it is difficult, for all sorts of reasons, to fulfill either aspect of our vocation perfectly, and indeed to fulfill both of them at the same time. Yet it holds both before us, and it does not allow us to make easy choices between them. We are to live, indeed, in anticipation of a time when not only *human* society will be ordered perfectly justly, but *the entire cosmos* will be redeemed; the time of a new natural order, indeed of a new heavens and a new earth (Isa 27:1; 65:17–18; 66:22; Ezek 47:1–12), when "the wolf will live with the lamb, the leopard will lie down with the goat ... They will neither harm nor destroy on all my holy mountain, for the earth will be full of the knowledge of the LORD as the waters cover the sea" (Isa 11:6–9); the time of the ultimate fulfillment of the words of Hosea 2:18:

> In that day I will make a covenant for them with the beasts of the field and the birds of the air and the creatures that move along the ground. Bow and sword and battle I will abolish from the land, so that all may lie down in safety.

It is this time that the apostle Paul has in mind in Romans 8:19–22, when he writes of creation waiting "in eager expectation for the sons of God to be revealed," so that these sons of God can do their job of earth-keeping properly and "the creation itself will be liberated from its bondage to decay." In the meantime our own task is not only to be light, illuminating the darkness of contemporary human society with respect to its true vocation, but also salt, slowing down and perhaps even preventing further creation-decay. People-keeping and earth-keeping are not different options. They are both part of the same Christian calling.

16

"'HOW CAN I UNDERSTAND, UNLESS SOMEONE EXPLAINS IT TO ME?' (ACTS 8:30-31): EVANGELICALS AND BIBLICAL HERMENEUTICS"

One of the consequences of emigrating to Canada in 1997 was that I began to encounter, at first hand, widely-endorsed North American ways of thinking about the Bible and how to read it, of which I was only dimly aware while living, teaching, and writing in Europe. Some of these are what can only be described as fundamentalist ways of thinking, and they are extremely unhelpful to the reading of the Bible that actually exists. It is for this reason that I have spoken and written just as robustly against the proponents of these "ways" as I have against others who disable the aspiring Bible-reader from reading the biblical texts well (e.g. as narrative, or as history)—others who are often, incidentally, just as "fundamentalist" in outlook on the "left" as are those on the "right," but in pursuit of different agendas. This particular essay was intended as a constructive critique of the Chicago Statement on Biblical Hermeneutics (1982), whose popularity in certain Christian circles in North America is quite astonishing in the light of its many and obvious deficiencies. I originally wanted the essay published in a journal where it might actually be read by the Statement's admirers, but in this quest I completely failed. It was turned down by the editor of the Journal of the Evangelical Theological Society *for no very coherent reason. It was accepted initially by the* Westminster Theological Journal, *but then the editor was removed, and the new editor told me shortly before publication that he was not, in fact, going to publish it (again, the reasons were entirely unconvincing). Eventually it appeared in the* Bulletin for Biblical Research *in 2007. I was glad to see it published, but I cannot help but think that in the end I got to preach only to the choir.*

"How can I understand, unless someone explains it to me?"

And Philip replied,

> WE AFFIRM that a person is not dependent for understanding of Scripture on the expertise of biblical scholars ... WE AFFIRM the necessity of interpreting the Bible according to its literal, or normal, sense. The literal sense is the grammatical-historical sense, that is, the meaning which the writer expressed ... WE AFFIRM that the Bible's own interpretation of itself is always correct, never deviating from, but rather elucidating, the single meaning of the inspired text. The single meaning of a prophet's words includes, but is not restricted to, the understanding of those words by the prophet and necessarily involves the intention of God evidenced in the fulfillment of those words.[1]

And the Ethiopian rode on none the wiser because, unfortunately, he *was* dependent on a biblical scholar for his grasp of the scriptural passage in question; he didn't himself understand its grammatical-historical sense—that is, the meaning that the writer had expressed. Moreover, he had an uneasy feeling that there was something wrong somewhere, when it was claimed that the Bible ought to be interpreted in terms of the meaning which the writer expressed and yet at the same time that "the single meaning of a prophet's words includes, but is not restricted to, the understanding of those words by the prophet and necessarily involves the intention of God evidenced in the fulfillment of those words." The more he thought about this last point, in fact, the more confused and troubled he became; and he was glad when at last the voice of the apostle, affirming still, faded into the distance, and he found himself alone once more in the desert, with only his mute charioteer and his puzzling text for company, his horizons still confused.

"Do you understand what you are reading?" (as Philip asked). The question has pressed itself upon the Christian Church throughout the centuries, perhaps especially in the case of Christians of the Protestant persuasion, with their emphasis on the importance of Scripture in the life of the believer and the believing community. For "conservative Protestantism ... looks on the Bible as *sola fidei regula* and not as just *prima fidei regula* ... In that conservative Protestantism takes *only* the Bible as authoritative, there is no secondary means of making clear the meaning of the Bible."[2] It has been of the greatest importance for Christians of this persuasion, then, to be sure that they truly do understand what they are reading in the Bible—the individual sentences and paragraphs and chapters, the various whole books as whole books, and the various parts of the Bible taken together. It has been particularly important that readers ensure that, rather than simply reading out of it what they have first brought to it, they are giving the biblical text its own voice so that the Bible does indeed have authority over the reader rather than vice versa. So it is that over the course of time various rules of Bible reading have emerged that are designed to guide the reader in respect of proper and improper ways of reading the Bible, in the hope that true rather than false interpretations of it will emerge; and a particular term has come to be widely employed as an "umbrella term" to refer to this rule-governed biblical interpretation. It is the term "hermeneutics," from the Greek verb *hermeneuein*, "to interpret, translate or explain." Bernard Ramm writes of the matter in these terms:

> Hermeneutics is the science and art of Biblical interpretation. It is a science because it is guided by rules within a system; and it is an art because the application of the rules is by skill, and not by mechanical imitation. As such it forms one of the most important members of the theological sciences.[3]

For Ramm, hermeneutics is as a theological discipline, "the science of the correct interpretation of the Bible."[4] The word has, in fact, often been used interchangeably with "interpretation" or indeed with "exegesis," with the emphasis falling upon how one's understanding of the biblical text could be achieved by the observance of the proper hermeneutical rules. In more recent times, however, it has sometimes been used more broadly of the entire process by which a biblical text comes to be understood, with the emphasis sometimes falling on the only partial adequacy of the application of "rules," as such, in the pursuit of understanding. The authors of the *Chicago Statement on Biblical Hermeneutics* reflect this more recent shift in emphasis, while not approving of certain aspects of it, when they affirm "that the term hermeneutics, which historically signified the rules of exegesis, may properly be extended to cover all that is involved in the process of perceiving what the biblical revelation means and how it bears on our lives."[5] In the background here lie philosophical questions about the interpretation of texts in general (not only biblical texts), most notably the question as to what the circumstances are that make the understanding of *any* text possible.[6] In this discussion, the role of the *interpreter* in *creating* or at least *participating in the creation* of meaning has tended to come to the fore, and it has become customary to speak of the "two horizons" that must be merged if an act of understanding is to take place—the horizon of the text, and the horizon of the interpreter. Understanding occurs when subject and object move into appropriate relationship with each other.[7]

What kind of biblical hermeneutics ought evangelical Christians to embrace for themselves and to advocate to others? That is the question at the heart of this article. In asking it, I take the term "hermeneutics" in the broader sense expressed in the *Chicago Statement*, to refer to "all that is involved in the process of perceiving what the biblical revelation means and how it bears on our lives." I take the term "evangelical Christian" to mean much the same as the terms "Protestant" or "conservative Protestant" in the earlier parts of this article. I recognize that it is a slippery term that has been used historically of various religious groups from a variety of Christian traditions, and that the diversity of the people and institutions to which it has been applied, both theological and ecclesiastical, has led some commentators to argue that the label is in fact meaningless.[8] At the heart of "evangelical" concern, nonetheless, and in the midst of much diversity of thought and practice, has been the preservation and promotion of what are regarded as foundational aspects of historic Christian faith, especially as these came to fresh expression in the Reformation. Fundamental here is the place of the Bible as God's inspired Word and as the final authority in all matters of Christian faith and life—the norm that cannot be corrected by other sources (*norma normans, non normata*, as the Reformers put it).[9] It is not the teaching of the Church, but the teaching of the Bible, that is paramount in the end, although evangelicals have no argument with much of the teaching of the Church throughout the ages, and indeed would claim to stand firmly for orthodox, historic Christian faith (properly understood) in the face of misunderstandings and perversions of it both ancient and modern and both within and without the Church. Particular evangelical emphases in response to such misunderstandings and perversions (although this is not an exhaustive list) have been: "Eternal salvation only through faith in Christ, a serious commitment to evangelism and missions, the necessity of personal conversion and a spiritually transformed life."[10] What manner of biblical hermeneutics should people with this kind of view of things embrace and advocate?

The Chicago Statement on Biblical Hermeneutics

I take as my starting point the *Chicago Statement*, for it remains to this day the only quasi-"official" statement that exists on evangelical hermeneutics. Norman Geisler indeed describes it, along with the earlier *Chicago Statement on Biblical Inerrancy* (1978), as representing "a consensus of evangelical scholarship on these fundamental topics."[11] The *Chicago Statement on Biblical Hermeneutics* consists of 25 articles, each of which contains an affirmation and a denial. These articles of affirmation and denial I wish to subject to critical scrutiny, as a way of clearing the ground for further reflection. I shall not comment directly and at length on every article, for reasons of space. I shall comment sufficiently, however, that an impression of the strengths and weakness of the whole emerges, along with some suggestions about the way ahead. This preliminary work will then provide the platform for a proposal as to which kind of biblical hermeneutic evangelicals should embrace and advocate to others.

Article I of the *Chicago Statement on Biblical Hermeneutics* (hereafter simply the *Statement*) affirms "that the normative authority of Holy Scripture is the authority of God Himself, and is attested by Jesus Christ, the Lord of the Church." It denies "the legitimacy of separating the authority of Christ from the authority of Scripture, or of opposing the one to the other." The concern here is to identify what Scripture says with what God says and to invest it with the very authority of God. The correct approach to the interpretation of the Bible begins with the recognition, gained from reflection upon biblical texts themselves, that we are dealing here with a book—a single book, albeit possessing many parts—in which and through which God speaks; and since it is God who speaks, the words carry authority in respect of the mortal and contingent reader. It is an uncontroversial beginning, from the point of view of historic Christian faith.

Article II affirms "that as Christ is God and Man in one Person, so Scripture is, indivisibly, God's Word in human language." It denies "that the humble, human form of Scripture entails errancy any more than the humanity of Christ, even in His humiliation, entails sin." This article requires more careful scrutiny. It proceeds by analogy, paralleling the dual aspects of divinity and humanity in Christ and in Scripture. The question is, however, whether the precise use made of the analogy is very convincing. Sin, after all, is ever and always moral fault, but errors in texts are not ever and always a matter of moral fault. It is certainly possible that they might arise from an intention to deceive (which would involve moral fault), but it is also possible that they might arise for some other reason, such as limitation of knowledge on the part of the writer (and this would *not* involve moral fault). What is it, then, about the biblical text in particular that inevitably leads to the equation of an error with a sin (for it appears to be an inevitable equation in the minds of the framers of the articles at this point)? Is it that there is no other explanation for error in a God-inspired text than that God has lied? Perhaps the thinking is that God, being God, is not limited in knowledge, and therefore that any such "errors" in the Bible could not be explicable otherwise than by divine deceit. Yet as plausible as this sounds when only logic is invoked, the fact of the matter is that the Bible presents to us a Christ who Himself, although without sin, was certainly not without limitation of knowledge (Mark 13:32).

It seems unwise to assume, therefore—if the analogy between Christ and Scripture is indeed to be pursued—that Scripture should be as unfettered as God by limitation of knowledge.[12] Indeed, the evidence is everywhere to be found in the Bible that the individual biblical authors *were*, like God-as-He-enters-the-world-in-Christ, limited in knowledge. It could hardly be otherwise, if they were (as they were) people of time and culture. And this limitation of knowledge is revealed in statements that, when measured by fuller knowledge gained from Scripture itself and from elsewhere, are surely not correct. The prophet Haggai tells his contemporary Zerubbabel, governor of Judah, that God will shake the heavens and the earth, overturn royal thrones and shatter the power of the foreign kingdoms, and make him the messianic king (Hag 2:22–23), yet this did not happen. Jesus describes the mustard seed as the smallest of all the seeds, but his statement does not correspond to scientific reality (Mark 4:30–31). All this is not very important. The reason it is not important is precisely because, first, it does *not* follow (as Article II implies) that biblical statements such as these somehow inevitably reflect negatively on the character or indeed the divinity of God; and second, it does not follow (which is the implication of following Article I with Article II) that biblical statements such as these inevitably undermine the normative authority of Scripture. On the contrary, it is the very wonder of the biblical understanding of God that God enters ever-changing history, accommodating Himself to its limitations and indeed to our sinfulness, in order not only to communicate with us but also to act on our behalf. If some so-called "errors" in regard to the full truth of things are the result, it is not a matter for concern,[13] and certainly not a reason for overall distrust of the Bible.[14]

It does, however, press upon us the question of hermeneutics; for clearly any proposed hermeneutic for the Bible, if it is to be regarded as the best and the truest, will need to be able convincingly to deal with the question of how we are to move from individual biblical statements, conditioned as they are by time and culture, to an overall understanding of the Bible as God's Word to us today. It will need to be able to help us to move from partial and limited individual texts—even some texts in which "error" might be alleged—to a reading of the whole. This may be relatively easy (it is not difficult to understand what Jesus meant by his parable in connection with the mustard seed, and how that fits into Jesus' and biblical teaching overall, and the precise size of the mustard seed in relation to all other seeds is, of course, irrelevant to the point at issue). It may be more difficult (the process by which Haggai's prophecy to Zerubbabel came to be seen as a prophecy that relates to the Church in Heb 12:26–29 merits some enquiry). Easy or difficult, hermeneutics must suggest how it is to be done. For

> the cultural trappings of the urbanized, technologized West of today are very different from those of the rural and pastoral Near East in the two millennia before Christ and also from those of Hellenistic towns in the first century AD— the worlds from which came our Old and New Testaments respectively ... noting the distance between their worlds and ours with regard to manners, customs, expectations, and assumptions about life is very necessary in interpreting Scripture, just as it is in all study of ancient documents

that present to us people of the past. To think of Jesus, or Socrates, or Julius Caesar, or the Buddha as if he were a man of our time and never to ask what was involved for him in being a man of his own time is bound to issue in grotesque misunderstanding.[15]

Moving on, Article III itself gives us one well-known hermeneutical key that has deep roots in Christian history. It affirms "that the person and work of Jesus Christ are the central focus of the entire Bible" and denies "that any method of interpretation which rejects or obscures the Christ-centeredness of Scripture is correct." It is not easy to argue with this article so long as the word "focus" indeed means just that, and there is no intention to collapse the entirety of biblical theology into Christology.[16] It would be difficult on any reading of the Bible to come to the conclusion that Jesus Christ is not the most important figure therein, and indeed that He is the center that makes ultimate sense of the remainder. Any reading of the "parts" of the Bible must keep in mind this center around which the parts coalesce.

Article IV affirms "that the Holy Spirit who inspired Scripture acts through it today to work faith in its message" and denies "that the Holy Spirit ever teaches to anyone anything which is contrary to the teaching of Scripture." This is closely related to Article V, which affirms "that the Holy Spirit enables believers to appropriate and apply Scripture to their lives" and denies "that the natural man is able to discern spiritually the biblical message apart from the Holy Spirit." These are again unexceptionable statements in themselves. It is difficult to see what they have to do with biblical hermeneutics directly, however. How does belief in the work of the Holy Spirit, so described, help us specifically in our quest to "read, understand, and apply" biblical texts? It is not made clear.

Article VI affirms "that the Bible expresses God's truth in propositional statements," and declares "that biblical truth is both objective and absolute," going on to explain "that a statement is true if it represents matters as they actually are, but is an error if it misrepresents the facts." It denies "that, while Scripture is able to make us wise unto salvation, biblical truth should be defined in terms of this function." It further denies "that error should be defined as that which willfully deceives." Here is substantive guidance about how the Bible should be read. It is somewhat problematic, however. In the first place it is perfectly clear that the Bible does not in fact always express God's truth in propositional statements. As J. I. Packer notes:

> Revelation is person-to-person communication (personal self-disclosure in and through the giving of information about oneself) ... revelation is embodied not only in propositions relayed by God's spokesmen on His behalf, but also in the attitudes, wishes, invitations, appeals, and reactions that they expressed by the way they put things ... divine revelation should not be thought of as if it were the kind of depersonalized conveying of information that one finds in official memoranda or company reports. Whether operating through verbal utterance, vision, sign, miracle, providence, or any other means, God's revelation was and is His personal self-disclosure, to which the only proper response is faith, worship, and obedience. Revelation is essentially God revealing *God*.[17]

It is one of the tasks of hermeneutics, indeed, to suggest how it is that God reveals himself to us in all kinds of biblical texts, whether they make propositions or not, and indeed *to what extent* God reveals Himself to us in any given text. For God is not revealed to us in equal measure in all parts of Scripture. "God spoke to our ancestors in many and various ways by the prophets, but in these last days he has spoken to us by a Son" (Heb 1:1–2), and most assuredly this latter speaking says more than all the former ones. In fact, all revelation of the divine self prior to the Incarnation must surely be regarded as partial and limited in respect of that great event. The Old Testament authors did not know as much about God as we know now.

This is the difficulty of the use of the word "absolute" of biblical truth in Article VI. Biblical truth taken as a whole may well be considered "absolute," but biblical truth considered in the particular is often presumably only *relatively* true. For example, it is not *absolutely* true that "as the cloud fades and vanishes, so those who go down to Sheol do not come up; they return no more to their houses, nor do their places know them any more" (Job 7:9)—as the New Testament resurrection narratives know. Nor is it *absolutely* true that "a slack hand causes poverty, but the hand of the diligent makes rich" (Prov 10:4)—as the Old Testament book of Job already knows. The first statement is only true in Job's limited experience of the world. The Church, having witnessed one person rise from the dead, hopes for something more for others. The second statement may reflect the limited experience of its author too, if it is intended to express a general truth. Whether it is so intended or not, it is certainly the case that the Bible knows of other causes of poverty than laziness (for example, oppression) and it is well aware that there is no universal connection between diligence and wealth (as, in fact, other proverbs show). A biblical hermeneutic needs to consider statements *in relation to others* in order to weigh how *far* they are true, so that Bible readers can come to a considered view on how absolute biblical Truth is to be expressed on topics such as the afterlife or wealth and poverty.

This necessary task is, however, denied to the reader by the article's apparent attaching of an ill-defined notion of "absolute truth" to all biblical statements *in their individuality*. Indeed, an impossible burden is thus laid on the reader's shoulders, for the definition of truth offered in Article VI makes no allowance at all for limitation of any kind arising out of the historical nature of divine revelation. On this definition a text like Job 7:9 "represents matters as they actually are," if true; if it does not represent matters as they actually are, it is in error. There is no room for any middle ground here, in which (for example) error might be defined "as that which willfully deceives" and the overall truth of biblical revelation might be affirmed while the limitations of particular biblical statements, taken by themselves, might be recognized. Yet the biblical interpreter *requires* such middle ground if she is to make sense of the Bible.

It is at this point that the reader of the Bible begins to wonder how far the Bible itself is truly guiding the principles of interpretation being advocated in the *Statement*, and how far other factors are far more determinative. For if the Bible itself were guiding the enterprise, how could anyone affirm that "the Bible expresses God's truth in propositional statements" that simply represent matters "as they actually are"? Article VII increases one's sense of unease, for it affirms "that the meaning expressed in each biblical text is single, definite, and fixed." Along with this article must be read Article XV, which affirms "the necessity of interpreting the Bible according to its literal, or normal, sense. The literal sense is the grammatical-historical sense, that is, the meaning which the writer expressed." It denies, further, "the legitimacy of any approach to Scripture that attributes to it meaning which the literal sense does not support." So the meaning expressed by the writer in each biblical text is single, definite and fixed; and that is the only meaning of importance to us as interpreters of the Bible. Yet the Bible itself does not encourage us to take this view of things. The Bible itself appears to suggest that God can mean things by Scriptural words that their human authors did not mean.

Let us return to the example of Haggai 2:20–23. As far as can be ascertained from the words employed, Haggai meant no more and no less than to promise Zerubbabel, governor of Judah, that on the day that God shook the heavens and the earth and overthrew the throne of kingdoms, he would take Zerubbabel and make him king. Yet the author of the epistle to the Hebrews (12:26–29) takes that divine promise to Zerubbabel as referring to his own time ("now he has promised, 'Yet once more I will shake not only the earth but also the heaven'"), and he looks forward from his own time to a future in which created things will be shaken, but not the kingdom of God. There is no reason to think that Haggai "meant" this by his words; yet his words are given that meaning in Hebrews.

Then again, let us consider the famous Immanuel prophecy in Isaiah 7:14 in its immediate Isaianic context. Isaiah promises King Ahaz a sign in regard to his current predicament, faced by the military might of the kings of Israel and Aram: a young woman will have a child and call his name Immanuel. Of whom does he speak? Clearly it is of a child to be born imminently, for "before the child knows how to refuse the evil and choose the good, the land before whose two kings you are in dread will be deserted. The LORD will bring on you and on your people and on your ancestral house such days as have not come since the day that Ephraim departed from Judah—the king of Assyria" (Isa 7:16–17). Isaiah means to refer to a contemporary child. Yet Matthew's Gospel (1:22–23) records the fulfillment of these words as taking place in Christ: "All this took place to fulfill what had been spoken by the LORD through the prophet: 'Look, the virgin shall conceive and bear a son, and they shall name him Emmanuel.'"

In neither of these examples is the meaning expressed by the writer—the grammatical-historical sense—of great interest to the later biblical author. The words are considered to carry another, far more significant meaning—at least, more significant for readers of the Bible who now share a different context from the original readers and hearers. One could multiply examples from the New Testament of the same kind of approach to biblical texts; and one would be hard pressed, from this cumulative New Testament evidence, to mount any argument that the meaning we are ultimately to be concerned with as biblical interpreters is any single, definite, and fixed meaning of a text that we can discern, as expressed by the original author. Indeed, one is led to worry that from the standpoint of the *Statement* our New Testament writers might be regarded as illegitimate interpreters of Scripture, for they appear clearly to attribute to it, from time to time, "meaning which the literal sense does not support."

Taking our lead from the Bible rather than the *Statement*, on the other hand, we might argue on the contrary that while interest in the grammatical-historical sense of an individual text may well be an important starting point for biblical interpreters, if they are to avoid reading anything they like into texts, far more important (surely) is the meaning of a text as it may be discerned within the entire canonical context of Scripture—its canonical sense. Biblical hermeneutics must give attention not just to what authors may have explicitly meant (so far as this can be ascertained), but also to ways in which the meanings of biblical texts elude their authors and take different shapes within the larger biblical and historical context, speaking now to *us* in very different terms to those in which they spoke to our *forebears*.[18]

Unsurprisingly, given the pressure of the biblical data, the authors of the *Statement* themselves evidently feel compelled to acknowledge to some extent this "gap" between words and meaning, for in Article VIII they deny "that the writers of Scripture always understood the full implications of their own words." Unfortunately they attempt to concede the point while still holding on to their impossible formulation with respect to single meanings, and the consequence is the most tortured prose of the entire document:

> WE AFFIRM that the Bible's own interpretation of itself is always correct, never deviating from, but rather elucidating, the single meaning of the inspired text. The single meaning of a prophet's words includes, but is not restricted to, the understanding of those words by the prophet and necessarily involves the intention of God evidenced in the fulfillment of those words.

The "single" meaning of the text now turns out to include meaning that was not in the mind of the original author at all. It is a desperate and unconvincing attempt to accommodate the biblical data to a frame of reference that is not in itself biblical. If Scripture "is its own best interpreter," we are surely obliged to pay it better attention than this when trying to discover in which ways it possesses "unity, harmony, and consistency" (Article XVII). We should not simply assume in advance that we know which kinds of unity, harmony, and consistency it *must necessarily* have. For that would presumably be to risk committing the error against which Article XIX rightly warns us: refusing to bring our preunderstandings of Scripture into harmony with what the Bible has to say, and indeed requiring Scripture to fit into alien preunderstandings. Article XIX only mentions a few of the alien preunderstandings—naturalism, evolutionism, scientism, secular humanism, and relativism. These are not the only possibilities, however. Modern readers of ancient texts must constantly keep in mind the distance between the reader and the text, and the danger of being blind to what we are bringing to our reading—in all respects.

One way of guarding against the ill-considered imposition of our own categories on biblical literature, of course, is to ask careful questions about what we may expect of these ancient texts, taken on their own terms, and what it might be anachronistic to expect of them. The authors of the *Statement* helpfully introduce this matter into their reflections in Article XIII, where they affirm "that awareness of the literary categories, formal and stylistic, of the various parts of Scripture is essential for proper exegesis, and hence we value genre criticism as one of the many disciplines of biblical study." Genre-recognition is indeed an indispensable aspect of biblical hermeneutics, as it is of the interpretation of any text, biblical or non-biblical. If we read a fictional work as if it were a historical work, or a poem as if it were a scientific treatise, we are going to make mistakes in our interpretation of these works of literature. Reflection on the genre or type of text with which we are dealing on any given occasion is a crucial part of the interpretive process. The denial that accompanies the affirmation in Article XIII is, however, curious: "WE DENY that generic categories which negate historicity may rightly be imposed on biblical narratives which present themselves as factual." It is a curious denial, because it seems *obvious* that no interpreter should *impose* a generic category on any text to which it is not suited—that would be an entirely counter-productive thing to do, if one were seeking understanding. Rather, one should endeavor to attach to every text the genre-label that best fits. It is still more curious that the interest of the *Statement* has at this point narrowed for no reason that is immediately apparent to "biblical narratives which present themselves as factual"—as if unfortunate genre-labeling were only a matter of serious concern to the interpreter of the Bible regarding these kinds of texts. I would have thought, on the contrary, that any misapprehension of genre with respect to any of our biblical texts should be a cause for concern—biblical narratives included.

And here I must register a concern with regard to the word "factual" in this denial. We have come across a concern with "facts" before, in Article VI, where we encountered the problematic claim "that the Bible expresses God's truth in propositional statements," allied to the assertion "that a statement is true if it represents matters as they actually are, but is an error if it misrepresents the facts." We noted how this way of looking at the Bible is not flexible enough to deal with the actual data of the Bible as they exist on the page. There is a lot more to biblical literature than "propositions" about "facts," and the propositions that do exist are always reflective of the circumstances of time and culture in which they are advanced. The examples I chose earlier to illustrate the point were taken from poetry and proverbs (Job and Proverbs); but exactly the same may be said of biblical narrative literature. We may well agree that this or that narrative appears to be intended as *historical* narrative by its authors, yet access to the history is still through the *narrative*, and there is more to the narrative than simply "factuality." This is true of all historical narrative, not just biblical historical narrative. Historiography is never merely a matter of stating "facts." All historiography is, on the contrary, purposefully designed narrative about the past that involves, among other things, the selection of material and its interpretation by authors who are intent on persuading themselves or their readership of certain truths about the past. This selection and interpretation is always made by people with a particular perspective on the world—a particular set of presuppositions and beliefs that do not derive from the facts of history with which they are working, but are already in existence before the narration begins—and these same people necessarily employ the customary literary convention and style of their time and culture in making their presentation of the past, which determines the precise way in which their story of the past is told.[19]

The author of the biblical conquest account of Joshua 9–12, for example, does not merely give us "the facts" of the matter with respect to the time period he is describing. He selects and interprets some facts from an innumerable array, and weaves them into a story about the past that is designed to teach his readers something, not only about the past, but about God and God's purposes in the world. It is further evident, when the broader context of second- and first-millennium BC conquest accounts from Assyria, Hatti, and Egypt is taken into consideration, that the biblical conquest account of Joshua 9–12 is a fairly typical example of this ancient form of writing, using commonly shared literary conventions to speak about that event.[20] This helps us greatly in reading the biblical text. It helps us to see, for example, what might already have been obvious to a careful reader of Joshua and Judges, that the summary of Joshua's southern campaign found in Joshua 10:40—Joshua "left no one remaining, but utterly destroyed all that breathed"—should be regarded as hyperbole indicating a very successful campaign, and not simply as a "fact" (although it is certainly a statement in a *historical* narrative). If indeed it were a "factual" statement, we should have to conclude within the terms of reference of the *Statement* that it is an error, for "a statement is true if it represents matters as they actually are, but is an error if it misrepresents the facts"—and there is plenty of evidence in the biblical texts themselves that many Canaanites survived the Israelite onslaught.

For these reasons it would have been much better if the authors of the *Statement* had avoided the word "factual" in Article XIII's denial, and instead employed the word "historical." For the current wording gives the impression that they are interested only in one manner of inappropriate imposition of generic category on biblical narrative historical texts, and not in others. Certainly we should not impose generic categories on these texts that lead us to devalue their historical referentiality; but should we not also avoid imposing on biblical historical narratives generic categories that conceal within them a particularly modern understanding of historicity and that, embracing this understanding, assume too readily and without due reflection that history-writing is only or mainly a matter of reporting "facts"? Should we not allow biblical narrative and historical texts, considered in their ancient environment, to lead us in our determination of the ways in which they intend to be historical, rather than accept what is perhaps an alien, modern preunderstanding of history (in the terms of Article XIX)?

The problem is that biblical hermeneutics must wrestle not only with what the biblical texts *say* but with what they *mean* in the saying of it, which is connected with the *form* in which it is said. Much interpretive trouble has followed from an inability among modern biblical interpreters to think well about this distinction, particularly in relation to the complex matter of "historicity." Unfortunately the *Statement* itself does not really help the interpreter in this regard. It seems less interested in helping us to read well—in their various dimensions as history, art and theology—"biblical narrative texts that present themselves as factual" than it is in ensuring that the historicity of such texts is safeguarded. Article

XIV is equally unhelpful in this way, while pursuing the same theme. It affirms "that the biblical record of events, discourses and sayings, though presented in a variety of appropriate literary forms, corresponds to historical fact," but it does not help us at all to know how "the variety of appropriate literary forms" impacts on our understanding of what the history is that the literature witnesses to, much less the theology that it teaches. It seems strange that a statement on hermeneutics should thus be content with telling us what to think *about* the biblical texts (or some of them), rather than helping us to *read* them; and indeed that it should apparently be more interested in certain preordained outcomes of our reading than in the process by which we arrive at the outcomes.

This "interest" is particularly clear in Article XXII, in which the main reason for the denial of Article XIII is perhaps to be found, and in the light of which we may well question the seriousness of the *Statement's* commitment to genre recognition as a fundamental aspect of biblical interpretation. If Article XIII denies "that generic categories which negate historicity may rightly be imposed on biblical narratives which present themselves as factual," Article XXII simply affirms "that Genesis 1–11 is factual, as is the rest of the book," proceeding to deny "that the teachings of Genesis 1–11 are mythical and that scientific hypotheses about earth history or the origin of humanity may be invoked to overthrow what Scripture teaches about creation." That Genesis 1–11 intends to provide us with "facts" I do not dispute. There are facts in it about God (for example, God is one and not many), about human beings (human beings, both male and female, are made in the image of God), and about the world in which we live (it is not itself divine, although it is blessed by God). Yet the question remains: in what *form* are these facts given to us? How has the final author of Genesis 1–11 selected his material and interpreted it, in line with his particular set of presuppositions and beliefs, and employed the literary conventions and style of his time and culture in presenting it to us? That we do not simply have "facts" in these chapters, in the sense in which the *Statement* uses the term, is obvious. It is presumably not *factually* the case, for example, that the man and the woman of Genesis 3 "heard the sound of the LORD God walking in the garden at the time of the evening breeze," as if God actually "walks." The narrative speaks of the fact of God's intimacy with human beings in the garden; but it does so in a "non-factual" way (if that is even the correct term—perhaps "nonliteral" would be better). Likewise, it speaks in the opening two chapters of Genesis of the fact of the creation of the world by the one God who will later reveal himself to Moses as Yahweh, but it does so in a way that shows little interest in a "factual" chronology of events.[21] To be sure, there are facts in Genesis 1–11—propositions about God, humans, and the world that may be derived from their content. But these "facts" are presented to the reader in a particular narrative form, and if one then presses on to discover more about the precise nature of that narrative form, one is driven relentlessly to the conclusion that it has been heavily influenced by its ancient Near Eastern environment.

Genesis 1–11 is in fact at all points in dialogue with the governing presuppositions about reality expressed in ancient Near Eastern literature outside the Bible, as well as in various nonliterary aspects of ancient Near Eastern culture such as architecture. So are other biblical texts of a non-narrative nature. Genesis 1, for example, is written against the background of, and alludes to, a common ANE cosmogony (that is, an account, usually in the form of a mythological tale, about the genesis or birth of the structured universe). The source of this cosmogony used to be understood as Mesopotamia, the location of the creation tale *Enuma elish* with its account of the battle between the god Marduk and the dragon goddess Tiamat; or Egypt, with its tale of combat between the creator god Re and the dragon Apophis. More recently, however, the mythological texts from Ugarit in Syria have demonstrated a more local version of this same myth, in which the god Baal Haddu (familiar as Baal in the Old Testament) battles the forces of chaotic destruction and death, called by such titles as Prince Sea (*yām*) and Judge River (*nāhār*), and sometimes Lotan (the equivalent of the biblical Leviathan) or the seven-headed serpent. The Bible reflects and alludes to this common ANE cosmogony in various ways and at different levels. For example, Psalm 29:10 portrays the victorious God of Israel enthroned upon the "flood." Psalm 74:13–14, in the midst of a section explicitly devoted to creation, tells of Yahweh's victory over "Sea" (*yām*) and the crushing of the heads of the "Sea Monster" (*tannînîm*) and of Leviathan. Another hymn to God as creator (Ps 89) refers to Yahweh's rule over the "Sea" (*yām*) after defeating the dragon Rahab. Psalm 104, which possesses various similarities with the Egyptian celebration of creation called the Hymn to the Aton, again alludes to the defeat of watery chaos, going on to describe the various positive uses to which water has been put within creation. We may also note Isaiah 51:9–13, where Yahweh is said to have killed Rahab the "Sea Monster" (*tannîn*), and dried up the waters of "Sea" (*yām*) and the "Great Deep" (*tĕhôm rabbāh*). The very brevity and allusiveness of the texts suggests familiarity on the part of their original authors and hearers with the cosmic battle pattern that we are describing here. So it is with Genesis 1:1–2. Watery chaos and darkness did already exist when God began to create the heavens and the earth, these verses tell us, but the forces of chaos posed no real threat to the one true and living God. They were simply "there," waiting to be organized into useful entities. If a battle took place to subdue them, it is of so little consequence to the author of Genesis that it is not even mentioned, and sea monsters (*tannînîm*) only appear in Genesis 1:21 as creatures of God like any other creatures.

The biblical authors do *propose* things about the nature of reality, and what they propose—about God, and the world, and the nature and vocation of human beings within this world—is radically different from what the surrounding cultures proposed.[22] The narrative in which the propositions are embedded, nonetheless, inevitably reflects the time and culture of its origin and speaks the language of its day. One of the tasks of biblical hermeneutics is precisely to clarify the propositions by clarifying the nature of the narrative in which they are embedded, and the nature of the time and culture in which the narrative was composed. It is of little help in this task to make the kind of facile distinction between "fact" and "myth" that is found in Article XXII; and while one must agree that "scientific hypotheses about earth history or the origin of humanity" should not "be invoked to overthrow what Scripture teaches about creation," this does of course beg the question about what it is that Scripture teaches about creation, which can only be settled by the sort of careful attention to the nature of the biblical texts about creation that I am advocating.[23]

Clearly some of the alleged "facts" of Genesis 1–2 are more problematic than others when the claims of modern science are considered, and there is muddled thinking on both sides of this debate—not just among those Bible readers who cannot understand the inevitable limitations, from a scientific point of view, of texts produced in ancient times by authors intent on refuting their neighbors' ideology rather than in producing a scientific textbook, but also among those scientists who suffer from the delusion that science can ultimately pronounce on the existence of a Creator, the nature of the human being, and the destiny of the world. Article XXI actually strikes the right note: "WE AFFIRM the harmony of special with general revelation and therefore of biblical teaching with the facts of nature. WE DENY that any genuine scientific facts are inconsistent with the true meaning of any passage of Scripture." All truth should cohere, but if it does not, the problem may lie *either* with one's grasp of the scientific facts *or* with one's understanding of Scripture. Both will need to be reviewed. The reluctance of many modern interpreters actually to engage in a review of this sort with regard to their interpretation of a book like Genesis is in striking contrast to a Reformer such as John Calvin, who well understood that we must be careful not to make the Bible into a modern rather than an ancient book and play it off against modern science, as this extract from his commentary on Genesis (on 1:16) reveals:

> I have said, that Moses does not here subtiley [*sic*] descant, as a philosopher, on the secrets of nature, as may be seen in these words. First, he assigns a place in the expanse of heaven to the planets and the stars; but astronomers make a distinction of spheres, and, at the same time, teach that the fixed stars have their proper place in the firmament. Moses makes two great luminaries; but astronomers prove, by conclusive reasons, that the star of Saturn, which, on account of its great distance, appears the least of all, is greater than the moon. Here lies the difference; Moses wrote in a popular style things which, without instruction, all ordinary persons, endued with common sense, are able to understand; but astronomers investigate with great labor whatever the sagacity of the human mind can comprehend. Nevertheless, this study is not to be reprobated, nor this science to be condemned, because some frantic persons are wont boldly to

reject whatever is unknown to them. For astronomy is not only pleasant, but also very useful to be known: it cannot be denied that this art unfolds the admirable wisdom of God. Wherefore, as ingenious men are to be honored who have expended useful labor on this subject, so they who have leisure and capacity ought not to neglect this kind of exercise. Nor did Moses truly wish to withdraw us from this pursuit in omitting such things as are peculiar to the art; but because he was ordained a teacher as well of the unlearned and the rude as of the learned, he could not otherwise fulfill his office than by descending to this grosser method of instruction ... Moses, therefore, adapts his discourse to common usage.[24]

Before Calvin, Augustine had expressed his own impatience with people who read Genesis in ways that contradicted the best science of the day:

Usually, even a non-Christian knows something about the earth, the heavens, and the other elements of the world, about the motion and orbit of the stars and even their size and relative positions ... and so forth ... Now, it is a disgraceful and dangerous thing for an infidel to hear a Christian, presumably giving the meaning of Holy Scripture, talking nonsense on these topics ... If they find a Christian mistaken in a field which they themselves know well ... how are they going to believe those books in matters concerning the resurrection of the dead, the hope of eternal life, and the kingdom of heaven ...? Reckless and incompetent expounders of Holy Scripture bring untold trouble and sorrow on their wiser brethren.[25]

Biblical texts must be understand on their own terms for what they are—ancient, and not modern, texts. A biblical hermeneutics that does not take seriously this necessity but pays only lip service to it will mislead the interpreter as to the biblical message. The presence of Calvin in our midst at this point in our article indeed prompts the question as to how "Reformed" such a hermeneutics would be. The question is relevant, because many evangelicals see their emphasis on literal interpretation of the Bible as in line with the practice of Luther and Calvin—that is, they claim that their hermeneutics represents only a recovery of forgotten Reformation emphases, not something essentially modern. The fact is, however, that while the rhetoric is often resolutely Reformed, the implicit reading theory is often resolutely modern, in the sense that its emphases are historical, empirical, and referential, and "literal reading" has in fact become—not the reading of the text by "the exegete [who] seeks to put himself in the writer's linguistic, cultural, historical, and religious shoes"[26] and to understand that writer's expressed meaning— but "literalistic reading."[27] This literalistic reading is not as Reformed as some people think, and it is certainly far from sensible. It is typically not even very consistent, for even while insisting that science should not be invoked to overthrow what Scripture teaches, reading of this kind has already and in all sorts of ways allowed its own interpretation of Scripture to be influenced by scientific discovery (as any comparison of what has been deduced about the world and its history by modern Christian readers when compared with ancient Christian readers of the Bible reveals). It simply chooses, somewhat arbitrarily, which science will be allowed to impact our understanding of a book like Genesis and which will not. Article XX reflects this arbitrariness, when it rather extraordinarily asserts "that in *some* [my italics] cases extrabiblical data have value for clarifying what Scripture teaches." This affirmation leaves in the hands of the interpreter, of course, which cases these might be. So it is that we find interpreters insisting that *this* detail of the text can only be taken "literally" by the person who truly regards the Bible as authoritative (for example, the "days" of Genesis 1 must be "real days"), whereas *that* detail need not be so taken (for example, the sun was not "really" created on the fourth day). It is apparently acceptable to allow modern heliocentric understandings of the nature of our solar system to influence our reading of Genesis, but not modern understandings of the way in which our world was created and came to be as it is.[28] It sometimes seems, indeed, that genre questions are only invoked in this way of approaching the Bible when it is convenient that they be so, in order to justify a decision that has already been taken on other grounds—when the interpreter simply cannot believe, as a person with at least one part of his mind rooted in modernity, that the Bible can really mean a certain thing "literally" (in his or her own narrow sense of the term).

It is of course in pursuit of this understanding of biblical texts on their own terms as ancient texts that biblical criticism in general (and not just genre-criticism) has been developed as a discipline. Article XVI recognizes the important place of critical method in biblical hermeneutics, affirming "that legitimate critical techniques should be used in determining the canonical text and its meaning," albeit refraining from telling us which critical techniques it considers legitimate. We deduce from the denial that follows, however, that once again *desired outcome* is the focus of concern, and that any critical method would be considered illegitimate by the authors of the *Statement*, at least in its *employment*, that did not produce this outcome: "WE DENY the legitimacy of allowing any method of biblical criticism to question the truth or integrity of the writer's expressed meaning, or of any other scriptural teaching." It is once again a curious denial, however. The desired outcome is that the writer's "expressed meaning" should be taken seriously, but how is the writer's expressed meaning to be grasped, if not through meticulous study of the text in its context, both literary and historical? Are we simply to imagine that we already "know" somehow what our biblical texts mean, without subjecting them to such meticulous study—without, indeed, countenancing suggestions from biblical critics that we may be mistaken? Yet if "God is the author of all truth ... biblical and extrabiblical" (Article XX), and truth is indeed everywhere to be found in God's world, how can one assume in advance that proposals made by biblical critics about biblical literature are untrue? They *may* be untrue, in whole or in part, but they may *not*, and their truth or untruthfulness must surely be discovered by measuring their explanatory power in any given case in terms of the biblical data that are the object of study—not by measuring their impact on our received interpretation of an author's "expressed meaning."

To return to our earlier example from Joshua 10:40, the "expressed meaning" of the text might well be assumed by the first-time reader of the book of Joshua to be that all Canaanites in the land were slain. The *Statement* would then apparently encourage this reader not to allow form criticism, with its emphasis on understanding the genre of the literature we read, "to question the truth or integrity of the writer's expressed meaning." Form-critical enquiry, however, suggests that this reader is not correct in her assumption as to the "expressed meaning" of Joshua 10:40, and presents a good case for reading the text as conventional hyperbole, which in turn makes excellent sense of the biblical data overall in respect of the Israelite settlement of the land. Measured in terms of its explanatory power in respect of the data, this proposal deserves to be regarded as true, in which case the first-time reader is found to be misunderstanding the "expressed meaning" of the text. The problem is that this reader will never discover her misunderstandings of Scripture, because she has been told in advance that conflicts between her current reading and any suggested new reading are always to be resolved in favor of the former.

Article XXIV compounds the problem with its weak advice not to "ignore the fruits of the technical study of Scripture by biblical scholars," accompanied by its strong affirmation "that a person is not dependent for understanding of Scripture on the expertise of biblical scholars." Quite how the authority of Scripture is upheld in all of this, as opposed to the authority of one's current interpretation of Scripture, is unclear. The proposed hermeneutic of the *Statement* in Article XVI and in other articles that we have examined appears heavily to favor the latter, or at least not to recognize in any significant way a possible difference between the two. A hermeneutic that takes the authority of the Bible itself more seriously would need to allow critical method to take its own course in helping to form our opinion on *everything* that is likely to be true about our biblical texts, on the way to trying to understand what it truly is that our biblical texts can be said to mean. It is, for example, crucial to the interpretation of the Gospels that the interpreter gain some clarity on what a Gospel is and is not by examining the four Gospels in relation to each other and to their ancient cultural context, if he is not to impose upon them improper expectations and ultimately derive from them indefensible readings. Clarity of interpretation is not aided by beginning with fixed conclusions about what the Gospels are and say, and then proceeding to argue what else *must* be the case in order to defend these conclusions.[29] It is indeed the task of any "method of biblical criticism," as such, not "to question the truth or integrity of the writer's expressed meaning" but to help to clarify this meaning by working patiently and intelligently with the text in question. All too often attacks from within the evangelical camp on modern biblical criticism, and indeed on modern hermeneutics generally, have had nothing in reality to do with faults in the method or approach being employed as such, but everything to do with covert attempts to defend traditional interpretive outcomes against disliked and competing readings of texts. A truly evangelical approach to the Bible must surely always place Scripture *over* tradition, and will wish to discover the truth of the matter as to how to *read* Scripture well *even if* in the process tradition (including traditional reading) is overturned.

It will readily be seen from this critical reflection on the *Chicago Statement on Biblical Hermeneutics* that I do not consider it a very satisfactory statement. It may be that I have not understood it in all respects as it means to be understood. I have certainly sought to read it, however, according to its literal, grammatical-historical sense, and I find its propositions, as written, in many respects problematic and sometimes plainly in error. In many ways it is not truly a statement on hermeneutics at all, for it focuses on telling the reader what to think *about* the Bible, rather than on helping the reader to *read* the Bible; and in fact, much of what is said in respect of the latter is so poorly stated that it is most unhelpful to the Bible reader who is seeking to understand actual biblical texts and to have them shape his or her life. The requirement to read an Old Testament psalm, for example, as making propositional statements conveying absolute divine truth (Article VI) will not get the reader very far in understanding that psalm. It is more likely to impart in equal measure reverence for the text and ignorance as to what to do with it. This may indeed help to explain why it has so often been my experience as a teacher of the Old Testament that students who are ready and willing to expound on why the Old Testament must be regarded as the Word of God nevertheless have not read very much of it, understand still less of it, and have little idea of what to do with it as Scripture in any practical, meaningful sense. That is the serious edge to my opening paragraphs, in which I playfully but with intent retell part of the story of Acts 8. If hermeneutics is about helping people to perceive "what the biblical revelation means and how it bears on our lives" (Article IX), the *Statement* is disappointingly inadequate.

The Way Ahead

What kind of biblical hermeneutic *should* evangelical Christians embrace and advocate to others, then? The various elements of my proposal are already evident in the critique above, but here I pull them together into one whole piece. We should certainly begin where the *Statement* begins: "The normative authority of Holy Scripture is the authority of God Himself, and is attested by Jesus Christ, the Lord of the Church" (Article I). We are dealing here with a single book that we receive from Christ and his apostles, in which and through which God speaks—the same Holy Spirit who inspired Scripture acting through it today to work faith in its message (Articles IV and V). The voice of God when it is heard is obviously to be taken deeply seriously in terms of what we should believe and how we should live as his creatures. It would be folly to behave otherwise. It is from this beginning point that hermeneutics launches itself, as "the study of the process whereby the Bible speaks to us (from God, as Christians believe)."[30]

What is the Bible that speaks to us from God? It is literature. More precisely, it is a *body* or *library* of literature—one book, and yet also many books; and the many books are of many different types or genres. The Bible is narrative, yet it is also poem and proverb. The many different types of book contain within them many different kinds of individual text and employ a great diversity of literary conventions. To hear God speak, all these texts through which he speaks must be understood for what they are, and we must be careful to identify what they are *not*. For we do not, for example, wish to find ourselves affirming that God wishes us to believe that floods possess hands, and hills voices, if it is not really so.[31] We do not wish to find ourselves misunderstanding what is *meant* as a result of adopting an insufficiently curious attitude toward what is *said*. This distinction is explored briefly but entertainingly by Father Brown in one of G. K. Chesterton's short stories:

> Have you ever noticed this—that people never answer what you say? They answer what you mean—or what they think you mean. Suppose one lady says to another in a country house, "Is anybody staying with you?" the lady doesn't answer "Yes; the butler, the three footmen, the parlour-maid, and so on," though the parlour-maid may be in the room, or the butler behind her chair. She says: "There is *nobody* staying with us," meaning nobody of the sort you mean. But suppose a doctor inquiring into an epidemic asks, "Who is staying in the house?" then the lady will remember the butler, the parlour-maid and the rest. All language is used like that; you never get a question answered literally, even when you get it answered truly."[32]

Biblical hermeneutics must give careful attention to the type of text with which it is dealing, as it seeks to affirm what God is saying (and meaning) through the human words on the pages of this literature.

This inevitably involves biblical hermeneutics in historical study, for the many-books-in-one of which we are speaking were written in places that are foreign to most of us, and over a lengthy period of history that predates our own period of history by between 2,000 and 4,000 years (depending on which books we are speaking of, and which precise dates we attach to these books). Language—as the Father Brown story reminds us with its words concerning country houses, butlers, footmen, and parlour maids—is always intrinsically connected with time and place. We cannot assume that the literary conventions of the ancients or their mode of writing—indeed, even their view of authorship and books—were the same as ours. Only historical study would make this clear, as the biblical texts were considered together as ancient texts and located within and measured against their times and their cultures, and their similarities to and differences from comparable texts came fully to light. This kind of study has often been called "historical-critical" study, and sometimes simply "literary-critical" study. These are labels that have often caused discomfort amongst conservative Christians who think that it is wrong to "criticize the Bible." Yet the enterprise is directed toward the same end as the "grammatical-historical" method—that is, understanding biblical texts in their historical context. And of course the word *critical*, which can mean "censorious" or "fault-finding," can also carry the more neutral sense of simply "skillful at or engaged in criticism." The *Concise Oxford Dictionary* refers to "textual criticism," for example, as the process by which people bring their minds to bear on texts and try to decide, by the use of reason and evidence, which is the correct text of an author. It differentiates this "lower criticism" from the so-called "higher criticism" that certain conservative Christians "know" they are supposed to be against, yet "higher criticism" is really nothing other than the further employment of the mind in enquiring into the nature and meaning of the biblical texts as historical artifacts. To be "against" it is to imply the possession of a docetic lack of interest in the texts as historical artifacts at all. As two authors have put it so well, "To deny that the Bible should be studied through the use of literary and critical methodologies is to treat the Bible as less than human, less than historical, and less than literature."[33] It is not clear on what grounds one would wish to do that. One would have thought, on the contrary, that Christians readers of the Bible would wish to discover as much as they can about the biblical texts in their historical context, precisely in order to hear God speak the more clearly through them and to avoid misunderstanding him.

I suggest, then, that it is a direct implication of the nature of the biblical texts themselves that biblical hermeneutics must employ a historically-oriented biblical criticism, since God must be heard in the "now" through a reading and appreciation of texts through which he first spoke "back then," and it is as we understand better what was said back then that we shall understand better what is said now. There is no knowledge about these texts as historical artifacts that is "too much" knowledge in this quest. Attention must be paid to what source and form criticism suggest about where our texts came from and how they may once have functioned *in situ* in ancient Israelite society. This may impact how they are to be read today. Consideration must be given to what redaction criticism claims about how our texts were put together and came to their present form, to what narrative and rhetorical criticism have to say about the art through which biblical texts communicate their message, and to what ideological criticism suggests about the specific "interests" in which individual texts were written, and the social contexts out of which they arose. Not everything that scholars employing these methods say about our texts will turn out to be true, and sometimes little of it may turn out to be true, but whatever *does* turn out to be true, or to be likely true, is important, and it must be factored into the larger Truth in which we are interested as Bible readers.

If narrative criticism discovers truly, for example, that biblical narrative is "scenic, subtle, and succinct"—that is, that biblical narrators "do more showing than telling ... are generally reticent to make their points directly, preferring to do so more subtly (and) ... accomplish the greatest degree of definition and color with the fewest brushstrokes"[34]—then hermeneutics must take these things seriously in attempting to say what the text means. If source criticism were to discover truly that the Pentateuch is based upon four major sources of different dates, ranging from the monarchic to the postexilic periods, then likewise hermeneutics would need to consider what impact that made (if any) on how the text is to be read.[35] It is all simply part of taking the biblical texts seriously as texts from the past. "Higher criticism" may or may not be flawed in all sorts of ways as it comments on and hypothesizes about the Bible, from its presuppositions to its conclusions. It is not flawed, however, in its commitment to historical-critical method, and it must not be ignored by any serious Bible reader when it turns up data important for the reading of biblical texts. Indeed, to attempt to move from biblical text to biblical meaning without taking seriously the nature of the text is to fall inevitably into the pit of incomprehension described once again by G. K. Chesterton in another of his short stories, in which the policeman Valentin "had come to the end of his chase; yet somehow he had missed the middle of it ... he had grasped the criminal, but still he could not grasp the clue."[36]

Biblical hermeneutics, then, must begin in its quest to know the meaning of the Bible for us *now* with the question: what did this or that biblical text mean back *then*? This question is of course more complex than is sometimes understood, precisely because many of our biblical books evidently have a history to them, in the course of which the context in which individual texts were read undoubtedly changed; and the true meaning of individual texts is certainly bound up with their context.

The Psalter, for example, evidently came into its present form over the course of considerable time, and contains texts from the monarchic (for example, Ps 2) as well as the exilic period (for example, Ps 137) and perhaps beyond. A sentence in a psalm meant what it meant first to the author of that psalm, and might be deduced from a careful reading of both the sentence and the whole psalm. What the sentence meant to the compilers of the section of the Psalter in which the psalm now sits, however—and to the compilers of the whole Psalter—might conceivably not have been quite the same. If Psalm 1:3 proclaims, for example, that in all that the righteous do they prosper, the meaning of that sentence for the author, as deduced from a reading only of Psalm 1, might reasonably be suggested to have been just that—in all that the righteous do, they prosper. The meaning of the sentence for the compilers of the Psalter, on the other hand, is only arrived at by way of reflection on the present suffering of the righteous and the present prosperity of the wicked in other Psalms, not only in book 1 of the Psalter (for example, in Ps 37, which gives us the most extensive discourse on the wicked and the righteous and their two ways outside Ps 1), but in later sections as well (for example, Ps 73). Read with attention to its *entire* context in the Psalter, in other words, Psalm 1:3 cannot be understood as telling the whole truth of the matter, at least in the sense that the reader might first have taken from it. The verse then affirms as a general truth that people who are obedient to God are blessed, but it is set in a context in which is acknowledged the reality of the obedient life all too often in present reality—the reality of lament and complaint.

Likewise, the proverb in Proverbs 26:4 ("Do not answer fools according to their folly, or you will be a fool yourself"), taken by itself, might be understood (and perhaps once was meant) to prohibit the wise from answering fools according to their folly. It is currently followed in the book of Proverbs (26:5), however, with the advice, "Answer fools according to their folly, or they will be wise in their own eyes." The whole truth of the matter from the perspective of the compilers of the book of Proverbs, it seems, is that one must make a judgment in each case when asking whether one should answer a fool, for there are risks on both sides. The whole truth is, however, only perceived when one considers not just the words of the first text, which offers only a limited perspective on the matter, but also the words of the second.

Perhaps in the case of both the Psalms text and the Proverbs text the author of the individual text already possessed the broader perspective described, and the compilers of the books in question have simply clarified this. Perhaps so; we cannot know. My point is only that the individual texts as such—whether or not their authors *thought* other things that they did not express—do not provide us internally with the clues that enable us in the end to avoid (from the point of view of the final form of the books) a mistaken understanding of them. And the purpose of this paragraph is to underline, in a context in which we often become confused about which "original meaning" of a text we are interested in, when seeking to determine "what a text meant," that it is indeed the "original meaning" of individual texts *within whole biblical books* with which biblical hermeneutics should be first concerned, since these are the primary contexts within which the individual texts are set and declare their meaning. Thus the careful reader of the book of Exodus, for example, when confronted with the story of Exodus

4:19–26 in which God first tells Moses to go back to Egypt, and then meets him on the road and tries to kill him, will resist the conclusion that the text reflects divine arbitrariness (that is, God cannot make up his mind whether he wants Moses to go or not), for this interpretation of God is not borne out by the remainder of the book, even though it is certainly the interpretation that the reader might first be drawn to by the passage in itself.

If individual texts provide only limited insight into the truth that a whole book spoke "back then" to its readers or hearers, however, it is equally true that entire biblical books also provide only limited insight into biblical truth overall as it was directed towards its ancient recipients—and also towards us. This limitation, too, biblical hermeneutics must reckon with. How is the book of Proverbs, for example, to be understood, with its advocacy of wise behavior that leads to life in all its fullness, its warnings about the foolish behavior that leads to destruction, its overall apparent belief that the way in which the world works is reasonably plain and that one can easily determine the way to go forward? It must be understood in relation to the book of Job, which denies that proverbial wisdom provides us with invariable rules about life, and specifically denies that we can deduce what God is doing in the world from observing who is suffering and who is prospering. It must also be understood in relation to the book of Ecclesiastes, which argues the weakness of an empirical approach to these matters even more vehemently. The truth of the Old Testament Scriptures is to be found by reflecting not on one of these books individually, but on all three in all their similarity and difference and on others besides. How is Old Testament law as it is described in the Pentateuch to be understood, in all its complexity and variety, as direction to the Old Testament people of God for living in God's world? It must be understood in relation to the Pentateuchal narrative, which presents the law, not as a means to redemption for God's people, but as a gift that follows redemption; and, within itself, to the Ten Commandments, which lay out certain great principles of behavior that ground and explain the various practical case-laws that surround them. It must further be understood in relation to passages like Isaiah 1, which makes clear that there are weightier and less weighty aspects of law, and that the practice of the lesser is of little worth in the absence of the practice of the former (as Jesus himself teaches in Matt 23:23); and Job 31, which makes clear that in any case the virtuous way of life to which an Israelite is called is not defined by law and cannot be contained within law.

Biblical truth, insofar as it is contained in the Old Testament Scriptures, can only be determined as text is compared with text, and as an overall picture emerges of what may be said and what may not be said about this or that matter. What the Old Testament has to say is itself limited in respect of the whole Bible, of course, and so its truth must also be measured by what is now known to Christians as a result of the divine revelation in Christ and the apostolic witness to that revelation. It turns out that there is more to be said of who God is, who we are, and what the world is like, than has ever been said before. It also turns out that the Old Testament people of God, when they spoke of these things, saw them far more dimly than they themselves imagined, so that the meaning of their words was often transformed by its new context into something of which they themselves apparently never conceived. Thus their prophecies of a king who was to come, for example, took on a significance far beyond their grasp in the coming of Christ; their expectation of a land to call their own was met in a land beyond our present physical existence; and their desire for a rebuilt temple was ultimately fulfilled in a new people of God that was international in composition.

Their hopes were not fulfilled literally, but truly nonetheless, as they peered into the future "through a glass darkly."

In summation of all the above, the kind of biblical hermeneutic that evangelical Christians should embrace and advocate to others begins with the understanding that we receive the Bible from Christ and his apostles as a book in which and through which God speaks to us, yet also with the understanding that God speaks in words written by people of old. This being so, biblical hermeneutics must seek to hear God's voice in the Bible by giving attention in the first instance, in the case of the individual text, to the meaning of words in their ancient literary context within the document of which they are part—which involves (among other things) attention to matters of genre and literary convention. It must use all the critical tools at its disposal in the effort thus to understand the text, in itself, in its historical context. It should then go on to clarify how that text is to be read along with other biblical texts—how those other texts impact on the matter of what the text in question can be said to mean. The ultimate measure of how texts are to be read is the divine revelation in Christ and the apostolic witness to that revelation. This revelation makes clear the only-partial grasp of the truth possessed by those biblical writers who preceded its time, and sets the context within which the true meaning of all biblical texts must be pursued. As Vanhoozer puts it, "the 'fuller meaning' of Scripture—the meaning associated with divine authorship—emerges only at the level of the whole canon."[37] The Reformers referred to this same process of "reading texts along with other texts" under the rubric "analogy of Scripture." Scripture should be interpreted by Scripture and certainly not set against Scripture. Indeed, individual Scriptures should always be read within the whole sweep of the canonical story, with due attention to what appears to be secondary, incidental, and obscure, and what appears to be primary, central, and plain.

Although it is common to contrast this approach with a pre-Reformation approach to biblical interpretation, especially because of the Reformation insistence on the literal sense of the text over against allegorical reading, the fact is that the differences are overstated[38]—or perhaps it would be more accurate to say that once the more problematic aspects of hermeneutical theory in both pre-Reformation and post-Reformation (especially post-Enlightenment periods) have been set aside or clarified, we can see more clearly what they share that is good rather than what distinguishes them. Mediaeval Christian exegetes, too, employed a canonical approach. They regarded the meaning of Scripture in the mind of the person who first uttered it as only one of its possible meanings. It might not be, in certain circumstances, even its primary or most important meaning. The literal sense of Scripture was regarded as basic, and as limiting the range of other possible meanings, but other meanings had to be considered when the literal sense of a particular passage appeared absurd. Sometimes a passage was required to be reinterpreted because it did not address directly the Church, or did not in general edify the Church, nurturing the three theological virtues of faith, hope and love. God, it was held, can mean things in speaking in the whole Bible that individual human beings do not mean of themselves, and what God means to say to the Church in any given case must be measured by what he means elsewhere, as the reader is led by the Spirit to read the Scriptures aright. Here, too, is a way of "reading texts along with other texts" and allowing Scripture to interpret Scripture within the whole sweep of the canonical story, with due attention to what appears to be secondary, incidental, and obscure, and what appears to be primary, central, and plain. This formulation of hermeneutics in fact explicitly reminds us of the important point that we read the Bible not only to *understand* it in itself, but to *understand how to live*, in relation to God and to our neighbor. The most simple rule to give to a first-time Bible reader who wants to know how to read, indeed, is to tell him or her to read with a view to loving God and neighbor more deeply and more truly, and to organize his or her thoughts about individual biblical passages around those two imperatives—as ancient Christians like Augustine advised.[39]

Is there more to be said? On the matter of hermeneutical "rules and procedures that enable us to grasp first of all what Scripture *meant* as communication from its human writers speaking on God's behalf to their own envisaged readers,"[40] perhaps not. It is the case, however, that "a man [or a woman] might possess all the linguistic and historical knowledge required in order to interpret a text, but still not be able to understand the text in question."[41] We are thus reminded that the existential grasping of a text in terms of "what it means" does not arise automatically from an understanding of "what it meant." As Anthony Thistleton explains:

> If a text is to be *understood* there must occur an engagement between two sets of horizons (to use Gadamer's phrase), namely those of the ancient text and those of the modern reader or hearer. The hearer must be able to relate his own horizons to those of the text. Gadamer compares the analogy of the 'understanding' which occurs in a conversation ... The nature of the hermeneutical problem is shaped by the fact that both the text and the interpreter are conditioned by their given place in history. For understanding to take place, two sets of variables must be brought into relation with each

other. Gadamer's image of a fusion of two horizons provides one possible way of describing the main problem and task of hermeneutics.[42]

"There is a reader horizon as well as a textual horizon when it comes to hermeneutics."[43] Biblical hermeneutics needs to take account of this fact, for "the heart of the hermeneutical problem does not lie in the determining of the historical meaning of each passage ... it lies, rather, in seeing how it applies to you, me, and us at the point in history and personal life where we are now."[44] We need not interpret the language of the "fusion of two horizons" to mean "that the message of Scripture derives from, or is dictated by, the interpreter's understanding," rather than by the biblical text (as does Article IX of the *Chicago Statement*). At the same time, however, an understanding of what a biblical text means does not arise in a self-evident manner from an understanding of "the expressed meaning of the Scripture," as the *Statement* might be read to imply. The task of translation from past to present is a real one. As J. I. Packer says on the matter of the fusion of horizons, "at the heart of the hermeneutical process there is between the text and the interpreter a kind of interaction in which their respective panoramic views of things, angled and limited as these are, 'engage' or 'intersect'—in other words, appear as challenging each other in some way." He comments further on Gadamer's insistence that "distancing" must precede "fusing" of horizons, thus:

> [W]e must become aware of the differences between the culture and thought-background out of which the words of the text come and that of our own thought and speech. Only so can we be saved from the particular naïveté that H. J.

Cadbury pinpointed when he wrote *The Peril of Modernizing Jesus*. The naïveté consists of treating people and words from the past as if they belonged to the present, thus making it impossible to see them in their own world and have our own horizons extended or redrawn by the impact of what they actually meant. Popular Bible study and preaching easily go astray here—indeed one might almost say inherit a tradition of going astray here—and anyone who highlights the danger deserves our thanks.[45]

It may well be the case that in a properly conceived biblical hermeneutics "the reader's understanding has no hermeneutically definitive role."[46] Yet definitive or not, the reader's understanding certainly possesses *a* hermeneutical role. This is indeed not only true of the process by which a text comes to *mean* something to the reader, but also of the process by which the reader assesses what was *meant*. It is, for example, intrinsic to the fact that Old Testament narratives are "scenic" that "the reader is seldom explicitly *told* by the narrator how this or that character, or this or that action, is to be evaluated (though this does occasionally occur). Instead, the reader is *shown* the characters acting and speaking and is thereby drawn into the story and challenged to reach evaluative judgments on his or her own."[47] Here too the reader follows the guidance of the text itself in making his/her judgments; nonetheless, it is the reader who is doing this. It does not happen by itself. It is an unfortunate aspect of the *Statement's* articulation of the hermeneutical task that it is so concerned to emphasize the objectivity of biblical interpretation that it can find no proper place for its subjectivity. Yet what are sometimes called "in-front-of-the-text" issues affect the interpretation of biblical texts as much as "behind-the-text" and "in-the-text" issues.[48] Biblical hermeneutics properly conceived must find a place for both, recognizing the necessarily personal elements that are part and parcel of interpreting the Bible, especially if it is to have genuine existential impact on modern readers and we are to avoid the pitfall of "honoring the Bible as embodying what God said to mankind long ago while failing to listen to it as God's word to us in the present."[49] The Bible itself does not tell us how to express the meaning of its words (first addressed to an ancient world) to the modern world. That is something that the reader must do—in prayer and under the guidance of the Holy Spirit, as Christians would insist, as well as in community with the Church both present and historic. Max Turner puts it in this way:

> We need fully to appreciate the importance of "in front of the text" issues, and how much they can, do, and must shape, not merely our appropriation of texts, but also (to a lesser extent) our exegesis of them. We can thus learn from even the most radical reader-response critics and ardent postliberals—though, in the final analysis, we need to avoid their temptation prematurely to fuse the horizons of author/text and reader. The canonical principle bids us join the apostolic conference table with the NT writers and give them due hearing. It does not invite us to gag and bind the apostolic authors and hustle them into our century, and into our churches, where they are able only to stutter out, in stifled whispers, the things we have already told them to say.[50]

Conclusion

It follows from everything above that biblical hermeneutics involves hard work, for it is possible to err in one's reading of the Bible, even as one is insisting that one is only articulating the plain meaning of a text.[51]

Sometimes these errors do not have great consequences; it is possible, however, to interpret biblical texts in harmful and even demonic ways, even while remaining faithful to their apparent historical-grammatical sense.[52] It is possible to err even while believing oneself to be under the guidance of the Holy Spirit, as all long-time readers of the Bible are able to attest, for "the Spirit works *through* human understanding, and not independently of it."[53] Biblical hermeneutics requires an enormous commitment to education;[54] it requires the embrace of discipline; it requires the arduous requirement of constant repentance from and revision of previous opinion, "for all of us make many mistakes" (Jas 3:2).[55] It requires all this and more from the reader.[56]

But those who wish to hear God speak through the Bible and to obey him have no alternative but to accept the challenge, and those who want *others* to hear God speak through the Bible and obey him must also accept it. For there are multitudes of "Ethiopian eunuchs" in the world who look for understanding and receive no help—not even from those who believe that correct biblical interpretation is important, and who even practice a version of it. These people need "someone to guide them" (Acts 8:31). There is a need, then, for many "Philips" who have wrestled with the Scriptures, understand what they mean, and are capable of "rightly explaining the word of truth" (2 Tim 2:15). The hermeneutical process by which I believe we should arrive at this "right explaining," in the case of any given biblical text I hope that I have now adequately described. The rest is practice, as we seek to give substance to biblical authority in our lives by listening to "Scripture communicating instruction from God about belief and behavior, the way of faith and obedience, and the life of worship and witness."[57] As Kevin Vanhoozer puts it: "Neither standing nor understanding ... is the final word in interpretation. The final word belongs to following."[58]

17

"UNSCRIPTED, ANXIOUS STUTTERERS": WHY WE NEED OLD TESTAMENT (HI)STORY

One of the really great things about moving to Canada has been getting to work with Professor Loren Wilkinson, Professor of Interdisciplinary Studies and Philosophy at Regent College. No doubt I have to some degree expanded Loren's horizons with respect to Bible-reading since arriving in Vancouver in 1997; however, he has greatly *expanded my horizons on almost everything else. I was therefore very glad to co-author this paper with him and to submit it for publication in 2008 to a brand new African journal of biblical research and interpretation,* Sapientia Logos. *It is a very broad paper, connecting the Old Testament story with many others and exploring its ultimacy for Christian pilgrims. The reader may assume that the breadth, in so far as it does not pertain to the ancient Near Eastern world, was largely supplied by Professor Wilkinson. I later reproduced quite a bit of this essay in the opening chapter of my 2014 book,* Seriously Dangerous Religion: What the Old Testament Really Says and Why It Matters, *because it introduces the argument of that book so very well.*

Towards the end of the second volume of J.R.R. Tolkien's *The Two Towers*, which forms part of *The Lord of the Rings*, we find ourselves in one of the darkest places in the story. The two Hobbits Frodo and Sam are preparing to enter the evil realm of Mordor, where they hope to be able to destroy the ring of power that will otherwise assure the victory of evil over good and the dominion of the dark lord Sauron. They sit down to eat together; and they talk about their journey—the story in which they find themselves—and about other famous journeys and stories of the past. "I wonder," muses Sam, "what sort of tale we've fallen into?" Frodo confesses that he does not know, but "that's the way of a real tale. Take any one that you're fond of. You may know, or guess, what kind of a tale it is, happy-ending or sad-ending, but the people in it don't know. And you don't want them to." This prompts in Sam a revelation, as he considers the old story of Beren and his Silmaril, a long tale that "goes on past the happiness and into grief and beyond it," and he realizes that some of the light of Silmaril lies close by them in the star glass gifted to Frodo by the Lady Galadriel: "Why, to think of it, we're in the same tale still! It's going on. Don't the great tales never end?"[1]

We each likewise find ourselves, as we begin to write or to read this essay, in the midst of a story. It could not be otherwise—it is just the way that human beings are. At the most personal level there is the story of our own life. Our telling of this story is an integral part of the way in which we not only relate to others, but also come to understand and to shape who we ourselves are. Yet we are only ever able to share *parts* of the story, for at least three reasons.

One reason is that there is usually a great deal of mystery about the beginning of each of our personal stories. Our own memory emerges out of the mist. We do not remember much at all of the things that first shaped us. We know these aspects of our past by hearsay, or through looking at pictures in old photo albums, interpreted in the first instance by other people. Direct memory of the first part of our individual stories is not available to us. And then we do have our own earliest memories. They are usually vivid; but they are almost always fragmented, disconnected, and dependent on the stories of others for a context that makes sense of them. We cannot usually organize them chronologically; and such chronology as we possess has no doubt been given to us mainly by others. We cannot say for sure how our childhood shaped the person we later became, except in the most general terms—and much of the story at that point depends upon adult reflection on stories told by others, not on memory. That is how it often is with our personal life stories; they usually begin in some forgottenness and mystery. Perhaps that is why we are so fascinated by stories of adopted people who set out to discover the identity of their birth mother and father—or by a different version of the same thing, stories of amnesia, in which people do not know anything at all about their past, but must solve the mystery not just of their first few years, but of a whole life. Even when we know the main details of our lives—as most of us do—most of us have also entertained the possibility that there might be more; that if there is not some mystery about us, there *ought* to be. Perhaps the details of our lives are not themselves enough to match the depth that we feel within us. We find ourselves in the position of the writer of Ecclesiastes 2:11: "He has set eternity in the hearts of men: yet they cannot fathom what God has done from beginning to end." We cannot fathom what God has done—from beginning to end.

There is of course an even greater degree of mystery about the *end* of our own story—the second and obvious reason that we are only ever able to share *parts* of our story with others. If the *beginning* of our story is wrapped in some mystery, the *end* of our story is even more unknown. There is much of the story still to be written, and we do not yet know where it is going to end up.

Thirdly, and finally: not only does the past escape our grasp and the future lie beyond our knowledge, but we are in fact "inextricably middled" in our own story—to use a fine phrase from the pen of David Lyle Jeffrey.² Being inextricably *middled*, we are often also comprehensively *muddled* about the present in which we find ourselves. One of the greatest stories in Western literature is Dante Alighieri's *Divine Comedy*—the medieval (but also very contemporary) story of one man's journey down into the pit of Hell, up the great mountain of Purgatory and out through all the circles of heaven until he is given a vision of the triune God. It is a physical journey; but it is also a journey that Dante takes into himself, to confront his own past and his own capacity for sin, for repentance, and for righteousness. Dante's story begins in this way: *Nel mezzo del camin di nostra vita, Mi ritrovai per una selva oscura, Che la diritta via era smarrita* ("Midway this way of life we're bound upon, I woke to find myself in a dark wood, where the right road was wholly lost and gone").³ This is the original midlife crisis. The speaker finds himself lost in the middle of a story whose end is a mystery. He is middled—in the middle of a story, in the middle of a journey—and he is muddled.

We each have our story to tell. Yet its beginning is shrouded in mystery, its end lies entirely beyond our grasp, and the middle that we inhabit is difficult to read. Our personal story seems curiously incomplete. It is a story that begs a larger story to make sense of it. Perhaps that is just the way that things are. Perhaps we are stuck with only our own story, even if it is unsatisfactory and incomplete; perhaps there is nothing more. That is what many would say who live in those parts of the world that have embraced with a passion the philosophy or mood known as "postmodernism." All that there is in the world, they would say, is stories—*my* story, and *your* story, and *your* story. These stories may well be unsatisfactory in all sorts of ways; they may well be unable to provide us with much meaning or direction in life, of themselves; but at least they are *our* stories. A contemporary Canadian T-shirt says it well:

"I'm starring in my own soap opera." Serious postmodernists are in fact typically and deeply suspicious of claims that there might be any kind of larger story beyond the individual stories that could make fuller sense of them because it holds more of the truth. In the words of the French thinker Jean-François Lyotard, they are possessed of "incredulity toward all metanarratives"—toward any "framing" story or story of stories that purports to be *the* true story that embraces and ultimately explains all others. They are suspicious of the story of science, for example, which has told with increasing clarity at least something of the truth of the nature of the universe. They are suspicious of economic metanarratives like Marxism or capitalism, and of religious metanarratives, like Christianity or Islam. These various large-scale narratives are rejected by postmodernists in terms of their large claims to universal truth. The trouble with metanarratives, say these critics, is that a story that purports to be universally true inevitably leads to tyranny: you push your story onto me, and you oppress me with it. Instead of one large story, then, we must be content (on this view) with multitudes of small stories, which perhaps help me to understand the one story that counts, *my* story—or perhaps more often *fail* to help me to understand my own story, leaving me eternally, rather than simply temporarily, middled and muddled.

This is the kind of reality explored in Tom Stoppard's amusing but tragic play, *Rosencrantz and Guildenstern Are Dead*. The play is derivative of Shakespeare's *Hamlet*, which represents traditional drama, in the sense that human actions in *Hamlet* are presented in a social context:

> The action characteristically moves from a normal situation which is upset, through a series of conflicts as the characters seek to cope with this upset, towards a final conclusion in which something is resolved and a normality (even if a

transformed one), is restored ... there is an overall logic to the action, and the plot has a discernible shape: a beginning, middle, and end. By the conclusion of the play, in other words, through the actions of the participants, something has been dealt with, resolved ... these traditional plays establish a "horizon of significance," a world ordered by certain normative understandings which, even if they are not ours, enable us to understand what is going on as a coherent and accessible vision. The horizon of significance comes to us through what the characters believe and how the story establishes for us a sense of moral meaning.[4]

In Stoppard's play, however, the action of the Shakespeare play *Hamlet* is seen through the eyes of two of its minor characters, Rosencrantz and Guildenstern; and these two men in fact inhabit a world completely beyond their comprehension. Unsure of where they are going (and even of who they are and where they have come from), they depend upon other characters to give their lives meaning. While awaiting instructions, they play games that rarely achieve their intended goals. In the end, they resign themselves to their fate, which is death; although Guildenstern does say this: "There must have been a moment, at the beginning, when we could have said—no. But somehow we missed it." *Rosencrantz and Guildenstern Are Dead* is a play in the tradition of the Theatre of the Absurd, where "protagonists are discovered in a world which they do not, indeed they cannot, understand. It has no reliable meaning."[5]

Perhaps this is the world in which we must live—a world in which there is only your story and my story, and nothing more. Yet it does not appear that most people are *able* to live very well in this world of individual, private stories, which partake in no larger story and can provide no meaning or direction to the human person. We are not wired in such a way that we can easily accept this reality; Christians would say that we are not "created" in such a way—but that is to get ahead of ourselves at this point. Let us simply concede that we all yearn for larger stories in which we can find significance—stories that give our life meaning. This yearning reveals itself in various ways, even in a resolutely postmodern culture. It reveals itself in the popular fascination with the stories of the rich and famous that litter our media, as people imagine themselves enviously into the seemingly more complete and satisfying stories of others and seek to live vicariously through these demi-gods and thus to gain some sense of meaning and purpose that their own story does not give them. It reveals itself in the modern obsession with TV soap operas and with movies, most disturbingly in the case of those many people who apparently cannot clearly distinguish between fantasy and reality. It reveals itself in the fascination of an increasing number of cultures with video games, designed to draw us into a story and provide us with an adventure in "virtual reality"—giving us the opportunity to play endlessly shifting roles and to experience in these roles a world complete in itself that makes sense and hangs together.

In their own ways these different phenomena are what sociologists of religion might call "signs of transcendence"—hints that we are wired to find our place in a larger story, and not to remain an island unto ourselves; hints that, as the writer of Ecclesiastes would have put it, God "has set eternity in the hearts of men." The truth of the matter is that if we have only "my story" we are, to paraphrase the apostle Paul, "of all men most miserable." And despite all the postmodern rhetoric regarding suspicion of metanarratives, none of us really believes it. All of us are looking for the larger story within which our lives can fit. As an ancient philosopher, the pre-Socratic Alcaemon of Crotona wrote, "men perish because they cannot join the beginning with the end."[6]

These reflections on postmodernity bring us back to Frodo and Sam, by way of moving us ahead. The old story that they recall, the story of Beren, Luthien and the Silmarils, is not itself told in *The Lord of the Rings* at all. It lies far behind it. It is in fact the presence of the almost forgotten past that gives these books in general such an extraordinary depth and power. The hobbits have a connection, through Lothlorien and Galadriel, with that old story; and the realization of this gives them hope: "Why, think of it—we're in the same tale still! It's still going on. Don't the great tales never end?" They discover that they are part of a larger story; and this clarifies what it is that they are doing, and *must* do. The larger story helps them to locate themselves in the present and move resolutely into the future. Without it, they would not be able to do so. As in fiction, so in life. As Alasdair MacIntyre puts it in *After Virtue*:

> I can only answer the question "What am I to do?" if I can answer the prior question "Of what story or stories do I find myself a part?" We enter human society, that is, with one or more imputed characters—roles into which we have been drafted—and we have to learn what they are in order to be able to understand how others respond to us and how our responses to them are apt to be construed. It is through hearing stories about wicked stepmothers, lost children, good but misguided kings, wolves that suckle twin boys, youngest sons who receive no inheritance but must make their own way in the world ... that children learn or mis-learn both what a child and what a parent is, what the cast of characters may be in the drama in which they have been born and what the ways of the world are. Deprive children of stories and you

leave them unscripted, anxious stutterers in their actions as in their words.[7]

I can only answer the question "What am I to do?" if I can answer the prior question "Of what story or stories do I find myself a part?" It is a profound point. Our great human question therefore is to find out which story we are in and what our place in it is. We find ourselves in the middle of a story—but which story? Is it only our own personal story? Or is there a larger tale of which I am a part? On the answer to these questions hangs everything else—my sense of who I am, where I should be heading, and what I should do next.

The orthodox Christian answer to the questions necessarily involves the Old Testament. Not-so-orthodox Christian faith has sometimes attempted to evade this conclusion, whether formally, in the Marcionite movement of the early centuries AD, and its intermittent descendants throughout history; or informally, in a lip service paid to the Old by those who were really only interested in the *New* Testament. Yet the Jesus Christ who stands at the center of the Christian metanarrative clearly took the Old Testament as his *own* reference point for understanding the story of which he found himself a part. It was those truth-telling Scriptures, he said, in whose context his truth (and his own person as Truth) was to be understood. They revealed who God is, and what His relationship is to the world—including His relationship to the world in history; and they did so authoritatively. This is easily seen to be the case if we simply note how many times in the course of His teaching and disputes Jesus prefaces what he is about to say with statements such as "It is written that" (e.g. Mark 14:27; Matt 11:10); or, more broadly, how many times we find Jesus basing his teaching or arguments on the Old Testament (e.g. Mark

12:28–31, virtually quoting Deut 6:4–5 and Lev 19:18; Mark 7:9–13, quoting Exod 20:12, 21:17 in the Septuagint). In the Sermon on the Mount, he explicitly teaches that these Old Testament scriptures have a lasting validity (Matt 5:17–20). His earliest followers unsurprisingly took the same view, correctly grasping that their discipleship committed them to this path.

In the writings of St. Paul, for example, we find again constant reference back to the Old Testament. For example, he often applies the ten commandments to the various ethical situations with which he is confronted in the churches (Rom 7:7, 13:9, Eph 6:2–3); and taking his lead from Jesus, he applies Leviticus 19:18 to what is left untouched by these commandments (Rom 13:9, Gal 5:14). In other places, too, he depends directly upon the Old Testament for ethical guidance (e.g. the injunction that two or three witnesses are necessary to establish a matter, 2 Cor 13:1, quoting Deut 19:15). Second Timothy 3:16 sums up the overall New Testament perspective: "All Scripture is inspired by God and profitable for teaching, for reproof, for correction and for training in righteousness." The Scripture predominantly in view is the Old Testament, for the New Testament did not yet exist as a gathered collection of apostolic writings.

Of which story do we find ourselves a part, then, as followers of Jesus Christ? It is a story that begins with one God, rather than with the many "gods" of the ancient or postmodern worlds. The story is not at this point historical, in the normal sense of the word—that is, it is not (it seems) a story constructed from historical records, deriving perhaps from eyewitnesses who were involved in the events they describe. Our biblical story overall is in fact a story that embraces many genres in its telling: parables, letters, love songs, and song of lament, laws and proverbs—to name but a few. It is a story that is as multifaceted in its telling as reality itself, as befits a story that claims to be true to all aspects of that reality. Its ending in the book of Revelation is articulated in apocalyptic language, heavy in metaphor and symbolism, and opaque to those who seek for accurate details about existence that is future. Its beginning, in Genesis 1–11, is apparently articulated in the language of ancient myth, especially Babylonian myth, as those who have come to know the Lord God in later times look back upon an earlier era and use the materials that lie to hand in order to tell the truth about existence that is past and present.[8] In Babylonian mythology the world begins when Marduk defeats the sea monster Tiamat, using the upper half of Tiamat's body to form heaven and the lower half to form earth. The primeval "waters" symbolize the powerful, chaotic threat to order that Tiamat represents. Genesis begins, on the other hand, with the waters under the sovereign control of the Spirit of the one God and has the sea monsters as creatures of this one God, playing in the oceans. In Mesopotamia and also in Egypt astral worship was common; the sun and the moon were among the most important gods in the pantheon, and the stars were often credited with controlling human destiny. This is reflected in the fact that in Genesis the creation of the sun, moon, and stars is described at much greater length than anything else save the creation of human beings. However, the luminaries of the heavens are only *creatures* in Genesis, and not gods. Sun and moon do rule over day and night, but only through God's permission; and in this "ruling" they are assigned merely the role of lighting the earth—a lowly function for them by ancient Near East standards. There is one God, the creator of all that is in heaven and earth; and there are no other gods beside Him.[9]

The world that this God creates is quite separate from God. While God is intimately involved with creation, creation is not itself divine. Creation is contingent and other-than-God. In Genesis 1 this is underlined by the fact that creation is by the divine word: God speaks and "over there," as it were, creation takes place. Creation is through effortless decree by a divine being who has no natural connection with what is being created. It is, of course, this belief about God and the world that shaped Israelite religion, which set its face against the magic or the empathetic religion as was found in the ancient fertility cults, where a basic connection *was* assumed between the stuff of the gods and the stuff of creation. Creation is not divine in the early chapters of Genesis. Creation *is*, however, a resolutely *good* place. It is indeed a good place precisely because it has been created by a single benevolent God who has no rival to disturb His plans to bless His creatures. All God's works obey Him; there is nothing to fear. This includes the seventh day.

The pattern of six days of similar acts followed by a change on the seventh day is well attested in Mesopotamian and Ugaritic literature; but in the Babylonian tradition in particular, the seventh day of the week was regarded as unlucky. This is not so in Genesis, where the seventh day is consecrated by God himself and declared holy. The significance of this is that the Israelite Sabbath is understood as quite independent of the phases of the moon—the moon has no "power" over human beings. The Sabbath, far from being unlucky, is blessed and sanctified by the creator, and it becomes clearer later in the Pentateuch story that this is connected with God's intention to bless creation by giving all creatures respite from work.

If "the gods" are not to be feared in this world that has been evacuated of deities excepting the good creator God, then we should not fear our fellow human beings either, even when they may aspire to deity. In the ideology of the ancient Near East, it was kings and kings alone (with occasional exceptions) who were made in the divine image—gods on earth, as their inscriptions often tell us. Other human beings were allegedly created as servants of the gods to keep them supplied with food; so says the Atrahasis Epic of Old Babylon, at least.[10] In Genesis, on the other hand, *all* human beings (both male and female) are made in God's image. There is ruling and subduing to be done on the earth, as kings often do; but it is the ruling and subduing of creation by humans beings in general. All are "kings," occupying a preeminent place in the created order. Human beings are not created for the benefit of the gods and certainly not to supply the gods (including the king) with food. Rather, *God* provides food for all his *creatures*, including his human creatures—an abundant supply of food that (implicitly) enables rest from labor once a week. The dignity of every human person is thus established.

There are no gods in the created order, except those "images of God" who are, in fact, all human beings. There is only one God; and all his human creatures are on the same level in terms of worth and dignity, and in terms of the blessedness of life that they should enjoy under God. This view of human beings involves thus a fundamentally egalitarian, communal view of life that is quite out of step with ancient Near Eastern ideology in general and with much political and religious ideology since; and the various ways in which it is out of step are apparent already in the remainder of the Old Testament story.[11]

This is how our story begins. It begins with one good God, above and beyond all other entities called "god," who out of love and not necessity creates a world that bears His marks and knows His presence but is not part of Him. It begins with creatures, among whom are human creatures who are called to look after the other creatures on God's behalf—who are made for love for God and for all their creaturely neighbors, and are given freedom to express this love (or not). Before these creatures lies the tree of the knowledge of good and evil, as they grow up from childhood into maturity with God; and the tree of life, as their mortality is clothed with immortality. A direction is in view, in this story; a process is envisaged. A happy ending is already intended—an ending that does not leave the world where it began, but takes it into a different dimension.

How does the story develop? In a complicated way! The reason is that the darkness, ordered by God in Genesis 1 so as to make it useful, breaks free of its bonds in Genesis 3 and insinuates its way into human experience. The world of unbroken communion with God, who walks in the garden and talks with his creatures—the world of childlike innocence and unselfconsciousness—becomes a fractured, alienated world. The serpent invites human beings to view God cynically and untrustingly, and they do. As a consequence they grasp at equality with God, and find themselves naked and ashamed. A broken relationship with God becomes a broken relationship also between the man and the woman, marked now by a desire for power rather than by love; and thus disabled, neither is able to look after the earth in the manner God intends. The alienation of Genesis 3 leads on to the bloodshed of chapter 4; and the world spirals downwards into the complete chaos and anarchy of Genesis 6, as violence fills the earth (6:11–13), and then later into the hubris of Genesis 11. There *is* adulthood (human beings have eaten from the tree of the knowledge of good and evil); but there is no maturity, and there is certainly no immortality.

The complication introduced by the evil serpent is, however, met with a remedy introduced by the good God, who is committed to His original plan for the world and sustains it throughout the mainly disastrous events of Genesis 1–11. The fragmentation of the human race is met with the promise to one of those fragments of land and nationhood, to the end that all the earth may still receive God's blessing, as He originally intended (Gen 12). Now in the story we leave the dialogue with Babylonian mythology and enter the world of historiography as such. The truth about the drama that Abraham enters has been articulated in one way; the truth about the ongoing drama itself is now told in quite another. The story shifts gears, moving from "great lyrical narrative of the world (Gen 1–11) ... [to] treasured family memories (Gen 12–36, 37–50)."[12] It is the promise to Abraham that occupies center stage for most of the remainder of the Pentateuch, as we wait to see whether this promise too will founder on the rocks of human folly, or whether God will soon succeed in his goal of blessing the created order through Abraham and his descendants. The promise survives, it turns out—but barely. It survives the character of Jacob; the childlessness of Rachel (Gen 29:31 ff.); severe famine in the land, and exile from it to Egypt (Gen 41:57). It is resurgent in the Exodus, as the living God confronts the false god Pharaoh and reveals who it is that controls creation, including human life itself. It is foundational to the formation of the people of Israel at Mount Sinai in Exodus 19, where they are reminded that the whole earth is the Lord's, in respect of which the Israelites are to be a "kingdom of priests," mediating the redemptive love of God to other creatures. The promise is resurgent and foundational, and yet in the closing chapters of Exodus it hangs by a thread, for while Moses is up on the mountain listening to God, the people are down at the foot of the mountain building idols (Exod 32:1–6).

The book of Numbers reveals that such behavior is not uncharacteristic of the Israelites; this is a people that will always want to go back to Egypt, whether literally or metaphorically (Num 14:1–3). Deuteronomy holds the promise still before them, but also outlines the obligations laid upon them—most particularly the obligation to display unswerving love and loyalty to God (Deut 6:4–9). The Pentateuch ends with little resolved, and we are propelled into Joshua through Kings to discover if the promise is fulfilled.

Moses dies; Joshua succeeds. The Promised Land is apparently entirely conquered (Josh 10:40–42), yet other texts suggest that this is not so (e.g. Judg 2:1–3). What has happened in the book of Joshua is not yet the kind of fulfillment of the promise that Genesis 12 expects. In the book of Judges the continuing military campaign falters because of sin, as the Israelites continually give in to apostasy and are given over by God to their enemies. They are rescued by "judges" of diverse character: righteous Othniel; ambiguous Gideon; foolish Jephthah; alarming Samson. The appendix to the book (Judg 17–21) describes an Israelite society that is corrupt at all levels. It is against this background that the books of Samuel describe the rise of the prophet Samuel and the reigns of Israel's first two kings, Saul and David. The monarchy is woven into the promise even though the monarchy itself arises out of sinful desire (1 Sam 8). Disobedient Saul is succeeded by David, a "man after [God's] own heart" (1 Sam 13:14), whose dynasty will be everlasting (2 Sam 7). David's reign does not see the promise fulfilled, however. Called to mediate blessing to the Gentiles, David brings only a curse, as he steals the wife of Uriah the Hittite and causes his death. The curse in turn destroys David's family (2 Sam 13–20). David evidently points forward beyond himself to someone who is still to come—a son of David who will in reality bring in God's kingdom.

The books of 1–2 Kings (and their partners, 1–2 Chronicles) describe a number of contenders. Solomon receives the wisdom of God (1 Kgs 3), and the people of Israel enjoy the prosperity and peace of his empire; there is even a degree of blessing upon the whole earth (1 Kgs 4:20–21, 24–25, 29–34). Yet Solomon is a fractured soul, and eventually turns away to worship other gods (1 Kgs 11). The glorious empire is dissolved, as Jeroboam son of Nebat leads northern Israel into independence from Rehoboam and Judah (1 Kgs 12:1–24). Sons of

David continue to reign in Judah, and some of them do relatively well, but the sins of Manasseh are ultimately too much for God to bear (2 Kgs 21) and the kingdom falls. Many Judeans are exiled to Babylon (2 Kgs 24–25). The threats of Deuteronomy have engulfed the promises, it seems, and Israel once again finds herself in a foreign country and under the dominion of a foreign king. The very future of the Davidic line hangs by the slender thread of a displaced ruler sitting at the table of the king of Babylon (25:27–30).

One thing is clear from this story: If there is to be a future, it will involve at its heart an individual Israelite leader of a particular character. He will be a Davidic king, yet have the strength of character of Joshua. He will be under prophetic authority (like David, not Saul), if he does not himself possess it; he will keep Torah (like Joshua, but not David). He will know how to combine Torah and Wisdom (unlike Solomon), rather than driving the two apart. If there is to be a future for the promise, such a character will be at its center; it is as a result of his reign that the kingdom of God will arrive and all the earth will be blessed. It is precisely this hope (as expressed, e.g., in Isa 9 and 11) that God's people hold onto in the midst of and in the aftermath of the exile, as Israelites either do (Ezra–Nehemiah) or do not (Esther) return to the promised land once the Persians have taken over the reins of empire from the Babylonians (2 Chronicles 36).

This, then, is the Old Testament section of the story of which we find ourselves a part, as followers of Jesus Christ. Here is the foundational section of that great all-biblical story that makes sense of our existence, as we in faith attach our own personal stories to it—the story that saves us from the fate of being "unscripted, anxious stutterers."

Here it is that we learn first, along with the Israelites, who God truly is—God who is for us, and not against us.[13] God is incomparable: "Who is like you, O Lord, among the gods? Who is like you, majestic in holiness, awesome in splendor, doing wonders?" (Exod 15:11).[14] God is the one and only God: "There is no one like you and there is no God but you" (2 Sam 7:22).[15] God is good, and His deepest intention is to bless: "The Lord bless you and keep you; the Lord make his face to shine upon you, and be gracious to you; the Lord lift up his countenance upon you, and give you peace" (Num 6:24–27).[16] God is a devoted, dependable lover: "O give thanks to the Lord, for he is good; his steadfast love endures forever" (1 Chr 16:34).[17] God saves: "I will give you as a light to the nations, so that my salvation may reach to the end of the earth" (Isa 49:6).[18] God is holy, dangerous to sinful beings because He is good: "I am God and no mortal, the Holy One in your midst" (Hos 11:9).[19] God is angry when He encounters wickedness: "Now let me alone, so that my wrath may burn hot against them and I may consume them" (Exod 32:10).[20] God forgives: "Who is a God like you, pardoning iniquity and passing over the transgression of the remnant of your possession? He does not retain his anger forever, because he delights in showing clemency" (Mic 7:18).[21] It is this God who comes at last to walk among us in Jesus Christ, the son of David who is like Joshua; the one who is keeper of Torah and teacher of Wisdom. It is this God who remains with us after Pentecost in the Holy Spirit—a God revealed as three, even though He is one. We first get to know this God, however, in the Old Testament.

Here it is in this Old Testament story that we learn secondly, along with the Israelites, who *we* truly are. We are beings made for relationship—with God, with each other, and with the rest of creation. We are divine image-bearers, "a little lower than the angels" (Ps 8), made for unbroken communion with God, who walks in the garden in which He has placed us and talks with us (Gen 3). We are gendered image-bearers, male and female, made for intimacy and mutual help, in a world in which there is to be no shame or guilt (Gen 2:24–25). As gendered image-bearers we are designed for joint governance of the rest of creation as God's representatives, just as ancient kings placed "images" of themselves in chosen territories in order to claim sovereignty over that territory. Like these kings we are called to look after the welfare of our subjects (note, e.g., Ps 72), the other creatures, many of whom (like us) come "from the ground" (Gen 2:7 and 2:19).

We are servant-kings; stewards of a greater Lord, accountable always and in every respect to the Owner of the Garden, the Creator (cf. Ps 24:1). The other creatures are our companions for the journey we are set upon by God, towards the tree of life. This journey having been subverted by the powers of darkness, we find ourselves also the recipients of divine grace—the subjects of God's passion to save, initially worked out on behalf of the world through one people, Israel. We are people who are pursued, so that the world will be, one day, the world that God always intended it to be—in the time when the Great Serpent is finally slain and the new heavens and the new earth are created (e.g. Isa 11:1–9; 27:1; 65:17–25).

It is this reality toward which we are pointed in Christ, as we "put on the new self, which is being renewed in knowledge in the image of its Creator" (Col 3:10; cf. Eph 4:24; Rom 8:29), emerging from the various fallen cultures that we currently inhabit, with all their distorted relationships (between God and us; among us humans; and between humans and the rest of creation), and finding a new Christlike Way ahead. It is a reality represented in the New Testament in terms of a city where there are trees of life and a river of life (Rev 22:1–5). That city in Revelation is only the endpoint of a journey, however, that begins in the garden of Genesis, which also has its tree of life and its river that gives life to everything round about it.

Here is the story, told through its manifold genres, that makes sense of our stories; "the same tale ... still going on," that explains our beginning and our end, so that we may begin to understand our muddled middle. Here is the Christian metanarrative. Its articulation need not involve the despising or rejection of any individual human story, in spite of what postmodern people fear—whether it is a story drawn from real life or more from the imagination (that is, whether we are dealing with fiction or nonfiction). It does not even require the wholesale despising or rejection of other large-scale metanarratives that compete with the Christian story for people's loyalty. There *is* a version of Christian faith that is somewhat totalitarian in these respects—that is so keen to stress the truth of the Christian story that it has a tendency to deny any truth at all in other stories, including competing metanarratives. It is, indeed, this version of Christian faith against which postmodernity is substantially reacting when it adopts its "incredulity toward metanarratives" and suggests that metanarratives produce only tyranny. Intolerance of other stories, it is claimed, has led to intolerance of other people; and there is certainly truth to that claim, with respect to Christian faith. For this totalitarian version of Christian faith defines itself fundamentally over *against* other stories: it is against the modern story of science; it is against the stories told by other religions; it is against the story told by Marxists (although strangely often enthusiastic about the story told by capitalists); and it has a tendency not only to be dismissive of personal stories drawn from real life (in so far as they do not support and confirm the metanarrative), but also to be hostile to art and fictional literature. It is formally similar to other totalitarian systems, like certain versions of Islam, in such respects. It finds no space for truth outside the barricade; it finds in other stories only a threat, and not a promise.

Yet Christian faith is not *inevitably* totalitarian in such ways. It is possible to take a different view, understanding (along with the Bible) that the whole world is *God's* place; that human beings, Christians or not, remain those who are made in God's image; and that the world at large is therefore a place in which truth can be found. A more truly Christian way in which to approach the world around us is in fact not to define ourselves over *against* other stories—the stories of science; of other religions; of economic and political systems; real life stories and fictional stories. A more truly Christian way in which to approach the world is surely to rejoice in truth wherever it may be found, and to expect that in its finding we shall also discover that it is deepened, and more fully understood, within the context of the Christian Gospel. For we do live in God's creation, and the truth that is found in God's creation can hardly be in conflict with the truth that is found in the Gospel which is also preached by God Himself incarnate. On the contrary, if the Christian metanarrative is truly true—if it is truly the story that explains and embraces all stories—then it should be able in principle to account for the truth that is found in other stories, and to explain it more fully than those stories; and it should be possible in principle to persuade other people of this fact, and to encourage them to embrace the Christian story of reality instead of holding on to their incomplete stories of reality. Creation itself reveals God's glory, rightly viewed; all the individual stories point towards the larger story.

This is true, for example, of the story of modern science. We now have solid evidence that the universe had a beginning in time—that we ourselves are midway through a complicated cosmic story whose telling embraces such realities as novae explosions, scattering throughout the galaxies the dust of stars of which (it turns out) we are made. We are star dust—that is how the carbon, iron, phosphorous and calcium in our bodies were formed. This "time" that has thus begun and moved on flows only one way—a remarkable cosmological oddity, much pondered by cosmologists, astrophysicists, and some mathematicians, because everything else in the universe is potentially symmetrical. Time flows only one way; and not all the science fiction stories or "back to the future" movies in the world will make it do otherwise. Story (beginning, development and end) seems to be built into the very structure of the universe. The current Archbishop of Canterbury, Rowan Williams, has said that this new understanding of the universe

> has put back into our understanding of the universe elements of narrative, elements of biography. The universe has a biography, a story of life. This is a story which moves forward, which accumulates, which points ahead. The stories that are visible in the lives of individuals are not some kind of aberration in a universe which basically goes around in circles.[22]

A cosmic story implies a storyteller, of course, as G. K. Chesterton well understood. Writing of his own coming to Christian faith, he tells us that he had always had a sense of the mystery and wonder of the universe—the longing that is a mixture of both sadness and joy, which the writer of Ecclesiastes calls "eternity in the heart." In the wonderful story of his conversion Chesterton writes:

> I had always vaguely felt facts to be miracles in the sense that they are wonderful; now I began to think them miracles in the stricter sense that they were *willful*. I mean that they were, or might be, repeated exercises of some will. In short, I had

always believed that the world involved magic: now I thought that perhaps it involved a magician. And this pointed to a profound emotion always present and subconscious; that this world of ours has some purpose; and if there is a purpose, there is a person. I had always felt life first as a story: and if there is a story there is a storyteller.[23]

The story of science points beyond itself to a greater story; so do all stories, large or small. They are all part, inevitably, of a greater story, without which they can in the end only help to illuminate our predicament, our lostness—until we come to be a conscious participant in the story that God is telling, which he invites us into through the Gospel of Jesus Christ. That is indeed what the Gospel is: a proclamation that the longing for eternity that we have in our hearts, manifested in all stories that try (however unsuccessfully) to connect the beginning and the end in one shining whole, is now met in the God who has entered into our human story in Christ.

Perhaps St. Augustine said it best, at the beginning of the long telling of the story of the first part of his life, in all its wandering and confusion: "You have made us for yourself," he says to God, "and our heart is restless until it rests in you."[24] The same point is made towards the end of 1 Corinthians 13. St. Paul himself alludes to the middled muddledness of our condition: "Now we see but a poor reflection...now I know in part." All good stories help us to "know in part" something more about ourselves and our condition. But in the future, St. Paul concludes, "I shall know fully, even as I am fully known." It is that great promise—that our story has an Author, who fully knows both our beginning and our end—that enables us to rest in the great benediction of all good stories: "And they lived happily ever after." It is that great promise that gives us hope.

ENDNOTES

All the abbreviations used for journals and series in the notes may be found in the *SBL Handbook of Style*.

CHAPTER ONE
[1] The paper was read at the Society of Biblical Literature International Meeting in Copenhagen, Denmark, August 1989.
[2] It could hardly be so, given the author's commitment to the method elsewhere: cf. I. W. Provan, *Hezekiah and the Books of Kings* (BZAW 172; Berlin: de Gruyter, 1988).
[3] J. Morgenstern, "Jerusalem – 485 BC," *HUCA* 27 (1956): 101–79; 28 (1957): 15–47; and 31 (1960): 1–29.
[4] M. Treves, "Conjectures sur les dates et les sujets des Lamentations," *Bulletin Renan* 95 (1963): 1–4.
[5] So, for example, N. K. Gottwald, *Studies in the Book of Lamentations* (SBT 14; London: SCM, 1954), 20–21; H.-J. Kraus, *Klagelieder (Threni)* (BKAT 20; 3d ed; Neukirchen-Vluyn: Neukirchener, 1968), 13–15 (tentatively); B. Albrektson, *Studies in the Text and Theology of the Book of Lamentations* (Studia Theologica Lundensia 21; Lund: CWK Gleerup 1963), 214–15; D. R. Hillers, *Lamentations* (AB 7A; Garden City: Doubleday, 1972), xviii–xix; O. Kaiser, "Klagelieder," in H. Ringgren et al., *Sprüche, Prediger, Das Hohe Lied, Klagelieder, Das Buch Esther* (ATD 16, 3d ed; Göttingen, 1981), 291–386 (300–302); R. Brandscheidt, *Gotteszorn and Menschenleid: Die Gerichtsklage des leidenden Gerechten in Klgl 3* (TThSt 41; Trier: Paulinus, 1983), 204–15;

J. Renkema, *"Misschien is er hoop ...." De theologische vooronderstellingen van het boek Klaagliederen* (Franeker: Wever, 1983), 43–58.

[6] W. Rudolph, *Die Klagelieder* (KAT 17/3; 2d ed; Gütersloh: Gerd Mobu, 1962), 209–11; M. Haller, "Die Klagelieder," in M. Haller and K. Galling, *Die fünf Megilloth* (HAT 1/18; Tübingen: Mohr Siebeck, 1940), 91–113 (94); A. Weiser, "Klagelieder," in H. Ringgren and A. Weiser, *Das Hohe Lied, Klagelieder, Das Buch Esther* (ATD 16/2; Göttingen: Vandenhoeck & Ruprecht, 1958), 39–112 (43).

[7] G. Brunet, *Les Lamentations contre Jérémie* (Bibliothèque de l'école des hautes études, section des sciences religieuses 25; Paris: Presses universitaires de France, 1968), 28–39, 114–25.

[8] According to Kraus, *Klagelieder*, 25, "One thing is certain: the whole song stands so near the events that one feels everywhere as if the terrible pictures of the destruction stand still immediately before the eyes of the one lamenting."

[9] Thus Kaiser, "Klagelieder," 300–302, argues that Lam 2 is literarily dependent upon prophetic texts and psalms, and that Lam 1, like the other poems in the book, shows knowledge of Lam 2. All the poems must therefore date from the fifth century or later. He further argues (311–13) that Lam 1 itself shows knowledge of prophetic texts and psalms.

[10] E. M. Forster, *Anonymity: An Inquiry* (London: Hogarth, 1925), 14.

[11] Morgenstern, *HUCA* 28, 16–18.

[12] For example, Kaiser, "Klagelieder," 312–13, says that a change in the status of Jerusalem–Judah as vassals of the Babylonians is *"unbedingt vorausgesetzt"* (absolutely presupposed) by Lam 1:1, 14c, using these verses to argue against Rudolph's notion of the background of the poem.

[13] This suggestion is that of T. F. McDaniel, "Philological Studies in Lamentations," *Bib* 49 (1968): 27–53, 199–220 (29–31), who notes the frequent occurrence of *rbt* with this meaning in Phoenician, Ugaritic, and Punic.

[14] A better rendering than that of the RSV, the city being identified with the area around it. The word *mdynh* is always used elsewhere in the Old Testament of the district of a kingdom or empire, as in 1 Kgs 20:14 ff. and especially Ezek 19:8, where it also appears alongside *gwym*, "nations."

[15] This interpretation of Lam 1:1 follows JB, which understands the verse as comprising two interpretive units rather than three (cf. RSV), dividing the second line between them. On this understanding, the verse hinges upon the double use (lines 1 and 2) of the Heb. *rbty*, "great" or "mistress."

[16] W. C. Gwaltney, Jr., "The Biblical Book of Lamentations in the Context of Near Eastern Lament Literature," in *Scripture in Context* II (ed. W. W. Hallo, J. C. Moyer and L. G. Perdue; Winona Lake, IN: Eisenbrauns, 1983), 191–211 (205–10); D. R. Hillers, "History and Poetry in Lamentations," *CurTM* 10 (1983): 155–61.

[17] Brunet, *Lamentations*, 1–27, attempts to draw a distinction throughout Lam 1–4 between the "foes" (*srym*) and the enemies (*'ybm*) of Jerusalem, whom he sees as external (foreign) and internal (Judean) opponents of the authors respectively. The latter are the erstwhile "friends" of Lam 1:2. The imagery of the poem, however, which portrays the city and the inhabitants of Judah and Jerusalem as closely identified (cf. vv. 3, 15, 17), and the latter as being possessed by and dependent upon the former (vv. 4–7, 11, 15–16, 18–19), makes it highly unlikely that "friends" (which implies a relationship between equals) in this verse does refer to Judeans; and careful consideration of other references to enemies (1:5, 9, 16, 21; 2:3, 7, 16, 17, 22; 3:46, 52; 4:12) makes clear that it is of foreign enemies of Judah that most of this material is also more naturally taken as speaking.

[18] LXX has "rams" here, implying a different understanding of the verse.

[19] P. R. Ackroyd, *Exile and Restoration* (Philadelphia: Westminster, 1968), 20–31.

[20] LXX seems to presuppose a Heb. verb *nhwgwt*, "led away," implying absence from Jerusalem. MT, on the other hand, reads *nwgwt*, which is usually taken to be a form of the verb *ygh*, "to suffer" which appears in Lam 1:5, 12; 3:32–33. Given the context, this is most probably a reference to grief (cf. NIV, JB): "Her maidens grieve, and she herself is in bitter anguish."

[21] It should be noted that, although much has been made of the likely length of the siege presupposed by Lam 1, nothing in the poem itself actually requires that a siege is in view at all. Indeed, the position of the references to hunger in the chapter, after descriptions of defeat and captivity, make it much more likely that famine is a consequence of these events rather than a prelude to them.

[22] It is often suggested by commentators (e.g. J. Gray, *I and II Kings* [OTL; 3d ed.; London: SCM, 1977], 344–45) that what is really in view here is simply the giving of tribute by Rehoboam to Shishak, rather than the latter's entry into Jerusalem. In large part this is because Egyptian records of Shishak's campaign do not mention any action against Jerusalem. It should be noted, however, that 1 Kgs 14:26 quite clearly implies that the pharaoh *took* treasure rather than being given it: compare the language of 2 Kgs 14:14; 24:13; 25:13–17, and contrast that of passages where the giving of tribute is described (1 Kgs 15:18; 2 Kgs 12:18; 16:8; 18:15–16). That this is historically accurate is quite possible, since the Egyptian records are not complete (cf. K. A. Kitchen, *The Third Intermediate Period in Egypt* (1100–650 BC) [Warminster: Aris and Phillips, 1973], 294–300, 432–47), and since, in any case, "entry," whether in this text or in Lam 1:10, does not necessarily imply conquest. It may be that Rehoboam simply acquiesced in the removal of the treasure from Jerusalem by Shishak's representatives.

[23] It is, for example, by no means improbable that Shishak took captives back to Egypt after completing his campaign in Palestine. Deportation frequently accompanied conquest throughout the ANE (cf. I. J. Gelb, "Prisoners of War in Early Mesopotamia," *JNES* 32 (1973): 70–98 [92]), and was certainly prac-

ticed by the Egyptian pharaohs (cf. Abd El-Mohsen Bakir, *Slavery in Pharaonic Egypt* [Supplément aux Annales du Service des Antiquités de l'Égypte 18; Cairo: L'institut français d'archéologie orientale, 1952], 109–17).

[24] See most recently R. B. Salters, "Lamentations 1:3: Light from the History of Exegesis," in *A Word in Season: Essays in Honor of William McKane* (JSOTSup 42; ed. J. D. Martin and P. R. Davies; Sheffield: JSOT Press, 1986), 73–89.

[25] S. J. D. Cohen, "The Destruction: From Scripture to Midrash," *Proof* 2 (1982): 18–39.

[26] This is how *Lamentations Rabbati*, a rabbinic commentary of the fifth to the seventh centuries AD, understands the book. It sets forth the eternal paradigm of Jewish suffering, Jeremiah having prophesied in detail of the various troubles which had fallen upon the Jewish people from his time to that of the reader.

[27] J. Barton, *Reading the Old Testament* (London: Darton, Longman and Todd, 1984), 159.

CHAPTER TWO

[1] The paper was originally read at the Summer Meeting of the Society for Old Testament Study, held in Sheffield, UK, in July 1989.

[2] F. H. W. Gesenius, *Hebräisches Elementarbuch* 1: *Hebräische Grammatik* (11th ed., Halle: Renger, 1834) § 124; G. H. A. Ewald, *Ausfürliches Lehrbuch der hebräischen Sprache des Alten Bundes* (5th ed., Leipzig: Hahn, 1844) § 223b; F. Böttcher, *Ausfürliches Lehrbuch der hebräischen Sprache* (2 vols., Leipzig: Barth, 1866, 1868) § 939g, 947g.

[3] W. M. L. de Wette, *Commentar über die Psalmen* (Heidelberg, 1811), 122. M. Buttenwieser, *The Psalms* (Chicago: University of Chicago Press, 1938), 24, is therefore not entirely accurate when he says that "Ewald and Böttcher ... were the first to recognize the existence of the precative perfect in Hebrew."

[4] F. E. König, *Historisch-kritisches Lehrgebäude der hebräischen Sprache* (vol. 3; Leipzig: Hinrichs, 1897), § 173; A. B. Davidson, *Introductory Hebrew Grammar*

(vol. 2; 3d ed., Edinburgh: T&T Clark, 1912), § 41, rem. 5; G. R. Driver, *Problems of the Hebrew Verbal System* (Edinburgh: T&T Clark, 1936), 147–48.

[5] M. J. Dahood, "Ugaritic-Hebrew Syntax and Style," *UF* 1 (1969), 15–36 (20–21); *Psalms I* (Garden City: Doubleday, 1970), 20; *III* (1970), 414–17.

[6] A. A. Anderson, *Psalms* (London: Marshall, Morgan & Scott, 1972), 77, and passim; P. C. Craigie, *Psalms 1–50* (Waco: Word, 1983), 77–78, and passim. The precative perfect had already been accepted as occurring in some instances in earlier work on the Psalms (e.g. Buttenweiser, 18–25, 905).

[7] S. R. Driver, *A Treatise on the Use of the Tenses in Hebrew* (Oxford: Oxford University Press, 1874; 3d ed., 1892), § 20. Among other older students of Hebrew grammar and syntax who rejected the idea (e.g. A. E. Cowley, ed., *Gesenius' Hebrew Grammar as Edited and Enlarged by the late E. Kautzsch* [2d ed., Oxford: Oxford University Press, 1910 = 28th German ed.] § 106 *n*, n2; C. Brockelmann, *Grundriss der vergleichenden Grammatik der semitischen Sprachen* [vol. 2; Berlin: Reuther and Reichard, 1913] § 16b; G. Bergsträsser, *Hebräische Grammatik* [vol. 2; Leipzig: Hinrichs, 1926] § 6h, i), Driver's work was regarded as foundational.

[8] S. E. Loewenstamm, "The Death of the Upright and the World to Come," *JJS* 16 (1956), 183–86 (185n6), for example, states that the evidence for a precative perfect is "precarious," citing S. R. Driver and Gesenius-Kautzsch.

[9] He was specifically concerned with Ewald's claim with regard to an Arabic parallel. Whereas in Hebrew the supposed examples of the precative perfect varied in the position which they occupied in the sentence and occurred in the context of concrete personal petitions, in Arabic precative perfects all but universally stood in first position in the sentence, and were not used to express concrete personal petitions.

[10] G. R. Driver, *Canaanite Myths and Legends* (ed. J. C. L. Gibson, 2d ed., Edinburgh: T&T Clark, 1978), 40n4; 62n2; 104n13; 123n11; 124n6; 127n4;

129n11, for example, recognizes the construction in *CTA* 2.i.12; 17.i.41; 23.25, 75–76; 24.50. I am grateful to Professor Gibson for helpful correspondence on the matter.

[11] W. H. Bellinger, *Psalmody and Prophecy* (Sheffield: JSOT, 1984), 109–10.

[12] H. Wiesmann, *Die Klagelieder* (Frankfurt: Philosophisch-theologische Hochschule Sankt Georgen, 1954), 194; W. Rudolph, *Das Buch Ruth, Das Hohe Lied, Die Klagelieder* (2d ed., Gütersloh: Gerd Mohn, 1962), 236–37; H. Lamparter, *Das Buch der Sehnsucht: Das Buch Ruth, Das Hohe Lied, Die Klagelieder* (Stuttgart: Calwer, 1962), 171; D. R. Hillers, *Lamentations* (Garden City: Doubleday, 1972), 4, 15, 52–53, 59–60; R. Gordis, *The Song of Songs and Lamentations* (3d ed., New York: Ktav, 1974), 186–187; H. Gottlieb, *A Study on the Text of Lamentations* (Aarhus: Aarhus University Press, 1978), 57–60.

[13] Gottlieb has already offered arguments along similar lines to those offered here. I believe, however, that a more detailed and still stronger case than his can be made, and in one important aspect (see below) I disagree with him. Gordis and Hillers, in their commentaries, assume the existence of the precative perfect in this passage more than they argue for it.

[14] H.-J. Kraus, *Klagelieder (Threni)*, (3d ed., Neukirchen-Vluyn: Neukirchener, 1968), 53–59; A. Weiser, "Klagelieder," in H. Ringgren and A. Weiser, *Das Hohe Lied, Klagelieder, Das Buch Esther* (Göttingen: Vandenhoeck & Ruprecht, 1958), 39–112 (76–77, 87–91); O. Kaiser, "Klagelieder," in H. Ringgren et al., *Sprüche, Prediger, Das Hohe Lied, Klagelieder, Das Buch Esther* (3d ed., Göttingen: Vandenhoeck & Ruprecht, 1980), 291–386 (349–51, 357–58).

[15] It could be argued, of course, that such searching for transition is misguided, and that what we have in this passage is much more complex, the author jumping from past to present and back again with no great concern with order and progress of thought. This is possible. The remainder of the book of Lamentations, and indeed the remainder of this chapter, do not, however,

give this impression of his literary style, and most scholars have thought that if two situations of distress are to be found here, then there must be a point at which the description of one ends and the description of the other begins.

[16] J. K. Zenner, *Beiträge zur Erklärung der Klagelieder* (Freiburg: Herder, 1905), 27; Wiesmann, *Klagelieder*, 197–98.

[17] The LXX and Peshitta both read the verb here as a perfect, perhaps reflecting a Hebrew *špṭt*. W. Rudolph, "Der Text der Klagelieder," *ZAW* 56 (1938): 101–22, suggests (115) that the consonantal MT *špth* may have been a variant spelling of *špṭt*, but admits that there are no other Old Testament examples of the proposed form.

[18] Gottlieb, 49, 58; Kraus, 53–57; Weiser, 76–77; Kaiser, 349–50, 357–59; R. Brandscheidt, *Gotteszorn*, 68–70; cf. the rendering of the NEB.

[19] For example, Ps 5:2; 10:17; 17:1, 6; 31:3; 39:13; 54:4; 55:2; 71:2; 80:2; 84:9; 86:1, 6; 88:3; 102:3; 130:2; 140:7; 141:1; 143:1.

[20] Albrektson, *Studies*, 163.

[21] D. Michel, *Tempora und Satzstellung in den Psalmen* (Bonn: Bouvier, 1960), 79–81.

[22] I can find no convincing evidence that the poem is not for the most part spoken by one voice, "the man" (Heb. *gbr*) of v. 1, though there does seem to be a second speaker in vv. 34–36 (cf. Rudolph [n12], 240–41), who is best taken as Zion or her people. The case for taking "the man" himself as Zion and her people as a collective (cf., for example, Albrektson, 126–28) is not strong. It is, first, not the natural way in which the reader who has approached the chapter via chs. 1 and 2 would take the term *gbr*, since Zion in those chapters is female, not male. This is an important point, since it seems likely that the third poem was never intended to be read independently of the second, but was composed with the second in mind (cf. K. Budde, "Die Klagelieder," in Budde et al., *Die fünf Megillot* [Freiburg im Breisgau, Leipzig and Tübingen: Mohr Siebeck, 1898], 70–108 (76–77, 93); Rudolph, 235). Secondly, Lam 3:48 and 51 clearly make a distinction between the one weeping and the people/city,

the statement of the former verse being very similar to that of the narrator in 2:11b. It is this narrator who is best taken as the main speaker here. We must differentiate, then, between the man and the people, though recognizing that the former feels himself to be closely identified with the latter. Their suffering is his suffering, and he can exhort them to join him in repentance (cf. vv. 40–47).

[23] It has often been suggested (e.g. by Kraus, 53, and Kaiser, 346) that the slightly longer line in v. 56 has been created by the addition of *lšw'ty* by an editor who wished to make clear the meaning of the less well known word. There is, however, no evidence from the Versions that there was ever a Hebrew text less full than the one now available to us. Like the Peshitta, the LXX clearly presupposes the presence of *lšw'ty* or a similar word, though both (cf. their references to "salvation") seem to have identified the root here as *yš'* rather than *šw'*.

CHAPTER THREE

[1] Note, for example, the influential S. Mowinckel, *He That Cometh* (ET; Oxford: Blackwell, 1956).

[2] M. Noth, *The Deuteronomistic History* (ET; 2d ed; JSOTSup 15; Sheffield: JSOT Press, 1991).

[3] We may note, e.g., H. W. Wolff, "The Kerygma of the Deuteronomic Historical Work," in W. Brueggemann and H. W. Wolff, eds., *The Vitality of Old Testament Traditions* (Atlanta: John Knox, 1975), 83–100, who contends that in the Deuteronomistic History as a whole there is a pattern of repentance and forgiveness which suggests that the author still held out hope for a restoration of God's blessing; and W. Dietrich, *Prophetie und Geschichte* (FRLANT 108; Göttingen: Vandenhoeck & Ruprecht, 1972), who argues that in the final redaction of Kings a future hope is envisaged for Israel if she is obedient to the Deuteronomic law.

[4] G. von Rad, *Old Testament Theology* (ET; vol. 1; London: SCM, 1962), 334–47.

⁵ A notable exception is B. S. Childs, *Introduction to the Old Testament as Scripture* (London: SCM, 1979), 281–301.

⁶ We may note among many examples J. Licht, *Storytelling in the Bible* (Jerusalem: Magnes, 1978); R. Alter, *The Art of Biblical Narrative* (London: SPCK, 1981); M. Sternberg, *The Poetics of Biblical Narrative: Ideological Literature and the Drama of Reading* (Bloomington: Indiana University Press, 1985); D. M. Gunn and D. N. Fewell, *Narrative in the Hebrew Bible* (Oxford: Oxford University Press, 1993).

⁷ Some recent commentaries on Kings reveal the influence of the change in climate in particularly obvious respects, e.g., B. O. Long, *1 Kings, with an Introduction to Historical Literature* (Grand Rapids: Eerdmans, 1984) and *2 Kings* (Grand Rapids: Eerdmans, 1991); T. R. Hobbs, *2 Kings* (Waco: Word, 1985); and R. D. Nelson, *First and Second Kings* (Louisville: Westminster/John Knox, 1987).

⁸ We may note here, e.g., two scholars who approach the question from quite different angles, but nevertheless share this skepticism to different degrees: Childs, *Introduction*, and J. D. Levenson, *The Hebrew Bible, the Old Testament, and Historical Criticism* (Louisville: Westminster/John Knox, 1993).

⁹ I mean by intertextuality the way in which individual books either share portions of text with other books (e.g., 2 Kgs 18:17–20:19 and Isa 36:1–38:8; 38:21–39:8; 2 Kgs 24:18–25:30 and Jer 52:1–34), or quote them (e.g., 1 Kgs 22:28 and Mic 1:2), or otherwise reveal that they are aware of them (e.g., by narrating stories in such a manner that they evoke other stories with which they might usefully be compared or contrasted). See further on the general topic M. Fishbane, *Biblical Interpretation in Ancient Israel* (Oxford: Oxford University Press, 1985); D. A. Carson and H. G. M. Williamson, eds., *It Is Written: Scripture Citing Scripture. Essays in Honor of Barnabas Lindars* (Cambridge: Cambridge University Press, 1988), 25–83.

¹⁰ For the detail of the argument here, and indeed for the exegesis *in extenso* which undergirds the whole argument of this essay, see I. W. Provan, *1 and 2 Kings* (Peabody, MA: Hendrickson, 1995).

¹¹ His pretensions to divinity are well expressed in 2 Kgs 19:23–24. He claims to have brought judgment—as only the LORD can do—upon the cedars of Lebanon (cf. Ps 29:5; Isa 2:12–13; Amos 2:9; Zech 11:1–3) and upon Egypt (Isa 19:1–15). He ascends the heights so that he can look God straight in the face (*mārôm*, "height" in both v. 22 and v. 23; cf. Ps 73:8; 75:4–5; Isa 14:13–15). It is he, and not the LORD, who brings or withholds fertility, creating springs and drying up rivers (Ps 36:8–9; Jer 2:13; 17:13; 51:36; Ezek 31; Hos 13:15).

¹² Mowinckel, *He That Cometh*, 123, 157.

¹³ I omit further consideration of Solomon in this essay for reasons of space; see further my commentary, cited above.

¹⁴ P. R. Ackroyd, *Studies in the Religious Tradition of the Old Testament* (London: SCM, 1987), 105–20, building on the work of R. F. Melugin, *The Formation of Isaiah 40–55* (Berlin: de Gruyter, 1976).

¹⁵ Childs, *Introduction*, 325–38.

¹⁶ So Ackroyd, *Studies*, 105–20.

¹⁷ Cf. also Jer 30:1–11, which looks forward more generally to a time when a descendant of David will once again sit on the throne of a united kingdom of Israel (cf. 1 Kgs 11:39).

¹⁸ On Josiah see further A. Laato, *Josiah and David Redivivus: The Historical Josiah and the Messianic Expectations of Exilic and Postexilic Times* (ConBOT 33; Stockholm: Almqvist & Wiksell, 1992); idem, *The Servant of Yhwh and Cyrus: A Reinterpretation of the Exilic Messianic Programme in Isaiah 40–55* (ConBOT 35; Stockholm: Almqvist & Wiksell, 1992).

¹⁹ On the structuring see G. H. Wilson, *The Editing of the Hebrew Psalter* (Chico, CA: Scholars Press, 1985); the various articles in *Int* 46 (1992) 117–55;

and J. C. McCann, ed., *The Shape and Shaping of the Psalter* (JSOTSup 159; Sheffield: JSOT Press, 1993). In general, however, insufficient attention has been paid to the way in which this shaping is bound up with messianic expectation.
[20] Hezekiah's significance as a paradigmatic king is, in fact, greater in Chronicles than in Kings, not least because of the Chronicler's direct equation of kingship in Israel with the kingdom of God and the much more explicitly hopeful note upon which 2 Chronicles ends. We may note here the significance of the fact that the Chronicler in 1 Chr 3:17–24 extends the Davidic line precisely in terms of a list of Jehoiachin's descendants, carrying still further the "logic" of 2 Kgs 25:27–30.
[21] D. Daube, *He That Cometh* (London: London Diocesan Council for Christian–Jewish Understanding, 1966).

CHAPTER FOUR

[1] For example, J. Gray, *1 and 2 Kings* (OTL; 3d ed.; London: SCM, 1977); G. H. Jones, *1 and 2 Kings* (NCB; 2 vols.; Grand Rapids: Eerdmans, 1984); and S. J. DeVries, *1 Kings* (WBC; Waco: Word, 1985).

[2] For example, M. Cogan and H. Tadmor, *2 Kings* (AB; Garden City: Doubleday, 1988); and D. J. Wiseman, *1 and 2 Kings* (TOTC; Leicester: InterVarsity, 1993).

[3] For example, J. Licht, *Storytelling in the Bible* (Jerusalem: Magnes, 1978); R. Alter, *The Art of Biblical Narrative* (London: Allen & Unwin, 1981); M. Sternberg, *The Poetics of Biblical Narrative: Ideological Literature and the Drama of Reading* (Bloomington: Indiana University Press, 1985); D. M. Gunn and D. N. Fewell, *Narrative in the Hebrew Bible* (Oxford Bible Series; Oxford: Oxford Univesity Press, 1993).

[4] The present article arose out of my own work on a new commentary on Kings which will be published in 1995 as *1 and 2 Kings* (NIBCOT; Peabody, MA: Hendrickson). I should like to take this opportunity to thank the staff

at Tyndale House for their excellent hospitality during the sabbatical that saw this work completed.

⁵ Much of what is currently being written about the history of Israel, for example, seems to me to reveal a profound failure to grasp the nature of historiography in general—the extent to which all historiography, whether ancient or modern, has a story-like quality; the extent to which all writing or speaking about the past involves turning happenings and people into events and characters; the extent to which all historiography is also in some sense ideological in character, involving selection and interpretation by authors intent on persuading their readership in some way. The fact that books like Kings may in some sense be "ideological" and "story-like" (as modern literature tends to describe them: cf., for example, N. P. Lemche, *Ancient Israel: A New History of Israelite Society* [Biblical Seminar 5; Sheffield: JSOT Press, 1988]; G. W. Ahlström, *The History of Ancient Palestine from the Palaeolithic Period to Alexander's Conquest* [JSOTSup 146; ed. D. V. Edelman; Sheffield: JSOT Press, 1993]; P. R. Davies, *In Search of 'Ancient Israel'* [JSOTSup 148; Sheffield: JSOT Press, 1992]; T. L. Thompson, *Early History of the Israelite People from the Written and Archaeological Sources* [SHANE 4; Leiden: Brill, 1992]) does not *ipso facto* render them incapable of speaking truly about the past, any more than this is necessarily true of other texts which plainly have historiographical intent. For a detailed discussion of the point, see my soon to be published *JBL* paper, "Ideologies, Literary and Critical: Reflections on Recent Writing on the History of Israel."

⁶ In the extreme form of this position, we find the assertion simply that there is no such thing at all as "the meaning of the text"; readers create their own meanings. There is not, in fact, any such thing as a text; there is simply a primeval chaos of words and phrases waiting for the divine actor (i.e., the reader) to bring it to order. It is difficult to explain the popularity of this position, since it is self-evidently both incoherent (if readers create their own meanings, how

do they know the meaning of statements like "readers create their own meanings"?) and politically unwise (what is the purpose of departments of Hebrew and Old Testament Studies in these days of market-forces ideology, if there are no Hebrew texts and their meanings to be studied?). The more moderate form of the argument runs as follows. Biblical narrative texts do have meanings, and their authors do have intentions, but these texts are nevertheless ideological entities. The task of the reader is not, therefore, simply to interpret what the authors are saying, and certainly not simply to accept it. Readers, rather, conscious of their own competing ideologies, must bring these same ideologies to the text and look for ways of making connections with the text at some level other than its surface meaning. The reader-as-consumer (deciding whose story to tell, and with what kind of meaning attached to it) must begin with a "hermeneutics of suspicion," moving on from there to penetrate beneath the surface meaning of the text to what is really going on, to lay it bare for what it is, and then to retell the story in more acceptable, indeed more politically correct terms. Again, it must be asked whether those aboard the good ship biblical scholarship can safely cut the anchor of authorial intention in this way, and still be able to claim that the ship has any real direction. If the text becomes simply the tool of this or that crusade—if it is talked about in terms of what it *should* have said rather than what it *does* say—then ultimately the text is dispensable, and will not sustain the study that used to be centered around it.

[7] This is particularly so when it is realized that Abiathar is, in fact, never described in the Hebrew text of Samuel as carrying the ark before David. I draw a veil here over discussion of ephods and the like.

[8] Joab's "guilt" may or may not be regarded by the reader as having been established. What is certain, however, is that in ordering his execution beside the altar, Solomon himself is guilty of breaking the law. Exod 21:12–14 quite clearly states that a murderer is to be *taken away* from the altar and put to death; and Benaiah certainly seems to be aware of this (note his instinctive

interpretation of Solomon's first command in 1 Kgs 2:29 as implying execution *outside* the sanctuary, v. 30). So who is really "guilty?"

[9] Solomon's willingness to ignore the letter of the law when it suits him (in the case of Joab) only throws into sharper relief his vindictive treatment of Shimei in 1 Kgs 2:36–46, where the letter of the law is crucial. Whether Shimei interpreted Solomon's instructions in 1 Kgs 2:36–37 to mean that he must *never* under any circumstances leave Jerusalem is not clear. It would be natural, rather, to interpret these words (particularly in view of the mention of Kidron in 2:37) as being intended specifically to prevent a potential troublemaker from operating within his own power base in Benjamin. In fact, Shimei quite clearly does not cross Kidron in vv. 39–40—the silence of the text on this point is deafening. He is going westward to Gath, not eastward to Bahurim. But Solomon takes the opportunity to have him executed anyway (2:46). David's instructions have been carried out. Solomon has proved himself to be a "wise" king (2:9).

[10] I understand the conflict in ch. 1 to be largely a conflict between old, Judah-based comrades of David from the Hebron days, and newer, Jerusalem-based associates. Adonijah was, of course, born in Hebron (2 Sam 3:2–5), while Solomon was born in Jerusalem (2 Sam 5:13–16). Joab appears early on as David's right hand man and the commander of his troops (e.g., 2 Sam 2–3; 11–12; 14; 18); Abiathar is also one of David's oldest associates (1 Sam 22:20–23). These are men with deep roots in David's Judean past. It seems likely, in view of the fact that the guest list for Adonijah's feast (1 Kgs 1:9) mentions only those royal officials who were men of Judah (and not also Israel), that their support for Adonijah represents at least in part a commitment to history and tradition, and to the continuing influence of Judeans at the centers of power. By contrast, only Benaiah of the individuals named in the opposing group has any claim to such a long-standing association with David (1 Kgs 1:8; cf. 2 Sam 20:23; 23:20–23), although we must include here also the men who made up

David's special guard (the "mighty men" of 2 Sam 23:8–39). Aside from these men and Rei (otherwise unknown), we find mentioned in this group Shimei, who does also appear in 2 Sam (16:5–14), but only as an antagonist of David from the house of Saul; and Nathan and Zadok, neither of whom appear in the narrative before 2 Sam 7:2 and 8:17 respectively (ie., after David's move from Hebron to Jerusalem, 2 Sam 5:6–10). It seems reasonable to assume that what unites at least these last three around the Jerusalem-born Solomon is a commitment to the present *in contrast* to the past—to a kingdom in which Jerusalem is centrally important and the northern tribes are more likely than under Adonijah to play their full part. We must understand the events of 1 Kgs 1–2, in other words, in the light of the Judah–Israel tensions already evident in Samuel (e.g., 2 Sam 20), and soon to explode into schism again in 1 Kgs 12 (cf., in particular, 2 Sam 20:1 and 1 Kgs 12:16).

[11] Commentators have been reluctant to identify the Shimei mentioned in 1 Kgs 1:8 with the man of the same name in 2 Sam 16:5–14 and 1 Kgs 2:8–9, 36–46, though why this should be is something of a mystery. The wording of 1 Kgs 2:8 ("you have *with you* Shimei son of Gera") clearly implies that it is indeed this same Shimei who has joined Solomon's party, and this is the natural assumption of the reader who has read thus far in Samuel–Kings. His presence for the moment in the Solomonic party is sufficiently explained by antipathy to the Judean Adonijah, a king not likely to favor someone from Saul's clan. Solomon is perhaps nothing more to him than the lesser of two evils.

[12] It is certainly interesting in this connection to note the way in which the "king's table" (1 Kgs 2:7) reappears later in the Solomon story, in 1 Kgs 4. It is the very center, in fact, of the account that we are given there of Solomon's glorious and peaceful rule over Judah/Israel and the nations (4:27): a period which Solomon can describe to Hiram in 5:4 [5:18] as one in which there is rest on every side, all enemies subdued. The symbolic value of the king's table to the authors of Kings is indeed illustrated not only by that passage, but also

by 2 Kgs 25, where the eventual end of Davidic rule over Judah/Israel, the obverse of Solomonic splendor, is given pathetic illustration by the fact that king Jehoiachin sits at the table of the king of Babylon (2 Kgs 25:29). The nations no longer flock to supply David with food. David is instead to be found as a dependant upon *them*.

CHAPTER FIVE

[1] The conference paper was delivered to the Society for Old Testament Study 1994 Summer Meeting held in Edinburgh, UK. It was offered in honor of the president of the Society in 1994, Professor J. C. L. Gibson, in the year of his retirement from the University of Edinburgh.

[2] I mean by this "literature in the modern sense," for the relation of history to literature has only become notably problematic in modern times, as "literature" increasingly has come to be associated with poetry and fiction and "history" has moved in the direction of the sciences (see L. Gossman, "History and Literature: Reproduction or Signification," in *The Writing of History: Literary Form and Historical Understanding* [ed. R. H. Canary and H. Kozicki; Madison: University of Wisconsin, 1978], 1–39). It is as interest in the Bible as literature in this sense has grown that we have seen in recent scholarship a corresponding movement among historians away from the text and toward a more "scientific" approach to the history of Israel—paradoxically just at a time when many historians outside the biblical field are calling for renewed attention to the relationship between historiography and literature (see, e.g., H. White, "The Historical Text as Literary Artifact," in Canary and Kozicki, *Writing*, 41–62; A. Cameron, ed., *History as Text: The Writing of Ancient History* [London: Duckworth, 1989]; A. Rigney, *The Rhetoric of Historical Representation: Three Narrative Histories of the French Revolution* [Cambridge: Cambridge University Press, 1990]), and some even feel able to say: "The old battle against those who wished to make history a science has been fought and

won" (J. Clive, *Not By Fact Alone: Essays on the Writing and Reading of History* [London: Collins Harvill, 1990], 34–35).

[3] That is to say, that this or that element of the biblical story, but not the whole, owes more to the conventions of narrative than to a concern to recount the past.

[4] Niels Peter Lemche, *Ancient Israel: A New History of Israelite Society* (Biblical Seminar 5; Sheffield: JSOT Press, 1988), 53.

[5] Gösta W. Ahlström, "The Role of Archaeological and Literary Remains in Reconstructing Israel's History," in *The Fabric of History: Text, Artifact and Israel's Past* (JSOTSup 127; ed. D. V. Edelman; Sheffield: JSOT Press, 1991), 116–41 (118).

[6] Ibid., 134.

[7] Gösta W. Ahlström, *The History of Ancient Palestine from the Palaeolithic Period to Alexander's Conquest* (JSOTSup 146; ed. D. V. Edelman; Sheffield: JSOT Press, 1993), 50.

[8] Philip R. Davies, *In Search of "Ancient Israel"* (JSOTSup 148; Sheffield: JSOT Press, 1992), 29.

[9] Ibid., 60.

[10] Thomas L. Thompson, *Early History of the Israelite People from the Written and Archaeological Sources* (SHANE 4; Leiden: Brill, 1992), 29.

[11] Davies, *Search*, 31.

[12] Ibid., 44–48.

[13] Ibid., 161.

[14] Thompson, *History*, 4.

[15] Ibid., 13.

[16] Ibid., 19.

[17] Ibid., 81.

[18] Ibid., 404.

[19] Ibid., 168–69.

[20] Ibid., 61.

[21] Ibid., 83.

[22] See, e.g., Jürgen Habermas, *Knowledge and Human Interests* (London: Heinemann, 1972); Mary B. Hesse, *Revolutions and Reconstructions in the Philosophy of Science* (Brighton: Harvester, 1980).

[23] Thompson, *Early History*, 83.

[24] Ibid., 116.

[25] Ibid., 171n1.

[26] Ibid., 177.

[27] This is so, of course, whether one is aware of it or not. Thompson is not the only recent historian of Israel who seems somewhat lacking in self-awareness in this respect, as we shall see. The most revealing comment of all surely belongs to Ahlström (*History*, 52n2), who confesses to responding thus to a question about the philosophy informing his study of Old Testament history and religion: "If I have a philosophy, it is that one cannot use any philosophical system." The real division in scholarship is not, of course, between those who have a philosophical system and those who do not. It is between those who realize that they have one, and those who are innocent of the fact. All historians, whatever their claims, "employ their intentions, their hopes and fears, their beliefs, their methodological, even metaphysical, principles, their grasp and use of language and of languages, their hermeneutic capacities" in their work (M. Stanford, *The Nature of Historical Knowledge* [Oxford: Basil Blackwell, 1986], 96).

[28] Ahlström, *History*, 23.

[29] Ibid., 31.

[30] Davies, *Search*, 13–14.

[31] Ernst A. Knauf, "From History to Interpretation," in Edelman, *Fabric*, 26–27. Knauf is equally perceptive later in his essay (50): "Every history, critical or uncritical, is constructed from a present point of view with a present purpose to serve."

[32] See, e.g., R. G. Collingwood, *The Idea of History* (Oxford: Oxford University Press, 1946), 231–49; P. Veyne, *Writing History: Essay on Epistemology* (Manchester: Manchester University Press, 1984); and Stanford, *Nature*, 96: "How a historian sees the past is only a part of how he or she sees the world. The final color and shape of a historian's construction is bestowed by his or her own *Weltanschauung* ... Dominating all technical considerations of evidence, method, interpretation and construction is the individual human being." And the individual human being is, of course, on a quest not only for the past but also for meaning (see R. Martin, "Objectivity and Meaning in Historical Studies: Towards a Post-Analytic View," *History and Theory* 32 [1993]: 25–50).

[33] See K. L. Younger, Jr., *Ancient Conquest Accounts: A Study in Ancient Near Eastern and Biblical History Writing* (JSOTSup 98; Sheffield: JSOT Press, 1990).

[34] See Thucydides, *History of the Peloponnesian War*; Bede, *Ecclesiastical History of the English People*.

[35] These are only some of the historians discussed entertainingly and illuminatingly by Clive (*Not By Fact Alone*)—himself a historian who understands very clearly the extent to which written history is "knowledge of the past filtered through mind and art" (see his Preface). Rigney (*Rhetoric*) further compares and contrasts Michelet with both Lamartine and Blanc, all of them having written histories some sixty years after the French Revolution that they describe; each of them having deployed their own particular discursive and narrative strategies to represent and give meaning to events; and each of them revealing, in so doing, their particular ideological presuppositions.

[36] Ahlström, *History*, 31.

[37] Ibid., 22–23.

[38] F. Brandfon, "The Limits of Evidence: Archaeology and Objectivity," *Maarav* 4/1 (1987): 30, 33. For similar points about the nature of archaeological data, and the creative role of the archaeologist and the historian in relation to them, see D. V. Edelman, "Doing History in Biblical Studies," in *Fabric*, 22–23; J.

M. Miller, "Is it Possible to Write a History of Israel without Relying on the Hebrew Bible?" in *Fabric*, 96–97, 100–101; and Lemche, *Ancient Israel*, 72: "Archaeological evidence ... does not consist of *objective data* (i.e. data whose meaning is immediately clear) like the data of the natural sciences. It consists instead of subjective data (i.e. they are the results of the interpretation of an archaeologist)." Whether Lemche's view of the nature of the natural sciences is defensible is, of course, open to serious question.

[39] Ahlström, "Role," 117.

[40] Ibid., 120, in the midst of a curious and not entirely intelligible critique of those who have hypothesized about archaeological sites on the basis of biblical texts—as if such hypothesizing were in itself invalid.

[41] Ahlström, *History*, 44.

[42] Ibid., 29.

[43] Ibid., 42.

[44] Ibid., 50.

[45] Ibid., 36.

[46] Ibid., 28–29.

[47] It is truly extraordinary how often in his writings Ahlström equates *selection* by the biblical authors (and apparently only by them) with *distortion*. For example: "It could be asked ... why the Judahite temple at Arad in the Negev is never mentioned in the Bible" (*History*, 43); or again, in respect of how the story of Ahab has been told: "The real events of time are of less importance or of no interest to the writer. Realizing the writer's attitude, it is quite in order that no mention is made of such a historic event as the battle at Qarqar ... It did not suit the author's purpose. In view of the foregoing considerations it is self-evident that we have no possibility of describing or analyzing with any *accuracy* [my italics] the history of the religion of the kingdom of Israel" ("Role," 132).

[48] See P. A. Roth, "Narrative Explanations: The Case of History," *History and*

Theory 27 (1988): 1–13.

⁴⁹ N. P. Lemche, *The Canaanites and Their Land: The Tradition of the Canaanites* (JSOTSup 110; Sheffield: JSOT Press, 1991), 16.

⁵⁰ Ibid., 151n1.

⁵¹ Ibid., 158, 159.

⁵² Aside from Ahlström and Lemche, we may note, for example, Knauf, "History," 46n1: "Ancient Near Eastern historiography (including biblical and early Islamic historiography) is not concerned with what actually had happened. Rather, it is interested in stating what should have happened in order to construct a 'correct' world"; and K. A. D. Smelik, *Converting the Past: Studies in Ancient Israelite and Moabite Historiography* (OtSt 28; Leiden: Brill, 1992), 15: "The aim of these biblical authors was not to record history."

⁵³ That is (lest there be any objection to the term), the sense in which the newer historians would like the rest of us to take their *own* works.

⁵⁴ Smelik, *Converting the Past*, 23.

⁵⁵ We may deduce also from the text, for example, that it has a didactic intention. It aims to teach its present readers about God and the world through its portrayal of the past.

⁵⁶ It seems clear that it is this perspective that at least partially explains the above-mentioned lack of "compelling arguments" about intentionality. The belief appears to be that, merely by describing the biblical text as narrative, one has also made it self-evident that the biblical authors did not intend to write history. Smelik, for example (*Converting the Past*, 11–15), characterizing "real" historiography as being of the annalistic sort, then moves on to suggest that the biblical author of Kings "was conscious that he was writing a text belonging to another literary genre" (14). Why we should believe that historiography cannot properly take the kind of narrative form we find in the Bible is never made clear. It cannot merely be because of the presence of fictionality in the biblical texts, since even in modern times fictionality is as likely to be found

in historiography as in fiction (see M. Sternberg, *The Poetics of Biblical Narrative: Ideological Literature and the Drama of Reading* [Bloomington: Indiana University Press, 1985], 28–30). Form, of itself, is not a sufficient criterion by which to differentiate history from fiction. Nor is it self-evidently the case (as some analytical philosophers have maintained) that narrative coherence is inevitably falsification of a past truly given to us only in the form of separate, isolated incidents. As A. P. Norman reminds us ("Telling It Like It Was: Historical Narratives on Their Own Terms," *History and Theory* 30 [1991]: 124): "Doing history is as much the breaking up of an initially seamless whole as it is the bringing together of initially unrelated events. World War II was no less real, no more a fiction, than was D-Day."

[57] Thompson, *History*, 82.

[58] Ibid., 353–54.

[59] Ibid., 356, 357.

[60] Ibid., 9n17.

[61] It is surprising that it should be so commonly assumed, without arguments being offered, that the case is otherwise. Many scholars (consciously or not) seem to have accepted without question the Rankean assertion that those texts that were produced in the course of events as they were happening are more worthy of the historian's attention than those texts which were produced afterwards (see, e.g., Knauf, "History," 45–47). A moment's reflection, however, should convince us of the facile nature of the distinction. There is simply no good reason to assume *a priori* that so-called primary sources are going to be more "reliable" than any others. The assumption itself has quite a bit to do with the naïve belief that eyewitnesses "tell it like it is," while others inevitably filter "reality" through various distorting screens. As in art, however, where close proximity to subject and canvas by no means guarantees a more "accurate" portrait (since the painter sometimes gets lost among the proverbial trees and loses sight of the overall shape of the forest), so in history. On the one hand,

"the recounting of what happened, even a few moments later, inevitably introduces simplifications, selections, interpretations" (P. R. Ackroyd, "Historians and Prophets," *SEÅ* 33 [1968]: 21). Eyewitnesses, like everyone else, have a point of view, as Thucydides recognized long ago (*History* 1.20–22). On the other hand, "the historian who writes at some distance from the events may be in a better position to give a true appraisal than one who is so involved as to see only a part of what makes up the whole" (Ackroyd, "Historians," 21). It is, indeed, one of the main tasks of the historian to discern and represent "the larger patterns, structures and meanings behind particular events and facts which contemporaries were not able to see" (J. Axtell, "History as Imagination," *The Historian: A Journal of History* 49 [1987]: 457).

[62] On this point, refer further to n53 above.

[63] Davies, *Search*, 13–14.

[64] Ibid., 16–17.

[65] Ibid., 22, 29.

[66] Ibid., 48.

[67] Ibid., 13.

[68] Ibid., 48.

[69] Ibid., 35.

[70] Statements of faith of this kind are fairly common in this literature, although it is never clear that those making them are conscious of their nature as such. We may note, for example, the following two quotations from Ahlström: "Religion can create whatever 'history' it wants or needs" (*History*, 28); and, "Any sacred literature is by nature religious propaganda. It uses historical events as it sees fit" ("Role," 129).

[71] Troeltsch's argument was that harmony with the normal, customary, or at least frequently attested events and conditions as we have experienced them is the distinguishing mark of reality for the events that criticism can recognize as really having happened in the past (see E. Troeltsch, "Über historische

und dogmatische Methode in der Theologie," in *Gesammelte Studien* [vol. 2; Tübingen: Mohr, 1922], 729–53). Followed through in a narrow sense, this is clearly too restrictive, since historians regularly accept the reality of events and practices that lie outside their own immediate experience. Yet it is not clear that widening the sense so that "general human experience" is taken into account helps us very much either. How do we ascertain, for example, what is in fact normal, usual, or frequently attested? And even if we could ascertain this, would it follow that what is not normal, usual, or frequently attested cannot have happened? Again, there appear to be events that historians would accept as having happened that do not conform to the criterion (e.g., the first climbing of Mount Everest, or the first human landing on the moon). The fact is that analogy never operates in a vacuum. There is "an intimate relation between analogy and its context or network of background beliefs" (W. Abraham, *Divine Revelation and the Limits of Historical Criticism* [Oxford: Oxford University, 1982], 105), and conclusions drawn from an application of the principle of analogy are only as valid as the background beliefs held by those drawing the conclusions.

[72] Miller, "Is it Possible?," 100.

[73] Much of the literature I have described shares to a greater or lesser extent in the kind of materialist/determinist approach to history that we find in such writers as Marx and the so-called Annales group of French historians (e.g., Braudel). Primary emphasis is placed on the role of impersonal processes in historical change (e.g., climate, geography, demographics, economic conditions—the "nomothetic" view of change), and only secondary emphasis on the individual personalities of the past. This is not unrelated, of course, to the stance taken by the newer historians of Israel in general with regard to the biblical texts, in which, of course, individuals and their actions are portrayed as vitally important in "making history." Narrative historiography was already regarded by the Annalistes "as a nonscientific, even *ideological representation*

strategy, the extirpation of which was necessary for the transformation of historical studies into a genuine science" (see H. White, "The Question of Narrative in Contemporary Historical Theory," *History and Theory* 23 [1984]: 1–33 [7]). It is no surprise to find that advocacy of the nomothetically inclined "new archaeology," marked by its reductionism and its environmental determinism, is similarly accompanied in many scholars by depreciation of the historical value of the Bible's more "idiographical" narratives. As Knauf puts it: "For those interested in this kind of history ... the historiographical heritage of the ancient world ... has become mute" ("History," 42). Those who in general take a more idiographic view of historical change, which allows that individual personalities may have exercised significant influence in shaping the past, will not have the same ideological difficulty with narrative texts. For an introduction to the broader debate among historians with regard to method, see the review article by C. Parker, "Methods, Ideas and Historians," *Literature and History* 11 (1985): 288–91.

[74] The tradition is represented, however, in such scholars as J. Wellhausen, W. Robertson Smith, H. Gunkel, S. Mowinckel, M. Weber, and others. For a convenient historical survey, see C. Osiek, "The New Handmaid: The Bible and the Social Sciences," *TS* 50 (1989): 260–78. For evidence from the newer historians themselves of a sense of roots, see Thompson, *History*, 1–8.

[75] Positivism is most famously incoherent, of course, precisely in its formulation of the verifiability criterion of meaning which lies at its heart—a criterion that cannot be meaningful in the light of its own standard. It is a self-defeating philosophy that cuts the ground from under its own feet, able to render itself comprehensible only through metaphysical concepts, yet declaring metaphysical assertions meaningless (see Habermas, *Knowledge and Interests*, passim; and further, the devastating analysis in J. Milbank, *Theology and Social Theory: Beyond Secular Reason* [Oxford: Basil Blackwell, 1990], esp. 49–143). A similar case can be made in relation to materialism, whose proponents have often been found

trying to change the world while at the same time telling the rest of us that individuals have little significant role to play in such change. The classic case, of course, is Marx himself, who not only tried, but self-evidently succeeded, with the help of other notable individuals who purported to espouse the same ideas about history (see C. B. McCullagh, *Justifying Historical Descriptions* [Cambridge: Cambridge University Press, 1984], 225–26).

[76] Why not assume the historicity of the Canaan/Israel polarity, for example, even though it is biblically based and unverified by extrabiblical evidence, unless and until it is shown to be *unhistorical*? Why insist, as Thompson does (*History*, 23–24), that external verification is required for the assumption of historicity? And what are we to make of the same author on p. 44? Here we read: "The fundamental weakness of the amphictyonic hypothesis is that it is only an analogy and not a historical reconstruction of early Israel based on evidence. It is in the final analysis really unimportant whether what exists in the Old Testament narratives is identical or similar to what is known to have existed in Greece or elsewhere ... no analogy can replace for us the lack of evidence for any bond of unity the alleged early tribes may have had." There could hardly be a better illustration of the manner in which all interpreters of the past inevitably reflect their underlying assumptions by what they select to serve as evidence. Here the text is simply discounted, even though what it appears to describe has historical analogies elsewhere. This is an exceedingly dogmatic approach to the text, allied to an exceedingly illiberal attitude to other scholars (note his critique of Mayes with regard to the history of the "Judges period" [96–100], because Mayes supposedly offers a hypothesis based on texts rather than on "evidence."

[77] See the excellent new book by V. P. Long, *The Art of Biblical History* (Foundations of Contemporary Interpretation 5; Grand Rapids: Academie Books, 1994), which I was privileged to read in prepublication form during a sabbatical in Cambridge in 1993, and which first alerted me to many of the

items of secondary literature cited in the footnotes of this article, as well as stimulating my own thinking enormously.

[78] Davies, *Search*, 76.

[79] Ibid., 86.

[80] He does not present it precisely as such, of course. The justification he offers (p. 86) is, first, that unlike the case with Iron Age Israel, the nonbiblical data do "to a degree" afford confirmation of "some" of the basic processes described in the biblical narrative at this point; and second, that processes of the kind described in Ezra–Nehemiah are "necessitated" by the subsequent developments in the emergence of Judean society and its religion. This is slippery language. What does "to a degree/some" mean in relation to such sparse nonbiblical data? What does "necessitated" mean? How does all this justify such a very different approach to this period of history over against earlier periods? The argument is entirely unconvincing. It seems that Davies is trying to maintain here (and only here) that once one has taken the literature seriously as such (and it is, of course, just as much ideological literature as any of the remainder), one can still take it along with the nonbiblical data as reflecting history. That is precisely the argument that other scholars would wish to frame in respect of other biblical texts as well—those very scholars who, when they proceed in this way, are accused by Davies of producing a sanitized version of the biblical story, rather than doing "proper history."

[81] See White, "Historical Text," 46–62.

[82] Cf., for example, the comments by Thompson, *History*, 126, 369, with the more extended section in Davies, *Search*, 87–133. For a brief but useful introductory discussion of ideology, see Younger, *Ancient Conquest Accounts*, 47–52.

[83] Knauf, "History," 30, 31. Similar sensitivity to the nature of things is displayed by Edelman—another of those scholars who understands very well that historiography is art, and not "science." We may note, for example, the emphasis in her description of historical method on the place of instinctive

understanding and imagination (borrowing from our daily experiences) and of historical "genius" ("Doing History," 15); and her citation of G. R. Elton's wise words (21): "The available evidence rarely necessitates our judgments but is at least consistent with them. Obviously, in such areas of interpretation, there is no one demonstrably correct 'explanation,' but very often competing, equally unfalsifiable, theories." We may note further in this connection Miller ("Is it Possible?," 100): "When it comes to the origin and early history of Israel, I think the best we can ever hope to do is make some guesses and offer some hypothetical scenarios. These scenarios, moreover, will reveal as much about how we understand our own historical circumstances as what we know about ancient Israel." On the slippery concept of "facts," see further Stanford (*Nature*, 71–74), who concludes (74): "The chief task of the historian is therefore to do two things: to establish as firmly as possible events and states of affairs in the past; and to find the most appropriate words in which to relate and describe—that is, to communicate—these findings to other people. Facts need not be mentioned, for 'fact' is a slippery concept and, unless carefully handled, may only obscure the issue."

CHAPTER SIX

[1] The Scriptures that thus lie before the author apparently do so usually in their Hebrew form, although sometimes in their Greek form as well. See R. H. Charles, *A Critical and Exegetical Commentary on the Revelation of St John* (ICC; Edinburgh: T&T Clark, 1920), I:lxvi–lxxxii; and G. K. Beale, "A Reconsideration of the Text of Daniel in the Apocalypse," *Bib* 67 (1986): 539–43, who helpfully categorizes Revelation's relation to the text(s) of Daniel in particular as of three sorts: clear dependence, probable dependence, and possible dependence or echo.

[2] The influence of the following is especially clear: the Babylon prophecies of Isa 13 and Jer 51; the Tyre prophecy of Ezek 26–27; the Edom prophecy of Isa 34; and the Nineveh prophecy of Nah 3. This by no means represents,

however, an exhaustive listing of the Old Testament passages whose echoes may be heard in the background of our chapter.

[3] See I. W. Provan, *Lamentations* (NCB; London: Marshall Pickering, 1991).

[4] Charles, *Revelation*, II:87–113.

[5] The same point can be made in relation to the arguments of, e.g., J. A. T. Robinson, *Redating the New Testament* (London: SCM, 1976), 221–53, who dates Revelation to the reign of Nero on the grounds that chs. 11, 17 and 18 have links with events in Jerusalem and Rome in AD 64–70, and that the vindictive intensity of the passages about Babylon drunk with the blood of Jesus' witnesses is only intelligible under the immediate impact of Nero's pogrom. He vastly underestimates the difficulties involved in disentangling "historical" allusions from literary allusions in literature of this type, and is somewhat naïve in the assumptions he makes about what "historical" allusions can in any case tell the reader about the date of composition. For some sane comment here, see J. P. M. Sweet, *Revelation* (TPINTC; London: SCM, 1979), 21–27, especially on the "stock" element in John's writing.

[6] Thus, whether or not we think we have access to what a zealous Jew after the destruction of Jerusalem might have expected, it is not clear that from the text of Revelation we can say that the author of Revelation was such a person. Charles is not the only scholar to assume rather too easily a correlation between what is found in the text and what is found in the author's mind or heart. A. Yarbro Collins, for example, claims to find evidence that a desire for revenge played a role in the composition of Rev 18 ("Revelation 18: Taunt-Song or Dirge?," in J. Lambrecht, ed., *L'Apocalypse johannique et l'Apocalyptique dans le Nouveau Testament* [BETL, 53; Leuven: Leuven University Press, 1980], 185–204 [204]), while Sweet (*Revelation*, 49–50) laments the "vindictive harping ... on torture and destruction" that is to be found in Rev 6–20, noting a spirit that is at home in the Old Testament but not in the New Testament, and that can possibly be explained in terms of the author's personal situation

and psychology. Whether this kind of distinction between the testaments can be defended must certainly be open to question. Old Testament scholars tend to be nervous at the least, in view of the history of biblical scholarship and indeed of the world, when confronted with arguments that rest on implicit and explicit distinctions between a theologically/morally inferior Old Testament and a superior New Testament, or between zealous Jews and (moderate? loving?) Christians. The ghost of Marcion still haunts the Christian mansion, and it is questionable whether he has ever been a benevolent presence. Be that as it may, the immediate question here is simply whether the nature of the language and the sources from which the language is drawn allows any sensible comment on what the author might have been thinking or experiencing while writing the book. How are vindictiveness or desire for revenge to be recognized? How are they to be distinguished, for example, from a desire for justice? Cf. E. Schüssler Fiorenza, *The Book of Revelation: Justice and Judgment* (Philadelphia: Fortress, 1985), 7–8, on Rev 15:5–19:10: "To misread this scene as hate for civilization or as resentment and revenge is a serious misunderstanding of the visionary rhetoric and theology of justice in Rev." For further bibliography on the issue, see Yarbro Collins, "Revelation 18," 185–86.

[7] J. Roloff, *The Revelation of John* (Continental Commentaries; trans. J.E. Alsup; Minneapolis: Fortress, 1993), thinks that the verse fits poorly into the context not only in form, but also in content, since "fruit hardly belongs to the luxury goods from overseas that are mentioned earlier." One is stunned into near silence by the level of literalism revealed in such a remark. The verse is a general and summarizing remark, and "fruit" in such a context presumably does not require a very narrow interpretation.

[8] The sayings in 13:9–10, 18; 14:12; 16:15 are analogous (Yarbro Collins, "Revelation 18," 194).

[9] Provan, *Lamentations*, 33–56.

[10] Indeed, the artfulness of vv. 13–14 taken together seems evident in the clever

play that we find there on the Greek *psyche*, the first in v. 13 speaking of the human soul *as* merchandise, and the second in v. 14 describing the deprivation of merchandise *for which* the human soul had longed.

[11] There are notable exceptions, such as W. M. Swartley, *Israel's Scripture Traditions and the Synoptic Gospels: Story Shaping Story* (Peabody, MA: Hendrickson, 1994).

[12] *Revelation*, 28n39.

[13] E.g. J. Fekkes III, *Isaiah and Prophetic Traditions in the Book of Revelation* (JSNTSup 93; Sheffield: JSOT Press, 1994).

[14] Cf. K. A. Strand, "Some Modalities of Symbolic Usage in Revelation 18," *AUSS* 24 (1986), 37–46 (37n1).

[15] R. Bauckham, "The Economic Critique of Rome in Revelation 18," in L. Alexander, ed., *Images of Empire* (JSOTSup 122; Sheffield: JSOT Press, 1991), 47–90. John has quite deliberately fashioned a prophetic oracle that gathers up all that his prophetic predecessors had said against Babylon and Tyre. Rome is the heir of Babylon in political and religious activity, of Tyre in economic activity; and it is Tyre that gives John the particular image of the harlot (cf. Isa 23:15–18), an image that does not appear in relation to Babylon in the Old Testament, but that speaks of association with other nations for the sake of profit.

[16] The two shorter laments of the kings and the sailors in vv. 9–10 and 17b–19 frame the much longer lament of the merchants in vv. 11–17a.

[17] G. R. Beasley-Murray, *The Book of Revelation* (NCB; London: Oliphants, 1974), 266–67.

[18] Sweet, *Revelation*, 270–71, makes a similar point about literary influence, while not seeing this as the sole reason for John's emphasis here: "If we ask why John for his dirge over Rome centers on trade, the answer may be partly that trade, with the foreign ties and wealth it brought, had in the eyes of the Old Testament prophets destroyed the primitive simplicity of Israel's national life."

[19] It differs both in its principle of organization (Ezekiel's is structured around countries, John's around types of cargo) and in its detail.

[20] Bauckham himself sees that this is so ("Economic Critique," 84), but argues that this is because John is setting his readers a hermeneutical trap, inviting them to share the perspective of Rome's mourners rather than John's own perspective with a view to alerting them to the peril in which they stand. The question here, of course, is how we know that what is described as John's perspective is not simply Bauckham's perspective imposed on John. How can it be established that a perspective that is not clearly expressed in the text (that Rome's economic activity is exploitative) is nevertheless the perspective of the author of the text?

[21] Viz., that slaves are not mere animal carcasses to be bought and sold as property, but are human beings.

[22] See Charles, *Revelation*, 2:103–105, for a detailed listing. He notes that gold, silver, precious stones, fine linen, purple, brass, iron, all spices, oil, wheat, cattle, sheep, horses, and the souls of men all appear in Ezek 27:12–24, representing at least half of the items in Rev 18 and probably more, depending on how precisely the counting is done.

[23] It would be possible, of course, to follow up this general point with reference to many other particular examples. Is gold, for example, at the head of the list in Rev 18 because of its prominence in Roman thinking (Bauckham, "Economic Critique," 60–61), or because of its prominence in the account of that part of Solomon's reign that reveals a slow slide into apostasy (1 Kgs 9:10–10:29; on this passage, see further I. W. Provan, *1 and 2 Kings* [NIBCOT; Peabody, MA: Hendrickson, 1995])? How can one say that the presence of wheat on John's list shows how the general population of Rome survived only at the expense of the rest of the empire ("Economic Critique," 72), when wheat appears on the very list in Ezek 27 that provides the basis for John's list? And if "great men of the earth" in Rev 18:23 is drawn from Isa 23:8, why is it that "John

must have selected it as corresponding to the reality of the Roman empire" ("Economic Critique," 81)?

[24] 2 Kgs 19:24; cf. Ps 36:8–9; Jer 2:13; 17:13; 51:36; Ezek 31; Hos 13:15.

[25] As he stands before the gates of Jerusalem, Sennacherib is thus to be found promising the besieged Judeans that if they surrender, their exile will not be harsh. They will find themselves in a new "promised land" very much like their own (2 Kgs 18:31–32; cf. Deut 8:7–9).

[26] We might also ask whether it allows us to deduce anything about the nature of the church first addressed by the book. Can it really be safely claimed, for example, that the economic material of Rev 18 "reflects the current situation of John's audience, which apparently has been either marginalized (cf. 2:9) or compromised (cf. 3:17) by the economic structures of the Roman world" (R. E. Wall, *Revelation* [NIBCOT; Peabody, MA: Hendrickson, 1991], 216)?

[27] The same may be asked of the very similar line pursued by C. R. Smith, "Reclaiming the Social Justice Message of Revelation: Materialism, Imperialism and Divine Judgment in Revelation 18," *Transformation* 7/4 (1990): 28–33, whose view is not only that Rome's economic sins are the central focus of this chapter, but that other sins are indeed subordinate to these. He believes that the presentation of the cargoes in 18:12–13 "is strictly literal; a symbolic depiction of Rome's commerce would almost be too lenient, when the reality is so graphic" (29). How does he know that the presentation is strictly literal? Too lenient for whom?

[28] Yarbro Collins, "Revelation 18," 203.

[29] It is puzzling that although Bauckham himself knows well ("Economic Critique," 56–57) that the primary Old Testament use of the harlot image is in reference to idolatrous religion, and indeed argues that John did wish in his use of this image to comment on the imperial cult, where the emperor was worshipped precisely as a divine saviour who brought blessings to his subjects (as in the Sennacherib story), yet he still insists that "the primary meaning of

the harlot image in Revelation 17–18 is economic." It is not clear how this can be established.

[30] Yarbro Collins, "Revelation 18," 202.

[31] J. Day, *God's Conflict with the Dragon and the Sea: Echoes of a Canaanite Myth in the Old Testament* (Cambridge: Cambridge University Press, 1985); C. Kloos, *YHWH's Combat with the Sea: A Canaanite Tradition in the Religion of Ancient Israel* (Leiden: Brill, 1986). For detailed consideration of Revelation as representation of the conflict between the rule of God and present reality, in which the struggle with Rome is presented in terms of the old conflict between order and chaos, note A. Yarbro Collins, *The Combat Myth in the Book of Revelation* (HDR 9; Missoula, MT: Scholars Press, 1976); and *Crisis and Catharsis* (Philadelphia: Westminster 1984).

[32] Note, e.g., Roloff, *Revelation*, 206: "Rome was neither a port city nor a shipping center. But here John hardly intended to copy precisely the real situation; rather he wanted to round off the scene of lament by means of a third group, and for that purpose he used the material that Ezek 27:29–33 provided him."

[33] On the (Mediterranean) sea as a negative image in Revelation, see K. Wengst, *Pax Romana and the Peace of Jesus Christ* (trans. J. Bowden: London: SCM, 1987), 130.

[34] Bauckham, "Economic Critique," 59.

[35] J. M. Court, *Myth and History in the Book of Revelation* (London: SPCK, 1979), 139. Others think the subject matter of the chapter equally self-evident. Yarbro Collins, "Revelation 18," 200–202, for example, discusses some of the images in Rev 17–18 and asserts: "All the images examined thus far not only describe Rome but give reasons for her predicted downfall." Some scholars have such certainty on the matter that they are even prepared to counter-read references to "the great city" elsewhere in the book that might be taken as pointing in a different direction (e.g. R. H. Mounce, *The Book of Revelation* [NICNT; Grand Rapids: Eerdmans, 1977], 226, who implausibly interprets

Rev 11:8 as referring to Rome "in view of the consistent use of the term elsewhere in the book as a *reference* to Rome" [my italics]), or simply to remove them (e.g. S. Giet, *L'Apocalypse et l'histoire: Etude historique sur l'Apocalypse Johannique* [Paris: University of Paris, 1957], 130, who argues that the phrase "where their Lord was crucified" in Rev 11:8 "must" be a gloss, since the verse really refers to Rome).

[36] A. J. Beagley, *The 'Sitz im Leben' of the Apocalypse with Particular Reference to the Role of the Church's Enemies* (BZNW 50; Berlin: de Gruyter, 1987), 27.

[37] It is intriguing that Court, *Myth*, 139–42, sees quite clearly the way in which Old Testament material on Israel's unfaithfulness to God has especially influenced the author of Revelation, noting in particular the similarity of ideas between Jer 3–4 and Rev 17. He nevertheless rejects the possibility that the Daughter of Zion has provided the model for John's picture of the harlot (147–53), on the ground that to make Israel the epitome of evil is to adopt a view more one-sided than the Old Testament ever seems to be, or to make the author of Revelation more violently anti-Jewish than the remainder of the book suggests. It may well be asked how the use of this kind of Zion imagery can possibly be construed as indicating one-sidedness or anti-Jewishness of any sort, especially when it is so closely associated with other kinds of Zion imagery in chs. 21–22. It must also be asked whether it is sensible to abandon the obvious model for John's picture of the harlot in favor of a somewhat speculative hypothesis about the goddess Roma (cf. also Yarbro Collins, "Revelation 18," 200–201, and others). Court himself asks a good question here (*Myth*, 151): if a definite reference to Roma is intended, "one might ask why did he not make the contemporary reference more explicit in the description of the woman, rather than relying so heavily in his description on the Old Testament material. At least one might expect a helmet, which seems to be a characteristic feature of the martial Roma."

[38] J. Massyngberde Ford, *Revelation* (AB; Garden City: Doubleday, 1975), 283–85.
[39] Ibid., 285, 301–302, 304–305.
[40] Ibid., 285–86.
[41] Ibid., 296–307.
[42] Beagley, *Sitz im Leben*, 31–36.
[43] Ibid., 36–48.
[44] Ibid., 48–71.
[45] Ibid., 90–92.
[46] Ibid., 92–100. Strand, "Modalities," also notes that it is Judah that is spoken of in terms of "doubling" of punishment (and restoration) in the Old Testament, not Babylon (cf. Isa 40:2; 61:7; Jer 16:18; 17:18; Zech 9:12).
[47] Beagley, *Sitz im Leben*, 113–50.
[48] Massyngberde Ford, *Revelation*, 300; Beagley, *Sitz im Leben*, 94.
[49] This is not the only respect in which Lamentations is recalled by Rev 18. We may note the following as some examples. Jerusalem is the fallen princess (Lam 1:1; Rev 18:2, 7), burned with fire like Sodom (Lam 2:1–4; Rev 18:8, 18; and esp. cf. Lam 4:6 with Rev 11:8), a haunt for wild animals (Lam 5:18; Rev 18:2). She has known the reversal of God's favor, especially symbolized in the use of vine and vineyard imagery to express God's wrath rather than God's blessing (Lam 1:15; 2:6; Rev 18:6; cf. Court, *Myth*, 143–144); and her wealthy people have suffered disaster and deprivation (Lam 4:5–9; Rev 18:14–17).
[50] So E. M. Humphrey, *The Ladies and the Cities: Transformation and Apocalyptic Identity in Joseph and Asenath, 4 Ezra, the Apocalypse and the Shepherd of Hermas* (JSPSup 17; Sheffield: Sheffield Academic Press, 1995), 115n97, who rightly points out that the function of Babylon as a foil to the righteous city in Revelation "makes it quite beside the point to enter into a debate regarding the intended historical identity of the city."

[51] It should be said, however, that during the 1995 AAR/SBL meeting itself, it became clear that Professor Massyngberde Ford has in fact changed her position on Babylon (among other matters) so that in fact it is now much closer to the position I am arguing for in this paper. Babylon is not a particular city, but a symbol of general decadence.

[52] L. L. Thompson, *The Book of Revelation: Apocalypse and Empire* (Oxford: Oxford University Press, 1990). This is a most insightful book where method is concerned.

[53] As Thompson puts it, "the conflict and crisis in the Book of Revelation between Christian commitment and the social order derive from John's perspective on Roman society rather than from significant hostilities in the social environment" (*Revelation*, 175).

[54] Thus in view of work like Thompson's we must certainly at the least be much more cautious in what is claimed about persecution in the Roman empire on the basis of the book of Revelation, like Schüssler Fiorenza, *Revelation*, 8–9, who places emphasis on what would have been *thought* of as persecution by Christians, rather than on what we might call (if we were speaking naïvely) the objective facts of the matter.

[55] Massyngberde Ford, *Revelation*, 281.

[56] C. Rowland, *Revelation* (Epworth Commentaries; London: Epworth, 1993), 24.

[57] L. Morris, *The Revelation of St John* (London: Tyndale, 1969), 180.

[58] On Rev 11:8 in particular see Sweet, *Revelation*, 187, for whom Babylon is only the most powerful image of "the city," the social and political embodiment of human self-sufficiency and rebellion against God, presently located in Rome, but with precursors in Sodom, Egypt and Jerusalem and with many successors; and also P. E. Hughes, *The Book of the Revelation* (Leicester: Inter-Varsity, 1990), 127, for whom the great city is not a particular geographical location or metropolis, but the worldwide structure of defiance and unbelief, whose prototype is Babel.

⁵⁹ Sweet, *Revelation*, 271.

⁶⁰ A. Farrer, *The Revelation of St John the Divine* (Oxford: Clarendon, 1964), 189.

⁶¹ J. Ellul, *Apocalypse: The Book of Revelation* (New York: Seabury, 1977), who applies the imagery of Revelation, not to a particular city and nation, but to universal collective human realities. I take the implication of what Thompson, *Revelation*, is saying to be similar, since his work suggests that Revelation is not so much about what Christians should believe and do in a particular situation, but about what Christians should believe and do "full stop." John presents a *vision* of the world, and not simply a reflection of or a reaction to the world as he knows it.

⁶² Beasley-Murray, *Revelation*, 23, makes the general connection between what it is possible to know and what is important rather nicely: "John's visions of the end are those of an impressionist artist rather than the pictures of a photographer. For the most part they defy precision in application. But they convey sufficient to warn men of the end of state-idolatry, and enough about the kingdom of God, to encourage them to faith and adoration of God."

CHAPTER SEVEN

¹ The paper was read at the "Bible and Theology" conference at King's College, London, in April 1995. I am grateful to Dr. Francis Watson for the invitation to read it, and to all those others who have since offered comments and suggestions which have improved it.

² The spirit of the times is well captured in the title of J. Semler's seminal work on the canon, *Abhandlung von freier Untersuchung des Canons* (*Treatise on the Free Investigation of the Canon*, 1771–1776), in which he argued that the theological approach to the Hebrew canon that regarded it as a unified body of authoritative writings, resting as it did upon historical misconceptions, should be replaced by a strictly historical approach that would establish its "true" historical development.

³ See B. C. Ollenburger et al., eds., *The Flowering of Old Testament Theology*, (Sources for Biblical and Theological Study 1; Winona Lake, IN: Eisenbrauns, 1992), 489–502, for an English translation of his original lecture.

⁴ W. Eichrodt, "Does Old Testament Theology Still Have Independent Significance within Old Testament Scholarship?," in Ollenburger et al., *Flowering*, 30–39; and *Theology of the Old Testament* (trans. J. A. Baker; 2 vols., Philadelphia: SCM, 1961 and 1967). Eichrodt himself could not consistently organize his Old Testament theology around the theme of covenant, for the very obvious reason that in those many parts of the Old Testament where religion is considered in more universalistic terms as a relationship between God and the world or God and humanity, rather than between God and Israel, there is scarcely any trace of that theme. The attempt by others to find a different theme that functions more happily as the center has resulted only in such a proliferation of centers that the concept itself is brought into question.

⁵ G. von Rad, *Old Testament Theology* (trans. D. M. G. Stalker; 2 vols.; Edinburgh: Oliver and Boyd, 1962 and 1965). It is clearly not the case across the broad sweep of Old Testament literature that Israel's faith is essentially concerned with the acts of God. There are many Old Testament books in which Yahweh's acts do not figure prominently at all. Salvation history can, in fact, be plausibly argued to be a direct concern of only about half the Old Testament.

⁶ B. S. Childs, *Biblical Theology of the Old and New Testaments: Theological Reflection on the Christian Bible* (Minneapolis: Fortress, 1993).

⁷ The task of biblical theology, on the other hand, is to explore the relation between Old Testament and New Testament witnesses in more serious dialogue with the traditions of dogmatic theology.

⁸ F. Watson, *Text, Church and World: Biblical Interpretation in Theological Perspective* (Edinburgh: T&T Clark, 1994), 32–33.

⁹ J. Barr, *Holy Scripture: Canon, Authority, Criticism* (Oxford: Clarendon, 1983); see also "Childs' Introduction to the Old Testament as Scripture,"

JSOT 16 (1980): 12–23.

[10] It has, in fact, received it, e.g. from M. G. Brett, *Biblical Criticism in Crisis? The Impact of the Canonical Approach on Old Testament Studies* (Cambridge: Cambridge University Press, 1991), 118–23.

[11] For the detail with regard to Kings, see I. W. Provan, *1 and 2 Kings* (NIBCOT; Peabody, MA: Hendrickson, 1995). On inter-textuality within the Old Testament in general, see D. A. Carson and H. G. M. Williamson, eds., *It Is Written: Scripture Citing Scripture. Essays in Honor of Barnabas Lindars* (Cambridge: Cambridge University Press, 1988), 25–83; M. Fishbane, *Biblical Interpretation in Ancient Israel* (Oxford: Clarendon, 1985); and many of the newer books on Hebrew narrative.

[12] This is a common distinction, already found in Semler (op. cit.) and often repeated in modern times, e.g. A. C. Sundberg, *The Old Testament of the Early Church* (Cambridge: Harvard University Press, 1964). Evidence of canon consciousness, it is often asserted—even by scholars who the stress the continuity of the tradition-process rather more than Barr does—is not to be found. Thus D. A. Knight, "Canon and the History of Tradition: A Critique of Brevard S. Childs' *Introduction to the Old Testament as Scripture*," *HBT* 2 (1980): 127–49, is happy to write of the shaping of the biblical materials, and to view their redactors as theologians, yet confesses himself "unconvinced that this 'shaping' should be considered explicit and intentional canonical activity" (137).

[13] That the silence is deafening is well illustrated by the fact that J. L. Mays ("What is Written: A Response to Brevard Childs' *Introduction to the Old Testament as Scripture*," *HBT* 2 [1980]: 151–63), after describing the New Testament canonization process, can actually pose as a question: "Is this process in any way analogous to what happened in ancient Israel and in early Judaism?" (162). It is curious, indeed, that in "Childs' Introduction" (21–22), Barr himself suggests that Childs might usefully have considered the process of New Testament canonization in forming his views about the Old Testament

process and its implications. This does not seem entirely consistent with his comments in *Holy Scripture*.

[14] Even Barr is not entirely clear on the point (*Holy Scripture*, 57), affirming that a clear distinction between scripture and non-scripture "very probably" did not exist even at the turn of the era, while maintaining that Sundberg's "wide religious literature without definite bounds" is "perhaps too vague" to capture the reality. Why he objects to the latter if he really believes the former is not at all clear. Does he believe that there were limitations set to the number of the Scriptures even before the line between Scripture and non-scripture had been finally drawn? But does that not, then, imply that the notion of limitation is built in to the notion of Scripture? And what are we to make of his later concession (*Holy Scripture*, 83) that there was "back into early Old Testament times, a sort of core of central and agreed tradition, a body of writings already recognized and revered, which … functioned … in the same general way in which the canon of scripture functioned for later generations," and his acceptance that "that the whole nature of Israelite religion was canonical, that it depended on the selection of a limited set of traditions which were accepted and were to be authoritative in the community"?

[15] Thus both J. A. Sanders, *Torah and Canon* (Philadelphia: Fortress, 1972) and J. Blenkinsopp, *Prophecy and Canon: A Contribution to the Study of Jewish Origins* (Notre Dame: University of Notre Dame Press, 1977) conceive of growing canonical consciousness as early as the exilic period, questions of authority and legitimation already arising then in connection with Israel's Scriptures.

[16] It is a curious feature of Childs' work that although he is not prepared sharply to distinguish Scripture and canon in general, he seemingly thinks of the era before the pre-exilic period as somehow different in kind from the remainder: note his objection to Leiman's position that authority and canonicity were in all likelihood bound up with each other in the case of Moses ("A Response," 201). It is not easy to find consistency here.

[17] The point about the continuity of the canonical process is underlined by R. Smend, "Questions About the Importance of the Canon in an Old Testament Introduction," *JSOT* 16 (1980), 45–51 (48): "We may well ask whether the Song of Deborah or any prophetic oracle or a law or a psalm ... do not contain within themselves a tendency towards the supra-individual, the authoritative, and the normative—and thus toward the canonical ... the identity of the material and its continuity in the course of changes make it difficult, in my view, to determine with any certainty the beginning of the canonical."

[18] B. S. Childs, *Introduction to the Old Testament as Scripture* (London: SCM, 1979), 69–106; cf. also the discussion on 659–71.

[19] Childs, *Biblical Theology*, 55–69.

[20] Barr, *Holy Scripture*, 42, makes the same point in a different way and to different purpose: "No one could reasonably suppose that the self-identity of the Roman Catholic Church would be materially affected if it dropped the Book of Ecclesiasticus from its canon, or even if it dropped all the books which Protestants have traditionally counted as Apocrypha. Nor would Protestant communities be materially changed if Ecclesiasticus or Wisdom were to be read in them as Old Testament lessons."

[21] B. S. Childs, *Old Testament Theology in a Canonical Context* (Philadelphia: Fortress, 1985), 6-7. The necessity of the distinction between Church and Old Testament is quite clear on these pages.

[22] "The Church has received this Septuagint as if it were the only translation; the Greek-speaking Christian peoples use it and most are not aware whether any other exists ... it is the judgment of the churches of Christ that no one person [i.e. Jerome] should be preferred over the authority of so large a body of men [i.e. the Seventy]" (Augustine, *City of God*, 18:43).

[23] "It is an obvious, but essential feature of the Old Testament," he tells us, "that the original addressee and tradent of this biblical witness was Israel, which sets this testament clearly apart from the New Testament." (Childs, *Biblical*

Theology, 91). A clear distinction is in fact maintained here between Greek language and Hellenistic culture, on the one hand, and the Hebrew-Aramaic Old Testament, on the other.

[24] This is well illustrated if one refers to his index of biblical references and notes the small number of references to the Apocrypha. Within the book itself, a curious ambivalence towards the Apocrypha is evident. Sometimes they are clearly not canonical (e.g. on p. 116, 4 Ezra is included among the "non-canonical Jewish writings"); sometimes they apparently are (cf. the discussion on 189–90); but often it is not clear (e.g. esp. 131, where both Wisdom of Solomon and Sirach are cited as coming from "Jewish Hellenistic circles," but the significance is not obvious).

[25] Childs, *Introduction*, 75–76.

[26] Cf. B. S. Childs, "A Response," *HBT* 2 (1980): 199–211 (207–11), where in reply to Knight's contention that every stage in the history of the literature has as much right to its own integrity as the final form he says: "[T]his scholarly conviction was not shared by the editors of the biblical literature, nor by the subsequent Jewish and Christian communities of faith. The whole intention in the formation of an authoritative canon was to pass theological judgments on the form and scope of the literature" (210). This is connected with the fact that the mode of divine revelation in Christ was not a process but an incarnation within a historical moment. Childs further notes in respect of the post-history (202, in response to Sanders) that the early church distinguished sharply between apostolic tradition and later church tradition precisely because it set apart the period of Christ's incarnation as *sui generis*—both canon and creed functioned as derivatives of Christology, the apostolic witness being regarded as unique testimony that was not to be extended.

[27] Childs, *Old Testament Theology*, 12–15.

[28] Note the use of the very word "coercion," for example, in Childs' review of Barr's *Holy Scripture* in *Int* 38 (1984): 66–70 (69).

²⁹ Childs, *Introduction*, 78–79.

³⁰ B.S. Childs, "Response to Reviewers of *Introduction to the OT as Scripture*," *JSOT* 16 (1980):52–60 (54–55).

³¹ Childs, *Introduction*, 77.

³² Childs, *Biblical Theology*, 18–20, 71–73.

³³ C. J. Scalise, *Hermeneutics as Theological Prolegomena: A Canonical Approach* (StABH 8; Macon, GA: Mercer University Press, 1994), 68–71.

³⁴ Brett, *Biblical Criticism*, 135–67.

³⁵ Childs, *Introduction*, 75.

³⁶ Note, for example, his comments on Ephesians in *The New Testament as Canon: An Introduction* (Philadelphia: Fortress, 1985), 322–23, where he insists that the letter's appeal to the modern reader should be taken seriously. It is "an essential part of the descriptive task to seek to understand how this ancient letter was transmitted, shaped, and interpreted in order to render its message accessible to successive generations of believers by whom and for whom it was treasured as authoritative."

³⁷ The same may be argued to apply to the language of Ricoeur, as useful as his work is in helping to explain how readers might grasp canonical intentionality through the reading process, "grounding a larger vision by referring specifically to the narrative shape ('configuration') of the texts themselves" (Scalise, *Hermeneutics*, 71). Canonical intentionality does not refer solely in Childs to "the theologically-construed shape ... of the texts themselves" (Scalise, *Hermeneutics*, 71). That is why even though his initial comments on Ricoeur in his *Biblical Theology* (19–20) are somewhat warmer than those, for example, in his *Introduction* (77), Childs still wishes to distance himself from the newer literary perspectives of Ricoeur and others, affirming that "the stress on the autonomy of a text, while freeing the text momentarily from the excessive burden of historicism, opens up a whole set of new problems for the biblical interpreter which threaten the very life of narrative theology. It has also demon-

strated that the emphasis on language can domesticate the Bible theologically just as quickly as the excessive stress on history did" (*Biblical Theology*, 205).

[38] Cf. H. R. Jauss, *Toward an Aesthetic of Reception* (Brighton: Harvester, 1982), 30–32.

[39] It is one thing to assert, as Gadamer does, that tradition is always in principle revisable. It is another thing to move from theory to practice. What would count as sufficient reasons for criticizing tradition? Given that one cannot criticize all traditions at the same time, what are the grounds upon which one might cease criticizing other traditions from one's present position, and move outside this position to criticize it also? Is it at all a sensible or coherent way in which to live, given one's finitude and historicality, to make oneself the measure of all things, jumping from position to position in order to offer accumulating criticisms of every point of view? Can or does anyone actually live in this way? To assert that tradition is always in principle revisable will certainly grant one a measure of respectability within the Academy, but one wonders what the point of the assertion really is, if it is not clear how or when the principle might be carried through into practice.

[40] Brett, *Biblical Criticism*, 146–47.

[41] Childs, "Response to Reviewers," 56.

[42] Brett, *Biblical Criticism*, 154.

[43] Childs' review of Barr's *Holy Scripture*, 69. We may note in further support of this interpretation of Childs' position his remarks in *Biblical Theology*, 335–336, where he first speaks of "the canonical guidelines for interpretation which have been structured into the biblical text" (cf. the identification of editors and canonical shapers on 334), moving on to speak of "reader response" to the coercion of the text (a Christian reader renders the Old Testament ultimately in a different way from a Jew because of the experience of the Gospel), but ending with the insistence that canonical restraints must be observed by the reader—that reader response must be critically tested in the light of the different witnesses of the whole Bible. Reader response has a legitimate role, but

the uniqueness of the biblical witness must not be compromised by "assigning an autonomous role to human imagination."

[44] Barr, *Holy Scripture*, 33–37, 122–23, 133.

[45] To choose but one famous example, we may note Karl Popper's emphasis (e.g. in *Objective Knowledge* [Oxford: Oxford University Press, 1972]) on the inevitable way in which all learning is guided by conscious or subconscious expectations, all knowledge is modification of previous knowledge—essentially, his emphasis on the way in which we all stand in a tradition while we do our "free" thinking.

[46] A good example is found in Eichrodt, who is so far from succeeding in his attempt at objectivity that he chooses as his center for an Old Testament theology a theme (covenant) that is radically absent from much of the Old Testament but just so happens to represent a fundamental way in which the Christian Bible in its two parts has been understood: as a book of two covenants. On the manner in which theoretically "neutral" historical research within the Academy has so often been in fact thoroughly Christian, note the perceptive book by the Jewish scholar J. D. Levenson, *The Hebrew Bible, the Old Testament and Historical Criticism: Jews and Christians in Biblical Studies* (Louisville: Westminster/John Knox, 1993).

[47] I. W. Provan, "Ideologies, Literary and Critical: Reflections on Recent Writing on the History of Israel," *JBL* 114 (1995), 585–606.

[48] It is not clear to me that Brett has grasped this important point, when he holds against Childs that his position does not allow critique from outside (*Biblical Criticism*, 150). In relation to Gottwald, he asks: "What if modern biblical studies discover that the communicative intention of the canonical texts is systematically distorted by precisely those 'hidden indices'—historical forces behind the text—that the canonical approach excludes on methodological grounds?" It is precisely the possibility of (presumably objective) "discovery" of what is behind the text, enabling the kind of critique of the text Brett has

in mind, that needs to be challenged.

[49] M. G. Brett, "Against the Grain: Brevard Childs' *Biblical Theology of the Old and New Testaments: Theological Reflection on the Christian Bible*," *Modern Theology* 10 (1994): 281–87 (283).

[50] It is precisely Childs' criticism of Brueggemann (*Biblical Theology*, 71–73), in fact, that he separates form and content, emphasizing the role of the canonical interpreter in shaping the theological content of the Bible.

[51] Watson, *Text*, 133–36, offers a reading, for example, that tends to emphasize Lindbeck's focus on intrasystematic truth rather than upon correspondence to extrinsic reality. Brett, *Biblical Criticism*, 156–67, argues, on the other hand, that Lindbeck is not uninterested in the question of correspondence to reality, but only concerned to say that reference to ontological reality is inseparable from the wider cultural-linguistic system in which it is perceived—that theological reality is encountered only through the witness.

[52] Childs, *Introduction*, 45.

[53] As Barr, "Childs' Introduction," 15, notes: "The canonical reading here presented makes no sense unless one already has a latish Deuteronomy, a Deutero-Isaiah, and so on." And again, on p. 20: "From a canonical point of view, there is no 'Deutero-Isaiah,' there are no concluding 'additions' to Daniel, no 'epilogue' to Qoheleth."

[54] Childs, "Response to Reviewers," 55.

[55] Ibid., 56.

[56] Childs, *Old Testament Theology*, 24–25 (23): Childs' analysis of the canonical process "is not to suggest that canonization changed profane literature into sacred by rendering it qualitatively different from its origins." See further Brett, *Biblical Criticism*, 150–53.

[57] Childs, "Response to Reviewers," 56.

[58] E.g., Childs, *Old Testament Theology*, 6; *Biblical Theology*, 71; cf. also *Exodus* (OTL; London: SCM, 1974), xiii.

⁵⁹ Childs' ambivalence towards historical-critical "results" has been spotted by more than one (nervous) reviewer of the *Introduction*; note, for example, G. M. Landes, "The Canonical Approach to Introducing the Old Testament: Prodigy and Problems," *JSOT* 16 (1980): 32–39, who laments that "in the face of the full thrust of the constantly reiterated shortcomings of historical-critical results which accompanies Childs' treatment of nearly every Old Testament book ... the unfortunate impression is liable to be left that canonical analysis can be successfully pursued without giving much if any serious attention to the fruits of historical-critical research" (35).

⁶⁰ Scalise, *Hermeneutics*, 67.

⁶¹ J. Blenkinsopp, "A New Kind of Introduction: Professor Childs' *Introduction to the Old Testament as Scripture*," *JSOT* 16 (1980), 24–27, also notes (24) the curious fact that although Childs is in fact much influenced in his general approach by "recent and not so recent trends in literary criticism," he makes only passing reference to these in his writing. Scalise, *Hermeneutics*, 71–74, argues that, aside from his background in traditional critical method, a theological concern also underlies Childs' lack of openness in this area: he is suspicious of any approach to biblical theology that does not emphasize the christological role of the Christian canon, fearful of the threat of reductionistic perspectives on Scripture. It is certainly striking that even in his *Biblical Theology*, where he is in certain respects quite warm towards the newer literary approaches to Scripture (18–22), Childs' main emphasis lies still upon the problem of extra-biblical referentiality. He seems to have great difficulty in seeing past this problem, as if it is somehow impossible for a well-crafted *story* (for example) nevertheless to refer to external reality both historical and divine.

⁶² For example, R. N. Whybray, *The Making of the Pentateuch* (JSOTSup 53; Sheffield: JSOT Press, 1987).

⁶³ Barr, *Holy Scripture*, 33–37.

⁶⁴ A decreasing number of Old Testament scholars, I imagine, would find

themselves able to agree with Barr, "Childs' Introduction," 16, who in attacking Childs' assertions as to the speculative nature of historical-critical reconstruction, affirms that "one could equally well say that it is the extrinsic referent, even if reconstructed, that is objective, and the canon that is illusion." This must rank as one of the more remarkable statements made in respect of Childs' work. Contrast R. Smend, "Questions About the Importance of the Canon in an Old Testament Introduction," *JSOT* 16 (1980): 45–51 (45–46): "The finalized texts are not imaginary entities. Here we are less under the influence of speculations, but can make observations on material that clearly lies before us."

[65] Childs, *Biblical Theology*, 416.

[66] It is precisely the fact that Childs concedes so much "objectivity" to historical-critical theories which encourages, for example, the kind of playing off of prior stages of the tradition against the final form that we find in Knight, "Canon," 143–46—a strategy that can make Childs' insistence on "the final form alone" seem somewhat arbitrary. The more that Childs questions, on the other hand, whether the tradents of tradition have left us sufficient information to reconstruct it (if reconstruction is even thought necessary), the more it becomes evident that playing off hypothetical "prior stages of the tradition" against the concrete final form is not a worthwhile exercise.

[67] Barr, "Childs' Introduction," 15, notes (though with characteristic overstatement) that "though the contributions made by critical study are acknowledged, practically nowhere does Childs concede that it has made a quite *decisive* difference to our understanding of scripture."

[68] Childs, *Introduction*, 421–26.

[69] Landes, "The Canonical Approach," 38–39. Matthew 12:41 and Luke 11:32 stress the repentance motif in referring to the Jonah story.

[70] Note, similarly Barr, *Holy Scripture*, 158, who writes of Childs' *Introduction* that it is "much less a meditation upon the canonical form than he thinks and much more a description of a *process*."

[71] Watson, *Text*, 42–45.

[72] It offers us the texts for use in the present, it tells us that we ought to use them in our own theological tasks, but it does not tell us how we are to do so. It does not tell us, for example, whether the texts are essentially all on a level or not, and whether the truth they offer lies not in the individual text but in complementarity and balance established by the whole collection.

[73] R. E. Murphy, "The Old Testament as Scripture," *JSOT* 16 (1980): 40–44.

[74] Childs, "Response to Reviewers," 55.

[75] Childs, *Old Testament Theology*, 15.

[76] Watson, *Text*, 188–201.

[77] Ibid., 279.

[78] We may note, for example, the two extended examples of canonical exegesis in Childs, *Biblical Theology*, 323–47, where it is explicit at least in the case of Gen 22:1–19 that Childs seeks to show how the passage has been shaped "in such a way as to provide important hermeneutical guidelines for its theological use" (326).

[79] That is to say, I do not believe (for example) that Childs grasps the extent to which the kind of narrative patterning he rejects in his response to Sanders ("A Response," 201–204 [203]) does in fact exist, not only in the New Testament in relation to the Old Testament, but within the Old Testament itself, and provides not only evidence of holistic reading over against Sanders but also hermeneutical guidelines for appropriating the material in the present. Having said that, Childs is surely quite correct to emphasize that hermeneutical practices found in the New Testament cannot be regarded as exhausting all the possibilities for Christian reading of the Old Testament in the present, for modern Christian readers come to the Bible as two testaments, whereas the earliest readers came to it as only one. The theological task of the Church is therefore of a different order from simply duplicating the practices of the Apostles (cf. also Childs, *Biblical Theology*, 76).

[80] The program I am suggesting here arises simply from taking with utmost seriousness Childs' own conviction that "the relation between the historical critical study of the Bible and its theological use as religious literature within a community of faith needs to be completely rethought" (*Introduction*, 15) and that biblical theology cannot be done "by adding a layer of icing on the historical critical Introduction" ("A Response," 206). It is precisely a *complete* rethinking that is required, allied with the kind of openness to literary criticism which Childs himself professes in his response to Landes on Jonah in "Response to Reviewers," 59–60.

[81] The real value of past historical-critical work for those pursuing the kind of program I am outlining here will lie, not in its provision of any so-called "depth dimension," but in its alerting them to interesting puzzles in the text which must be taken into account in offering a final form reading. Thus, for example, the strangeness of the "psalm" on the lips of Jonah (Jonah 2; see above), rightly noted by historical critics, will form part of the data that must be accounted for in the construal of the whole in its present form. The multiplication of plausible readings of this kind is, in fact, the only thing that in the long run will bring to an end the wearisome habit among scholars of responding to Childs' whole program in terms of individual favorite examples that "prove" that the historical-critical approach is absolutely indispensable if we are to understand the Old Testament, and therefore "prove" that Childs cannot be wholly right in his approach. Thus, for example, if Barr (*Holy Scripture*, 82), claims that the use of Ps 82 in John 10:34 shows that the New Testament did not read the Old Testament "canonically," because the canonical shape of Ps 82 "makes it plain that the reference is not to men hearing the Word of God, but to gods," it would be helpful to show that there is nothing "plain" about this reading of Ps 82 at all, *especially* when it is read in its canonical context within the Psalter, where the divinity of kings is presupposed (e.g. Pss 2, 45).

We may note that Ps 82:2–4 refers precisely to the responsibilitites of kings (cf., for example, Ps 72).

[82] Childs, unfortunately, is not so aware of this as he should be, and he thus gives standard text-critical positions just as much excessive respect as standard historical-critical positions. In doing so he gets himself into some difficulty, insisting that even a "mutilated" text like MT 1 Sam 1:24 should be preferred as the canonical text over against a better reading attested elsewhere (Childs, *Introduction*, 105; cf. Murphy, "The Old Testament," 40–41). A more fruitful line of argument would have begun by pursuing a little further than Childs does the question of how much "objectivity" attaches to the text-critical task, noting how the most casual of glances at any critical commentary or textual apparatus reveals the extent to which text-critical decisions are no more "objective" than those of historical critics, are indeed entirely bound up with numerous presuppositions about the text that "ought" to be there (e.g., the text ought to be one that makes immediate sense to me) and about the people who "failed" to deliver it (e.g. they, being pre-critical, could and did live with nonsense; cf. Barr, "Childs' Introduction," 17). It is a mistake, therefore, simply to concede that a text like 1 Sam 1:24 contains "an obvious textual error" and to invite the implication that to read this text as the canonical text is to allow nonsense to prevail. There is nothing "obvious" about it—the text makes perfectly good sense as "the boy was only a lad" or as "the child became a servant" (of Samuel). It is in fact the common experience of those who come to the MT prepared to think about it for more than a few moments that it "makes sense," even where it has generally been dismissed as "corrupt." It is one of the tasks of the canonical exegete to spend time thus thinking about the text, rather than conceding too readily that some other text should be read instead, on the entirely reasonable assumption that the Masoretes "saw their task as one of handing down a meaningful text" (J. F. A. Sawyer, *Semantics in*

Biblical Research [London: SCM, 1972], 14; note to the contrary Barr, *Holy Scripture*, 86n11, on grounds unstated, other than "it seems to me").

[83] Provan, *1 and 2 Kings*.

[84] Childs, *Old Testament Theology*, 17.

[85] Ibid.

[86] That is, the only things worth knowing about are what you can think about; the only things worth thinking about are what you can see, touch, handle etc.; and the proper way in which to pursue understanding is to take things to pieces.

[87] Watson, *Text*, 58–59, has nicely captured the sense of disillusionment felt by many.

[88] Cf. Watson, *Text*, 124–36, for a number of examples.

[89] As Barr (*Holy Scripture*, 111) rightly points out: "To perceive that the Bible is canonical Christian scripture, or canonical Jewish scripture, is an insight attainable by anyone, with or without any personal involvement in the Jewish or Christian religions."

[90] At the very least it might be possible to persuade others to change their starting point—to begin with the final form of the text—in order to see which of the various historical-critical hypotheses are any longer perceived to be really necessary, and which are redundant. It might then be possible to suggest (with Childs) that even if they are necessary, perhaps we should not dwell on hypothetical reconstructions for too long a time, but still focus on texts that we actually have.

CHAPTER EIGHT

[1] K. W. Whitelam, *The Invention of Ancient Israel: The Silencing of Palestinian History* (London: Routledge, 1996).

[2] See further I. W. Provan, "Ideologies, Literary and Critical: Reflections on Recent Writing on the History of Israel," *JBL* 114 (1995): 585–606.

[3] T. L. Thompson, *Early History of the Israelite People from the Written and*

Archaeological Sources (SHANE 4; Leiden: Brill, 1992), 13.

[4] Ibid., 81. I cite and refer to Thompson with some trepidation, since recent experience suggests that he is apt to react to citation and reference by claiming (in what I consider a quite unjust and tendentious way) that he has been misunderstood or misrepresented (see his response to my *JBL* article, cited in n2 above, in *JBL* 114 [1995]: 683–98). I am content, however, that I have not misrepresented him in my *JBL* article, and his response only further confirms to me that this is so. I therefore take the risk of citing and referring to him again.

[5] P. R. Davies, *In Search of "Ancient Israel"* (JSOTSup 148; Sheffield: JSOT Press, 1992).

[6] Whitelam, *Invention*, 222.

[7] That is, the idea that because there are few written materials to hand, the region cannot have a history.

[8] It is, for example, important to consider whether and to what extent in past reconstructions of ancient Israel modern scholars have indeed been working anachronistically with a model in their minds of the modern European nation state and modern expressions of imperial power. It is no less important, of course, to consider at the same time whether it is really appropriate to employ a model of the growth of and decline of imperial power in the modern world when trying to understand the ancient world (note Whitelam, *Invention*, 169 ff., and especially the unargued assertion that although Kennedy's study is concerned with the modern period, "his findings are also germane to any consideration of power shifts in the ancient world").

[9] Whitelam, *Invention*, 33.

[10] Ibid.

[11] Ibid., 119.

[12] Ibid., 161–62.

[13] Provan, "Ideologies."

[14] Whitelam, *Invention*, 177, reporting on views in recent scholarly writings

among which he numbers his own; and more explicitly, 204–205.

[15] Indeed, it might be considered rather a bold and confident statement, to assert that the "picture of Israel's past as presented in much of the Hebrew Bible is a fiction, a fabrication like most pictures of the past constructed by ancient (and, we might add, modern) societies" (*Invention*, 23).

[16] Whitelam, *Invention*, 119; compare the comment on Gottwald towards the end of 118.

[17] See my discussion of Ahlström, for example, in "Ideologies," 593–95.

[18] Whitelam, *Invention*, 181 ff.

[19] Ibid., 206–10.

[20] It is, for example, the case that the stele remains as early evidence of an identifiable Israel in Palestine, no matter what the situation with regard to the material culture of "Israelites" and "Canaanites" turns out to be (and that is one complicated matter in the midst of a set of wider complications, as Whitelam himself notes, 228–31). Whitelam's critique of some of the argumentation in this matter (ch. 5) is compelling, yet one wonders if too much emphasis has not been placed by scholars on all sides of this debate on a connection between material culture and identity, as if distinct identity (perceived by a people themselves and by outsiders) implied distinct culture (both existing, and perceivable and quantifiable by us). Is it right to assume that people thinking of themselves as Israelites (assuming for the moment that such existed) would necessarily have had a material culture very different from other people previously or concurrently living in the same region? Wherever such a people originated, their material culture would surely have been influenced by the topographic and economic realities of their dwelling place that others also encountered. At the very least one would not expect the situation on the ground as we find it to be uncomplicated. Nor do we.

[21] Whitelam, *Invention*, 210.

[22] Ibid., 207.

²³ Ibid., 202, referring to Elon.

²⁴ See, for example, *Invention*, 256n34.

²⁵ Ibid., 183.

²⁶ He needs to tell us, in other words, how he moves logically from the observation that archaeology provides us with a series of partial texts to this statement: "Even so, this trend [i.e. towards regional surveys and away from single-site excavations] is the most promising development for the historian desperate to understand the settlement, organization, and economy of ancient Palestinian society" (*Invention*, 181). Why are these partial texts of use to the historian and the biblical partial texts not?

²⁷ We are told, for example (*Invention*, 167), that an isolated reference in a stele like the Tel Dan stele "may confirm the existence of a dynasty which is traced back to a founder named David but it cannot confirm the biblical traditions in Samuel about this founder." This is obviously true, but it does raise the question as to what sort of "confirmation" Whitelam is looking for from archaeology at this point, and whether his expectations in respect of that discipline are reasonable. Conversely, it raises the question as to whether it is sensible to adopt a general attitude to biblical texts that one should not depend on them unless there is "corroborative evidence" (see n39 below). What exactly does "unambiguous evidence to confirm the dominant construction" look like to a scholar who takes Whitelam's position on ideology and scholarly subjectivity (*Invention*, 174)?

²⁸ Whitelam, *Invention*, 33.

²⁹ E.g. ibid., 162–63.

³⁰ Ibid., 236–37.

³¹ It is, for example, likely that scholars who make the occasional foray into the discourse of biblical studies that is generally perceived as somewhat flawed are going to remain marginal voices within that discourse (see Whitelam's own comments on Garbini in *Invention*, 161).

³² Whitelam, *Invention*, 1.

³³ Ibid., 9, noting also 179–82. It is of some interest in connection with a projected attempt to write such a history while consciously not paying undue regard to texts that we read on p. 227: "The painfully slow, but perceptible, shift towards a regional history of Palestine has been obstructed by the lack of an appropriate rhetoric with which to represent this alternative past." Is what is being conceded here that there has been no *narrative*, and that one cannot do much history without narrative (in spite of assertions elsewhere to the contrary)?

³⁴ Nor is it clear that the choice of language in the book helps readers to gain an accurate impression of academic reality in this respect. For example, the current situation is represented as one in which the writing of a history of Palestine has been "obstructed" by the discourse of biblical studies (Whitelam, *Invention*, 10), the study of Palestinian history has not yet quite broken free of the "stranglehold" of the biblical traditions (ibid., 205), and the discourse of biblical studies exercises "tyranny" from which Palestinian history requires to be set free (ibid., 233).

³⁵ Whitelam, *Invention*, 23. See also p. 10 ("It has been difficult to uncover or document sufficiently the subtle political and ideological influences which have shaped historical research in biblical studies"), and p. 148 ("The influences are subtle, not easy to substantiate"). One rather wonders at Whitelam's willingness, in the light of this, to implicate scholar after scholar in a "passive collaboration" that has silenced Palestinian history (148).

³⁶ For example, I find it generally unclear how the discussion in ch. 3 moves us from the very tentative "not easy to make these connections" of p. 23 to the very definite statement on p. 120 that "all the models have invented ancient Israel in terms of contemporary models." He has in this chapter, to my mind, not demonstrated at all that the direction of influence is generally from present to past (the invention of ancient Israel in terms of contemporary models) rather than from past to present (an understanding of ancient Israel, on the

basis of what is perceived as evidence, influencing current understandings of Palestine), and even in the latter case one struggles to find very much clear evidence of a direct connection between scholarly views of the past and their present attitude to Palestine. The questions arises, then, as to when an implicit connection is really a nonexistent one, or at least one that is so weak as to be quite insignificant in terms of implications.

[37] Thus Albright is criticized (Whitelam, *Invention*, 79 ff.) for justifying the slaughter by the ancient Israelites of the indigenous population of Palestine (84); yet the passage cited is very far from doing any such thing. He no more "justifies" this slaughter than he "justifies" the other slaughters mentioned, but rather offers the view in connection with such events that every deed of brutality and injustice is infallibly visited upon the aggressor. He does offer the opinion that there is an inevitable historical process by which "inferior" peoples disappear before "superior" peoples; but he patently does *not* say (as Whitelam alleges, 84) that "superior" peoples have/had the *right* (my emphasis) to exterminate "inferior" ones, and to claim that he does so in a sentence that refers to the Holocaust is entirely out of order. No doubt Albright can be criticized for many things, but it is important that he is criticized justly. The connection that Whitelam makes, moreover, between a preparedness to make value-judgments in respect of different cultures and a dehumanization that allows the extermination of native populations also requires some critical reflection, since the connection does not seem necessary either in logic or in the history of human thought and action. It has proved perfectly possible for people to hold to evolutionary views of human society, whether convincing or not, while combining this with a general belief system and a code of ethics that demanded the highest respect for all human life in present thought and action. Albright himself appears to have been one such person, and to characterize him as having a "racist philosophy" (88) because of his views on social evolution appears to go well beyond the evidence. In point of fact Whitelam's whole

attempt to demonstrate that Albright's "construction of Israel's past mirrors important perceptions of developments in the Palestine of his own day" (80) is most unconvincing, since it seems fairly clear that even if Albright *were* justifying genocide of the Canaanites (which he is not), there is little connection between his "conquest picture" of the past and his known views on the Israel/Palestine questions of his day. Nowhere does Whitelam tell us that Albright "justified" Israeli genocide of the Arab population of Palestine, nor indeed what might be the other specific "implications of his justification for the Israelite slaughter of the Palestinian population in the conquest of the land" (88).

[38] It is after all not surprising that certain words and themes appear both in histories of Israel and in modern discussions about Israel, given that the past impinges always on the present and that the number of ideas and words that could be used in reference to issues of people and land is in any case not unlimited. The real issue is not whether parallels occur, but whether particular views of the past are adequately grounded in evidence, or are simply read back from the present.

[39] In this respect, too, there are some highly curious readings of other scholars in this book. So far as I can see, for example, Meyers does not say or imply that other indigenous powers were *incapable* of the uncharacteristic achievement of David and Solomon (so Whitelam, *Invention*, 146, apparently implying that Meyers has an "attitude problem" with regard to non-Israelite peoples), but only that (so far as the *evidence* suggests) they did not in fact achieve what David and Solomon achieved. Whitelam's discussion of Herrmann just beforehand (ibid., 143–45) provides a good example, in fact, of the way in which it is constantly implied in this book that ideology rather than evidence is driving the discourse of biblical studies, when in fact the dispute is really about what counts as evidence. Hermann's whole treatement of the question of the ancient Israelite state is characterized as imbued with significance when read in the modern context. It is stressed, on the other hand, that the "only" evidence for

the uniqueness of this state is what is characterized as "a self-serving narrative of the Davidic bureaucracy." Herrmann "offers no corroborative evidence." Thus is it implied, it seems to me, that Hermann is not truly driven by "the evidence" at all. There is simply no discussion of why texts that in part can be imagined to have apologetic intention are nevertheless not to be regarded as proper evidence, nor why evidence has to be corroborated in order to be regarded in the first instance as reliable. It would be interesting to see how far anyone could get with Whitelam's projected history of Palestine if this attitude to evidence were consistently adopted.

[40] "The growth of Palestinian nationalism has not resulted in an attempt to reclaim the past similar to the movements in India, Africa or Australia" (Whitelam, *Invention*, 7).

[41] Ibid., 38.

[42] Ibid., 72.

[43] Ibid., 128.

[44] Ibid., 220.

[45] It is striking just how often Whitelam appears to have at the back of his mind a definite *picture* of ancient Palestine that somewhat exceeds the available *evidence* in respect of ancient Palestine. For example, he criticizes biblical scholarship for failing to say that the Canaanites had a national consciousness, but does not go on to show what evidence there is that they had (*Invention*, 57). He also criticizes Gottwald and others (ibid., 116–18) for assuming that Israel's political system was different from and fundamentally superior to that of the indigenous culture, and for undervaluing the indigenous value system in expressing the view that it required transformation from outside. Gottwald, however, is at least working from what he perceives as evidence, whether Whitelam accepts that it *is* in fact evidence or not. Leaving aside the question of superiority, on the basis of what evidence would Whitelam wish to argue that Israel's political system was *not* different from that of the indigenous culture, and that Gottwald

is indeed *undervaluing* the indigenous value system in expressing the view that it required transformation from outside? Returning to the question of superiority, Whitelam himself does seem prepared, if I read p. 117 correctly, to make at least some value-judgments in respect of different political systems. On this point, finally, how does Whitelam know in advance that a rhetoric of Palestinian history would provide a much more positive appreciation of the material and cultural achievements of the inhabitants of the region as a whole (233–34)? How does he know, for example, that the concern for the marginalized and underprivileged that is promoted in some indigenous religious systems would be found also in Palestine? Has his narrative already been written, quite independently of anything that might be called evidence?

[46] It is perhaps as well to make it unambiguously clear at the same time, in the context of this discussion, that I am certainly not one who offers or seeks to offer support to the modern state of Israel where it has behaved or currently behaves unjustly and immorally. I should like for my part to be clearer on the significance of the line in *Invention*, 116, where Whitelam refers to Israel "striking back against what it *perceives* (my emphasis) as terrorist actions," in a context where the striking back is characterized as "foreign adventures." This seems to me very committed language indeed. It would also be interesting to know which view of the present situation in Palestine is implied by his discussion of Gottwald (ibid., 115 ff.), where Whitelam criticizes Gottwald for his failure to articulate a Palestinian history even though Gottwald's view is that Israel had its roots fundamentally in the conscious and free choice of indigenous individuals and groups to reject Canaanite centralization of power and move in a different direction. If it is not Palestinian history even when Palestinians are conceived of as freely choosing a particular way of being, then what is being said? To put this question another way: is one of the implications of the view that we should not under any circumstances conceive of a distinctive *ancient* Israel within Palestine (even where this is associated with Palestinian consent)

that we should also not under any circumstances conceive (or continue to conceive) of a *modern* Israel within Palestine either? It is a reasonable question to ask, when Whitelam so frequently associates the "imagining" of ancient Israel with the oppression of the Palestinians, stressing the important role of history in the shaping of identity.

[47] They are, indeed, already recognized by some authors as influenced by ideology, as the first citation from Eden in Whitelam, *Invention*, 12, makes clear.

CHAPTER NINE

[1] Again, I am very happy to remember and to state for the record that my ability to reside in Germany at all and to write this essay there was due to the fact that I was the beneficiary of a grant from the Alexander von Humboldt-Stiftung.

[2] Those interested in an overview of such scholarship might consult, e.g., S. L. McKenzie, *The Trouble with Kings: The Composition of the Book of Kings in the Deuteronomistic History* (VTSup 42; Leiden: Brill, 1991), 1–19.

[3] I note the following among the many books which have raised questions like these and in the process contributed to a change in climate within biblical studies where narrative is concerned: J. Licht, *Storytelling in the Bible* (Jerusalem: Magnes, 1978); R. Alter, *The Art of Biblical Narrative*, (London: Allen & Unwin, 1981); and M. Sternberg, *The Poetics of Biblical Narrative: Ideological Literature and the Drama of Reading* (Bloomington: Indiana University, 1985). For detailed examples from Kings in which passages are read from both a historical-critical and a narrative-critical point of view, see I. W. Provan, *1 and 2 Kings*, (OTG, Sheffield: Sheffield Academic Press, 1996).

[4] See further on these points I. W. Provan, *1 and 2 Kings*, ch. 2.

[5] This is well-illustrated in Kings if one simply compares with their historical-critical predecessors such recent commentaries as take narrative issues much more seriously: T. R. Hobbs, *2 Kings* (Waco: Word, 1985); R. D. Nelson, *First and Second Kings* (Louisville: John Knox, 1987); B. O. Long, *1 Kings*, and *2*

Kings (Grand Rapids: Eerdmans, 1991); I. W. Provan, *1 and 2 Kings* (Peabody, MA: Hendrickson, 1995).

[6] P. R. Davies, *In Search of "Ancient Israel"* (JSOTSup 148; Sheffield: Sheffield Academic Press, 1992), 29.

[7] J. M. Miller and J. Hayes, *A History of Ancient Israel and Judah* (London: SCM, 1986).

[8] K. W. Whitelam, *The Invention of Ancient Israel: The Silencing of Palestinian History* (London: Routledge, 1996), for example, argues that it is not simply the information provided by the biblical texts *about* ancient Israel which is problematic, but the very *idea* of ancient Israel itself, which all these texts (and not just Joshua–Samuel) have put in the scholarly as well as the popular mind. In thus inventing ancient Israel, Western scholarship has contributed to the silencing of Palestinian history.

[9] Ibid., for example on p. 207: "The appeal to what is reasonable is part of the rhetoric of objectivity in order to support the dominant construction of Israel's past within the discourse of biblical studies." See further I. W. Provan, The End of (Israel's) History? A Review Article on K. W. Whitelam's *The Invention of "Ancient Israel," JSS* 42 (1997): 283–300.

[10] G. W. Ahlström, *The History of Ancient Palestine from the Palaeolithic Period to Alexander's Conquest* (JSOTSup 146; ed. D. V. Edelman; Sheffield: JSOT Press, 1993), 561.

[11] Ibid., 477.

[12] S. A. Wiggins, *A Reassessment of Asherah: A Study According to the Textual Sources of the First Two Millennia B.C.E.* (AOAT 235; Neukirchen-Vluyn: Neukirchener Verlag, 1993), 163–81.

[13] B. S. Childs, *Old Testament Theology in a Canonical Context* (Philadelphia: Fortress, 1985), 115–21.

[14] Among Childs' several critics see, for example, J. Barr, *Holy Scripture: Canon, Authority, Criticism* (Oxford: Clarendon, 1983).

¹⁵ See, e.g., V. P. Long, *The Reign and Rejection of King Saul: A Case for Literary and Theological Coherence* (SBLDS 118; Atlanta: Scholars Press, 1989).

CHAPTER TEN

¹ C. S. Lewis, *The Last Battle* (Harmondsworth: Puffin, 1964), 124–35.
² Ibid., 135.
³ I. W. Provan, "Ideologies, Literary and Critical: Reflections on Recent Writing on the History of Israel," *JBL* 114 (1995): 585–606.
⁴ P. R. Davies, "Method and madness: Some remarks on doing history with the Bible," *JBL* 114 (1995): 699–705 (700), is thus quite mistaken. My objection to his approach to the history of Israel does not stem from my regarding the Bible (because it is inspired Scripture) as a specially privileged source so far as historical reconstruction is concerned, but rather from the conviction that his approach is intellectually indefensible. This should have been clear to Davies from my original article, where I do in fact explain (contrary to his claim on 699–700) what I mean by "positivism" and "materialism," focusing especially on verification (cf. "Ideologies, 601–603). These labels were, incidentally, intended to be descriptive rather than pejorative (*contra* W. G. Dever, "Revisionist Israel Revisited: A Rejoinder to Niels Peter Lemche," *CurBS* 4 [1996], 35–50 [41]; R. P. Carroll, "Madonna of Silences: Clio and the Bible," in L. L. Grabbe, ed., *Can a 'History of Israel' be Written?* [JSOTSup 245; Sheffield: Sheffield Academic Press, 1997], 84–103 [97n28]).
⁵ L. L. Grabbe, "Are historians of ancient Palestine fellow creatures—or different animals?," in Grabbe, *History*, 19–36 (28–29), is apparently to be numbered among those who interpret my position as involving such a commitment, if juxtaposition of text and footnote 25 is any guide. It is not religious belief that drives such conservatism as I possess, however, but the kind of healthy regard for testimony in general (including biblical testimony) for which I shall argue below, in the course of outlining once again what I hold to be an entirely

rational and critical approach to history. What I find reason to be "annoyed" about (29) is precisely that scholars who happen to differ in their view of what is rational and critical should characterize such an approach as "naïve" (28), "apologetic" (28) and "insidious" (29), when it is none of these. Why, exactly, should one go down any "road" (defined as "critical" or not) further than necessary? Is the demand for logic or for a blind faith-commitment?

⁶ It does serve to confirm me in my suspicion, however, that some of the scholars concerned are working with an exceptionally narrow vision of the world, in which there live in the end only two sorts of persons: the critical scholar (for which read "scholars who broadly agree with oneself") and the religious fundamentalist. To be perceived as not one is thus inevitably to be perceived as the other.

⁷ T. L. Thompson, "A neo-Albrightean school in history and biblical scholarship?," *JBL* 114 (1995): 683–98 (esp. 695, beginning of second para.; 697, end of first para.); Grabbe, "Creatures," 21n6.

⁸ Thus Grabbe, "Creatures," 21, asserts rather than argues for the centrality of the "basic ground rules" of the game, moving seamlessly into a subsequent sentence about biblical fundamentalists which implies that only such people truly question these rules.

⁹ Thompson, e.g., apparently believes ("School," 696–97n37) that long footnotes indicating the company he allegedly keeps are any substitute for a rational and measured response to criticism of the general position that he adopts. The whole argument of his pp. 693–97 is in fact extraordinarily confused. He both denies that there is any broad school of thought regarding Hebrew Bible and history such as I described in "Ideologies" and yet accepts the adjective "neo-Albrightean" for the group of scholars to whom he belongs and describes the methodology of this group in terms similar to my own description of it (note especially the emphasis on the verification of sources on 694, para. 2, and 697, para. 1). He seems to imagine that this is not truly a particular school of

thought both because scholars in the group do not agree with each other on individual aspects of Israel's history (693–95), and yet also because so many people in so many different countries now think in the same way about how to approach that history—there has been a "paradigm shift" in the field of history since the 1960s (696–697). It is for these reasons that my "conspiracy theory" cannot be right (696). I never suggested, in fact, that there was any conspiracy. I suggested only that a broad prejudice currently seemed to exist with regard to the usefulness of large sections of the Hebrew Bible to the historian of Israel. It is an inadequate response to that critique to remind me of the diversity of scholarly views on individual matters (of which I am naturally aware: cf., e.g., "Ideologies," 589, opening sentence), and that the paradigm under discussion is widely adhered to (since a paradigm is only a paradigm, and not by virtue of that fact beyond criticism—although it is abundantly clear that it is regarded as such by many of those working within it). On the question of whether there has in reality been any recent paradigm *shift* see further below. The extent to which the paradigm is indeed widely adhered to among scholars is in any case constantly and massively exaggerated by Thompson, who appears to believe that repeated assertion (combined with the repeated suggestion that those scholars who do differ are not truly scholars at all) will make it so; see now T. L. Thompson, "Historiography of ancient Palestine and early Jewish historiography: W. G. Dever and the not so new biblical archaeology," in V. Fritz and P. R. Davies, eds., *The Origins of the Ancient Israelite States* (JSOTSup 228; Sheffield: Sheffield Academic Press, 1996), 26–43 (33, 36 with nn36, 37–38 and passim).

[10] Grabbe, "Creatures," 29n25.

[11] For illustration of these points, see further the extended example discussed later in this essay.

[12] *Contra* Grabbe, "Creatures," 29n25. Grabbe himself provides a good example of how it is possible both to articulate some of the epistemological problems

involved in writing history (as he does throughout his paper) and yet to make a fundamental error of the sort I describe when dealing with sources in respect of a particular era of *Israel's* history. Comparing the Hebrew Bible and other ancient Near Eastern texts in respect of their testimony concerning the later monarchy (24–26), he seems to assume that the latter, as "literature or inscriptions approximately contemporary with the events purported to be described," and notwithstanding the word "purported," simply describe for us the facts of the matter. Only thus can we understand how it is that the biblical text is thought to be "judged" by the extra-biblical information (24), and how it is that Grabbe can go on to assert that "the text is reasonably accurate about the framework" but that the details are at times "demonstrably misleading or wholly inaccurate and perhaps even completely invented" (26). It is entirely unclear, however, why one should embrace such a straightforward view of the Assyrian sources, nor grant them such epistemological primacy: cf., e.g., the brief summary discussion of the highly ideological nature of Assyrian scribal compositions in M. Z. Brettler, *The Creation of History in Ancient Israel* (London: Routledge, 1995), 94–97, with extensive footnote references. Other scholars are in my view similarly muddled on epistemological questions, and I do not accept that in seeking to demonstrate this muddle I have misrepresented any of them, including Ahlström (*contra* Grabbe again, 29n25). *Of course* my quotation is "selective" (what else could it be?); I disagree, however, that my selection somehow distorts Ahlström's position. What Grabbe must demonstrate in order to substantiate his accusation of "misreading" (leaving aside the speculative and offensive "willful") is that Ahlström (a) does not in fact believe that there is such as thing as "what history really looked like"; (b) does not regard the ideology and selectivity of the biblical texts as presenting a serious problem to the modern historian who wishes to reconstruct the past; and (c) does not believe (albeit with gross inconsistency in the argument) that archaeology grants us much more reliable access to the past than do the biblical texts. I do not believe that Grabbe can in fact demonstrate this. For comments on Ahlström's work which are somewhat consistent with my own, see H. M. Barstad, "History and the Hebrew Bible," in Grabbe, *History*, 37–64 (47–48).

[13] The fact of the matter appears to be that modern historians of Israel are on the whole not very well informed about the broader philosophical debates of the last several centuries regarding epistemology in general and historical knowledge in particular, and are thus seemingly unaware of just how far it is *not* self-evident that a historical method inherited from 19th century Germany is the only way (or indeed the best way, intellectually considered) in which to approach the past. Only thus is it possible to explain why this kind of "scientific" approach, founded as it is on a starkly developed but indefensible Cartesian dualism, can be advanced as the only properly critical approach to the history of Israel without the slightest hint that the position needs to be argued for rather than simply asserted (along with references to others who agree), and in studied ignorance of the important critiques of it in scholars like H.-G. Gadamer, *Truth and Method* (ET; London: Sheed and Ward, 1975) and W. Pannenberg, *Basic Questions in Theology* (ET; vol. 1; London: SCM, 1970).

[14] Cf. F. Brandfon, "The limits of evidence: Archaeology and objectivity," *Maarav* 4 (1987): 5–43, the implications of which, not to mention the extensive bibliography touching on archaeology and theory, have seemingly (if recent discussion of the history of Israel is any measure) still to be digested by biblical scholars in general.

[15] For an excellent theoretical discussion of history, ideology and literature which ranges much more broadly than Provan, "Ideologies" and provides voluminous bibliographical referencing, see Brettler, *Creation*, 8–19.

[16] This is again as true of the archaeologist as it is of anyone else. Cf. C. Schäfer-Lichtenberger, "Sociological and biblical views of the early state," in Fritz and Davies, *Origins*, 78–105 (79–80): "Data derived from archaeological artifacts exist only in linguistic form. Being elements of a linguistic structure,

however, they are subject to interpretation as well. The description of archaeological findings is already interpretation and it is subject, like any other literary form of expression, to the singular choice of the narrative procedure, to the concept of explanation, as well as to the value-orientation of the descriptive archaeologist."

[17] The constraints of space prevent a more detailed outworking of the epistemological stance outlined here, and this is in any case rendered unnecessary by the excellent C. A. J. Coady, *Testimony: A Philosophical Study* (Oxford: Clarendon, 1992) as well as many of the other works mentioned in these footnotes which do not adopt a positivist view of the historian's task.

[18] I naturally accept (*contra* the impression given by Davies, "Method," 701) that not all stories are intended to refer to a real past, and that even stories which generally are so intended may for various reasons not do so in specific instances or for specific reasons. My observation in "Ideologies," nevertheless, was that biblical stories about the past have been *without good reason* increasingly marginalized in recent discussion on the history of Israel. Davies' comments here are, therefore, very much beside the point.

[19] This is, on the basis of a reading of the content of most of the narrative texts, at least as clear as any other purpose that may be suggested by a reading of the same texts. I find no basis at all for Grabbe's assertion ("Creatures," 32–33) that theological or religious intent is clearer than historical intent in the biblical text. In respect of his argument on these pages I grant that writers may in fact fall short of what they intend, or indeed that their communication may exceed their intention. Nevertheless, it is fundamental to the task of taking literature seriously that the reader try to form some judgment as to what the author is seeking to do; and it requires some narrowness of perception, in my view, to miss the obvious fact that biblical narrative overall is seeking to speak about Israel's past. The question as to whether every narrative seeks to do this in precisely the same way is a different question. I certainly see no reason to accept the (again unargued) assertion that "the biblical writer would have made

no distinction between the account of creation in Genesis 1, the narrative of the exodus, or the story of Solomon's accession" (32; cf. also Barstad, "History," 45, but contrast B. Halpern, *The First Historians: The Hebrew Bible and History* [San Francisco: Harper and Row, 1988], 266–78). Whether it were true or not, of course, we should still have to make our own decisions (having sought to grasp the author's communicative intentions) as to how, precisely, to receive the testimony offered.

[20] Barstad, "History," 62. I have struggled, but failed, to find an *argument* in Thompson, "Historiography," 38–43, which might provide some basis for his rather different view of the biblical texts, discovering instead only assertion. We are apparently to believe simply that the character of the texts as theologically-shaped narratives precludes any intention on the part of their authors to refer to a real past and any access for us via the texts to such a past.

[21] J. M. Miller and J. Hayes, *A History of Ancient Israel and Judah* (London: SCM, 1986), 74, 129, 159.

[22] For the crucial nature of verification, cf. Miller and Hayes, *History*, 78: for examples of virtual apology, cf. 129, 159–60.

[23] J. A. Soggin, *A History of Israel: From the Beginnings to the Bar Kochba Revolt, AD 135* (London: SCM, 1984), e.g., 98 on the patriarchal narratives; 110 on the Exodus.

[24] E.g., P. R. Davies, "Whose history? Whose Israel? Whose Bible? Biblical histories, ancient and modern," in Grabbe, *History*, 104–22 (104–105), asserts that "the use of biblical historiographical narrative for critical reconstruction of periods that it describes (rather than periods in which it was written) is precarious and only possible where there is (*sic*) adequate independent data." I can see nothing in his preceding discussion, however, that justifies this conclusion, and indeed, I find his earlier assertion that "the historical testimony of any work will be relevant in the first instance to the time in which it was written" itself ungrounded and out of step with both logic and experience. *Why* should

we believe (if not simply for the reason that Wellhausen asserted it: cf. for a discussion, Halpern, *First Historians*, 26–29) that the historical testimony of texts is relevant in the first instance to their own times, and can only be used in a secondary respect "to build a picture of the periods *which they claim to be describing*"? It is from this (itself precarious) starting point in assertion that Davies once more moves on to criticize those who in constructing a history of Israel synthesize biblical texts and extra-biblical data. He truly has no adequate *grounds* for such criticism, however. For ungrounded assertion of the same kind, in defence of the same view of texts, cf. T. L. Thompson, "Defining history and ethnicity in the south Levant," in Grabbe, *History*, 166–86 (180): "We all know that the real world which such so-called [ancient] 'historiographies' reflect is that of their author's; and they are never any better than that."

[25] The general possibility, e.g., that the biblical authors *may* have been rather like James Macpherson, who is alleged to have invented the Celtic poet Ossian (Carroll, "Madonna," 86–88), or Shakespeare, who recontextualized historical figures in fictional works (91), does not demand that we take a general stance against presumption in favor of reading the Bible as historical (cf. 87, and the remainder of the article). Examples like these merely help us to form some idea of the range of possibilities that might exist in respect of any individual text (whether biblical or non-biblical) that "looks" historical in some way. A particularly intriguing aspect of much of this kind of citation of possible analogues to stories in the Hebrew Bible with a view to demonstrating its problematic nature is the way in which it is so readily forgotten that the "knowledge" we possess about the analogues has itself often been accumulated by scholars who operate with precisely that "scientific method" whose viability is here in question. It is thus naturally the case that the "evidence" brought to bear on the discussion of the history of Israel should favor biblical scholars committed to this same method. Whether that "method" gives us any more reliable access to historical reality when applied to non-biblical rather than biblical

texts is, however, entirely open to question. The nonexistence of Ossian, e.g., is by no means universally accepted among Scottish historians. More to the point, Grabbe, "Creatures," 31–32, thinks that Herodotus showed "wonderful critical acumen" in questioning (on the basis of an Egyptian tradition) the "quasi-canonical" Homeric version of the story of Helen of Troy, and indeed that Herodotus placed the burden of proof on those who wished to continue to accept it at face value. I, on the other hand, can find no reason to think that one version of the story is more or less likely to be true than the other, and would indeed be interested in exploring further the relationship between Herodotus' "critical acumen" and his attitude to women ("and no nation would allow itself to be besieged for ten years for the sake of a mere woman," 32). The burden of proof has not, in fact, been moved one inch in any direction whatsoever by Herodotus' expression of his opinion.

[26] Cf., again, Brandfon, "Limits."

[27] This is most clearly illustrated by the recent discussion of the Tel Dan inscription. For a convenient summary, cf. F. C. Cryer, "Of epistemology, northwest-Semitic epigraphy and irony: The BYTDWD/house of David inscription revisited," *JSOT* 69 (1996): 3–17; and for an even more recent reassessment, K. A. Kitchen, "A Possible Mention of David in the late Tenth Century B.C.E. and Deity *Dod as Dead as the Dodo," *JSOT* 76 (1997): 29–44; A. Lemaire "The Tel Dan Stela as a Piece of Royal Historiography," *JSOT* 81 (1998): 3–18.

[28] This is to my mind well-illustrated in the debate between W. G. Dever, "The identity of early Israel: A rejoinder to Keith W. Whitelam," *JSOT* 72 (1996): 3–24, and K. W. Whitelam, "Prophetic conflict in Israelite history: Taking sides with William G. Dever," *JSOT* 72 (1996): 25–44, concerning material culture and ethnicity. The debate is ostensibly about what it is that the archaeological data reveal to be true about the inhabitants of the central highlands of Palestine during the late 13th and early 12th centuries BC. Decisive for the positions ultimately adopted in each case, however, is the attitude

of each scholar to the biblical traditions, in terms of their usefulness to the historian as interpretative keys for the archaeological data. Cf. further Thompson, "Defining history," 167–76, with whose comments on the difficulty of deducing ethnicity from material remains I tend to agree; and more generally, Brandfon, "Limits." It would greatly help scholarly discussion about what it is that *particular* archaeological data "suggest" or "prove" if scholars were able to articulate more clearly their views on what it is that such data are *generally* able to "suggest" or "prove," and on what part their own interpretative theory plays in producing "suggestion" or "proof."

[29] Knowing any history aside from the history in which we are personally involved in fact requires trust in unverified and unverifiable testimony. Selectivity in application of the verification principle is thus an essential prerequisite for writing about the past; and so every historian of Israel is to be found selectively applying it. The testimony of archaeologists, above all, has been privileged by a lack of suspicion until fairly recently, although there are signs that this is at least partially changing (cf. K. W. Whitelam, *The Invention of Ancient Israel: The Silencing of Palestinian History* [Routledge: London, 1996]; and my review article on this book, I. W. Provan, "The End of (Israel's) History? A Review Article on K. W. Whitelam's *The Invention of Ancient Israel*," *JSS* 42 [1997]: 283–300). The testimony of extra-biblical texts has also been privileged in many quarters and continues to be so (cf. n11 above on Grabbe and the Assyrian texts). It is naturally essential that some sources of information should be exempted in this way from any rigorous demand for verification; otherwise nothing remains to be appealed to in respect of verification of the data being "tested."

[30] I do not myself believe that an historian should always feel honored when called a "skeptic" (Davies, "Whose history?," 109)—see further below. If skepticism is indeed to be the denoting feature of the historian, however, (s)he should at least attempt to be consistent about it.

[31] Note, e.g., N. P. Lemche, "Clio is Also Among the Muses! Keith W. Whitelam and the History of Palestine: A Review and a Commentary," in Grabbe, *History*, 123–55 (147–48), who paints a portrait of scholars "forced" successively to lower the time of composition of the biblical narrative; of scholars innocently engaged in "looking for traces" of early Israel, but compelled by lack of evidence to abandon use of the biblical narrative for historical purposes. I have no reason to think that Lemche does not sincerely believes this story, but it is, I believe, a fiction. It is the method itself that has determined the outcome of the enquiry, not such empirical evidence as has been gathered along the way. The fuller narration in N. P. Lemche, "Early Israel revisited," *CurBS* 4 (1996): 9–34 (in which Lemche himself figures particularly prominently among the heroes of the story), makes this especially clear. It is above all a decisive "shift of emphasis" (17) in recent years, rather than any decisive shift in the evidence, that has led to the current state of the debate about the history of Israel; and it is a shift of emphasis in relation to historical method that was already committed in large measure to the verification principle, particularly in respect of archaeological investigation. The precise character of the "shift" in respect of the Old Testament traditions is transparently clear in the closing pages of Lemche's essay (25–28), marked as they are throughout by the presence of ungrounded assertion and the absence of convincing argument. The last (if not entirely comprehensible) word here, however, must go to T. L. Thompson, "Historiography of ancient Palestine and early Jewish historiography: W. G. Dever and the not so new biblical archaeology," in Fritz and Davies, *Origins*, 26–43 (32): "It may well be ironic that it is this recognition of our ignorance of this period's history—indeed that the recognition of such ignorance is the hallmark of our field's cutting edge—that marks the most conclusive results of this generation's historical research!" That ignorance would be the inevitable endpoint of the "method" employed could have been safely predicted some time ago.

[32] It is characteristic of Thompson's response to my *JBL* article that he fails to address the substantive issue here and contents himself simply with assertions about the centrality of verification to historical method ("School," 694, para. 2; 697, para. 1). Acceptance of the verification principle is indeed apparently one of the tests of orthodoxy in respect of critical scholarship. To express doubt about it is to be a dreaded "fundamentalist" (694). Naked assertion aside, a central feature of his strategy in attempting to avoid addressing the main thrust of my argument is to suggest that I have engaged in deliberate and widespread distortion of his and others' views. I entirely reject this accusation. There is, for example, no case in which I have attributed a quotation to Thompson that belongs to an author he is citing or discussing (*contra* "School, 683–84), and he never demonstrates that I have. Nor is he very accurate even in describing that which I have indeed placed in quotation marks (cf. his 685, line 17, with "Ideologies," 586, line 12; and especially his 685n5 with "Ideologies," 586, lines 6–7, where the phrases in question are neither placed by me in quotation marks nor attributed to anyone). My use of what he calls "dots" in abbreviated quotations, moreover, in no case leads to misrepresentation of what he or anyone else has written (*contra* "School," 687 lines 28–33; 688 lines 24–32; 689 lines 18–33; 690 lines 7–11; 693 lines 23–27). Apparently uneasy about resting his entire case against me on allegations of misreading his *Early History*, he characterizes those sections of the book from which I quote as "rhetorical ... often originally designed as much to provoke as to enlighten," and blames me for not reading some other writings of his instead (684). It is true, of course, that I do expect scholars writing serious books to say what they mean. This appears to me to be a reasonable expectation. As to Thompson's other writings, there is in fact nothing to be found in them which suggests that my sketch portrait of his approach to the history of Israel is in the least degree unfair.

[33] Thus, e.g., E. A. Knauf, "From history to interpretation," in D.V. Edelman, ed., *The Fabric of History: Text, Artifact and Israel's Past* (JSOTSup 127; Shef-

field: JSOT Press, 1991), 26–64 (45–47), accepts that the historian should be first and foremost concerned with primary sources, produced in the course of the events as they were happening, rather than with sources produced after the events, which he (tendentiously) describes as designed "to clarify for future generations how things were *thought* [my emphasis] to have happened" (46).

[34] Thus, e.g., G. W. Ahlström, "The role of archaeological and literary remains in reconstructing Israel's history," in D.V. Edelman, ed., *The Fabric of History: Text, Artifact and Israel's Past* (JSOTSup 127; Sheffield: JSOT Press, 1991), 116–41.

[35] Thus, e.g., P. R. Davies, *In Search of "Ancient Israel"* (JSOTSup 148; Sheffield: JSOT Press, 1992), 32–36: cf. further the discussion of these pages below.

[36] My view on dating and its implications in summary is as follows. I do not believe that those who have plausibly argued for the ongoing shaping of, e.g., Genesis–Kings in the postexilic period have thereby demonstrated that Genesis–Kings is essentially and substantially itself late, and there are on the contrary many good reasons for thinking that it is not. There is in any case no good reason to think that the late date of a composition (if it were established) would inevitably imply that the composition would be less helpful than other sources of information to the modern historian interested in Israel's past. No implication follows from dating in itself.

[37] B. Becking, "Inscribed seals as evidence for biblical Israel? Jeremiah 40:7–41:15 *par example*," in Grabbe, *History*, 65–83 (68), asserts that a detective pursuing a murder inquiry is better off than an historian, since the former is in a position to check eyewitness reports. I cannot see, however, how mere access to eyewitness reports places one person in a better or worse position in respect of the other. There is no necessary correlation between the sort of interaction that "witnesses" have with events and the quality of access to events provided to others through it.

[38] H. Niehr, "Some aspects of working with the textual sources," in Grabbe,

History, 156–65 (157), insists that a clear distinction between primary and secondary sources must be upheld, on the ground that the primary sources "did not undergo the censorship exercised by, for example, the Deuteronomistic theologians nor were they submitted to the process of canonization." This is to assume that we already know that the Hebrew Bible is problematic in respect of the way in which it mediates the past (because of "censorship" and "canonization") and that other sources of information are not. Niehr believes, in fact, that the historical reliability of the Assyrian sources has recently been "shown" to be very high (158). The delusion of knowledge thus returns to wreak its havoc on rational argument. In relation to which "facts" do we "know" that Deuteronomistic redaction and canonical process have distorted the past in passing it on, and that Assyrian sources have not? What real basis is there for a distinction between these two kinds of data?

[39] Thompson's view, e.g., is that an "understanding of the coherence of the biblical tradition, as arising out [*sic*] first within intellectual milieu [*sic*] of the Persian period, causes great difficulty in affirming the historicity of the Israel of tradition at all" (T. L. Thompson, *Early History of the Israelite People from the Written and Archaeological Sources* [SHANE 4; Leiden: Brill, 1992], 353–54; cf. my "Ideologies," 597, for reference to other comments along the same lines). I do not myself believe that he has demonstrated (or can demonstrate) that the coherence of the biblical tradition overall indeed arises only at such a late date. Even if he is correct, however, there is simply no reason to assume that a particular rendering of earlier tradition at a later date cannot also be a truthful rendering, any more than there is reason to assume that an early rendering cannot be false. Certainly modern historians have typically wished to argue that *their* very late renderings of earlier tradition are truthful—and indeed, more truthful than earlier attempts—even though (and precisely because) they supply fresh coherence in articulating the tradition.

[40] Davies, "Method," 703, para. 4, objects to this same point in "Ideologies," defending the reliability of (demonstrably late) modern historians over against (allegedly late) biblical writers by referring to both archaeological excavation reports and comparative ancient Near Eastern materials in terms of their capacity to provide the "possibility of confirmation." The fallacy of verification thus rears its head once more (as it does throughout his response: e.g. 701, last three lines; 702 lines 4–6, 19–20, 34–36). It is not (as Davies suggests) that I "dislike" the possibility of confirmation at all. It is, rather, that I consider the whole notion of "confirmation" problematic.

[41] The idea that archaeologists' "texts" are no more "objective" than others in respect of the past is slowly imposing itself on biblical studies (cf., e.g., Carroll, "Madonna," passim), albeit that there is little consistency in the way that scholars are handling the idea. It is mainly appealed to when scholars wish to question possible correspondence, rather than possible conflict, between archaeology and the Bible (cf. esp. my comments on Whitelam in "End," 289–92). That Syro-Palestinian archaeologists themselves should generally have failed hitherto to see the need for epistemological reflection on their own discipline is nothing short of astonishing (cf. Brandfon, "Limits," 37; Dever, "Identity," 9n8). For an excellent brief discussion in this area, see Schäfer-Lichtenberger, "Sociological and biblical views," 79–82, whose closing words on the limited usefulness of archaeology to the historian of Israel in respect of the 10th c. stand in stark contrast to many of the statements from those of a more positivistic orientation: "It is not up to archaeology to decide an essentially theoretic debate, whose course until now has demonstrated only that the so-called hard facts are determined by the discussants' perspectives" (82).

[42] There has been a general tendency among historians both recent and not so recent, and whether focusing on biblical or extra-biblical material, to view material which "looks" less ideological (e.g. annalistic material) than other

material (e.g. narrative material) as if it really were so in reality. The assumption is a curious one, as Barstad, ("History," 45–46n25) points out.

[43] There is no reason to think, for example, just because the narrative of David's rise to power is pro-Davidic, seeking to acquit David of guilt, and follows a literary pattern found elsewhere in the ancient Near East, that "the traditional materials about David cannot be regarded as an attempt to write *history* as such" and do not grant us access to the real past (N. P. Lemche, *Ancient Israel: A New History of Israelite Society* [Biblical Seminar 5; Sheffield: JSOT Press, 1988], 52–54). This is a straightforward *non sequitur* (of the kind also found, e.g., in Carroll's puzzling discussion of Omri, "Madonna," 95–96). The fact that we are dealing with apologetic material here, with what Lemche calls "an ideological programmatic composition," does not of itself demonstrate that what the text claims is untrue (e.g., and centrally, that David was indeed innocent); cf. the balanced comments of Brettler, *Creation*, 143. Thompson ("School," 686) seeks to redeem Lemche from the *non sequitur* by having him say (which he does not) that the stories, being ideological, cannot be *assumed* to be historiographical, suggesting that in "Ideologies" I misrepresent Lemche by lifting a quotation out of context. I assuredly do not; cf. further now Lemche, "Clio," 140n25, where Lemche himself makes clear, in addressing the same point in my article and in spite of his objection to it, that he does not allow for the possibility that ideological literature can truly represent the past—he allows only the possibility that historical information is *concealed* (my emphasis) in Old Testament historical narrative (cf. also the text with which his n25 is associated: the fact that the history of Israel in the Old Testament is a religious story "ensures that simple-minded paraphrases of it will, from a historian's point of view, never lead to anything but a false understanding of ancient Palestinian society, including also the two historical states of Israel and Judah").

[44] Cf. my comments on analogy in "Ideologies," 601n71. It is worth under-

lining here the intellectual incoherence of that modern approach to the past, reaching back at least as far as Hume, that claims to eschew dependence upon testimony, yet moves on to ground its beliefs about the past in "common human experience." This latter can itself only ever (at best) be a construct dependent upon testimony (that which some others whom we happen to believe have claimed to be their experience), and appeal to it often seems in fact to represent nothing other than a smokescreen in which it is hoped that the very limited nature of the writer's individual experience might be lost sight of. Real human experience (as opposed to the construct "common human experience") is vast, differentiated and complex.

[45] One occasionally comes across the assertion in current debate on our topic that, even if some of our biblical authors are indeed properly called historians, the fact that they are not *critical* historians (like some of the Greeks) makes access to the past for us through their texts problematic. This is a proverbial red herring. It is questionable enough to "deduce" from the *claims* of certain ancient Greeks about their critical intentions and the *absence of such claims* in ancient Hebrew texts (as in other ancient Near Eastern literary traditions) that there is inevitably a substantive difference *in reality* between (some) Greeks and (all) Hebrews. What is entirely curious, however, is the assumption that there is any necessary correlation between the *stated intentions* of an historian and the usefulness of his account of the past to *us*. One can as well imagine an author whose intentions to be critical caused him to fail to pass on important testimony about the real past, as one can imagine an author who uncritically passed such testimony on. Perhaps the imagination of some modern contributors to the debate on the history of Israel is limited at this point, however, as a result of an incapacity to believe that any gulf is possible between *their* intention to be critical, on the one hand, and their grasping of and transmission of historical truth, on the other.

[46] I thus stand much closer to the position adopted by, e.g., Brettler, *Creation*,

142–44, than to that adopted by, e.g., Thompson: note in particular the former's n53, which itself helpfully distinguishes the two positions. Cf. also Halpern, *First Historians*, 28: "history cannot base itself on predictability … Lacking universal axioms and theorems, it can be based on testimony only"; and, anticipating my next paragraph, "Our understanding of human history resembles our knowledge of the contemporary world."

[47] It is naturally the case that our approach to the past will be very much tied up with our approach to and experience of the present (cf. D. V. Edelman, "Doing history in biblical studies," in Edelman, ed., *Fabric*, 13–25 [15, 19]; J. M. Miller, "Is it possible to write a history of Israel without relying on the Hebrew Bible?," in Edelman, *Fabric*, 93–102 [100]). In this sense we always tell our own story in the course of attempting to tell others' stories. It is, indeed, a good test of the worth of any "method" adopted in respect of external reality, whether past or present, to consider whether we are in fact able to (and do) live with it consistently. The running of such a test in relation to everyday life, I submit, would have saved more than one historian of Israel (and indeed more than one literary critic) from adopting implausible positions on a whole range of matters. Sufficient *contemplation* of everyday life in all its complexity, indeed, would have increased the capacity for imagination in historiographical work far beyond that which is often apparent. Narrowness of vision in the present can only ever produce narrowness of vision in respect of the past. Cf. further D. Edelman, "Saul ben Kish in history and tradition," in Fritz and Davies, *Origins*, 142–59 (143): "Most histories are created by linking together individual data into chains of cause and effect based on logical processing; real life does not necessarily operate by the same neat, rational principles. What is plausible, then, is not necessarily what actually happened." The whole discussion of method on pp. 142–48 is most perceptive and illuminating, underlining the complexity of the historian's task.

[48] It is just as possible to lose confidence in external textual reality as it is in

any other sort of reality, if we press our doubts in respect of it further than is sensible and are not epistemologically open to the text as "other." The recent history of literary criticism more than adequately illustrates this point.

[49] Thus, to answer Thompson's question in "School," 687, I certainly have no objection in principle to returning to what he calls "Nothian paraphrases," or the "uncritical harmonizations" linked to the old Albright school, if what he means is a careful synthesis of biblical and non-biblical data to produce a composite portrait of the past which takes the biblical testimony about that past with great seriousness. I do not think that Noth, e.g., was always right; but he had a far more sensible approach than Thompson to the relationship between biblical and extra-biblical evidence (cf., e.g., M. Noth, *History of Israel* [ET, 2d ed.; New York: Harper and Row, 1960], 42–49).

[50] As the remainder of this essay itself should make clear, I am not here suggesting a distinction between those who approach reality with sets of general beliefs already in place about it, and those who do not. No one is "epistemologically open" in the sense that they possess no such beliefs. A rational person will, nevertheless, recognize the provisional nature of all beliefs, and will wish to be sufficiently open to the entire realm of reality external to him/her that false belief stands some chance of being discovered.

[51] An associated reason has to do, I believe, with the particular socio-historical location of the historians. It is clear enough, as Barstad argues ("History," 50–51, 63), that there has not in fact been any "paradigm shift" among historians since the 1960s of the kind claimed by Thompson and Lemche. What there *has* clearly been is an increase in skepticism with regard to the Bible as historical source. In reflecting upon the reasons for this, I find Thompson's comments ("School," 694–695n32) quite fascinating, in as much as they reveal how far a romantic attachment to "1968" shapes his approach to reality. It is not surprising, in the light of these comments, that biblical tradition, as well as scholarship predating the 1960s that depended so much upon it in formulating its ideas about

Israel's history, should attract such emotionally-charged skepticism from him. Nor is it surprising, indeed, that an academic culture shaped directly or indirectly by the *Zeitgeist* of the 1960s should have been in general so devoted to individual "freedom" and so antagonistic to "tradition." Some of us who are younger scholars, on the other hand, find ourselves wondering whether this anti-conservative, anti-traditional passion aids clarity of thought any more than the anti-liberal, anti-critical thought that it opposes, and indeed whether it is has noticeably improved the world. "1968" is long ago, and those of us who did not experience it as adults find it difficult to see any reason why it should be taken as a (the?) defining moment in history.

[52] There is a particular prejudice against *religiously motivated* testimony (cf., e.g., the two quotes from Ahlström cited in "Ideologies," 600n70, to which may be added Becking, "Seals," 70: "In view of the religious character of the composition, DtrH cannot be viewed as a primary historical source" [cf. also p. 71 on Jeremiah]). I am not unaware that this prejudice is of long standing (Grabbe, "Creatures," 21n6). I am only surprised that the length of time it has survived is thought to be sufficient justification of it, doubting as I do that scholars would allow the defence of any other prejudice on similar grounds. Are there any good *reasons* why this tradition of reading should be maintained? The prejudice in question is, in my view, not unrelated to the commonly found prejudice against religiously inclined *scholars* (magnificently expressed in Carroll, "Madonna," 85–86).

[53] Thompson, "School," 697, following Davies, *Search*, while ignoring my criticism of Davies' argument ("Ideologies," 599–600). Becking, "Seals," 68, rightly notes (consistent with my own criticism of Davies) that: "He, correctly, sees 'ancient Israel' as a product of the mind of biblical scholars. He fails to see, however, that what he calls 'historical Israel' is a product of the mind too."

[54] Thompson is right to say ("School," 690, lines 17–18) that he himself never explicitly stated that "events … may be directly observed," and it was careless

of me to word my criticism of his position on "knowledge" in the way I did, not least because it has given him the opportunity to distract attention from its weaknesses. What he explicitly said (Thompson, *Early History*, 61) was that the heart of historical science is "the specific and unique *observation* [my emphasis] of what is known," distinguishing this from processes involving probability and analogy. He appears to repeat the distinction a few lines further on in his response to me ("School," 690), when he differentiates between knowledge (connected with texts and potsherds) and speculation (moving beyond these and beginning to guess), as if the process of "observing" were a straightforward one. Events, he claims, "can be *directly described* [my emphasis] on the basis of evidence." It is precisely this sharp contrast between hypothesis, on the one hand, and direct access to events, on the other hand—between guesswork and knowledge—that I question. One does not have to read far into Thompson's writings to discover that the distinction, however questionable, is fundamental to his thinking (cf., e.g., "Defining history," 182, where "independent historical knowledge" will one day supposedly enable us to make judgments about the biblical tradition; or T. L. Thompson, "The intellectual matrix of early biblical narrative: Inclusive monotheism in Persian Period Palestine," in D. V. Edelman, ed., *The Triumph of Elohim: From Yahwisms to Judaisms* [Kampen: Kos Pharos, 1995], 107–24 [108]). As Barstad ("History," 50–51) rightly points out: "Lemche and Thompson, apparently unaware of the fact that what we may call a conventional concept of history today is *highly* problematic, still work within the parameters of historical critical research, assuming that history is a science and that one must work with 'hard' facts."

[55] Thus, e.g., Grabbe, "Creatures," 24–26, and implicitly in his closing comments on 29n25. In respect of his challenge to me here to deal with Josh 1–15, I respond thus (in the context of this section of my current paper): I will accept his challenge to measure the distance between story and history if he will first of all tell me where the history is, outside the story, in respect of which I am to

measure this distance. Presumably he is referring here to testimony embodied in non-biblical sources.

[56] Cf. Davies, "Whose history?," 105: "If we have no positive grounds for thinking that a biblical account is historically useful, we cannot really adopt it as history. True, the result will be that we have less history than we might. But what little we have we can at least claim to know (in whatever sense we 'know' the distant past); this, in my opinion, is better than having more history than we might, much of which we do not know at all, since it consists merely of unverifiable stories." The fact of the matter, however, is that history *is* the telling and retelling of unverifiable stories (Collingwood's "reenactment" of the past), and that the kind of historical knowledged beyond tradition and testimony that Davies seeks is a mirage. We should certainly expect the story now told to have internal coherence and comprehensiveness in terms of the "evidence" that is drawn into it; but that is all that we can sensibly ask. To press the point in respect of Davies himself: is the story that he tells of the Assyrian invasion of Judah (see further below) itself truly a *verifiable* story?

[57] Cf. Halpern, *First Historians*, 3–29, who characterizes scholarship in this mode as "negative fundamentalistism."

[58] It is encouraging, in the aftermath of "Method," to find now such a healthy emphasis on pluralism in historiography in Davies, "Whose history?," 117–20. The essay itself, one must say, still leaves the impression that the generosity implied by this section of it is not to be extended to those who think it acceptable, for good reasons, to use the Hebrew Bible as their major source in composing their historiography. The theoretical pluralism stands in some tension with the total argument. I am happy to accept the author's verbal assurance to me, however, that broad pluralism is indeed what he now advocates.

[59] For a clear and helpful summary of the number and character of the Assyrian data relating to Sennacherib's third campaign, see A. R. Millard, "Sennacherib's attack on Hezekiah," *TynBul* 36 (1985): 61–77.

[60] Cf. O. Borowski, "Hezekiah's reforms and the revolt against Assyria," *BA* 58 (1995): 148–55, for a convenient summary. With regard to "Hezekiah's tunnel," J. Rogerson and P. R. Davies ("Was the Siloam Tunnel built by Hezekiah?," *BA* 59 [1996]: 138–49) allow only that Warren's Shaft may be Hezekian, arguing that the tunnel is Hasmonean, although I find convincing the rejoinders on the basis of the palaeography of the Siloam inscription by R. S. Hendel ("The date of the Siloam inscription: A rejoinder to Rogerson and Davies," *BA* 59 (1996): 233–37) and on the basis of the archaeology and history by J. M. Cahill ("A rejoinder to 'Was the Siloam Tunnel built by Hezekiah," *BA* 60 (1997): 184–185). For discussion of the economic context of Hezekiah's revolt, cf. D. Hopkins, "Bare bones: Putting flesh on the economics of ancient Israel," in Fritz and Davies, *Origins*, 121–39.

[61] Those who do require it can consult, for a brief account of the Kings and Isaiah passages, I. W. Provan, *1–2 Kings* (OTG; Sheffield: Sheffield Academic Press, 1997), 57–60. The Chronicler, in pursuit of a vision of Davidic kingship relating to the future messiah, tends to avoid mentioning the failures of Judean kings. This perhaps explains the omission of the attempted Hezekian compromise. Aside from that, however, his message is much the same as Kings. Faithfulness to the living God and his laws makes a difference to Israel's historical experience; Israel knows blessing in obedience, even in the face of overwhelming odds (the addition of 32:7–8 makes this explicit). For a fuller discussion of the ideology of Chronicles, see H. G. M. Williamson, *1 and 2 Chronicles* (NCB; London: Marshall, Morgan and Scott, 1982), 24–33; S. Japhet, *The Ideology of the Book of Chronicles and Its Place in Biblical Thought* (BEATAJ 9; ET; Frankfurt: Peter Lang, 1989).

[62] K. L. Younger, Jr. *Ancient Conquest Accounts: A Study in Ancient Near Eastern and Biblical History Writing* (JSOTSup 98; Sheffield: JSOT Press, 1990), 61–124.

[63] 2 Chronicles provides further information on these preparations (32:3–5),

and there is no good reason to doubt its account.

[64] This is unsurprising, when it is realized that according to Sennacherib's own account the coalition had already early in the campaign collapsed. Luli king of Sidon had fled and his cities had been brought to submission; others had also submitted, or in the case of Sidqia of Ashkelon had been deported to Assyria.

[65] This move is not unparalleled. The practice of besieging a major city while continuing operations elsewhere in the surrounding region is known also from Tiglath-pileser's campaigns in Syria in 743–740 BC Lachish was itself soon overwhelmed by Sennacherib, as implied by 2 Kgs 19:8; claimed also by the Assyrian reliefs and associated text which portray the siege and conquest of the city; and illustrated by the discoveries of archaeologists: cf. W. Dever, "Archaeology, material culture and the early monarchical period in Israel," in Edelman, *Fabric*, 103–15 (106–108). I am puzzled by Dever's assertion, however, that we cannot "sidestep" the challenge of archaeology to biblical historiography here "by insisting that we simply have two differing but complementary versions of what really took place." I see nothing in the data that he describes that leads me to think it *is* "sidestepping" anything to suggest such a reading of our sources.

[66] I take the opportunity here to correct a misunderstanding in Carroll, "Madonna," 90n19. I have never argued that any narrative event is "historical rather than legendary because the 'miraculous' must be factored into any competent historical reading of the Bible by historians today." One cannot (should not) short-circuit the genre issue, nor indeed any other issue, by the appeal to miracle, and one certainly cannot ignore, even in a case where one is convinced that the text overall means to refer to past reality, the question of how far narrative art and theology are playing their part in shaping the text. There is no reason to think, on the other hand, that past reality will always conform to the expectations we may have of it, and that unusual or unique (and even unexplainable) events cannot occur. Everyday reality, I suggest, is likewise a mixture of the "normal" and the surprising. I do not press the word

"miracle" in the context of a general discussion with others whom I know do not share my religious worldview, any more than I press, in the particular case under discussion here, the interpretative "the angel of Yahweh ... struck down." I certainly assert, however, that anyone seriously interested in the past rather than only in their own ideology should be as open to the possibility of "highly unusual events" in the past as they are sensitive to issues of literary genre, and should not foreclose consideration of individual cases as a result of a method which in practice (if not always in theory) equates improbability with impossibility. On the importance (and rationality) of openness to the "incredible report," see further Coady, *Testimony*, 178–98.

[67] The Kings account differs from the Assyrian account in what it has to say about the timing and content of the tribute paid by Hezekiah to Sennacherib; and it may well be the case that here we must make a decision about how far what one or both accounts has to say on this point has more to do with the overall purposes of the texts than with the past which they describe (see, e.g., Younger, *Conquest Accounts*, 122–24, for some interesting comments on the significance of material goods in the Assyrian texts). There is no reason to think, however, that Hezekiah did not indeed both attempt to buy Sennacherib off before the siege and provide future security for himself after it was over. In this case our texts are simply selecting differing aspects of the events for their narratives.

[68] Davies, *Search*, 32–36.

[69] Provan, *Kings*, 57–64. I choose this example again because it is an especially good one, and not because I have any particular reason to concentrate on Davies' unique contributions to recent debate on the history of Israel. I take the opportunity to comment, however, on his response to my *JBL* article, in which he at one point joins Thompson in his accusations of distortion, and with just as little justification (Davies, "Method," 704). His claim that I have engaged in "outright falsification" of his argument fails to note that I myself

refer to one of the passages Davies cites (on 704) precisely to show that, while he *claims* to have given reasons for his distinction between earlier biblical texts and Ezra–Nehemiah, these reasons are not convincing ("Ideologies," 604n80).

[70] Davies, *Search*, 34 (top).

[71] Ibid., 35.

[72] Ibid., 34: "Sennacherib's account belongs with a number of other similar texts which serve the vanity of the Assyrian monarchs, sustain the loyalty and cohesion of the Assyrian nation, and probably intend to cow would-be rebels into renouncing thoughts of rebellion."

[73] It is worth recalling in this context that Leopold von Ranke (1795–1886), to whom scholars often refer when they articulate the ideal of seeking *wie es eigentlich gewesen ist*, was himself "the foremost mythmaker of the Bismarckian National State" (A. Richardson, *History Sacred and Profane* [London: SCM, 1964], 175).

[74] Davies, "Whose history?," 109.

[75] Davies himself elsewhere appears to accept the wisdom of this approach to life, if not to history: P. R. Davies, "Introduction," in Fritz and Davies, *Origins*, 11–21 (13).

[76] P. Ricoeur, *Freud and Philosophy: An Essay on Interpretation* (ET; New Haven: Yale University Press, 1970), 15.

[77] Lewis, *The Last Battle*, 135.

CHAPTER ELEVEN

[1] This involves among other things, of course, acknowledging that the version of Christianity that Nietzsche was attacking is not particularly biblical. Biblical faith does not privilege soul *over* body, mind *over* senses, duty *over* desire, reality *over* appearance, and the timeless *over* the temporal. It is not surprising that versions of Christianity which do should alienate those who take humanness seriously. Nietzsche's critique of Christian *religion* must be heard, even if we do

not in the end accept that it is a valid critique of Christian *faith*, and even if we see all too clearly the darkness into which Nietzschean philosophy leads us.

[2] Walter Brueggemann, *Theology of the Old Testament: Testimony, Dispute, Advocacy* (Minneapolis: Fortress, 1997), 184–85.

[3] Ibid., 185.

[4] I am not claiming that the ten commandments themselves tell us everything there is to know about the good society and about loving our neighbor. In particular, it is apparent that they largely comprise negative commandments that in the first instance tell certain kinds of Israelites (i.e. they do not address women and slaves) what they *should not* do, rather than telling all Israelites what they *should* do. Biblical ethics are not contained within commandments of this kind, as Jesus constantly made clear (e.g. Luke 18:18–22). The correction between worship of God and treatment of fellow human beings is nevertheless a fundamental one in biblical thinking, and it is well-illustrated in the ten commandments as elsewhere.

[5] We note verses like Matt 10:25; 12:24, 27; Mark 3:22; Luke 11:15, 18, 19, e.g., which refer to "Beelzebub" or "Beelzebul" (depending on the ms.) and remind us of Old Testament verses like 2 Kgs 1:2, where we read of "Baal-Zebub," lit. "Baal/lord of the flies." Baal-Zebub may itself be a deliberate Hebrew corruption of "Baal-Zebul" ("Baal the exalted"), intended to express the biblical authors' scorn of or hostility towards this "deity."

[6] Leland Ryken, James C. Whilhoit and Tremper Longman III, eds., *Dictionary of Biblical Imagery* (Downers Grove: InterVarsity, 1998), 9.

[7] The passage is cited from Herbert Schlossberg, *Idols for Destruction: Christian Faith and its Confrontation with American Society* (Nashville: Nelson, 1983), 40.

[8] David Lyon, *The Steeple's Shadow: On the Myths and Realities of Secularization* (Grand Rapids: Eerdmans, 1987), 2.

[9] Ibid., 46.

[10] Ibid., 96.

[11] For a full discussion, see Schlossberg, *Idols*, ch. 5, from whose pages the Hegel citation is taken (178); and Jacques Ellul, *The New Demons* (trans. C. Edward Hopkin; New York: Seabury, 1973), chs. 3 and 6.

[12] For a concise treatment of the "war of myths" in which Christians are, and should consciously be, involved, see Ched Myers, *Binding the Strong Man: A Political Reading of Mark's Story of Jesus* (Maryknoll, NY: Orbis, 1988), 14–21.

[13] Cited from Moshe Habertal and Avishai Margalit, *Idolatry* (trans. Naomi Goldblum; Cambridge: Harvard University Press, 1992), 243.

[14] Schlossberg, *Idols*, 311.

[15] Ibid.

[16] Ibid., 139.

[17] Myers, *Binding*, 15.

[18] Lyon, *Shadow*, 106.

[19] Schlossberg, e.g., examines alongside idols of power and mammon those of history, humanity, nature, and religion, and others have their own favorite selection, which can include household gods such as sports. There is nothing in creation that cannot be the focus of idolatrous worship.

[20] On the last of these professional groups, see in particular Paul C. Vitz, *Psychology as Religion: The Cult of Self-Worship* (Grand Rapids: Eerdmans, 1977); and *idem*, "Leaving Psychology Behind," in Os Guinness and John Seel, eds., *No God But God* (Chicago: Moody, 1992), 95–110.

[21] Schlossberg, *Idols*, 40, recalls Arnold Toynbee's conclusion, having studied civilizations across the whole span of history, that self-worship has always been the paramount religion of humankind.

[22] Lyon, *Shadow*, 109.

[23] Schlossberg, *Idols*, 228–29.

[24] Alan Richardson, *History Sacred and Profane* (London: SCM, 1964), 249.

[25] Ellul, *Demons*, 228.

[26] On work and family as idols, see J. A. Walter, *Sacred Cows: Exploring Contemporary Idolatry* (Grand Rapids: Zondervan, 1980), 25–84; and Janet Fishburn, *Confronting the Idolatry of the Family: A New Vision for the Household of God* (Nashville: Abingdon, 1991), 19–87.

[27] Os Guinness, "Sounding Out the Idols of Church Growth," in Guinness and Seel, *No God But God*, 151–74.

[28] David F. Wells, "The D-Min-ization of the Ministry," in Guinness and Seel, *No God But God*, 174–88.

[29] See further Vinoth Ramachandra, *Gods That Fail: Modern Idolatry and Christian Mission* (Carlisle: Paternoster, 1996), esp. chs. 2 and 8.

[30] M. Buber, *I and Thou* (trans. R. G. Smith; 2d ed.; Edinburgh: T&T Clark, 1959), 104–106—the English slightly altered and clarified by myself. I am grateful to my friend and colleague Craig M. Gay for drawing my attention to this passage and take this opportunity to mention his important recent book, which is directly relevant to the topic of this paper: *The Way of the (Modern) World: Or, Why It's Tempting to Live as if God Doesn't Exist* (Grand Rapids: Eerdmans, 1998).

[31] Eugene H. Peterson, *Subversive Spirituality* (Grand Rapids/Vancouver: Eerdmans/Regent College, 1997), 30.

CHAPTER TWELVE

[1] The substance of this essay represents my inaugural lecture as Marshall Sheppard Professor of Biblical Studies at Regent College in Vancouver, delivered on 22 February 1998. I am delighted to be able to contribute it in honor of my esteemed friend and colleague Ron Clements, with particular gratitude for his kindness and support during my first tenure of an academic position at King's College London during 1986–88. I should like also to thank my teaching assistant, Ian Scott, for his help in preparing this essay for publication.

² I shall spare the reader long footnotes in respect of what follows—the tedious listing of scholars who have taken this or that view of the hypothetical entities now under discussion. Those who do not know the field may consult either of the following recent books: S. L. McKenzie, *The Trouble with Kings: The Composition of the Book of Kings in the Deuteronomistic History* (VTSup 42; Leiden: Brill, 1991); and G. Keys, *The Wages of Sin: A Reappraisal of the "Succession Narrative,"* (JSOTSup 221; Sheffield: Sheffield Academic Press, 1996).

³ Keys, *Wages*, 14. The emphasis is my own.

⁴ P. R. Ackroyd, "The Succession Narrative (so-called)," *Int* 35 (1981): 383–96 (396).

⁵ It is indeed striking that even those readers who have moved in the direction of "complex unity" have often found themselves unable quite to leave the past behind. Thus even D. M. Gunn, *The Story of King David: Genre and Interpretation* (JSOTSup 6; Sheffield: JSOT Press, 1978), whose overall approach to the content of 2 Samuel is quite different from that of many preceding scholars, nevertheless offers his reflections within the Rost framework (note his apology for so doing, 13–16), opining that the narrative begins with 2 Samuel 2. Likewise J. P. Fokkelman, *Narrative Art and Poetry in the Books of Samuel: A Full Interpretation based on Stylistic and Structural Analyses. I. King David (2 Sam. 9–20 & 2 Kings 1–2)* [SSN 20; Assen: Van Gorcum, 1981]), thoroughly unconvinced of the Rost hypothesis in terms of the thematic question—claiming that Rost's spell has already been broken, and evidently not entirely comfortable with the traditional delimitation of the text as including only 2 Samuel 9–20 and 1 Kings 1–2—nevertheless accepts precisely this material as the subject matter upon which he is to work (pp. 1–20), and this despite some scathing commentary on the treatment of the text to which the Rost hypothesis has led (e.g. 417–19). The intervening years have not seen much change, in this respect, to scholarly approaches to this section of text (see further below).

⁶ Thus R. A. Carlson, *David the Chosen King: A Traditio-Historical Approach to*

the Second Book of Samuel (Uppsala: Almqvist and Wiksell, 1964) still stands out as an oddity in his thoroughgoing rejection of the Rost hypothesis. Subsequent scholarship has generally sought to marginalize Carlson more than it has sought to engage with his arguments—one notable exception being Ackroyd, "Succession Narrative," who has himself been largely ignored to this point.

[7] Keys' view (*Wages*) is that there is indeed a major textual unit to be found in 2 Samuel, but that it stretches only from chapter 10 to chapter 20, and is not particularly about any succession. The idea of the "textual unit" survives, even though the idea of succession does not; and yet Keys herself assembles in one volume most of the evidence that calls into question any Rost-like approach to the text, and herself presents her position as a departure from the Rost paradigm (see in particular 213–16, where she refers with approval to Ackroyd).

[8] Intriguingly, Ackroyd himself ("Succession Narrative," 396) already refers, in the context of his plea that we should not read the text too narrowly, to the possibility that the wisdom aspects of the text might point, explicitly or implicitly, to the significance of the stories. It is this intuition, I believe, that is confirmed by the less rigid reading of 2 Samuel–1 Kings that he advocates.

[9] Thus, e.g., G. H. Jones, *1 and 2 Kings* (NCB; 2 vols.; Grand Rapids: Eerdmans, 1984), straightforwardly accepts the existence of a Succession Narrative without raising any fundamental questions about it. Rost is said to have "established" that 2 Samuel 9–20 and 1 Kings 1–2 originally formed an unbroken narrative, and a detailed discussion of this source is then provided (Jones, *1 and 2 Kings*, 1:48–57). Later, at the beginning of his detailed discussion of 1 Kings 1–2, Jones has this to say: "For reasons noted in the Introduction ... these first two chapters are to be separated from the account of Solomon's reign in 3:1–11:43" (88). The fact that we so obviously have a source in chapters 1–2 means that there is to be "separation" between chapters 1–2 and 3–11; and indeed, later in the commentary it is the latter chapters only, treated as a block and independently of 1–2, that are included under the heading "The

Reign of Solomon" (119–247).

[10] I. W. Provan, *1 and 2 Kings* (NIBCOT; Peabody, MA: Hendrickson, 1995), 41–98. My reading of Solomon in this commentary builds upon and extends the insights of various other scholars noted therein.

[11] For an excellent brief treatment of the biblical wisdom theme, see R. E. Clements, *Wisdom in Theology* (Grand Rapids: Eerdmans, 1992).

[12] I refer to literature that contributes directly to an understanding of the wisdom theme in 2 Samuel 9–20 and 1 Kings 1–2, and/or helps us to understand more fully the overall narrative as an artistically-constructed piece of work and thus to appreciate how its various wisdom elements function. Aside from the volumes by Carlson, Gunn and Fokkelman already cited, I am thinking chiefly of: J. Blenkinsopp, "Theme and motif in the Succession History (2 Sam. XI 2 ff.) and "The Yahwist Corpus," in G. W. Anderson et al., eds., *Volume du Congrès: Genève 1965* (VTSup 15; Leiden: Brill, 1966), 44–57; L. Delekat, "Tendenz und Theologie der David-Salomo-Erzählung," in F. Maass, ed., *Das ferne und nahe Wort* (L. Rost Festschrift; BZAW 105; Berlin: Töpelmann, 1967), 26–36; W. Brueggemann, "The Trusted Creature," *CBQ* 31 (1969): 484–98; R. N. Whybray, *The Succession Narrative: A Study of II Sam. 9–20 and 1 Kings 1 and 2* (SBT; London: SCM, 1968); J. L. Crenshaw, "Method in Determining Wisdom Influence upon 'Historical' Literature," *JBL* 88 (1969): 129–42; H.-J. Hermisson, "Weisheit und Geschichte," in H. W. Wolff, ed., *Probleme biblischer Theologie: Gerhard von Rad zum 70. Geburtstag* (Munich: Chr. Kaiser, 1971), 136–54; W. Brueggemann, "On Trust and Freedom: A Study of Faith in the Succession Narrative," *Int* 26 (1972): 3–19; J. S. Ackerman, "Knowing Good and Evil: A Literary Analysis of the Court History in 2 Samuel 9–20 and 1 Kings 1–2," *JBL* 109 (1990): 41–60; and R. Polzin, *David and the Deuteronomist: A Literary Study of the Deuteronomic History* (Bloomington: Indiana University Press, 1993). A considerable amount of insight into the way in which wisdom functions within the story can be gained from this

literature, even though the authors mentioned are sometimes so interested in other questions (such as *Tendenz* or genre) that they themselves do not develop the insights, and are sometimes so captivated (in my view) by a romantic view of David that they do not develop the insights rightly.

[13] Ackerman, "Knowing," 42.

[14] Fokkelman, *Art*, 126–47.

[15] Fokkelman himself resists this reading (*Art*, 142–44), arguing for the cleverness of David and the sincerity of the woman. He is only able to defend this position, however, by introducing the most extravagant of speculations about what is implicit in the text. Far more convincing is the reading of Whybray, *Succession Narrative*, 36–37, who writes of David's "absurd ineptitude" when confronted (among other things) with the fictions of 2 Samuel 12 and 14.

[16] Ackerman, "Knowing," 52.

[17] Polzin, *David*, 141.

[18] The way in which David adheres to the letter of the oath regarding Absalom in 2 Samuel 14:21–24, while failing to adhere to its spirit, also foreshadows his advice to his son about Shimei, and Solomon's subsequent behavior in respect of the latter, in 1 Kings 2. See further Provan, *1 and 2 Kings*, 31–42; and *idem*, "Why Barzillai of Gilead (1 Kgs 2:7)?: Narrative Art and the Hermeneutics of Suspicion in Kings 1–2," *TynBul* 46 (1994): 103–16.

[19] Fokkelman, *Art*, 156–57.

[20] Ibid., 158–61.

[21] Polzin, *David*, 169.

[22] The theme continues in passages like 1 Kings 22, where it is demonstrated that false prophets are as hopeless from this point of view as counsellors.

[23] Polzin, *David*, 168.

[24] Ackerman, "Knowing," 42, 51.

[25] The phrase is Carlson's, *David*, who places the entire second part of 2 Samuel (chs. 9–24) under this heading. This precise division of the book at ch. 9

owes more to Rost's theory that Carlson disavows, of course, than to his own analysis of the content (since David does not, in fact, come under the curse until chs. 11–12)—a further indication of the tenacity of critical tradition.

[26] On this point, see further W. Brueggemann, *First and Second Samuel* (Int; Louisville: John Knox, 1990), 312–13.

[27] Ackerman, "Knowing," 60.

[28] Ibid., 56.

[29] I note, for example, that Ackerman ("Knowing," 56–57), almost a decade after Ackroyd and for all his perceptiveness about the ways in which the books of Samuel constitute a unified work, cannot quite bring himself to believe in one author for the work, but posits instead a Court History that deliberately continues themes and elements from the History of David's Rise. I note further that Polzin (*David*), whose wonderful treatment of the David story provides countless examples of the art and ambiguity, the theological complexity of the book, cannot prevent himself speaking about a Deuteronomist, even though his description of the story bursts through the boundaries that exist in most people's minds regarding what this term means.

CHAPTER THIRTEEN

[1] See, e.g., Robert Gordis, *The Song of Songs and Lamentations* (rev. and aug. ed.; New York: Ktav, 1974), 16–18; Marcia Falk, *Love Lyrics from the Bible* (Bible and Literature 4; Sheffield: Almond, 1982), 62–70; John G. Snaith, *The Song of Songs* (NCB; London: Marshall Pickering, 1993), 6–8.

[2] Roland E. Murphy, *The Song of Songs* (Hermeneia; Minneapolis: Fortress, 1990), 151.

[3] Nothing is in fact generally made of it in modern writing on the Song: cf. Snaith, *Song*, 45–57; Tom Gledhill, *The Message of the Song of Songs: The Lyrics of Love* (BST; Leicester: InterVarsity, 1994), 143–52; Othmar Keel, *The Song of Songs* (CC; trans. F. J. Gaiser; Minneapolis: Fortress, 1994), 119–37. George

A. F. Knight and Friedemann W. Golka, *Revelation of God: A Commentary on the Books of the Song of Songs and Jonah* (ITC; Grand Rapids: Eerdmans, 1988), 20–22, at least hints at the kind of reading of 3:6–11 for which I shall be arguing, when Knight suggests that the "editor has assumed it wise to contrast at this point the pomp and worldliness of a royal wedding with the simplicity and holiness of the union of two lovers from a village situation" (21); but the point is not made in pursuit of a link with 3:1–5.

[4] For the sake of convenience and accessibility to the nonspecialist in Hebrew, I shall refer to the NIV as the base English text in the following exegesis, although as we progress I shall offer various alternative translations.

[5] The mother's house is the natural home of the woman who is not married (cf. Gen 24:28; Ruth 1:8).

[6] If the word *love* in the charge is taken to refer to one of the lovers themselves, the charge could in principle be understood as a less ominous request not to disturb the beloved as he sleeps but to leave him in peace until he is eager to arise. Yet the focus of Song 8:6–7 is the terrible power of love, which follows closely on a similar aside to the daughters of Jerusalem in 8:4, so this suggests that we are to understand the charge as a warning. Because love can be devastating and overpowering, these young women should ensure that it is awakened only when the timing and circumstances are right. There is, in effect, "a time to embrace and a time to refrain" (Eccl 3:5). To awaken love when it does not desire to be woken is as dangerous as rousing the sleeping animal of modern proverbial tradition. The oath laid upon the Jerusalem women refers, appropriately, to gazelles (*ṣĕḇā'ôt*) and does (*'ayyālôt*); see also Song 2:7. The man himself is portrayed as a gazelle (*ṣĕḇî*) or young stag (*'ayyāl*) in Song 2:8–9, 17 and 8:14, whereas 4:5 and 7:3 compare the woman's breasts to two fawns of a gazelle (*ṣĕḇiyyāh*); cf. Prov 5:19, where the woman is "a loving doe, a graceful deer." The emphasis of the imagery falls upon, among others things, grace and beauty (underlined by the fact that *ṣĕḇî* also means "beauty," as in Ezek 7:20).

In shifting the focus from the singular "gazelle" and "doe" to the plural, the oath appears to set the particular relationship that is described in Song 3:1–4 (and in 2:3–6) in the context of all other similar relationships. The daughters of Jerusalem are to think of the "gazelles and does" generally (i.e., all lovers) as they consider whether to arouse or awaken love. The verse thus has a "love your neighbor as yourself" aspect to it, for these daughters of Jerusalem are themselves some of the "does" who might in the future be found embracing their "gazelles." They swear as those who have common cause with our speaker and his or her beloved.

[7] See also Gordis, *Song*, 18–23.

[8] See Marvin H. Pope, *Song of Songs* (AB 7C; Garden City: Doubleday, 1977), 441–42, for a discussion.

[9] See, e.g., Gillis Gerleman, *Ruth: Das Hohelied* (BKAT 18; 2d ed.; Neukirchen-Vluyn: Neukirchener, 1965). The Targum already thinks of it as a fixed structure, namely the Temple.

[10] Thus, e.g., Exod 8:3 [MT 7:28], where the *miṭṭāh* is in Pharaoh's *ḥăḏar miškāḇ*; cf. Song 3:1, 4 above.

[11] That is, "sixty" to David's "thirty"—itself a round number, cf. 2 Sam 23:24, 39.

[12] 1 Kgs 6:29–35; cf. also Ezekiel's temple in Ezek 40–42.

[13] The "bed" of v. 7, being a feminine noun, could itself in principle be connected with the pronoun *zōʾt*, and v. 7 could be the answer to the question in v. 6: "Who is this? ... The bed!" We might then understand *mî* (normally "who?") as meaning "what?" following Akkadian usage; or we might simply think of the bed itself as personified. It is by far the most natural reading of v. 6, however—when both normal Hebrew grammar and syntax and the similar question in 8:5 are considered—to understand the question as referring to a woman *on* the bed rather than to the bed itself. See further P. B. Dirksen, "Song of Songs 3:6–7," *VT* 39 (1989): 219–24.

[14] For example, Ps 107:33–38; Isa 32:15; Jer 4:26.

[15] See Leland Ryken, James C. Wilhoit, and Tremper Longman III, eds., *Dictionary of Biblical Imagery* (Downers Grove: InterVarsity, 1998), 315–17, 948–51.

[16] It should be noted that the women in v. 11 are invited to view only the crown, not a wedding. The word *'ăṭārāh* is itself ambiguous and could refer to a royal crown or a wedding garland (cf. Isa 61:10). Given the passage's satirical edge, it is possible that the intended picture is of Solomon reposing on his ridiculously overstated bed wearing nothing *but* his crown (cf. Amos 6:1–7 and Ezek 23:40–41, with its interesting association of illicit sexual conduct and misuse of sacrificial incense and oil). The invitation is, in essence, to view a pathetic spectacle.

[17] The speakers in Song 8:8–9 are not explicitly identified, but the mention of "little sister"; the role of brothers in overseeing the arrangements for the marriages of sisters elsewhere in the Old Testament (e.g., Gen 24:29–60; Judg 21:22), and the earlier reference to brothers in Song 1:6, lead us to think of the woman's brothers as the contributors at this point. It is not their precise identity that is the focus here, however, but their attitude toward their sister. They regard her as their possession ("we *have* a young sister") as well as their responsibility ("what shall we do for our sister for the day she is spoken for?"— that is, the day when her hand is requested in marriage, 1 Sam 25:39). They see their task, in other words, both as ensuring that men stay away from their sister until the proper time and as making sure that she is a prize catch when that time comes. They themselves are, evidently, the arbiters of what the proper time might be. Possession is also the focus of 8:11, 12b. Here Solomon himself owns something: a "vineyard" in Baal Hamon, which is entrusted to others so that they may "tend" its fruit (*nṭr*). The verbal root also appears twice in 1:6, where the woman tells the daughters of Jerusalem that her brothers made her "take care" of the vineyards, although she did not "take care" of her own. This particular Solomonic vineyard is extraordinarily valuable: "A man would bring for its fruit one thousand silver pieces" (8:11). The fantastic price alerts us to

the fact that we are not dealing here with a literal vineyard. The "vineyard" is, characteristically, simply a metaphor for a woman, one of the most valuable of Solomon's possessions in "Baal Hamon." The place name is interesting: not only does it mean "husband of a multitude" (alluding to Solomon's harem, as the phrase "one thousand" possibly also does; cf. 1 Kgs 11:3), but it also evokes through its use of Baal (the Canaanite deity so often mentioned in 1–2 Kings and elsewhere in the Old Testament) the story in 1 Kgs 11, where Solomon's many wives lead him into idolatry. Here is one prized possession among the many possessions of the idolater king (cf. Song 6:8).

[18] The most natural assumption is that the woman speaks throughout ch. 3, being the one who refers to the king in the third person also in 1:4, 12. It may even be that we are to think of 3:6–10 as a continuation of the dream in 3:1–4, as she invites the group of females around her ("daughters of Jerusalem," in v. 5; "daughters of Zion" in v. 11, probably in order to avoid immediate repetition of "daughters of Jerusalem" from v. 10) to consider the nature of these relationships in which she is alternately eager participant and reluctant victim (like the woman she observes in v. 6). The dream of vv. 1–4 bespeaks her fear of loss and even her longing to return to the safety and security of her youth.

[19] A second dream, possessing obvious points of contact with ch. 3 (although on this occasion the lover is lost and *not* found), is recounted in 5:2–7. Between the two dream sequences we find the intriguing verses in 4:1–5:1, the appropriateness of whose location in the book has not been sufficiently discussed. Responsive to the unsettling dream and distasteful vision of ch. 3, the beloved man now showers the woman with intimate affirmations, placing the "events" of ch. 3 in the context of their special relationship. He commends her for her beauty while respecting her as one who has her own boundaries and who must be wooed so that their physical acts of love will be truly mutual. The imagery is once again gentle and pastoral, in contrast to the imagery of the frightening dream and the fortified palace of ch. 3. What is striking about 4:3–4 in par-

ticular is the way in which the verses echo 3:6–11 not only in the reference to the warriors (*gibbôrîm*, 3:7, 4:4), but also in their use of the unique *miḏbār* in 4:3 (where presumably it means "mouth" in parallel to "lips"), which reminds us of the common *miḏbār*, "wilderness," in 3:6. It is as if the lover is recontextualizing his beloved's traumatic experience, placing it once again in a larger and more familiar framework (4:1, 5–6; referring back to 1:13, 15; 2:16–17). The fearsome warriors who guard the king's bed are now stripped of their weapons, which hang like trophies around the beloved's neck. The thought of the barren wilderness, which is the same royal bed, is replaced now by the thought of the beloved's mouth, described as "lovely" (*nā'weh*) but also evoking the image of the pastures (*ne'ōṯ*; sing. *nāwāh*) in which sheep and goats graze. Here is a "wilderness" (the beloved's mouth) that is fertile and inviting to one who is a "gazelle" (cf. 2:8–17). The idea of fertility may also be hinted at in the use of *śĕpāṯayim*, "lips," which is often used of riverbanks (e.g., Gen 41:3, 17) and in the use of *rimmôn*, "pomegranate," a well-known symbol of fertility. The connections between the chapters only serve to emphasize the contrast of the two relationships described therein. The woman is to Solomon only one among many daughters of Jerusalem—readily available and coerced to join him in his desert prison—but to her lover she is an expansive and fertile landscape, magnificent, flawless (v. 7), and self-possessed. She is to be affirmed and enjoyed rather than controlled. See further my commentary on Ecclesiastes and Song of Songs in the NIV Application series (Grand Rapids: Zondervan, 2001).

[20] On this and other aspects of the ambiguous presentation of Solomon's reign in 1–2 Kings, see Iain W. Provan, *1 and 2 Kings* (NIBCOT; Peabody, MA: Hendrickson, 1995), 23–102.

[21] For further details here, see again my commentary on Ecclesiastes and Song of Songs in the NIV Application series.

[22] The Hebrew phrase is *šiddāh wĕšiddôt* (NIV's "and a harem as well"), the

correct interpretation of which is arrived at, in my view, via Judg 5:30a, *raḥam raḥămāṯayim lĕrōʾš geḇer*: "a womb or two for each man." A phrase like this is often explained in terms of synecdoche, whereby part of something can stand for the whole; thus the NIV translation of Judg 5:30a: "a girl or two for each man." It is not always clear, however, that the intention is to refer to the whole female person rather than to the part in which the men, whose perspective dominates the text, are interested (whether "womb," because of child-bearing potential, or "breast," where it is perhaps the potential for sexual fulfillment that is in mind). In the context of Eccl 2:4–8, which is focused resolutely on possessions, we are thus led to the following translation of the second part of Eccl 2:8: "I acquired for myself male and female singers and the delights of the male—a breast or two." Even if translated "a girl or two," of course, the line would be no less offensive.

[23] Rikk E. Watts, "Women in the Gospels and Acts," *Crux* 35 (1999): 22–33.

CHAPTER FOURTEEN

[1] This "Theonomic" position is well outlined, for those interested in pursuing this topic, in G. L. Bahnsen, *Theonomy in Christian Ethics* (2d ed.; Phillipsburg, PA: Presbyterian and Reformed, 1984).

CHAPTER FIFTEEN

[1] This essay was conveniently reproduced in I. G. Barbour, ed., *Western Man and Environmental Ethics* (Reading: Addison-Wesley, 1973), 18–30. The quote is taken from p. 25.

[2] Gordon J. Wenham, *Genesis 1–15* (WBC; Waco: Word Books, 1987), 21.

[3] Lynn White, "The Historical Roots of our Ecologic crisis," *Science* 155 (1967):1203–7. This essay is conveniently reproduced in *Western Man and Environmental Ethics* (ed. I. G. Barbour; Reading, Mass.: Addison-Wesley, 1973) 18–30, and the quote comes from the latter (29).

⁴ Ibid., 25.

⁵ Psalm 8 further says that humans, having been created a little lower than the angels, are crowned with glory and made to rule the works of God's hands.

⁶ Wenham, *Genesis 1–15*, 33.

⁷ Whatever the significance of the fact that the creation of the woman is mentioned after the creation of *'ādām* in ch. 2, no interpretation of this fact which is not consistent with the basic thrust of Genesis 1:27–31 can be defended—at least, not if one is interested in reading Genesis 1–2 together. It is precisely joint identity as image of God and joint authority over creation that is in view in Genesis 1. That general statement about the image of God having been made, it is very difficult then to think that we are meant to draw any theological conclusion simply from the order of events as described in ch. 2. Certainly the mere fact that the woman apparently comes "after" the man of itself cannot be said to prove anything in particular about the importance of the man vis-à-vis the woman, nor about the authority that the man is alleged to have over the woman, since *'ādām* itself comes last in the chain of creation in Genesis 1 and is formed out of the ground in Genesis 2, and yet *'ādām* is not said on that basis to be less important than the rest of creation or indeed subordinate to it.

⁸ W. G. Lambert, Alan R. Millard and Miguel Civil, eds., *Atra-Hasis: The Babylonian Story of the Flood* (Oxford: Clarendon Press, 1969), 43.

⁹ This is contrary to the interpretation found in the NIV's translation of Genesis 6:12, which renders "all flesh" as "all the people"; cf. Genesis 6:19, 7:16, 8:17, and 9:16 for "all flesh" as referring to both humans and animals.

¹⁰ Ambrose, *De Nabuthe Jez.* 53, quoted in Justo L. Gonzalez, *Faith and Wealth: A History of Early Christian Ideas on the Origin, Significance and Use of Money* (New York: Harper & Row, 1990), 191.

¹¹ Ambrose, *De Nabuthe Jez.* 11, quoted in Gonzalez, *Faith and Wealth*, 191.

CHAPTER SIXTEEN

[1] *The Chicago Statement on Biblical Hermeneutics* (1982), Articles XXIV, XV and XVIII. The *Statement* is available in E. D. Radmacher and R. D. Preus, eds., *Hermeneutics, Inerrancy, and the Bible: Papers from ICBI Summit II* (Grand Rapids: Zondervan, 1984), 882–87.

[2] B. Ramm, *Protestant Biblical Interpretation: A Textbook of Hermeneutics* (3d rev. ed.; Grand Rapids: Baker, 1970), 1.

[3] Ibid.

[4] Ibid., 11.

[5] *Statement*, Article IX.

[6] Thus for Paul Ricoeur, "hermeneutics ... relates the technical problems of textual exegesis to the more general problems of meaning and language" (cited in A. C. Thiselton, *The Two Horizons: New Testament Hermeneutics and Philosophical Description with Special Reference to Heidegger, Bultmann, Gadamer and Wittgenstein* [Exeter: Paternoster, 1980], 8). See further D. E. Klemm, "Hermeneutics," in *Dictionary of Biblical Interpretation* (ed. J. H. Hayes; 2 vols.; Nashville: Abingdon, 1999), 1:497–502.

[7] See further K. J. Vanhoozer, *Is There a Meaning in This Text? The Bible, the Reader and the Morality of Literary Knowledge* (Grand Rapids: Zondervan, 1998), 15–35. Vanhoozer distinguishes three "ages" of criticism, which he labels "the age of the author" (characterized by interest in the author's intention); "the age of the text" (where the focus shifts to the question of what methods enable us to gain knowledge of the text); and "the age of the reader" (where the role of reader in construing or creating meaning is at the forefront).

[8] T. P. Weber, "New Dimensions in American Evangelical Theology: The Mainstreaming of Evangelical Theological Education," in *New Dimensions in Evangelical Thought: Essays in Honor of Millard J. Erickson* (ed. D. S. Dockery; Downers Grove: InterVarsity, 1998), 148–83 (149).

[9] This comes to expression, for example, in J. I. Packer, "Infallible Scripture

and the Role of Hermeneutics," in *Scripture and Truth* (ed. D. A. Carson and J. D. Woodbridge; Grand Rapids: Zondervan, 1983), 325–56 (327): "By evangelicalism I mean that multi-denominational Protestant constituency within the worldwide church that combines acknowledgment of the trustworthiness, sufficiency, and divine authority of the Bible with adherence to the New Testament account of the gospel of Christ and the way of faith in Him."

[10] Weber, "Dimensions," 150.

[11] Radmacher and Preus, *Hermeneutics*, ix. I do not myself believe this bold statement to be true. Perusal of the papers presented at the conference itself gives rise to doubts, because these papers not only disagree with each other in significant ways, but also because they often cite other evangelical scholars with whom they disagree. Geisler also provides a commentary on the *Statement* ("Explaining Hermeneutics: A Commentary on the Chicago Statement on Biblical Hermeneutics Articles of Affirmation and Denial," in Radmacher and Preus, *Hermeneutics*, 889–904) that is written in such a way as to suggest that it is *the* interpretation of the *Statement* rather than simply Geisler's own. For the sake of clarity in respect of what follows, I need to declare that I see no reason to concede this—not least because, again, the contributors to the conference do not give the impression of unanimity on various points, whether in their conference papers or in their other writings. I have not depended on Geisler's exegesis of the *Statement*, therefore, in seeking to understand what it is saying. I have remained focused on what the words of the *Statement* themselves appear to imply, taken in their grammatical-historical sense. I shall also occasionally refer, however, to Geisler's own views.

[12] The framers of the 1978 *Chicago Statement on Biblical Inerrancy* (available in W. Grudem, *Systematic Theology: An Introduction to Biblical Doctrine* [Leicester/Grand Rapids: InterVarsity/Zondervan, 1994], 1203–1207) explicitly state that divine inspiration does not confer omniscience on the biblical authors (Article IX). Yet at least some of those who argue the inerrantist position appear to

believe that this does not mean that a lack of omniscience is reflected in their *words*. Witness J. S. Feinberg's opposition to scholars who argue that the biblical writers, being time-bound in their statements, made some statements that are formally inaccurate, in his essay "Truth: Relationship of Theories of Truth to Hermeneutics," in Radmacher and Preus, *Hermeneutics*, 1–50 (15): "The Holy Spirit is also the author of Scripture. The Holy Spirit as omniscient is not time-bounded in His knowledge. Moreover, He obviously will not willfully deceive us … If the Holy Spirit refuses to deceive us in regard to whatever he knows, and if He knows everything … then His participation in the production of Scripture as co-author eliminates both willful deception, factual error, and doctrinal error of any kind." This view of things amounts to an extraordinary refusal to take seriously in practice, if not in theory, the genuine historicality of divine revelation. Note further the unconvincing nature of the same author's argument in "A Response to Adequacy of Language and Accommodation," in ibid., 377–90. Here he appears to argue that while God does necessarily accommodate himself to human ignorance in communicating with us, in order that we may understand what is said (e.g. "the realm of nature is spoken of in terms of physical properties and human emotions," 388), yet the writers of Scripture were able to transcend the ignorance of their day in inscripturating God's revelation. It is very difficult to understand how this could possibly be so, and indeed, a reading of the Bible itself does not encourage one in the belief that it *is* so. The words that our biblical authors use arise out of the world in which they live, and reflect what they understand at that point in time and culture—about God, about the world, and about human beings. For a similar problematic formulation of the matter, see Geisler, "Explaining Hermeneutics," 895, where he concedes that "God adapted Himself through human language so that his eternal truth could be understood by man in a temporal world," yet affirms that "while there is a divine adaptation (via language) to human finitude there is no accommodation to human error," failing to understand that the human understanding, expressed in human language, of one era may turn out to be inadequate when considered in relation to the human understanding, expressed in language, of a later one.

[13] Indeed, we should be more concerned about the implicitly Docetic view of Christ that often lies in the shadows of robust affirmations of inerrancy in the Bible that draw the kind of analogy between Christ and the Bible that the *Statement* draws.

[14] It would be entirely irrational, in fact, to "distrust the Bible" simply because it shares in the nature of all historical documents—that what it says, it says in time and culture. It would be worthy of our distrust only if it were shown to be intent on deceiving us or if, despite a lack of intent, it were found in fact to be misleading, once the implications of its time-bound statements were fully understood in relation to each other.

[15] Packer, "Infallible Scripture," 330–31. I cite this passage from this essay in full awareness that the author was himself a member of the drafting committee that produced the *Statement*, whose wording I am here criticizing. I do so because I believe that it is an excellent passage—one of many in the essay—whose implications lead in a direction that the *Statement on Biblical Hermeneutics* itself does not appear to take. Indeed, I am convinced that a *Statement* formed on the basis of the essay would look very different from the *Statement* that we actually have—which I assume to be, like all committee products, a patchwork of compromises made between different views.

[16] *The Chicago Statement on Biblical Inerrancy* appears to fail to avoid falling into this trap in its only reference to hermeneutics, albeit in the exposition that accompanies it (under "Authority: Christ and the Bible") rather than in any of the articles: "No hermeneutic ... of which the historical Christ is not the focal point is acceptable. Holy Scripture must be treated as *what it essentially is—the witness of the Father to the incarnate Son* [my italics]."

[17] Packer, "Infallible Scripture," 334–35. The *Statement on Biblical Hermeneutics*'

emphasis on propositions is very curious especially when one considers that Article X clearly states that "Scripture communicates God's truth to us verbally through a wide variety of literary forms," and that Article XIII affirms "that awareness of the literary categories, formal and stylistic, of the various parts of Scripture is essential for proper exegesis, and hence we value genre criticism as one of the many disciplines of biblical study." Geisler's commentary on Article X does not aid us in clarifying the matter (Geisler, "Explaining Hermeneutics," 895), for he appears to equate the term "propositional" in Article VI (although he erroneously refers to it as Article II) with the terms "verbal" and "sentential," in the course of acknowledging that "the Bible is a human book which uses normal literary forms." This is extremely confusing.

[18] It is consistent with the ways in which our biblical authors have a far more flexible understanding of the relationship of words to meanings that John in his Gospel can report the following (11:49–53): "But one of them, Caiaphas, who was high priest that year, said to them, 'You know nothing at all! You do not understand that it is better for you to have one man die for the people than to have the whole nation destroyed.' He did not say this on his own, but being high priest that year he prophesied that Jesus was about to die for the nation, and not for the nation only, but to gather into one the dispersed children of God." Caiaphas assuredly did not himself *mean* this; but he prophesied of it nonetheless.

[19] See I. W. Provan, V. P. Long, and T. Longman III, *A Biblical History of Israel* (Louisville: Westminster/John Knox, 2003), 3–104, for a thorough discussion of the nature of history, including the history of Israel.

[20] See K. L. Younger, Jr., *Ancient Conquest Accounts: A Study in Ancient Near Eastern and Biblical History Writing* (JSOTSup 98; Sheffield: JSOT Press, 1990).

[21] The structure of Genesis 1 is designed to emphasize what is important from the author's point of view—that the earth is ordered by God to allow habitation, specifically habitation of the earth by its creatures, including human creatures

who are the pinnacle of God's creation. There is no evidence that the interest is at all chronological (for example, day and night exist before there is a sun and moon), except in the logical sense that habitability must precede habitation. Genesis 2 clearly implies that the interests of the author of Genesis were indeed *no more chronological than that*. For if 1:11–13 tells us of the creation of plants and trees on the third day, the creation of birds and other creatures on the fifth day, and the creation of humankind just after cattle and so on on the sixth day, ch. 2 tells us of the absence of plants and herbs (v. 5) before the creation of Adam from the ground (Heb. *'ădāmāh*), and only mentions the creation of trees, animals and birds after this creation of Adam as well (vv. 9, 19 ff.). The interest of both passages has little to do with chronology, but everything to do with different strategies for emphasizing the importance of Adam in the context of creation. Chapter 1 does it by mentioning Adam as its pinnacle, while ch. 2 does it by having Adam as the center of creation around which everything else revolves.

[22] See the helpful chart in J. H. Walton, *Genesis* (NIVAC; Grand Rapids: Zondervan, 2001), 33–35, which summarizes the differences.

[23] One assumes, for example, that we are not to regard Isa 51:9–13 as teaching us that Yahweh really did kill a sea monster called Rahab at the time of creation.

[24] J. Calvin, *Genesis* (trans. and ed. by J. King; 2 vols., Edinburgh: Banner of Truth, 1965), I:86–87.

[25] Augustine, *The Literal Meaning of Genesis* (trans. J. H. Taylor; 2 vols., New York: Newman, 1982), 1:42–43, as cited in M. A. Noll, *The Scandal of the Evangelical Mind* (Grand Rapids: Eerdmans, 1994), 202–203.

[26] Packer, "Infallible Scripture," 345.

[27] See further on this point J. I. Packer, "Understanding the Bible: Evangelical Hermeneutics," in *Honoring the Written Word of God: The Collected Shorter Writings of J. I. Packer, Volume 3* (Carlisle: Paternoster, 1999), 147–60 (153): literalistic reading "can produce unhappy mistakes: celebrations of the created

order get read as lessons in science (e.g. Gen 1–2), apocalyptic symbolism as prosaic prediction (e.g. Rev 6–20), the Gospels as ventures in biography." See also Vanhoozer, *Is There a Meaning*, 113–26, for a most helpful discussion of "literal reading," in the course of which a *literalistic* reading is defined as one that insists on "staying on the level of ordinary usage, even when another level is intended" (117); and later on 303–35, in the course of which he proposes that we "define literal meaning as 'the sense of the literary act' ... literal interpretation is less a matter of identifying objects in the world than it is specifying communicative acts—their nature and their objects ... only when we consider the text as a literary act requiring a number of levels of description can we give an account of what the author is doing in the text." (304–305). And again (311): "Literal interpretation ... is more like a translation that strives for dynamic equivalence and yields the literary sense."

[28] Geisler's commentary on Articles XX to XXII is interesting in this regard ("Explaining Hermeneutics," 901–903). "Scientific knowledge of the spherical nature of the globe" is allowed to correct a faulty interpretation of Isa 11:12 (902). Yet it is denied "that we should accept scientific views that contradict Scripture or that they should be given an authority above Scripture," and it is especially important that a literal hermeneutic should be applied to Gen 1–11, with the result that "belief in macro-evolution, whether of the atheistic or theistic varieties" is excluded (903).

[29] For example, the recent book edited by R. Thomas and D. Farnell, *The Jesus Crisis: The Inroads of Historical Criticism into Evangelical Scholarship* (Grand Rapids: Kregel, 1998), begins with a particular view of what is entailed in affirming the historical veracity of the Gospels (for example, that the Gospels must give us word-for-word transcripts of what Jesus said) and proceeds to argue for the absolute necessity of believing that the Gospel writers worked independently from one another, and against the employment of redaction criticism on the Gospels (because any view of literary dependence by one author

on another will lead to a denial of historicity). The theory that they propose cannot deal at all adequately with the data of the Gospels themselves, however, and certainly not as well as the standard modern redaction-critical hypothesis: see the excellent, measured response to the book by G. R. Osborne, "Historical Criticism and the Evangelical," *JETS* 42 (1999): 193–210. Commenting on Thomas's work, I. H. Marshall says ("Evangelicalism and Biblical Interpretation," in *The Futures of Evangelicalism* [ed. C. Bartholomew, R. Parry and A. West; Leicester: InterVarsity, 2003], 100–23 (106): "Some scholars want to start from a position which rules out the possibility of *what they regard* [my italics] as error in Scripture. Therefore any method which might find errors is ruled out as inappropriate in principle. Clearly a lot hangs on what one understands as an error." Indeed so; and reading the Gospels carefully on their own terms, trying to account coherently for the data with which they present us, might well prompt some reflection (if one is at all open to it) on whether one's understanding of an error, or indeed of "historical veracity," is correct.

[30] Packer, "Infallible Scripture," 332.

[31] "Let the floods clap their hands; let the hills sing together for joy" (Ps 98:8).

[32] G. K. Chesterton, "The Invisible Man," in *The Complete Father Brown Stories* (Ware: Wordsworth, 1989), 64–77 (76).

[33] D. A. Black and D. S. Dockery, *New Testament Criticism and Interpretation* (Grand Rapids: Zondervan, 1991), 14.

[34] Provan, Long, and Longman, *History*, 91–93.

[35] Having examined the matter, I do not myself believe that source criticism *has* discovered truly that the Pentateuch is based upon four major sources of different dates, ranging from the monarchic to the postexilic periods; but *if* I did believe that this was the best explanation of the biblical evidence, I would be bound to accept this view of the composition of the Pentateuch. I would then need to explore what implications existed for my reading of the final form of the text that we have (although it seems obvious that the *mere fact* that the

Pentateuch were composed using these sources would not of itself necessarily alter my reading of it *at all*). Any theory about the nature of our biblical texts requires to be thus assessed on its merits; a commitment to truth (rather than merely an attachment to one's current beliefs) requires such an approach. I find it troubling, therefore, that when B. K. Waltke argues for the *plausibility* of the Documentary Hypothesis's analysis of Gen 1–2 ("Historical Grammatical Problems," in Radmacher and Preus, *Hermeneutics,* 69–129), A. A. MacRae's first and lengthiest response is not to the substance of the argument in respect of Gen 1–2, but to note that he is "disturbed" because (a) there has been no movement more effective in destroying Christian faith than higher criticism; (b) to many readers, use of Wellhausen's symbols "P" and "J" for the sources in Genesis seems to imply that his antichristian reconstruction of Bible history is true; (c) source-critical endeavor of this type has largely been abandoned in secular scholarship; and (d) source-critical positions held by biblical scholars vary ("A Response to Historical Grammatical Problems," in ibid., 143–62). We may respond to the response thus: (a and b) if any view produced by "higher criticism" were true, it could only have destroyed faith that was in part false. This being so, it is not the effects of believing this or that higher-critical position that should be the concern, but the truth or error of the position itself; (c) the helpfulness of an approach to texts is not measured by its current popularity; and (d) the fact that source-critical positions held by biblical scholars vary does not of itself mean that none of them is right. One is reminded of the novelist Thomas Hardy's response to criticism that his writings were marked by "pessimism": "Existence is either ordered in a certain way, or it is not so ordered, and conjectures which harmonize best with experience are removed above all comparison with other conjectures which do not so harmonize. So that to say one view is worse than other views without proving it erroneous implies the possibility of a false view being better or more expedient than a true view; and no pragmatic proppings can make that *idolum specus* stand on its feet" (preface to the final revision of his novels in 1912, available in T. Hardy, *The Return of the Native* [Harmondsworth, Middlesex: Penguin, 1978], 475–80 [479]).

[36] G. K. Chesterton, "The Blue Cross," in *The Complete Father Brown Stories* (Ware: Wordsworth, 1989), 9–23 (19).

[37] Vanhoozer, *Is There a Meaning*, 264. He goes on to say this (265): "A text must be read in light of its intentional context, that is, against the background that best allows us to answer the question of what the author is doing. For it is in relation to its intentional context that a text yields its maximal sense, its fullest meaning. *If we are reading the Bible as Word of God, therefore, I suggest that the context that yields this maximal sense is the canon, taken as a unified communicative act.* The books of Scripture, taken individually, may anticipate the whole, but the canon alone is its *instantiation*" [italics in the original].

[38] As M. Silva notes in *Has the Church Misread the Bible? The History of Interpretation in the Light of Current Issues* (Grand Rapids: Zondervan, 1987), 63: "Allegorical interpretations are very difficult to avoid for a believer who wishes to apply the truth of Scripture to his or her life" (cited from Vanhoozer, *Is There a Meaning*, 143n76, whose own comments on 113–20 underline the difficulty of any facile distinction between Reformation and pre-Reformation interpretation).

[39] Vanhoozer, ibid., 117: "When confronted with a range of interpretive options, Augustine's advice is to choose the one that best fosters love of God and neighbor."

[40] Packer, "Infallible Scripture," 337.

[41] Thiselton, *Two Horizons*, 5, referring to Schleiermacher's view. Note similarly Vanhoozer's summary of Kierkegaard's view that "linguistic and historical scholarship is not yet genuine reading. It is rather like examining and working on the mirror itself—looking *at* the mirror rather than *in* it. Such, he suggests, is the danger of modern biblical criticism" (Vanhoozer, *Is There a Meaning*, 16).

[42] Thiselton, *Two Horizons*, 15–16.

[43] C. H. Pinnock, "New Dimensions in Theological Method," in Dockery, *Dimensions*, 197–208 (205).

[44] Packer, "Infallible Scripture," 346.

[45] Ibid., 339–40.

[46] Geisler, "Explaining Hermeneutics," 894.

[47] Provan, Long, and Longman, *History*, 91.

[48] It would be unfair to suggest that it is by any means alone in this. It is in fact the common assumption of what we might call "modernist" biblical scholarship (and, for example, the sort of preaching that shares the same perspective), of whatever theological complexion, that the task of interpretation is all but done when the "expressed meaning" of a text in its historical context has been objectively articulated. C. R. Seitz, "Scripture becomes Religion(s): The Theological Crisis of Serious Biblical Interpretation in the Twentieth Century," in *Renewing Biblical Interpretation* (ed. C. Bartholomew, C. Greene and K. Möller; Carlisle/Grand Rapids: Paternoster/Zondervan, 2000), 40–65 (42n5), draws attention to the common preface to the Hermeneia commentary series, which states that "the editors ... impose no systematic-theological perspective upon the series ... It is expected that the authors will struggle to lay bare the ancient meaning of a biblical work or pericope. In this way the text's human relevance *should become transparent, as is always the case in competent historical discourse*" [italics in the original].

[49] Packer, "Infallible Scripture," 325, of Barth. As Packer notes (326), "Bultmann, too, shared with Evangelicals a concern that the Word of God be heard today, though Evangelicals have judged that his account of revelation makes this formally impossible."

[50] M. Turner, "Historical Criticism and Theological Hermeneutics of the New Testament," in *Between Two Horizons: Spanning New Testament Studies and Systematic Theology* (ed. J. B. Green and M. Turner; Grand Rapids/Cambridge: Eerdmans, 2000), 44–70 (69).

[51] Ramm (*Interpretation*, 2) provides some examples: "The following has been urged as the *voice of God*: in that the patriarchs practiced polygamy we may practice it; in that the Old Testament sanctioned the divine right of the king of Israel, we may sanction the divine right of kings everywhere; because the Old Testament sanctioned the death of witches, we too may put them to death … because the Old Testament declared that some plagues were from God, we may not use methods of sanitation, for that would be thwarting the purposes of God." The text is read "plainly," but it is misunderstood, in part within its own context but more seriously within the entire biblical context, with no attention to the flow of the entire biblical story and the point at which the reader sits within it. The entire system of dispensationalism is founded on the same error. Packer refers more generally to "groups whose interpretative style, though disciplined and conscientious, is narrow, shallow, naïve, lacking in roots, and wooden to a fault," citing as a reason the "want of encounter with the theological and expository wisdom of nineteen Christian centuries" ("Infallible Scripture," 352). This comment underlines just how far much modern Christian interpretation is indeed an unreflecting product of modernity, even as it claims that is simply "biblical." It involves a "literalism" that has little justification in the Christian tradition.

[52] Satan himself interprets Scripture demonically, but in accordance with its plain sense, in Matt 4:6 (citing Ps 91:9–12). Jesus's response is not to correct him with respect to the plain sense, but to place that text in its broader scriptural context.

[53] Thiselton, *Two Horizons*, 440.

[54] It has often been claimed within conservative Protestantism that Scripture is "perspicuous"—that is, "plain to the understanding especially because of clarity and precision of presentation" (*Merriam-Webster's Collegiate Dictionary*). The defense of the perspicuity of Scripture has often been presented, indeed, as essentially the defense at the same time of the notion of the priesthood of

all believers, in contexts where biblical scholars are presented as potentially forming a "priest-scholar class" that will teach everyone else how to read the Bible; so Geisler, "Explaining Hermeneutics," 904, and L. I. Hodges, "New Dimensions in Scripture," in Dockery, *Dimensions*, 209–34 (223–28). It simply does not follow, however, from the fact that the entire community of Christian believers is called to mediate God's blessing to the world as "priests" that all believers are equally well-equipped to understand the Bible (not least because not all believers have invested equal amounts of time and effort in the task). It is also manifestly clear that believers all through the ages have in fact *often* made mistakes in reading the Bible, even on matters of central importance to the Christian faith, through want of education (as well as other reasons), which calls into question just how "perspicuous" Scripture really is. Perspicuous to whom? We should certainly affirm that those who seek will find; but we should also refrain from giving the impression in our speech about biblical interpretation that the task is an easy one (any more than Jesus did). If indeed "a person is not dependent for understanding of Scripture on the expertise of biblical scholars" (*Statement*, Article XXIV), then what are biblical scholars and others doing writing a long and complicated *Statement* on biblical hermeneutics? Or is it only *some* (other) biblical scholars who are in mind? In all truth, the rhetoric about Scripture's perspicuity often seems to represent merely a convenient and effective way in which to encourage selective anti-intellectualism among Christians. At its worst, the argument almost becomes, "anything about the Bible that requires some intelligence to understand cannot really be important and probably is not true, because the ordinary Bible reader might not find it there for himself, and would need to depend on someone else for help." See further on this topic R. C. Van Leeuwen, "On Bible Translation and Hermeneutics," in *After Pentecost: Language and Biblical Interpretation* (ed. C. Bartholomew, C. Greene and K. Möller; Grand Rapids: Zondervan, 2001), 284–311 who notes (300): "Literature in general reveals a spectrum of 'open' and 'closed' functions. An instruction manual is 'closed' in that it wishes to preclude 'interpretation' ... the Bible is in most of its parts and as a whole an 'open' book collection: the task of interpretation is demanded, the whole is dialogic (as in Job) and the truth arises and is to be found in the interaction of the complex whole and its parts. Can the gospel be stated simply? Yes, and some parts of the Scriptures do that. But even the 'simple' parts of the Bible have depths, nuances and wisdom that readers are meant to 'grow' into. We grow in our knowledge of Scripture just as we grow in the knowledge of a friend, a musical composition, or of God and creation itself." See further the excellent discussion of the Reformers and the perspicuity of Scripture in A. C. Thiselton, *New Horizons in Hermeneutics* (Grand Rapids: Zondervan, 1992), 179–85, who notes that "in some strands of post-Reformation Protestant thought the concept of the perspicuity of Scripture ... became more capable of being invoked ... as a defensive slogan against the need for strenuous thought concerning biblical interpretation. But this departs from Luther's usage" (185). Vanhoozer's formulation is appropriately careful (*Is There a Meaning*, 315–17): "Clarity means that the Bible is sufficiently unambiguous in the main for any well-intentioned person with Christian faith to interpret each part with relative adequacy ... The clarity of Scripture means that understanding is possible, not that it is easy."

[55] Packer, "Infallible Scripture," 349: "There are no *a prioris* in an Evangelical's theology, and nothing in it is 'already accepted" in the sense of not being open to the possibility of theological challenge and biblical reassessment—not even his view of Scripture."

[56] See Vanhoozer, *Is There a Meaning*, 367–452, on "reforming the reader."

[57] Packer, "Infallible Scripture," 326. Packer's own definition of biblical infallibility and inerrancy as relating to this biblical authority as expressed in this essay (351–52) is interesting and somewhat at odds, it seems, with the *Statement*: "By affirming biblical infallibility and inerrancy, one commits oneself

in advance to receive as God's instruction and obey as God's command whatever Scripture is already known to teach and may in the future be shown to teach. They entail no *a priori* commitments to specific views, whether of the nature of knowledge or of the correct exegesis of biblical passages that touch on natural and historical events. They indicate only a commitment to the three interpretative principles set out above [that is, adoption of the grammatical-historical method in exegesis, the principle of harmony in synthesis, and the principle of universalizing in application]." If this were the broadly-accepted understanding of the terms "biblical infallibility" and "inerrancy," one imagines that many people who regard the Bible as authoritative for faith and life would have less difficulty than they currently do with these terms (particularly the second).

58 Vanhoozer, *Is There a Meaning*, 467.

CHAPTER SEVENTEEN

1 J. R. R. Tolkien, *The Lord of the Rings* (London: Harper Collins, 1991), 738–39.

2 David L. Jeffrey, "The Self and the Book: Reference and Recognition in Medieval Thought," in D. L. Jeffrey, ed., *By Things Seen: Reference and Recognition in Medieval Thought* (Ottawa: University of Ottawa, 1979), 1–17 (2).

3 Dante Alighieri, *The Comedy of Dante Alighieri, the Florentine*, Cantica I: *Hell* (trans. Dorothy L. Sayers; Harmondsworth: Penguin, 1949), 71.

4 Ian Johnston, "Lecture on *Rosencrantz and Guildenstern are Dead*," accessed from www.mala.bc.ca/~johnstoi/introser/stoppard.htm, April 11 2008.

5 Ibid.

6 Cited in D. L. Jeffrey, *People of the Book: Christian Identity and Literary Culture* (Grand Rapids: Eerdmans, 1996), 145–46.

7 Alasdair MacIntyre, *After Virtue: A Study in Moral Theory* (Notre Dame: University of Notre Dame, 1981), 216.

⁸ That is to say: our biblical authors propose things about the nature of reality, in dialogue with their contemporaries, and the narrative in which the propositions are embedded inevitably reflects the time and culture of its origin and speaks the language of its day. Yet what the biblical authors propose in the course of this dialogue—about God, and the world, and the nature and vocation of human beings within this world—differs from what their dialogue-partners propose, not least in being *true*. This true account of things is in fact *radically* different from the accounts proposed by the surrounding cultures.

⁹ See John H. Walton, *Genesis* (NIVAC; Grand Rapids: Zondervan, 2001), 19–387, for an excellent commentary which explains the similarities and differences between Genesis and ancient myth, and their significance, throughout Genesis 1–11.

¹⁰ William W. Hallo, *The Context of Scripture 1: Canonical Compositions from the Biblical World* (Leiden: Brill, 1997), 450–53.

¹¹ We may note by way of example the constitutional nature of kingship in Deuteronomy 17, the warnings of Samuel about the economic and social consequences of adopting a king "like the other nations" in 1 Samuel 12, and the manner in which the narrative texts of the Old Testament go out of their way to show that kings were entirely fallible and open to severe criticism.

¹² Walter Brueggemann, *Theology of the Old Testament: Testimony, Dispute, Advocacy* (Minneapolis: Fortress, 1997), 590.

¹³ The summary that follows is based upon the helpful analysis of Ralph L. Smith, *Old Testament Theology: Its History, Method and Message* (Nashville: Broadman and Holman, 1993), 167–233.

¹⁴ Cf. Ps 77:13–15; Ps 89:6.

¹⁵ Cf. Deut 4:35, 39; Isa 44:6–8.

¹⁶ Cf. Gen 12:1–3; Num 23:8; Deut 7:13–16; Job 1:10; 42:12.

¹⁷ Cf. Exod 34:6; Ps 36:5; 119:64; Lam 3:22–24; Isa 66:9, 12–13; Jer 31:15–20.

¹⁸ Cf. Hos 13:4; Isa 45:22.

[19] Cf. Isa 6:1–8; Zech 14:20.

[20] Cf. Deut 7:4; 2 Kgs 23:26; Ezek 7:4.

[21] Cf. Exod 34:6–7; Neh 9:17; Ps 65:3; 86:5.

[22] Cited in Angela Tilby, *Soul: God, Self and the New Cosmology* (New York: Doubleday, 1992), 108.

[23] G. K. Chesterton, *Orthodoxy* (San Francisco: Ignatius Press, 1995), 66.

[24] Augustine, *Confessions* (trans. Henry Chadwick; Oxford World's Classic; Oxford: Oxford University, 1998), 3.

INDEX OF AUTHORS

While authors or titles may be referenced many times in the essays in this volume, this index lists only substantive discussions and at least one instance of the full bibliographical details of each title.

Abraham, W., *Divine Revelation and the Limits of Historical Criticism*, 83n71
Ackerman, J. S., 269
  "Knowing Good and Evil," 263n12–n13, 264n16, 267n24, 269n27–271n29
Ackroyd, P. R., 253, 258
  Exile and Restoration, 9n19
  "Historians and Prophets," 80n61
  Studies in the Religious Tradition of the Old Testament, 47n14, 48n16
  "The Succession Narrative," 253n4, 254n6–258n8, 271n29
Albrektson, B., *25*
  Studies in the Text and Theology of the Book of Lamentations, 4n5, 25n20, 25n22
Alexander, L., ed., *Images of Empire*, 93n15
Alighieri, Dante, 396
  The Comedy of Dante Alighieri, the Florentine, 396n3
Alter, R., *The Art of Biblical Narrative*, 32n6, 53n3, 167n3
Ahlström, G. W., 65, 72, 74–76, 77n52, 153n17, 186n12, 197n52
  The History of Ancient Palestine, 54n5, 65n7, 72n27–n29, 74n36–n37, 75n41–76n47, 83n70, 173n10–n11
  "The Role of Archaeological and Litetary Remains," 65n5–n6, 75n39–n40, 192n34
Ambrose, 343
  De Nabuthe Jez., 344n10–n11

Anderson, A. A., 18
  Psalms, 18n6
Anderson, G. W., et al., eds., *Volume du Congrès: Genève 1965,* 263n12
Augustine, 122, 371, 388, 388n39, 415
  City of God, 122n22
  Confessions, 415n24
  The Literal Meaning of Genesis, 371n25
Axtell, J., "History as Imagination," 80n61
Bakir, A. El-Mohsen, *Slavery in Pharaonic Egypt,* 10n23
Barbour, I. G., ed., *Western Man and Environmental Ethics,* 321n1
Barr, J., 113–16, 124n28, 128n43, 129, 133
  "Childs' Introduction," 113n9, 117n13, 131n53, 134n64, 135n67, 140n82
  Holy Scripture: Canon, Authority, Criticism, 113n9, 117n12–n14, 121n20, 129n44, 133n63, 135n70, 140n81–n82, 143n89, 179n14
Barstad, H. M., "History and the Hebrew Bible," 186n12, 188n19–n20, 194n42, 197n51, 198n54
Bartholomew, C., C. Greene, and K. Möller, *After Pentecost, Renewing Biblical Interpretation,* 390n48, 392n54
Bartholomew, C., R. Parry, and A. West, eds., *The Futures of Evangelicalism,* 375n29
Barton, J., *Reading the Old Testament,* 14n27
Bauckham, R., 93–95, 98–99
  "The Economic Critique of Rome in Revelation 18," 93n15, 95n20, 97n23, 98n29
Beagley, A. J., 99–103
  The 'Sitz im Leben' of the Apocalypse, 100n36, 101n42–102n48
Beale, G. K., "A Reconsideration of the Text of Daniel," 91n1
Beasley-Murray, G. R., 94
  The Book of Revelation, 94n17, 107n62

INDEX OF AUTHORS

Becking, B., "Inscribed Seals as Evidence for Biblical Israel?," 194n37, 197n52–198n53
Bede, 73
  Ecclesiastical History of the English People, 73n34
Bellinger, W. H., 19
  Psalmody and Prophecy, 19n11
Bergsträsser, G., *Hebräische Grammatik*, 18n7
Black, D. A. and D. S. Dockery, *New Testament Criticism and Interpretation*, 380n33
Blenkinsopp, J., "A New Kind of Introduction," 133n61
  Prophecy and Canon, 117n15
  "Theme and Motif in the Succession History," 263n12
Borowski, O., "Hezekiah's Reforms and the Revolt against Assyria," 201n60
Böttcher, F., 17, 20
  Ausfürliches Lehrbuch der hebräischen Sprache, 17n2–n3
Brandfon, F., 74
  "The Limits of Evidence," 75n38, 187n14, 190n26, 191n28, 194n41
Brandscheidt, R., 5, 22
  Gotteszorn and Menschenleid, 4n5, 22n18
Brett, M. G., 125, 127, 130
  "Against the Grain," 131n49
  Biblical Criticism in Crisis?, 114n10, 125n34, 127n40, 128n42, 130n48, 131n51, 132n56
Brettler, M. Z., *The Creation of History in Ancient Israel*, 186n12, 187n15, 194n44, 195n46
Brockelmann, C., *Grundriss der vergleichenden Grammatik der semitischen Sprachen*, 18n7
Brueggemann, W., 124, 131n50, 219–20
  "On Trust and Freedom," 263n12

First and Second Samuel, 268n26
Theology of the Old Testament, 219n2, 220n3, 407n12
"The Trusted Creature," 263n12
Brueggemann, W. and H. W. Wolff, eds., *The Vitality of Old Testament Traditions,* 31n3
Brunet, G., 4
Les Lamentations contre Jérémie, 4n7
Buber, M., 244, 246
I and Thou, 245n30
Budde, K., "Die Klagelieder," 25n22
Budde, K. et al., *Die fünf Megillot,* 25n22
Buttenweiser, M., *The Psalms,* 17n3
Cahill, J. M., "A Rejoinder to 'Was the Siloam Tunnel Built by Hezekiah?'," 201n60
Calvin, J., 370–72
Genesis, 371n24
Cameron, A., ed., *History as Text,* 64n2
Canary, R. H. and H. Kozicki, *The Writing of History,* 64n2
Carlson, R. A., *David the Chosen King,* 254n6, 263n12, 268n25
Carroll, R. P., "Madonna of Silences: Clio and the Bible," 183n4, 190n25, 194n41, 197n52, 205n66
Carson, D. A. and H. G. M. Williamson, eds., *It Is Written: Scripture Citing Scripture,* 33n9, 116n11
Carson, D. A. and J. D. Woodbridge, eds., *Scripture and Truth,* 350n9
Charles, R. H., 91–92
Revelation, 91n1, 91n4, 92n6, 96n22
Chesterton, G. K., 378, 381, 414
The Complete Father Brown Stories, 378n32, 381n36
Orthodoxy, 415n23

Childs, B. S., 47, 108–43, 113n9, 117n12–n13, 118n16, 130n48–131n49, 131n53, 132n59, 133n61, 134n64, 135n66–n67, 135n70, 139n79, 140n81–n82, 143n90, 163, 175–79, 179n14
"A Reponse," 123n26, 139n79–140n80
"Barr's *Holy Scripture*," 124n28, 128n43
Biblical Theology of the Old and New Testaments, 110n6, 119n19, 122n23, *Exodus*, 132n58
Introduction to the Old Testament as Scripture, 32n5, 33n8, 47n15, 118n18, 123n25, 124n29, 124n31, 126n35, 127n37, 131n52, 135n68, 140n80, 140n82
The New Testament as Canon, 127n36
Old Testament Theology in a Canonical Context, 122n21, 123n27, 132n56, 132n58, 137n75, 141n84–142n85, 178n13
"Response to Reviewers," 124n30, 127n41, 131n54–132n55, 132n57, 137n74, 140n80
Clements, R. E., *Wisdom in Theology*, 260n11
Clive, J., *Not By Fact Alone*, 64n2, 73n35
Coady, C. A. J., *Testimony: A Philosophical Study*, 187n17, 205n66
Cogan, M. and H. Tadmor, *2 Kings*, 53n2
Cohen, S. J. D., "The Destruction: From Scripture to Midrash," 13n25
Collingwood, R. G., *The Idea of History*, 73n32, 199n56
Court, J. M., 99
Myth and History in the Book of Revelation, 99n35, 100n37, 103n49
Cowley, A. E., ed., *Gesenius' Hebrew Grammar*, 18n7
Craigie, P. C., 18
Psalms 1–50, 18n6
Crenshaw, J. L., "Method in Determining Wisdom Influence," 263n12
Cryer, F. C., "Of Epistemology, Northwest-Semitic Epigraphy and Irony," 191n27

Dahood, M. J., 18
  Psalms, 18n5
  "Ugaritic-Hebrew Syntax and Style," 18n5
Daube, D., *He That Cometh*, 49n21
Davidson, A. B., 18, 20
  Introductory Hebrew Grammar, 18n4
Davies, P. R., 63–89, 86n80, 146, 168, 190n24, 201–10
  In Search of "Ancient Israel," 54n5, 66n8–n9, 67n11–n13, 72n30, 81n63–83n69, 85n78–86n79, 87n82, 146n5, 168n6, 192n35, 198n53, 205n68, 206n70–208n72
  "Method and Madness," 183n4, 188n18, 194n40, 205n69
  "Whose history? Whose Israel? Whose Bible?," 190n24, 191n30, 199n56, 201n58, 210n74
Day, J., *God's Conflict with the Dragon and the Sea*, 98n31
Delekat, L., "Tendenz und Theologie der David-Salomo-Erzählung," 263n12
Dever, W. G., 184n9, 191n28, 191n31
  "Archaeology, Material Culture and the Early Monarchical Period," 204n65
  "The Identity of Early Israel," 191n28, 194n41
  "Revisionist Israel Revisited," 183n4
DeVries, S. J., *1 Kings*, 53n1
de Wette, W. M. L., 17
  Commentar über die Psalmen, 17n3
Dietrich, W., *Prophetie und Geschichte*, 31n3
Dirksen, P. B., "Song of Songs 3:6–7," 282n13
Dockery, D. S., ed., *New Dimensions in Evangelical Thought*, 350n8, 380n33, 389n43, 392n54
Driver, G. R., 18
  Canaanite Myths and Legends, 19n10
  Problems of the Hebrew Verbal System, 18n4

Driver, S. R., 18, 20
A Treatise on the Use of the Tenses in Hebrew, 18n7
Edelman, D. V., "Doing History in Biblical Studies," 75n38, 89n83, 195n47
The Fabric of History, 65n5, 73n31, 192n33–n34, 195n47, 204n65
"Saul ben Kish in History and Tradition," 195n47
The Triumph of Elohim, 198n54
Eichrodt, W., 109–10
"Does Old Testament Theology still have Independent Significance?," 109n4, 130n46
Ellul, J., 107
Apocalypse: The Book of Revelation, 107n61
The New Demons, 233n11, 242n25
Ewald, G. H. A., 17–18, 20
Ausfürliches Lehrbuch der hebräischen Sprache, 17n2–n3, 18n9
Falk, M., *Love Lyrics from the Bible,* 273n1
Farrer, A., 106
The Revelation of St John the Divine, 107n60
Feinberg, J. S., "Truth: Relationship of Theories of Truth to Hermeneutics," 353n12
Fekkes, J., III, *Isaiah and Prophetic Traditions in the Book of Revelation,* 93n13
Fishbane, M., *Biblical Interpretation in Ancient Israel,* 33n9, 116n11
Fishburn, J., *Confronting the Idolatry of the Family,* 243n26
Fokkelman, J. P., 265–66
Narrative Art and Poetry in the Books of Samuel, 254n5, 263n12, 263n14–264n15, 266n19–n20
Forster, E. M., 6, 13
Anonymity: An Inquiry, 6n10
Fritz, V. and P. R. Davies, eds., *The Origins of the Ancient Israelite States,* 184n9, 187n16, 191n31, 195n47, 201n60, 210n75

Gadamer, H.-G., 125, 127–29, 388–89
  Truth and Method, 127n39, 186n13, 349n6
Gay, C. M., *The Way of the (Modern) World,* 245n30
Gelb, I. J., "Prisoners of War in Early Mesopotamia," 10n23
Gerleman, G., *Ruth: Das Hohelied,* 278n9
Gesenius, F. H. W., 17, 26
  Hebräisches Elementarbuch, 17n2
Giet, S., *L'Apocalypse et l'histoire,* 99n35
Gledhill, T., *The Message of the Song of Songs,* 274n3
Gonzalez, J. L., *Faith and Wealth,* 344n10–n11
Gordis, R., 20
  The Song of Songs and Lamentations, 20n12–21n13, 273n1, 277n7
Gossman, L., "History and Literature," 65n2
Gottlieb, H., 20, 22, 26
  A Study on the Text of Lamentations, 20n12–21n13, 22n18
Gottwald, N. K., 5, 130, 132
  Studies in the Book of Lamentations, 4n5, 130n48, 153n16, 161n45–n46
Grabbe, L. L., ed., *Can a 'History of Israel' be Written?,* 183n4–n5, 183n7–184n8, 185n10, 186n12, 188n19, 190n24–n25, 191n29, 191n31, 194n37–38, 197n52, 198n55
Gray, J., *I and II Kings,* 10n21, 16n1
Green, J. B. and M. Turner, eds., *Between Two Horizons,* 391n50
Grudem, W., *Systematic Theology,* 353n12
Guinness, O., "Sounding Out the Idols of Church Growth," 243n27
Guinness, O. and J. Seel, eds., *No God But God,* 238n20, 243n27–n28
Gunn, D. M., 151
  The Story of King David, 254n5, 263n12
Gunn, D. M. and D. N. Fewell, *Narrative in the Hebrew Bible,* 32n6, 53n3
Gwaltney, W. C., Jr., "The Biblical Book of Lamentations," 8n16

INDEX OF AUTHORS

Habermas, J., 70
    Knowledge and Human Interests, 70n22, 84n75
Habertal, M. and A. Margalit, *Idolatry,* 234n13
Haller, M., 5
    "Die Klagelieder," 4n6
Haller, M. and K. Galling, *Die fünf Megilloth,* 4n6
Hallo, W. W., *The Context of Scripture,* 405n10
Hallo, W. W., J. C. Moyer and L. G. Perdue, eds., *Scripture in Context II,* 8n16
Halpern, B., 77
    The First Historians, 188n19, 190n24, 195n46, 199n57
Hardy, T., *The Return of the Native,* 381n35
Hayes, J. H., ed., *Dictionary of Biblical Interpretation,* 349n6
Hendel, R. S., "The Date of the Siloam Inscription," 201n60
Hermisson, H.-J., "Weisheit und Geschichte," 263n12
Hesse, M. B., *Revolutions and Reconstructions in the Philosophy of Science,* 70n22
Hillers, D. R., 5, 20
    "History and Poetry in Lamentations," 8n16
    Lamentations, 4n5, 20n12–21n13
Hobbs, T. R., *2 Kings,* 32n7, 167n5
Hodges, L. I., "New Dimensions in Scripture," 392n54
Hopkins, D., "Bare bones: Putting Flesh on the Economics of Ancient Israel," 201n60
Hughes, P. E., *The Book of the Revelation,* 106n58
Humphrey, E. M., *The Ladies and the Cities,* 103n50
Japhet, S., *The Ideology of the Book of Chronicles,* 202n61
Jauss, H. R., *Toward an Aesthetic of Reception,* 127n38
Jeffrey, D. L., 396
    People of the Book, 399n6
    "The Self and the Book," 396n2

Jeffrey, D. L., ed., 396
  By Things Seen, 396n2
Johnston, I., "Lecture on *Rosencrantz and Guildenstern are Dead*," 398n4–n5
Jones, G. H., *1 and 2 Kings*, 53n1, 259n9
Kaiser, O., 5, 21–22
  "Klagelieder," 4n5, 5n9, 7n12, 7n14, 8n18, 10n23
Keel, O., *The Song of Songs*, 274n3
Keys, G., 252, 254
  The Wages of Sin, 251n2, 252n3, 254n7
Kitchen, K. A., "A Possible Mention of David," 191n27
  The Third Intermediate Period in Egypt, 10n22
Klemm, D. E., "Hermeneutics," 331n6
Kloos, C., *YHWH's Combat with the Sea*, 98n31
Knauf, E. A., 72, 89
  "From History to Interpretation," 73n31, 77n52, 80n61, 84n73, 89n83, 192n33
Knight, D. A., "Canon and the History of Tradition," 117n12, 123n26, 135n66
Knight, G. A. F. and F. W. Golka, *Revelation of God*, 274n3
König, F. E., 18
  Historisch-kritisches Lehrgebäude der hebräischen Sprache, 4n4
Kraus, H.-J., 5, 21–22
  Klagelieder (Threni), 4n5, 5n8, 7n14, 8n18
Laato, A., *Josiah and David Redivivus*, 49n18
  The Servant of YHWH and Cyrus, 49n18
Lambert, W. G., A. R. Millard, and M. Civil, eds., *Atra-Hasis: The Babylonian Story of the Flood*, 334n8
Lambrecht, J., ed., *L'Apocalypse johannique*, 92n6

INDEX OF AUTHORS

Lamparter, H., 20
Das Buch der Sehnsucht, 20n12
Landes, G. M., 135
"The Canonical Approach to Introducing the Old Testament," 132n59, 135n69, 140n80
Lemaire, A., "The Tel Dan Stela as a Piece of Royal Historiography," 191n27
Lemche, N. P., 65, 73, 77, 183n4, 197n51, 198n54
Ancient Israel, 54n5, 65n4, 75n38, 194n43
The Canaanites and Their Land, 77n49–n51
"Clio is also among the Muses!," 191n31, 194n43
"Early Israel revisited," 191n31
Levenson, J. D., *The Hebrew Bible, the Old Testament, and Historical Criticism,* 33n8, 130n46
Lewis, C. S., 181
The Last Battle, 181n1–n2, 210n77
Licht, J., *Storytelling in the Bible,* 4n6, 53n3, 167n3
Loewenstamm, S. E., "The Death of the Upright and the World to Come," 18n8
Long, B. O., *1 Kings, with an Introduction to Historical Literature,* 32n7, 167n5
2 Kings, 32n7, 167n5
Long, V. P., *The Art of Biblical History,* 85n77
The Reign and Rejection of King Saul, 179n15
Lyon, D., 232–33, 238
The Steeple's Shadow, 232n8–n9, 233n10
Maass, F., ed., *Das ferne und nahe Wort,* 263n12
MacIntyre, A., 400
After Virtue, 401n7
MacRae, A. A., "A Response to Historical Grammatical Problems," 381n35

Marshall, I. H., "Evangelicalism and Biblical Interpretation," 375n29
Martin, R., "Objectivity and Meaning in Historical Studies," 73n32
Martin, J. D. and P. R. Davies, eds., *A Word in Season*, 11n24
Massyngberde Ford, J., 99–105
    Revelation, 100n38–101n41, 102n48, 103n51, 105n55
Mays, J. L., "What is Written," 117n13
McCann, J. C., ed., *The Shape and Shaping of the Psalter*, 49n19
McCullagh, C. B., *Justifying Historical Descriptions*, 84n75
McDaniel, T. F., "Philological Studies in Lamentations," 7n13
McKenzie, S. L., *The Trouble with Kings*, 165n2, 251n2
Melugin, R. F., *The Formation of Isaiah 40–55*, 47n14
Michel, D., 25
    Tempora und Satzstellung in den Psalmen, 25n21
Milbank, J., *Theology and Social Theory*, 84n75
Millard, A. R., "Sennacherib's Attack on Hezekiah," 201n59, 334n8
Miller, J. M., 84
    "Is it Possible to Write a History of Israel?," 75n38, 84n72, 89n83, 195n47
Miller, J. M., and J. Hayes, 168, 188
    A History of Ancient Israel and Judah, 168n7, 188n21–n22
Morgenstern, J., 4, 7
    "Jerusalem – 485 BC," 4n3, 7n11
Morris, L., 106
    The Revelation of St John, 106n57
Mounce, R. H., *The Book of Revelation*, 99n35
Mowinckel, S., 45
    He That Cometh, 31n1, 45n12, 84n74
Murphy, R. E., 136, 274
    "The Old Testament as Scripture," 136n73, 140n82
    The Song of Songs, 274n2

Myers, C., *Binding the Strong Man,* 234n12, 236n17
Nelson, R. D., *First and Second Kings,* 32n7, 167n5
Niehr, H., "Some Aspects of Working with the Textual Sources," 194n38
Noll, M. A., *The Scandal of the Evangelical Mind,* 371n25
Norman, A. P., "Telling It Like It Was," 78n56
Noth, M., 31, 256
    The Deuteronomistic History, 31n2
    History of Israel, 197n49
Ollenburger, B. C., et al., eds., *The Flowering of Old Testament Theology,* 109n3
Osborne, G. R., "Historical Criticism and the Evangelical," 375n29
Osiek, C., "The New Handmaid," 84n74
Packer, J. I., 356, 389
    Honoring the Written Word of God, 372n27
    "Infallible Scripture and the Role of Hermeneutics," 350n9, 355n15, 356n17, 372n26, 377n30, 388n40, 389n44–390n45, 391n49, 391n51, 392n55, 392n57
    "Understanding the Bible," 372n27
Pannenberg, W., *Basic Questions in Theology,* 186n13
Parker, C., "Methods, Ideas and Historians," 84n73
Peterson, E. H., *Subversive Spirituality,* 246n31
Pinnock, C. H., "New Dimensions in Theological Method," 389n43
Polzin, R., *David and the Deuteronomist,* 263n12, 265n17, 266n21, 267n23, 271n29
Pope, M. H., *Song of Songs,* 277n8
Popper, K., *Objective Knowledge,* 129n45
Provan, I. W., *Ecclesiastes,* 285n19, 286n21
    Song of Songs, 285n19, 286n21
    "The End of (Israel's) History," 170n9, 191n29
    Hezekiah and the Books of Kings, 2n2

"Ideologies, Literary and Critical," 130n47, 144n2, 152n13, 182n3, 187n15

1 and 2 Kings, 38n10, 97n23, 116n11, 141n83, 167n3–n5, 202n61, 205n69, 259n10, 265n18, 286n20

Lamentations, 91n3, 92n9

Provan, I. W., V. P. Long, and T. Longman III, *A Biblical History of Israel*, 364n19, 381n34, 390n47

Radmacher, E. D. and R. D. Preus, eds., *Hermeneutics, Inerrancy, and the Bible: Papers from ICBI Summit II*, 347n1, 351n11–353n12, 381n35

Ramachandra, V., *Gods That Fail*, 244n29

Ramm, B., 349

Protestant Biblical Interpretation, 321n2–326n4, 391n51

Renkema, J., 5

"Misschien is er hoop…" 4n5

Richardson, A., *History Sacred and Profane*, 209n73, 240n24

Ricoeur, P., 124–25, 210

Freud and Philosophy, 127n37, 210n76, 331n6

Rigney, A., *The Rhetoric of Historical Representation*, 64n2, 73n35

Ringgren, H., et al., *Sprüche, Prediger, Das Hohe Lied, Klagelieder, Das Buch Esther*, 4n5, 21n14

Ringgren, H. and A. Weiser, *Das Hohe Lied, Klagelieder, Das Buch Esther*, 4n6, 7n14

Robinson, J. A. T., *Redating the New Testament*, 92n5

Rogerson, J., and P. R. Davies, "Was the Siloam Tunnel built by Hezekiah?," 201n60

Roloff, J., *The Revelation of John*, 92n7, 98n32

Roth, P. A., "Narrative Explanations," 76n48

Rowland, C., 106

Revelation, 106n56

INDEX OF AUTHORS 553

Rudolph, W., 4–5, 7n12, 20, 23
    Das Buch Ruth, Das Hohe Lied, Die Klagelieder, 20n12
    "Der Text der Klagelieder," 22n17
    Die Klagelieder, 4n6, 25n22
Ryken, L., J. C. Whilhoit, and T. Longman III, eds., *Dictionary of Biblical Imagery*, 225n6, 282n15
Salters, R. B., "Lamentations 1:3," 11n24
Sanders, J. A., *Torah and Canon*, 117n15, 123n26, 139n79
Sawyer, J. F. A., *Semantics in Biblical Research*, 140n82
Scalise, C. J., 125, 132
    Hermeneutics as Theological Prolegomena, 124n32, 127n37, 133n60–n61
Schäfer-Lichtenberger, C., "Sociological and Biblical Views of the Early State," 187n16, 194n41
Schlossberg, H., 235
    Idols for Destruction, 227n7, 233n11, 235n14–n16, 237n19, 238n21, 239n23
Schüssler Fiorenza, E., 93
    The Book of Revelation, 92n6, 105n54
Seitz, C. R., "Scripture Becomes Religion(s)," 390n48
Semler, J., *Abhandlung von freier Untersuchung des Canons*, 109n2, 117n12
Silva, M., *Has the Church Misread the Bible?*, 387n38
Smelik, K. A. D., *Converting the Past*, 77n52
Smend, R., "Questions About the Importance of the Canon," 118n17, 134n64
Smith, C. R., "Reclaiming the Social Justice Message of Revelation," 98n27
Smith, R. L., *Old Testament Theology*, 409n13
Snaith, J. G., *The Song of Songs*, 273n1
Soggin, J. A., 188
    A History of Israel, 189n23
Stanford, M., *The Nature of Historical Knowledge*, 72n27, 73n32, 89n83

Sternberg, M., *The Poetics of Biblical Narrative,* 32n6, 53n3, 78n56, 167n3

Strand, K. A., "Some Modalities of Symbolic Usage in Revelation 18," 93n14, 101n46, 392n54

Sundberg, A. C., *The Old Testament of the Early Church,* 117n12–n13

Swartley, W. M., *Israel's Scripture Traditions and the Synoptic Gospels,* 93n11

Sweet, J. P. M., *Revelation,* 92n5–n6, 94n18, 106n58

Thiselton, A. C., *New Horizons in Hermeneutics,* 392n54

    The Two Horizons: New Testament Hermeneutics, 331n6, 388n41–389n42, 392n53

Thomas, R., and D. Farnell, *The Jesus Crisis,* 375n29

Thompson, L. L., 104

    The Book of Revelation, 104n52–105n54

Thompson, T. L., 66–68, 70–71, 72n27, 73, 79–80, 145, 197n51, 198, 205n69

    "Defining History and Ethnicity in the South Levant," 190n24

    Early History of the Israelite People, 54n5, 66n10, 67n14–69n21, 71n23–n26, 79n57–n60, 84n74, 85n76, 87n82, 145n3–n4, 194n39, 198n54

    "Historiography of Ancient Palestine," 184n9, 188n20, 191n31

    "The Intellectual Matrix of Early Biblical Narrative," 198n54

    "A Neo-Albrightean School?," 183n7, 184n9, 192n32, 194n43, 197n49, 197n51, 198n53–n54

Thucydides, 73

    History of the Peloponnesian War, 73n34, 80n61

Tilby, A., *Soul: God, Self and the New Cosmology,* 414n22

Tolkien, J. R. R., 393

    The Lord of the Rings, 394n1

Treves, M., 4

    "Conjectures sur les dates et les sujets des Lamentations," 4n4

Troeltsch, E., 83

"Über historische und dogmatische Methode in der Theologie," 83n71
Turner, M., 391
"Historical Criticism and Theological Hermeneutics," 391n50
Vanhoozer, K. J., 386, 392
Is There a Meaning in This Text?, 333n7, 372n27, 386n37–388n39, 388n41, 392n54, 392n56, 392n58
Van Leeuwen, R. C., "On Bible Translation and Hermeneutics," 392n54
Veyne, P., *Writing History: Essay on Epistemology*, 73n32
Vitz, P. C., "Leaving Psychology Behind," 238n20
Psychology as Religion, 238n20
von Rad, G., 31–33, 110
Old Testament Theology, 31n4, 110n5
Wall, R. E., *Revelation*, 98n26
Walter, J. A., *Sacred Cows*, 243n26
Waltke, B. K., "Historical Grammatical Problems," 381n35
Walton, J. H., *Genesis*, 369n22, 403n9
Watson, F., 112–13, 136, 138–39
Text, Church and World, 108n1, 112n8, 131n51, 136n71, 138n76–139n77, 142n87–n88
Watts, R. E., "Women in the Gospels and Acts," 292n23
Weber, T. P., "New Dimensions in American Evangelical Theology," 350n8, 351n10
Weiser, A., 5, 21–22
"Klagelieder," 4n6, 7n14, 22n18
Wells, D. F., "The D-Min-ization of the Ministry," 243n28
Wengst, K., *Pax Romana and the Peace of Jesus Christ*, 99n33
Wenham, G. J., 321
Genesis 1–15, 321n2, 331n6
White, H., "The Historical Text as Literary Artifact," 64n2, 87n81

"The Question of Narrative," 84n73
White, L., 320–32
"The Historical Roots of our Ecologic Crisis," 324n3–326n4
Whitelam K. W., 144–61, 191n28–191n29, 191n31, 194n41
The Invention of Ancient Israel, 144n1, 146n6, 150n8, 151n9–n12, 152n14, 153n16, 153n18–162n47, 168n8–170n9, 191n29
"Prophetic Conflict in Israelite History," 191n28
Whybray, R. N., *The Making of the Pentateuch,* 133n62
The Succession Narrative, 263n12, 264n15
Wiesmann, H., 20, 24
Die Klagelieder, 20n12, 21n16
Wiggins, S. A., *A Reassessment of Asherah,* 174n12
Williamson, H. G. M., *1 and 2 Chronicles,* 202n61
Wiseman, D. J., *1 and 2 Kings,* 53n2
Wilson, G. H., *The Editing of the Hebrew Psalter,* 49n19
Wolff, H. W., "The Kerygma of the Deuteronomic Historical Work," 31n3
Wolff, H. W., ed., *Probleme biblischer Theologie,* 31n3, 263n12
Yarbro Collins, A., 92, 98
The Combat Myth in the Book of Revelation, 98n31
Crisis and Catharsis, 98n31
"Revelation 18: Taunt-Song or Dirge?," 92n6, 92n8, 98n28, 98n30, 99n35, 100n37
Younger, K. L., Jr., 202
Ancient Conquest Accounts, 73n33, 87n82, 202n62, 205n67, 364n20
Zenner, J. K., 21, 24
Beiträge zur Erklärung der Klagelieder, 21n16

SELECT LIST OF IAIN PROVAN'S PUBLICATIONS, 1988–2014

Books

1988 *Hezekiah and the Books of Kings*. Beiheft zur Zeitschrift für die alttestamentliche Wissenschaft 172. Berlin: De Gruyter, pp. xiii, 218.

1991 *Lamentations*. New Century Bible Commentary. London: Marshall Pickering, pp. xviii, 140.

1995 *1 & 2 Kings*. Understanding the Bible. Grand Rapids: Baker Books, pp. xiv, 305 (originally published by Hendrickson/Paternoster).

1997 *1 & 2 Kings*. Old Testament Guides. Sheffield: JSOT Press, pp. 125. Chinese translation 2003.

2001 *Ecclesiastes and Song of Songs*. NIV Application Commentary. Grand Rapids: Zondervan, pp. 399.

2003 *A Biblical History of Israel*. Co-authored with V. P. Long and T. Longman III. Louisville: Westminster John Knox, pp. xiv, 426. Chinese translation 2010 (Hong Kong: TienDao Publishing); Korean translation 2013. This book won the Biblical Archaeology Society "Best Popular Book on Archaeology" in 2005. The judges said that it made "an important contribution to the debate about the use of the Bible in writing a history of Israel… It is both scholarly and accessible to the general reader. Its interdisciplinary approach, utilizing archaeological sources, ancient texts and the Bible itself, makes the book compelling."

2012 *Let Us Go Up To Zion: Essays In Honour of H. G. M. Williamson on the Occasion of his Sixty-Fifth Birthday*. Co-edited with Mark Boda. Supplements to Vetus Testamentum 153. Leiden: Brill, pp. xxxix, 515.

2013 *Convenient Myths: The Axial Age, Dark Green Religion, and the World That Never Was*. Waco: Baylor University Press, pp. xii, 159.

2014 *Seriously Dangerous Religion: What the Old Testament Really Says, and Why It Matters.* Waco: Baylor University Press, pp. x, 502.

Contributions to Books

1990 "Kings" and "Lamentations." Pages 377–79 and 382–83 in *A Dictionary of Biblical Interpretation*. Edited by R.J. Coggins and J. L. Houlden. London: SCM Press.

1995 "The Messiah in the Book of Kings." Pages 67–85 in *The Lord's Anointed: Interpretation of Old Testament Messianic Texts*. Edited by P. E. Satterthwaite, R. S. Hess, and G. J. Wenham. Carlisle: Paternoster/Baker Academic.

1997 "Hezekiah" and "Kings (1 and 2): Theology of." Pages 703–707 and 846–54 in vol. 4 of the *New International Dictionary of Old Testament Theology and Exegesis*. Edited by W. A. VanGemeren. Grand Rapids: Zondervan.

1998a "The Historical Books of the Old Testament." Pages 198–211 in *The Cambridge Companion to Biblical Interpretation*. Edited by J. Barton. Cambridge: Cambridge University Press.

1998b "War and Warfare." "The Kings of Israel and Judah" and "Josiah." Pages 88–89, 134–35, and 144–45 in *The Complete Bible Handbook: An Illustrated Companion*. Edited by in J. Bowker. Willowdale, ON: Firefly Books.

1998c "Babylon," and "Nineveh." Pages 68–69 and 595–96 in the *Dictionary of Biblical Imagery*. Edited by L. Ryken, J. Wilhoit and T. Longman III. Downers Grove, IL: InterVarsity.

2000a "In the Stable with the Dwarves: Testimony, Interpretation, Faith and the History of Israel." Pages 281–319 in *Congress Volume: Oslo 1998*. Papers of the 16th Congress of the International Organisation of the

Societies for Old Testament Study. Edited by A. Lemaire and M. Sæbø. Leiden: Brill.

2000b "On 'Seeing' the Trees While Missing the Forest: The Wisdom of Characters and Readers in 2 Samuel and 1 Kings." Pages 153–73 in *In Search of True Wisdom: Essays in Old Testament Interpretation in Honour of Ronald E. Clements*. JSOTSup 300. Edited by E. Ball. Sheffield: Sheffield Academic Press.

2000c "The Terrors of the Night: Love, Sex and Power in Song of Songs 3." Pages 150–67 in *The Way of Wisdom: Essays in Honor of Bruce K. Waltke*. Edited by J. I. Packer and S. K. Soderlund. Grand Rapids: Zondervan.

2000d "Kings," "Solomon" and "Elisha." Pages 183–88, 788–89, and 456–58 in the *New Dictionary of Biblical Theology*. Edited by D. Alexander et al. Leicester: IVP.

2001 "1 and 2 Kings." Pages 487–575 in *The New Oxford Annotated Bible*. 3d ed. Edited by M. D. Coogan. Oxford: Oxford University Press.

2003a "Daniel." Pages 665–75 in the *Eerdmans Commentary on the Bible*. Edited by J. W. Rogerson and J. D. G. Dunn. Grand Rapids: Eerdmans.

2003b "Knowing and Believing: Faith in the Past." Pages 229–66 in *'Behind' The Text: History and Biblical Interpretation*. Edited by C. Bartholomew et al. Grand Rapids: Zondervan.

2003c "Why Bother with the Old Testament Regarding Gender and Sexuality?" Pages 25–41 in *Christian Perspectives on Gender, Sexuality & Community*. Edited by M. Hancock. Vancouver: Regent College.

2008 "1–2 Kings." *ESV Study Bible*, Wheaton, IL: Crossway.

2009 "2 Kings." Pages 110–219 in vol. 3 of *The Zondervan Illustrated Bible Backgrounds Commentary*. Edited by J. Walton. Grand Rapids: Zondervan.

2010 "1–2 Kings." Pages 215–38 in *The New Interpreter's Bible One Volume Commentary*. Edited by D. L. Petersen and B. R. Gaventa. Nashville: Abingdon.

2011 "'Who is the Prophet Talking About, Himself or Someone Else?' (Acts 8:34): A Response to Lester Grabbe's Review of *A Biblical History of Israel*." Pages 235–52 in *Enquire of the Former Age: Ancient Historiography and Writing the History of Israel*. Library of Hebrew Bible/Old Testament Studies Series (European Seminar in Historical Methodology 9). Edited by L. L. Grabbe. London: T&T Clark.

2012a "Pain in Childbirth? Further Thoughts on 'An Attractive Fragment' (1 Chronicles 4:9–10)." Pages 285–96 in *Let Us Go Up To Zion: Essays In Honour of H. G. M. Williamson on the Occasion of his Sixty-Fifth Birthday*. Supplement to Vetus Testamentum 153. Edited by Iain Provan and Mark Boda. Leiden: Brill.

2012b "Hearing the Historical Books." Pages 254–76 in *Hearing the Old Testament: Listening for God's Address*. Edited by C. G. Bartholomew and D. J. H. Beldman. Grand Rapids: Eerdmans.

2013 "Qoheleth for Today." Pages 401–16 in *The Words of the Wise are like Goads: Engaging Qoheleth in the 21st Century*. Edited by M. Boda, T. Longman III and C. Rata. Winona Lake, IN: Eisenbrauns.

Journal Articles

1990a "Reading Texts Against an Historical Background: The Case of Lamentations 1." *Scandinavian Journal of the Old Testament* 4: 130–43.

1990b "Feasts, Booths and Gardens (Thr 2,6a)." *Zeitschrift für die alttestamentliche Wissenschaft* 102: 254–55.

1991 "Past, Present and Future in Lamentations 3:52–66: The Case for a 'Precative Perfect' Re-examined." *Vetus Testamentum* 41: 164–75.

1995a "Why Barzillai of Gilead (1 Kings 2:7)? Narrative Art and the Hermeneutics of Suspicion in 1 Kings 1–2." *Tyndale Bulletin* 46: 103–16.

1995b "Ideologies, Literary and Critical: Reflections on Recent Writing on the History of Israel." *Journal of Biblical Literature* 114: 585–606.

1996 "Foul Spirits, Fornication and Finance: Revelation 18 from an Old Testament Perspective." *Journal for the Study of the New Testament* 64: 81–100.

1997a "Canons to the Left of Him: Brevard Childs, his Critics, and the Future of Old Testament Theology." *Scottish Journal of Theology* 50: 1–38.

1997b "The End of (Israel's) History? A Review Article on K. W. Whitelam's *The Invention of Ancient Israel*." *Journal of Semitic Studies* 42: 283–300.

2000 "To Highlight All our Idols: Worshipping God in Nietzsche's World." *Ex Auditu* 15: 19–38.

2002 "'All These I Have Kept Since I Was A Boy' (Luke 18:21): Creation, Covenant, and the Commandments of God." *Ex Auditu* 17: 31–59.

2003a "Pyrrhon, Pyrrhus and the Possibility of the Past: A Response to David Henige." *JSOT* 27: 413–37.

2003b "(Perhaps the) Last Comments on the Davies–Dever Exchange." *Bible and Interpretation* (http://www.bibleinterp.com/articles/Last_comments.htm)

2006a "Literary Competence and Biblical Authority." *Word and World* 26: 375–82.

2006b "The Land is Mine and You are Only Tenants (Leviticus 25:23): Earth-Keeping and People-Keeping in the Old Testament." *Crux* 42 no. 3: 3–16.

2007 "'How Can I Understand, Unless Someone Explains It to Me?' (Acts 8:30–31): Evangelicals and Biblical Hermeneutics." *Bulletin for Biblical Research* 17: 1–36.

2008 "'Unscripted, Anxious Stutterers': Why We Need Old Testament (Hi) story." Co-authored with Loren Wilkinson. *Sapientia Logos* 1: 12–36.

2013 "The Eclipse of Biblical Narrative, 1648–2013: How Did We Get Here And What Are We To Do?" *Virtue Online: The Voice for Global Orthodox Anglicanism*, (http://www.virtueonline.org/portal/modules/news/article.php?storyid=17355#.UU96zlfzuzc).

2014 "The Violent Legacy of Monotheism? Truths, Half-Truths, and Downright Lies about Religion and Culture." *Bible and Interpretation* (http://www.bibleinterp.com/articles/2014/03/pro388006.shtml).

www.ingramcontent.com/pod-product-compliance
Lightning Source LLC
Chambersburg PA
CBHW031842220426
43663CB00006B/470